D0754473

A Tibetan Revolutionary

A Tibetan Revolutionary

The Political Life and Times of Bapa Phüntso Wangye

Melvyn C. Goldstein,
Dawei Sherap, and
William R. Siebenschuh

UNIVERSITY OF CALIFORNIA PRESS
Berkeley · Los Angeles · London

Unless otherwise noted, all photographs in this book
are from the collection of Phünwang.

University of California Press
Berkeley and Los Angeles, California

University of California Press, Ltd.
London, England

© 2004 by the Regents of the University of California

Library of Congress Cataloging-in-Publication Data
Goldstein, Melvyn C.
    A Tibetan revolutionary : the political life and times
of Bapa Phüntso Wangye / Melvyn C. Goldstein, Dawei
Sherap, and William R. Siebenschuh.
       p.   cm.
    Includes index.
    ISBN 0-520-24089-8 (cloth : alk. paper)
    1. Tibet (China)—History—Autonomy and inde-
pendence movements.   2. Tibet (China)—Politics and
government—1951–   3. Phüntso, Wangye, 1922–
I. Sherap, Dawei, 1922–   II. Siebenschuh, William R.
III. Title.
DS786.G637   2004
951'.505'092—dc21
[B]   2003055224

Manufactured in the United States of America

13   12   11   10   09   08   07   06   05   04
10   9   8   7   6   5   4   3   2   1

The paper used in this publication meets the minimum
requirements of ANSI/NISO Z39.48–1992 (R 1997)
(Permanence of Paper). ♾

Tibetans are ruined by hope
Chinese are ruined by suspicion

བོད་རེ་བས་འཕུང་

རྒྱ་དོགས་པས་འཕུང་

—*Traditional Tibetan saying*

Contents

Illustrations

MAPS

Preface

Melvyn C. Goldstein

In a sense this book began in the summer of 1993. Phüntso Wangye (known as Phünwang)[1] was visiting Lhasa at the same time that I was there interviewing former Tibetan officials for a history of Tibet in the 1950s. When I heard Phünwang was in Lhasa, I was excited by the opportunity to include him in the study, and I telephoned him. Initially he said he was too busy, but after I had telephoned him several times he finally agreed to meet me in his hotel room. In the course of the interview, he mentioned a number of interesting and, I thought, important incidents in his own youth, so at the end of the meeting I asked him if I could return to ask some follow-up questions on the 1950s and on his own life.

Phünwang laughed and said, "Professor Goldstein, please come again and ask your questions on the 1950s, but as to my life, it is not of interest." Undeterred, I thanked him but pressed again, saying, "For our next meeting, please think a little about how you got from a village in Kham[2]

---

1. Tibetan personal names typically consist of two names comprised of four syllables, e.g., Phün-tso Wang-gye. Tibetans sometimes use both names together (Phüntso Wangye) but also sometimes use only the first name (Phüntso) or the second name (Wangye) or, as with the subject of this book, a combination of the first syllable of each name (Phün-wang).

2. During this period, ethnic Tibetans were divided between "political" Tibet—the kingdom ruled by the Dalai Lama—and "ethnographic" Tibet, those areas inhabited by ethnic Tibetans lying to the east of political Tibet and to the west of the Han Chinese areas of China proper. Ethnographic Tibet consisted of small principalities nominally under the authority of China but ruled day to day by traditional chiefs. Culturally, the Tibetan areas in ethnographic Tibet were divided into two major subcultural and linguistic areas, called Kham and Amdo. Amdo Tibetans were found in the northern part of ethnographic Tibet

to Chiang Kaishek's elite academy in Nanjing. I have been studying this period for a long time, and you are the first person I have met who accomplished that." Phünwang smiled and said, "We'll see."

Two days later I returned to Phünwang's hotel and started by asking him about his early years. Phünwang thought for what seemed a very long time—but was probably only a few seconds—and then said slowly, "Well, you are a persistent scholar with a long involvement in studying Tibetan history, so I will answer some of your questions about this."

So began a series of visits and questions about what turned out to be the life of a remarkable Tibetan. Over the next decade, I visited Phünwang whenever I passed through Beijing on my many research trips to Tibet. There were continuing questions about and clarifications of historical incidents during the 1950s, but also more and more about his life. At some point in late 2000, as I sat in my office at Case Western Reserve University reading through the transcripts of our conversations, I realized that the material was much more than anecdotes and footnotes to modern history. The story of Phünwang's life was historically and politically important in its own right and deserved to be told.

I then asked my good friend and university colleague Professor William Siebenschuh to join me in writing Phünwang's story (as he had for an earlier book on the life of a very different kind of Tibetan, *The Autobiography of Tashi Tsering*). I also asked Dawei Sherap, a Tibetan intellectual in Beijing who had authored a book on Phünwang, to collaborate, and over the next two years we set about converting over one hundred hours of disjointed taped interviews and re-interviews into this book.

Phünwang did not narrate the book in a formal sense. However, he used the first person in the interviews, and we decided to do the same and, in effect, let him tell his own story. This decision had obvious consequences. Because the book that resulted is highly autobiographical, it reflects Phünwang's strong views on matters that of course can be viewed differently. There are also many details that could not be independently corroborated, and some of his recollections differ from other accounts, but where possible, every effort has been made to insure historical accuracy.

Phünwang's life is more than a story of great individual courage under extraordinary privation. And it is more than just a window onto an im-

---

in today's Qinghai and Gansu provinces. Kham was located south of Amdo in today's Sichuan and Yunnan provinces (although some ethnic Khampas were also part of political Tibet). The term *Khampa* refers to a person from Kham. In 1939, the Khampa areas of Sichuan were officially organized into a new Chinese province called Xikang.

portant period of modern Tibetan history. An individual's life experiences often can illuminate the nature of a general problem with great clarity, and Phünwang's life and times provide just such a powerful spotlight on the nature of the Tibet Question—the conflict over the status of Tibet vis-à-vis China. The literature on modern Tibet has been monopolized by the voices of monks, lamas, and aristocrats, i.e., people who dominated the traditional semifeudal society and generally opposed modernization and change. They present the conflict in stark black-and-white images—good Tibetans against malevolent Chinese communists—and have come to represent the face of Tibetan nationalism in Western literature. However, the story of modern Tibet is far more complex, and there were other types of Tibetans fighting for their people and for a different kind of Tibet. Phünwang is one of the most important of these.

A strong nationalist who was already educated and "modern" in the late 1930s, Phünwang dedicated his life to the struggle to create a socialist Tibet that would encompass all Tibetans in Kham, Amdo, and Tibet proper and would be ruled by Tibetans. He worked tirelessly, at great personal risk, to achieve this, first through his own Tibetan Communist Party and then through the Chinese Communist Party, in which he was the leading Tibetan cadre in Tibet from 1951 to 1958.

Ultimately, Phünwang and his comrades failed, and Phünwang ended up spending eighteen years in solitary confinement in the Chinese equivalent of the Bastille—Qingchen Number One Prison in the northern suburbs of Beijing. He was released in 1978, after Deng Xiaoping came to power, and rehabilitated politically two years later. This terrible ordeal, however, did not extinguish his courage and vision, and after his release, he continued to speak and write about nationalities policy in China, becoming a critic within the Chinese Communist Party of its policies in Tibetan areas.

Phünwang's life suggests that the problem in China/Tibet is not so much a clash between incompatible ideas and values—the forces of "modernization" versus "religion" and "traditionalism." Rather, it is predominately a clash between the political dominance of a majority nationality, the Han, and the political subordination of a minority nationality, the Tibetans. It is, in essence, a clash about the very idea of what kind of a nation the People's Republic of China (PRC) is and should be. The PRC considers itself a multiethnic state in which all groups have equal rights and power. Phünwang suggests it really operates too much like a Han Chinese state.

Phünwang's life and thoughts convey powerful insights into the Tibetan Question from someone within the Chinese Communist Party. It is a Tibetan voice that should be heard by all who are concerned about this and other ethnic conflicts.

Writing the life story of someone still living in China raised troubling issues about possible negative consequences for him, even though Phünwang was not cognizant of our project. One day in 2002, therefore, while visiting Phünwang and his wife, Tseden, in Beijing, I mentioned to him that my colleagues and I had just finished writing a book about his life and views and asked whether he thought he might have problems when the book was published. He laughed and said no, he didn't, and in any case, he wasn't afraid. "I don't know exactly what you wrote, but everything I have told you over the years is true, so I am sure that the book will be fine. And if it isn't and they want to put me back in prison again, I am not afraid." And then he changed the subject, smiling, and invited me to have more tea and another cookie. Phünwang is that kind of person.

Acknowledgments

Melvyn C. Goldstein, Dawei Sherap, and
William R. Siebenschuh

Many people in the United States and China graciously assisted our research. All cannot be mentioned here, but we would especially like to thank Sandra Siebenschuh for carefully editing the manuscript, the University of California Press's two reviewers for their helpful comments, T. N. Shelling of Case Western Reserve University's Center for Research on Tibet for his help in clarifying Tibetan and Chinese spellings and terms, and the Yuthok family and Phünwang for providing photographs from their family collections.

We also would like to thank the National Endowment for the Humanities and the H. Luce Foundation for their support of Goldstein's research on modern Tibet (during which the interviews with Phünwang were conducted). Throughout this project, Case Western Reserve University provided important assistance by allowing Goldstein release time for the research and by supporting the Center for Research on Tibet.

Note on Romanization
and Abbreviations

Tibetan written and spoken forms diverge considerably, the written form containing consonant clusters that are not pronounced: e.g., the Tibet name Chagö Tomden is actually spelled (romanized) *bya rgod stobs ldan.* Throughout this book, the spoken (phonetic) pronunciation is used for Tibetan proper names and titles, with the correct spellings given in romanization in the "Glossary of Correct Tibetan Spellings" at the end of the book. However, in some cases, Tibetan terms or phrases mentioned in the text are accompanied by the correct Tibetan spelling. These are placed in brackets and preceded by "tib.": for example, "the Spark Association [tib. *me stag tshogs pa*]." Since the Tibetan language does not distinguish between capital and lowercase letters, all correct Tibetan spellings are cited with lowercase letters.

Chinese names and terms are cited in the standard pinyin system used in the People's Republic of China, with the exception of the established older spelling of Chiang Kaishek. Chinese pinyin terms or phrases are introduced by "ch.": for example, "the Spark Association [tib. *me stag tshogs pa;* ch. *xing huo she*]."

The following abbreviations are used in the text:

CCP   Chinese Communist Party

GMD   Guomindang Party/Government of Chiang Kaishek (also called the Chinese Nationalist Party/Chinese Nationalist Government)

NPC   National People's Congress
PLA   People's Liberation Army
PRC   People's Republic of China
TAR   Tibet Autonomous Region

Key Persons

Basu	Head of the Indian Communist Party in Calcutta
Chagö Tomden	A leading Tibetan official from Derge in Kham
Che Jigme	A leading official in the Panchen Lama's administration
Cheng Jingbo	PLA official and Phünwang's secretary
Chen Yi	Marshal in the PLA and vice premier of the PRC
Chömpel	Phünwang's brother
Dawa	Childhood friend of Phünwang and member of the Tibetan Communist Party
Deng Xiaoping	Political commissar of the Southwest Military and Administrative Bureau; later paramount leader of the PRC
Dramdul	Khampa from Batang; original member of the Spark Association in Derge

Fan Ming	Important Northwest Bureau official who was deputy secretary of the Tibet Work Committee in Lhasa
Fei Delin	First secretary of the Soviet Embassy in China and Phünwang's main Soviet contact
Fu Dequan	Guomindang military commander in Batang
Gora Ashi	Phünwang's father
Gyalo Thondup	The Dalai Lama's older brother
He Long	Marshal in the PLA and vice premier of the PRC
Hua Guofeng	Chairman of the CCP after Mao's death
Hu Yaobang	Reformist general secretary of the CCP in the 1980s
Janglojen	Progressive Lhasa aristocrat
Kapshöpa Sey	Progressive Lhasa aristocrat
Kesang Tsering	Tibetan who led a revolt against the local Chinese authorities in Batang
Kheme	Commander in chief of the Tibetan army and participant in Seventeen-Point Agreement negotiations
Lhalu	Governor-general in Chamdo after Yuthok and member of the Kashag (Council of Ministers)
Li Jingquan	Head party secretary in Sichuan Province
Liu Bocheng	Head of the Southwest Military and Administrative Bureau
Liu Chun	A deputy director of the State Nationalities Affairs Commission
Liu Geping	A deputy director of the State Nationalities Affairs Commission; in-

	vestigated the implementation of reforms in Sichuan in 1956
Liu Shaoqi	President of the PRC
Liushar (Thubden Tharpa)	Senior Tibetan aristocratic official
Liu Wenhui	Chinese warlord who ruled Kham (Xikang)
Li Weihan	Senior party official involved in nationalities affairs; head of the Chinese delegation to Seventeen-Point Agreement negotiations and director of the United Front Work Department
Lobsang Thundrup	Phünwang's uncle who was sent to Batang from Nanjing by Chiang Kaishek in 1935 and led an uprising there
Lukangwa	Anti-Chinese acting prime minister of Tibet, 1950–1952
Ngabö	Tibetan council minister and governor-general in Chamdo when the PLA attacked; head of the Tibetan delegation to the Seventeen-Point Agreement negotiations in Beijing
Ngawang Kesang	Phünwang's classmate and friend; early member of the Tibetan Communist Party
Ou Gen	Commander of communist forces in Yunnan in 1949
Panda Tobgye	Khampa leader and businessman
Peng Dehuai	Head of the Northwest Military and Administrative Bureau and a marshal in the PLA
Peng Zhen	Chairman of the standing committee of the NPC and Politburo member
Phüngang	Phünwang's eldest son

Phüntso Tashi   The Dalai Lama's brother-in-law
                             and general in the Tibetan army

Ragashar   Aristocrat and member of the
                             Kashag (Council of Ministers)

Sherap   Phünwang's friend at school; early
                             member of the Tibetan Communist
                             Party

Shökhang   Progressive Lhasa aristocrat

Sun Yatsen   Father of the Chinese revolution
                             against the Manchu dynasty

Surkhang   Aristocrat and member of the
                             Kashag (Council of Ministers)

Tharchin Babu   Publisher of the *Tibetan Mirror,* a
                             Tibetan-language newspaper in
                             Kalimpong

Thuwang (Thubden Wangchuk)   Phünwang's younger brother

Tian Bao   One of the first Tibetan cadre;
                             joined the Long March as it passed
                             through Kham

Topden   Khampa from Batang; original
                             member of the Spark Association
                             in Derge

Trendong Sey   Progressive Lhasa aristocrat and
(Tomjor Wangchuk)   close friend of Phünwang

Trinley Nyima   Khampa member of the Tibetan
                             Communist Party

Tsadrü Rimpoche   Well-known Tibetan lama and
                             scholar

Tseden Yangdrön   Phünwang's second wife

Tsilila   Phünwang's first wife

Tsögo   Tibetan aristocrat who was
                             Ngabö's aide in Chamdo

Ulanhu   Ethnic Mongolian who was direc-
                             tor of the United Front Work
                             Department

Wang Feng	A deputy director of the State Nationalities Affairs Commission
Wang Guangmei	Wife of Liu Shaoqi
Wang Qimei	A senior commander in the 18th Army in Tibet
Wu Zhong	Commander of the 52nd Division of the 18th Army
Xi Zhongxun	A high party official from the Northwest Bureau who was involved in nationalities affairs and became vice premier of the PRC
Xu Danlu	Head of intelligence operations for the 18th Army in Tibet
Xue Jianhua	Director of the Nationalities Bureau of the United Front Work Department
Ya Hanzhang	Northwest Bureau cadre who was a member of the Tibet Work Committee in Lhasa
Yang Jingren	Head of the State Nationalities Affairs Commission in the early 1980s
Yangling Dorje	Tibetan cadre from Batang who was a deputy secretary in the TAR government in the 1970s and 1980s
Ye Jianying	Senior official at the 8th Route Army office in Chongqing in 1939–1940
Yin Fatang	18th Army officer who was head of the party branch office in Gyantse in the 1950s; in 1980, became the head party secretary of the TAR
Yuthok	Tibetan governor-general of Chamdo
Zhang Guohua	Commander of the 18th Army and

	deputy secretary of the Tibet Work Committee in Lhasa
Zhang Jingwu	Representative of the Central Committee to Tibet and head of the Tibet Work Committee in Lhasa
Zhao Ziyang	Premier and member of the Standing Committee of the Politburo
Zhou Enlai	Premier of the PRC
Zhu Dalfen	Well-known Chinese revolutionary writer and publisher
Zhu De	Commander in chief of the PLA

Map 1. China and surrounding areas.

Map 2. Eastern Tibet.

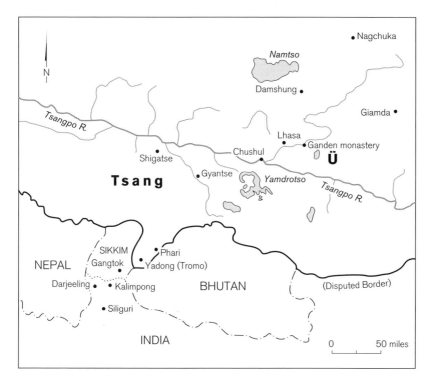

Map 3. Central Tibet.

A Brief Historical Context

Melvyn C. Goldstein

The people of Batang, Phünwang's home town, are part of the Eastern Tibet ethnic subgroup called the Khampa. They use the same written language as Tibetans in Central Tibet and are Tibetan Buddhists, but they speak a dialect that is very different from that used in Lhasa. Their customs are also somewhat different. They are a proud and aggressive people who are straightforward in talk and independent in character. They love horses and guns and are quick to seek vengeance for harms and insults. Traditionally, the area of eastern Tibet known as Kham was divided into twenty or so principalities, each ruled by its own local chief. Batang was one of the more important of these.

The rise to power of the Manchu dynasty in the second half of the seventeenth century changed the power structure in East Asia and the Tibetan Plateau. By the early eighteenth century, the Manchu had sent armies to Lhasa and established a loose protectorate over Tibet. At the same time, it formally established the boundary between Tibet and China as the watershed between the Drichu (Upper Yangtse) and Dzachu (Mekong) Rivers. Batang and much of Kham, therefore, fell on the Chinese side of the frontier (see map 2).

The Manchu dynasty, however, did not try to administer Kham directly. Instead it allowed the various Khampa kings and chiefs to continue to rule their territories, giving them titles such as *tusi* that confirmed their traditional authority.

Batang was one of these Tibetan "states." It was ruled by two chiefs called *depa* who were nominally under the authority of the Manchu dynasty via its officials in Sichuan Province. Sichuan Province maintained a commissariat office and a small garrison there, but on a day-to-day basis, Batang was autonomous and was ruled in accordance with local laws and customs.

This local autonomy policy changed in 1903–1904 when the Manchu moved to incorporate the Tibetan areas of Kham directly into their state. The new policy sought gradually to replace the local Tibetan rulers with Chinese officials and to undermine Tibetan religious and secular institutions.

In response to this policy, in early 1905, the people of Batang rose up and seized control over their area, killing a number of Manchu/Chinese troops and officials in the process. This uprising spread to surrounding Tibetan principalities but ultimately failed after Beijing sent an army of 7,500 troops from Sichuan to suppress it. By June 1905, the Manchu had ended the revolt and retaken Batang. They exacted a swift retribution, beheading Batang's two rulers along with a number of lesser leaders and burning Batang's famous Chöde monastery to the ground.

Over the next few years, new laws were imposed changing the administration of Batang. All inhabitants were placed under the direct authority of Chinese magistrates (appointed from Sichuan), restrictions were placed on the numbers of monks, new offices and garrisons were established, and a system of compulsory education in Chinese schools was started. At the same time, immigration by Chinese farmers was encouraged. Batang became one of the most important administrative and military centers for the Manchu/Chinese government in Kham.

The Manchu dynasty hoped ultimately to expand this policy to the Kingdom of the Dalai Lama (Tibet) and in 1909–1910 sent an army of several thousand troops from Sichuan to Lhasa. In the process, the Manchu dynasty redefined the existing Tibet-China border, claiming all the ethnic Tibetan territories up to Giamda, a town located only a few hundred miles east of Lhasa (see map 1). In 1910, as this Chinese army was entering Lhasa, the Thirteenth Dalai Lama fled into exile in India. Angered by this defiant act, the Manchu Emperor deposed the absent Dalai Lama; Tibet was well on the way to becoming, like Batang, another administrative unit in China.

But this never occurred because the Manchu dynasty itself was overthrown in 1911–1912. A new Chinese "Republican" government was set up in Beijing under Yuan Shikai that in 1927–1928 became the

Nationalist or Guomindang (GMD) government, headed by Chiang Kaishek.

Tibetans took the fall of the Manchu dynasty as an opportunity to revolt against the Manchu/Chinese officials and troops. In Kham, they took control over most areas, and the Dalai Lama returned from exile in India to Lhasa in Tibet proper, expelled all Chinese and Manchu troops and officials, and declared self-rule.

The new government in Beijing, however, was unwilling to permit the Tibetan areas in Kham to go their own way and in 1912 launched a military expedition from Sichuan to reestablish its control. Many Tibetans were killed and several large monasteries were destroyed. By 1914, China had regained military control over all these territories in Kham.

Back in Lhasa, the Thirteenth Dalai Lama considered the Chinese military victories in Kham a threat to Tibet per se and responded by sending a Tibetan army to the frontier to defend against possible Chinese military moves. In 1917–1918, fighting broke out between the Tibetan and Chinese frontier forces. The Tibetan troops, armed with new rifles recently obtained from Britain, defeated the Chinese and began to push them back beyond the Drichu River. Local Khampas took this opportunity to again rise against the Chinese garrisons in their areas. In the midst of this turbulence, in mid-1918, a truce was negotiated and a new Sino-Tibetan frontier was established. Batang (and the ethnic Tibetan areas to its east) was left under Chinese control. Thus, by the time Phünwang was born in 1922, Batang was firmly under Chinese rule.

PART I

Growing Up in Kham and China

CHAPTER I

Childhood in Batang

I was born in January 1922 in Batang, a remote and beautiful village in Kham (Eastern Tibet) roughly five hundred miles from Lhasa and twelve hundred miles from Beijing [see map 1]. Batang is located in a valley at about eighty-five hundred feet, sandwiched between the tiny Ba River on the west and a range of mountains to the east. It has a relatively mild climate for Tibet and is predominantly agricultural. Though rugged and beautiful, the area has always been politically troubled, and my later life as a Tibetan revolutionary is rooted in its turbulent history and the experiences of my childhood there.

Had things gone the way my parents planned, I would have been a monk, not a revolutionary. When I was four years old I went to live in the local monastery with my uncle, a learned monk who had studied at Ganden, one of Lhasa's great monasteries. In our area it was common for older monks to recruit a young nephew to live with them, and I loved being with him. I didn't take any formal monastic vows, but I remember that they cut my hair like a monk's and I began to memorize prayer books. In fact, I was well on my way to a life of religious study and practice when my uncle suddenly died. I don't recall the circumstances clearly, but his death resulted in my leaving the monastery, since I was very young and we had no other relative there to look after me. Not long afterward, my parents enrolled me in the Batang government school, a decision that dramatically changed the course my life would take.

Batang was unusual for Tibetan areas because it had a formal school

Figure 1. Panorama of Batang town, 1940.

system. The Chinese government had built a modern school there in 1907 and made attendance compulsory for Tibetans. Surprisingly, Batang also had an American missionary school (and orphanage) that a number of Bapas [people from the Batang area] attended as well. Because of these schools, many Bapas learned Chinese and even English, and some became important officials in the Chinese government.

I began attending the Chinese school when I was about seven years old and continued until I was twelve. My teachers were Tibetans who were fluent in Chinese, and the curriculum we studied included Chinese, Tibetan, and mathematics. The routine was relatively simple. We had class for about two hours in the morning and then for two hours in the afternoon after a break for lunch. We didn't have homework like children do now, and we had no clocks; we judged the time by the position of the sun.

I liked school and learning, and I worked hard. My parents wanted me to be proficient in the Tibetan language and therefore arranged for me to take extra language instruction from a former monk who had set up the first library in Batang. Because one of my best friends lived in

Figure 2. Gora Ashi, Phünwang's father (date unknown).

the Christian orphanage, I also learned many Christian songs and Western stories that the missionaries had translated into Tibetan. I remember delighting in songs like "Silent Night" and in the tales of Ali Baba.

For a while it looked like I was going to have a more or less normal, happy childhood. But the current of events in the region was simply too strong. Our people—the Khampas—have always deeply resented being ruled by outsiders, and there were repeated uprisings against the Chinese officials and troops in our area. My father was active in the anti-Chinese resistance, and I grew up hearing stories of past battles and brave Khampa heroes. I can pinpoint fairly exactly the time when I began to develop my earliest feelings about issues like independence, autonomy,

and resistance. It was when Kesang Tsering came to Batang in 1932. I
was ten years old at the time.[1]

I remember Kesang Tsering's arrival in Batang vividly. He rode into
our village on a large Chinese horse, looking glorious in his shiny government uniform. His official mission was to set up a GMD Party headquarters in Batang, but he had his own agenda, which included overthrowing the region's warlord, Liu Wenhui, and returning the governance
of Kham and Batang to Tibetans. He lost no time in securing the support
of the key Tibetan political forces in Batang: the Chöde monastery and
the local Tibetan militia (a volunteer organization comprised of about
150 men who came together only when there was a war or a disturbance). But even with their support, gaining control of Batang required
defeating a Chinese garrison of three hundred to four hundred troops.
Kesang therefore decided to use guile, not force, and he chose a classic
ploy: he invited the Chinese commander and his officers to a banquet.

Kesang was an important central government (GMD) official, and the
garrison had to take his invitation seriously. The commander was away,
but the next in command, Captain Zhou, came with some top aides. As
soon as they arrived, Kesang ordered them to hand over their weapons,
telling Zhou that if he complied, he and his men could leave peacefully,
but if they did not, they would all be killed. Zhou had no choice and
complied, but the Chinese soldiers stationed at the garrison refused to
turn over their weapons or let the Tibetans enter the garrison. It was a
standoff, and the fighting began early next morning.

Our house was not far from the garrison, and I was terrified when the
shooting began. It was the first time I had heard the gunfire of battle, and
the noise was so deafening that my younger brother and I covered our

---

1. In 1927–1928, the Nanjing-based Guomindang (GMD), or Nationalist government, led by Chiang Kaishek, set out to subordinate the many "warlords" who controlled
much of China. One of these warlords was Liu Wenhui, the ruler of Kham (or Xikang
Province, as the Chinese called it).

In 1931, Chiang Kaishek sent a Tibetan from Batang named Kesang Tsering to bring
Liu Wenhui into line. Kesang Tsering had graduated from the Batang government school
and had gone on to high school in Yunnan Province and then to the Provincial Officers'
Training Institute. He was bright and ambitious and joined the GMD Party in 1924 as its
first Tibetan member. By 1927 he had moved to Nanjing, then the capital of China, and
was appointed a commissioner in the Mongolian and Tibetan Affairs Commission (ch.
Meng Zang weiyuanhui), the Chinese government office that dealt with Tibetans. At
twenty-nine, he was sent back to Batang with the title of Xikang (Kham) Party Affairs Special Commissioner. Officially, his task was to strengthen the authority of the GMD Party
central government by organizing a Xikang GMD Party branch there, but for Chiang
Kaishek, this was to be the first step in weakening Liu's control.—*Goldstein, Sherap, and
Siebenschuh*

heads with our quilt. My mother was also frightened because my father was with the local militia, and she immediately made offerings to the protective gods in our family's chapel.

The fighting continued long into the morning hours before the Chinese troops finally surrendered. When the smoke of battle had cleared, Kesang summoned everyone to the Chöde monastery. When he was ready to speak to the crowd, he fired his pistol into the air several times to get everyone's attention. He then proceeded to tell us that he was the governor now and that Tibetans again ruled Batang.

Not long after the victory celebration, Kesang summoned everyone to the school and taught us a new song he had composed called "The Song of the New Kham." I don't remember all the words, but the idea was that we Tibetans should adhere to Sun Yatsen's "Three Principles of the People" [ch. *san min zhu yi*—nationalism, democracy, and livelihood] and that a new era had arisen for the people of Batang and Kham.

Spirits were high, and there was much to celebrate. None of the Tibetan (or Chinese) soldiers had been killed, and literally overnight Kesang had obtained six hundred to seven hundred rifles, with ammunition. Tall and strong, with a dark mustache, Kesang was a heroic figure to me and the other youths. (The people used to say of him, "Commander Kesang's mouth is like the central government's order" [ch. and tib. *zhongyang gi ga, kesiling gi kha*].) But of course it wasn't that simple, and that was part of my learning process, too. The fighting wasn't over. The Chinese weren't going to take such a defeat lightly, and other forces began to gather against Kesang almost immediately.

In our politically volatile region, alliances were shifting and unstable and promises unreliable. Kesang had come to Batang via Yunnan and Tsakalo, an autonomous Khampa area in Tibet, southwest of Batang on the Yunnan frontier [see map 2]. On the way, he had discussed his plans with the Gonggar Lama, an important lama whose support would have been valuable to him. At the time, the lama had appeared to approve Kesang's actions, but when he heard that Kesang had disarmed the Chinese soldiers and driven them out of Batang, he had a sudden change of heart. To hedge his bets, he secretly sent a letter to Liu Wenhui at Liu's headquarters/garrison in Tartsedo disavowing any support for Kesang's activities.

Events moved swiftly after that. By a series of coincidences, Kesang's men caught the lama's messenger and found the letter. Kesang was so furious when he read it that he shot the messenger on the spot and immediately began making plans to mobilize the Batang militia and move against the Gonggar Lama, who he felt had betrayed him. Things quickly went from bad to worse.

Intent on teaching the traitor a lesson, Kesang sent his militia—including my father—across the Drichu River and south toward Tsakalo. Unbeknownst to him, however, the Gonggar Lama had learned of the impending attack, mobilized the Tsakalo militia, and, critically, secured the support of a regiment of the Tibetan army that was stationed in Markam. Then they set a trap for Kesang.

Kesang and his soldiers suspected nothing. When they crossed the Drichu and headed south toward Tsakalo, they noticed Tibetan government troops at the foot of a mountain in the distance, but they didn't think anything about it because the main Tibetan army base was just beyond that mountain range and the territory here was part of political Tibet. However, as they started to move up toward the pass that led to Tsakalo, they suddenly found themselves under heavy fire from the Tsakalo militia, who were deployed above them.

Immediately realizing the weakness of their position, the Batang militia quickly began to retreat down the mountain. However, when they reached the valley, they were shocked to find the Tibetan government troops they had noticed before now shooting at them from the flanks. The Tibetan government troops had also flooded the fields behind the Bapas to impede their retreat. Kesang's main force managed to escape across the Drichu only because some of his militia stayed behind and fought an effective rear-guard action that temporarily kept the pursuers at bay.

When word of the defeat reached Batang, my family had a more immediate worry, because we were told that our father was part of that rear-guard force and that a number of that unit had been killed. (We were also told that the Tibetan government troops had cut off the heads of our dead fighters and had taken them back to display in their garrison at Markam.) It is a painful memory. As the main body of militia returned, my mother and I watched, hoping that my father would appear, but he was not among them.

After the last of the stragglers returned, she started crying and told me she was sure he was dead. She organized the final prayers for him and told me that now it was my responsibility to take over his job of doing the family's morning prayer rites, which involved cleaning and filling the religious water bowls and butter lamps. I was proud to be doing a man's job but also so very sad and angry. It was hard to accept the idea that my father was dead. I remember taking an oath before our protector deity that I would avenge his death, and I prayed to the Buddha each day to tell me the names of the people who had killed him. Fortunately, however, our sorrow was short-lived. A few weeks later our sadness turned to elation when a local trader from Markam told us that my father was alive and wounded. He had been shot in the leg in the battle and taken to Markam to recover. His wound was not serious; he was improving and would eventually come home.

Kesang Tsering's problems, however, continued to multiply. Not satisfied with driving him away, the Tibetan government soldiers pursued him across the Drichu River and, together with the Tsakalo militia, attacked Batang itself. Kesang's forces regrouped at the outskirts of the town and stopped them there. But they could not drive them back. Fighting continued for the next three months (roughly mid-April to July 1932), neither side able to gain an advantage. The fighting was so near and went on for so long that I actually learned to differentiate the sounds of the guns. I remember that the Tibetan army's English guns made a different sound than the Chinese ones our militia used.

The stalemate ended abruptly when word arrived that Liu Wenhui had sent an army from Tartsedo to retake Batang. Kesang had counted on Liu being too busy with challenges from rivals in Sichuan to move on him, but he had miscalculated. When word came that Liu's army was approaching the mountain pass into Batang, Kesang realized that the situation was hopeless and fled, taking about twenty soldiers with him. We heard afterward that he went to Yunnan and then back to Nanjing. I have no idea what he told his superiors in the GMD, but after a while he managed again to secure a position of authority in the Chinese government bureaucracy. For the people he left behind in Batang, however, there were hard days ahead.

The Chinese soldiers took possession of the town uncontested. When they approached, the Tibetan government troops withdrew across the Drichu River and returned to the garrison at Markam. Again we were under the direct control of the Chinese, who took their revenge on us by executing Yangsin, the head of the local militia, and two other leaders.

I did not actually see the executions, but I remember the day vividly. I was playing with Yangsin's son at the time. His name was Dawa, and we had gone to knock down walnuts from a huge tree. While we were laughing and having fun throwing rocks into the tree, I heard some shots but paid no attention. The fighting was over, and I thought it was just someone testing a rifle. A few minutes later a villager saw us and called me over. I knew something was wrong the minute I looked at him. In a lowered voice he told me not to take Dawa home by the same road we had come. I asked him why, and he said that Dawa's father had been executed and that the execution site was on that road. I did as he asked, of course, but I was shocked and sickened by the news.

I got details about the execution later. With their hands tied behind their backs and heavy placards hung around their necks, the condemned were paraded through the streets of the town and then shot. But they died proudly and defied the Chinese by loudly singing the "Song of the New Kham."

After the executions, Batang went back to normal and I returned to my classes and household routines. (Soon after this, my father was released by the Tibetan government in Markam and returned home.) However, feelings were running high about the killings and the rule of General Liu. I hated Liu Wenhui and dreamed about someday getting revenge. I also dreamed about following in the footsteps of these great heroes and fighting for the rights of Khampas to rule themselves. The whole episode made a deep impression on me, and I think my desire to become a modern, educated Tibetan like Kesang Tsering began to form itself at that time.

CHAPTER 2

The Coup of
Lobsang Thundrup

A few years later our people made another effort to achieve self-rule. This time, my family was even more directly involved.

One day after school, my parents told me that my uncle Lobsang Thundrup was coming from Nanjing. Like Kesang Tsering, he had been educated in our local school, gone on to middle school, and then joined the GMD Party. Some years before, he had been recruited to work in the Chinese government's Mongolian and Tibetan Affairs Commission. I felt especially close to him because his daughter had been living with our family for the past eight years and had become like a younger sister. When I learned that he was coming, I was excited and eager to see him because of all the stories I had heard about his great success in China.

He arrived in Tartsedo in 1935, together with two other Tibetans, Gara Lama and Panda Tobgye.[1] They had been sent by Chiang Kaishek

---

1. Gara Lama was originally from Riwoche, a part of Kham west of the Drichu River that was held by the Tibetan government. He had sided with the Chinese in the Sino-Tibetan war of 1917, and so had been arrested and imprisoned by the Tibetan government. In 1924, however, he escaped to China and made his way to Nanjing. By the late 1920s, he had been appointed a commissioner in the Mongolian and Tibetan Affairs Commission and then in 1935 was sent to Kham.

Panda Tobgye was a member of the wealthy and powerful Pandatsang family. They were from Trayab, a part of Kham that was under the Tibetan government (north of Markam). His father became a prominent trader in Lhasa, and one of his brothers was allowed to become a Tibetan government official, a right normally limited to Tibet's hereditary aristocracy. In 1934, Panda Tobgye launched a revolt and succeeded in capturing a Tibetan government regimental headquarters with all of its rifles and cannons. However, a large uprising did not develop, and when Tibetan government troops moved against him, he fled across the border with his militia and captured weapons and was permitted by the Chinese commander in Batang to resettle in that county. The Tibetan government asked Chiang Kaishek to deport Tobgye, but China refused. — *Goldstein, Sherap, and Siebenschuh* to persuade Tibetan leaders to oppose the Chinese Communists' Red Army (which was then passing through Kham on their "Long March," which ended in Yan'an) and to expand the presence of the GMD Party in Xikang. But, like Kesang Tsering, they had their own agenda—to eliminate the local Chinese administration and establish self-rule for Khampas.

My uncle traveled to Batang via Derge, an important Tibetan principality located to our north. His plan was similar to that of Kesang Tsering. Having secured a commitment from the Derge leaders to provide militia support, he planned to organize the Batang monks and militia—as quietly and unobtrusively as possible. While he was doing this, Panda Tobgye would ready his militia. When the groundwork had been laid and the monks and militia in Batang were prepared for battle, my uncle envisioned a coordinated attack from within and without. The revolt would begin in Batang, supported by the militias of Panda Tobgye and Derge. In theory it wasn't a bad strategy, but unfortunately, nothing turned out the way he planned.

When my uncle reached the outskirts of Batang, he was unexpectedly detained at a checkpoint set up by Fu Dequan, the local Chinese commander. There was no evidence that Fu knew anything about my uncle's plans; however, some apparently unrelated incident had put him on the alert, and my uncle was stopped and told he could not go on to Batang.

He did everything he could think of to get to the town and finally insisted he would not leave without seeing his daughter, whom he hadn't seen for eight years. The Chinese still would have none of it, although they eventually agreed to let my father bring his daughter out to meet him at the checkpoint. When my father arrived, Lobsang sent a message through him to the key figures in Batang about the revolt. Then he pretended to return to China but actually went only to the next relay station, where he waited, planning to sneak into Batang when the Batang monks and militia were ready to support him.

When Panda Tobgye's militia commanders learned that my uncle had been prevented from entering Batang, they attacked without waiting for either my uncle or the Derge troops. They should have waited, but they didn't. Perhaps it was overconfidence, or perhaps they feared the Chinese suspected an attack and did not want to give them time to reinforce their troops; or perhaps they just wanted to get all the credit for the victory themselves. Whatever the reason, they launched the rebellion on their own.

They persuaded the Laga Lama, the chief incarnation in the Batang monastery, to invite the Chinese leader to the monastery. When Fu and his bodyguards arrived, Lobsang, like Kesang Tsering before him, immediately took them prisoner. Fu was ordered to instruct his garrison to surrender and turn over their weapons; he agreed but insisted that to do so he would need to be released because his troops would never believe that he had given orders to surrender unless he was there in person to issue them. The Tibetans were reluctant to let him go, but they also wanted to avoid, if possible, a full-scale battle with the Chinese troops, which might result in heavy casualties. As the discussion went back and forth, Fu, who had been stationed in Kham for a long time and knew Tibetan customs well, came up with a clever ruse.

Using the Tibetans' belief in the power of their protector deities, he told his captors that he would be willing to swear an oath before the monastery's chief protective deity stating that when he got to the garrison he would keep his promise to deliver the guns within three days. Had my uncle, who was more sophisticated, been there, I doubt they would have let him go, but the other Tibetan leaders didn't think anyone would dare lie before a protector deity, and so they agreed.

Fu returned to the garrison, but after three days had passed and the Chinese had not surrendered, the Tibetan troops reiterated their demand that they turn in their weapons immediately. Once again Fu outsmarted them. He replied amiably that he fully intended to keep his word, but that he needed more time because there was disagreement among his troops over whether to take the eastern or southern route out of Batang when they departed. The deadlock, Fu suggested, could best be broken by having the Laga Lama come to the garrison and do a divination ritual. Despite much advice not to go, the Laga Lama went.

It was a colossal mistake. No sooner did he enter the Chinese garrison than Fu seized and detained him, neatly turning the tables on the Tibetans. Then Fu quickly dissolved the unity between Panda Tobgye's militia and the local monks and militia by threatening to kill the Laga Lama if they continued to oppose him. He knew the local people had deep faith in the Laga Lama, and correctly judged that they would not ignore Fu's threat. The local Batang force therefore withdrew from the siege, leaving Panda Tobgye's militia on its own, facing a garrison of seasoned Chinese soldiers who outnumbered them.

With the odds in their favor, the Chinese troops prepared to go on the offensive, and as part of their preparations, they performed a terrible ritual to increase their bravery and confidence. They tied a Tibetan prisoner to a wooden post in the center of their garrison's courtyard and systematically began to stab him with their bayonets. When the victim's screams became too distressing, they gagged him. They stabbed him everywhere, but not too deeply, because the idea was to allow each of the hundreds of Chinese soldiers to wet his bayonet with the blood of a living enemy. This, they believed, would bring good luck in the coming battle.

By evening he was dead, and well after dark, the Chinese poured out of the garrison and attacked Panda's militia. It was a bitter fight, with heavy casualties. Eighty-five Chinese troops and fifteen or sixteen of Panda Tobgye's militia were killed before the latter were forced to retreat to their home base in Po, two days' ride from the town.

Fu did not try to pursue them. Instead, he went immediately to Panda Tobgye's large house in Batang and looted it. After taking all the items of real value, Fu set out a number of boxes containing less valuable items, such as clothing and tea, and told the Batang people to take whatever they wanted. Sadly, there was a scramble for the goods. Thus Fu achieved a double victory. He made off with a fortune from Panda Tobgye's estate, and by cleverly dividing the rest of the goods among the villagers, he indirectly involved the local people in the looting, making it less a Chinese-Tibetan issue. (Panda's militia, however, scored one success. As they withdrew, they went to Fu's private house and captured his wife. Using her as a hostage, they were able to work out a deal whereby Fu returned some of Panda's possessions and did not take further reprisals against any of his people.)

At the time of the battle, my uncle was waiting at the next relay station. When he learned of the defeat, he immediately went to meet Panda Tobgye, who was not with his militia then but in Litang, a Tibetan nomad area east of Batang. They decided to regroup, coordinate their activities more carefully, and try again. This coincided with a change in Fu's thinking, as he now allowed my uncle to return to Batang. After arriving in Batang, my uncle Lobsang outwardly maintained cordial relations with Fu while covertly organizing the next attack, which began a few weeks later.

The town of Batang was surrounded by a wall that was too high for horses to jump over but could be scaled by men, and so was carefully guarded by Fu's troops. When they were ready to begin the attack, my uncle and Panda Tobgye chose not to launch a frontal attack. Instead, they began a siege of the town to prevent the inhabitants and the Chinese from leaving and, more importantly, to cut off their access to firewood, which was collected by donkey from the surrounding mountains.

After a few weeks of stalemate, sporadic gunfire, and little movement, my uncle and Panda made three direct attacks. On the third attempt, about fifteen of Panda's militia successfully scaled the wall and fought their way into the part of the town near the Chinese garrison. Fierce fighting erupted there, and for a while things looked bad for the Chinese, who at one point actually decided to flee. But just as Fu was dousing buildings with gasoline in preparation to set them on fire, a Chinese trader married to a local Tibetan girl persuaded Fu not to flee, arguing that if he tried to run, he and his men would almost surely be harassed and killed by the Tibetan horsemen. Fu reconsidered, and the Chinese went back to the fight, which slowly began to go their way because the initial incursion was not followed up by more Tibetan troops entering the town or by the townsfolk rising up. The Chinese soon were able to kill or drive off the Tibetans who had made it over the wall. Many wounded Tibetans were finished off by Chinese soldiers, who hit them on the head with rocks to save their bullets.

The failure of this attack did not put an end to the siege, and my uncle and Panda Tobgye had begun planning a fourth attack when news arrived that a division of Chinese central government troops had arrived at the Dunglung Pass, to the east of Batang. It was late summer 1935, and the communists' Red Army was in the midst of their famous Long March, which took them through many Tibetan areas of Kham. Although they didn't enter Batang, they crossed the ridge to our east, and I remember hearing that some outlying villagers actually captured some stragglers.[2]

The Chinese Nationalist general heading this army ordered both Fu and my uncle to stop fighting and join forces with him to pursue the Red Army. At this point my uncle felt he no longer could continue the attack against the local Chinese warlord, so he decided to stop the battle and

2. Years later, in 1950, Phünwang met General He Long of the People's Liberation Army, who told him that he had seen Batang from the mountain pass east of the town when his force was passing by during the Long March. He joked with Phünwang, saying that on his maps Batang was a large town, so he was surprised when he looked down and saw it was so tiny. They had a good laugh about this, and it spurred Phünwang to write a poem:

On Batang's Dunglung Pass
General He Long looked down.
The monastic land [Batang] between the two rivers
Oh my goodness, it was like a small grain of barley.

'ba' gi mdung lung la khar
dmag dpon ho lung spyan gzigs
chu gnyis bar gyi dgon yul
a tse 'bru chung lta bu

— Goldstein, Sherap, and Siebenschuh

return to China. It was the end of the fighting, but the beginning of a new life for me.

I was only fourteen, but even before the fighting was over I had made a major decision about my life. I wanted to follow in the footsteps of Kesang Tsering and Lobsang Thundrup by going to China to study, so I too could become a leader in the fight for the freedom of our Tibetan people. I wasn't in any way discouraged by the defeats. I was proud of the attempts. I remember how I felt at the beginning of Panda Tobgye's militia's first attack. When I saw his soldiers standing guard every five feet along the route from the town to the monastery, they looked fierce and imposing, and I was proud of our people. I still remember how my heart rose when I saw Kesang Tsering fire his pistol in the air and proclaim to the world that Batang was now going to be ruled by Tibetans. I wanted to be like my uncle and Kesang Tsering, and so the first time I heard my uncle mention leaving, I eagerly asked him to take me with him to Nanjing to school.

He laughed and said that he wasn't leaving for China then. He said he was just going to visit his colleague Gara Lama, who was seriously ill in another part of Kham, and that he would be back in a few weeks. He told me not to worry, but I *did* worry. I knew now that I wanted more than anything else to get an education in China. I didn't admire Kesang Tsering and my uncle simply because they defied the Chinese. I admired them because they were educated, sophisticated, and modern, as well as committed to the belief I now also strongly held—that Khampas had to rule Kham. Going to study in China therefore had become the focus of my dreams, and I feared that my uncle's insistence that he would return soon was simply empty words intended to placate me.

The more I worried that my uncle would not return, the more I became convinced that unless I took prompt action I would lose my only chance to study in China. So when I learned he had left, I decided to run away from home, catch up with him on the road, and make him take me with him. I persuaded a young friend of mine to join me, and with his help I stole some food from my family's storage room and gave it to him with instructions that he should meet me early the next morning with the provisions. I got up early and waited at the appointed spot, but my friend did not come on time. I waited a few minutes, but when he didn't arrive, I decided not to waste time going to look for him, and I left alone, without any food or money.

I walked as fast as I could to the next relay station, where I arrived hungry and extremely tired. But I was too late. The innkeeper told me that my uncle had already gone. I was crestfallen and wanted to follow him at once, but the innkeeper persuaded me to have a meal and spend the night. He promised he would send a rider ahead to tell my uncle I was there. Unbeknownst to me, he also sent someone to tell my family.

The next morning, first my uncle arrived, and then my father. My uncle was amused by my fears and again promised that he would return to Batang soon and that when he finally returned to China he would definitely take me with him. My father also assured me that he would let me go to China to study, so I felt better. I returned with my father. I had some lingering doubts, but deep down I believed them. Now I felt it was just a matter of time.

The ride home with my father is a painful memory. He had brought only one horse, so on the return trip I sat on the saddle in front of him. As we rode, he asked me to tell him the truth about why I had run away. I thought for a few moments about whether I should speak candidly. I decided that I ought to, and so I told him that the main reason was that I wanted to go to study in China and be educated like my uncle, but then I also I told him that I was unhappy with life in our household.

Perhaps it was presumptuous or disrespectful, but I told him that he drank too much. I reminded him that when he had come home from Markam—after we had thought he had been killed—he was so drunk that he could scarcely stay seated on his horse. And my aunt had had to clap her hands over his mouth to prevent him from yelling insults that would have antagonized the Chinese. I also said that I didn't like it when he got drunk and hit my mother. So, I said, I was running away because of these things as well.

My father said nothing. I was facing forward and couldn't see his face, so I had no idea what he was thinking. The silence began to get uncomfortable, and suddenly I felt something warm and wet on the back of my neck. When I turned in the saddle to see what was happening, I was shocked to see tears flowing freely from his eyes. I had never seen him cry.

After we got home, I wondered many times if I had done the right thing in being honest. I didn't know the answer, but I had said what I had said, and my life was now pulling me in a new direction. My uncle was as good as his word. He returned to Batang, and when the fighting was over, he took me with him to China as he had promised. For better or for worse, I would not see Batang again for nearly ten years.

CHAPTER 3

School Years

We left Batang for China on horseback. We were a small party consisting of my uncle, his daughter and younger sister, a servant, and myself. Because my uncle worried that Liu Wenhui might try to arrest him, for the first leg of the journey—between Batang and Liu's headquarters at Tartsedo—he pretended to be a trader, and we traveled with about thirty yaks loaded with goods. I spent most of the time daydreaming about what school in China would be like. I remember that I wasn't apprehensive at all. I was excited. I was going to become educated and modern. I couldn't wait to get started and see a new world.

At Tartsedo, my uncle sent the yaks back, and we went on foot from there. This portion of the trip was a nightmare. We stayed off the main roads, choosing remote mountain trails and passes that were exhausting and dangerous. My uncle hired two porters, who carried the girls on their backs, and we often had to go for a day or more on short rations because we were passing through areas with no villages. My uncle's feet blistered and swelled, and it took us about twelve days to reach Leshan, where we were able to take a boat directly to the city of Chongqing and finally get beyond Liu's reach.

In Chongqing we were in ethnic China, and after we arrived, my uncle had us change into Chinese clothing. He also had us clean up. We had been on the trail for several weeks, and the two girls had so many lice in their hair that my uncle hired a Chinese woman to help them wash it.

(In the end, we all had to have our heads shaved.) But it didn't bother me at all.

I was thrilled to be in the midst of this fantastic new world. I was naïve and full of wonder. I had never imagined there were places with so many people and buildings that seemed as large as mountains. The first time my uncle took me for a ride in a car and I saw the scenery whizzing by, I thought it was the buildings that were moving! I was also amazed by the sight of rickshaws pulled by people—something I had never seen or imagined—and by the endless shops selling all kinds of odd and wonderful things. Although I had studied Chinese in primary school, people spoke quickly here, and I had a hard time understanding them. I found that at first I could communicate effectively only about simple everyday things, and then only with difficulty. Obviously I had a lot to learn. But I was in the modern world, and I loved it. At fourteen, I thought my life had finally begun.

While we waited to secure passage on a boat going down the Yangtse River to Nanjing, we stayed in a house my uncle rented. He went to work in another part of the city during the day, and we stayed around the house and took our meals in Chinese restaurants.

Although I later came to find Chinese food delicious, at first I found it strange and unsatisfying. In Tibet we were used to eating a lot of butter and meat, but the restaurants where we ate served mainly rice and vegetable dishes, which did not fill us up. I amazed the restaurant workers because I would eat six or seven bowls of rice at a sitting (and the girls ate five or six). In truth, even after eating all this, we usually went out and bought some bread from street vendors in the afternoon.

After about two weeks in Chongqing, we finally got seats on a boat to Nanjing. My uncle had to stay behind, but he made special arrangements with the boatmaster to look after us. The trip was to take four or five days, and I wasn't afraid at all. We dressed like the Chinese now, but everyone on the boat knew we were Tibetan. Actually, it was a lot of fun. The boatmaster had never seen Tibetans before, and he treated us with special concern and care. He sometimes invited us to eat with him and the crew, and in general went out of his way to be kind to us. We didn't know enough Chinese to have extended conversations with the other passengers, but we could talk among ourselves, and we made the whole trip into an adventure.

When we arrived in Nanjing, my uncle's brother and his wife met us at the dock. He was a student at Chiang Kaishek's military academy—

actually he was the first Tibetan to enroll there. His wife was a translator in the Mongolian and Tibetan Affairs Commission, the branch of the Nationalist government that dealt with minority nationalities. She had gone to the Batang missionary school and knew English as well as Chinese and Tibetan.

The school program we were planning to attend was part of Chiang Kaishek's Central Political Institute that had been established by the Mongolian and Tibetan Affairs Commission to train Tibetans and other minorities to work in the government. There were approximately three hundred students, of whom fifteen to twenty were Tibetans (some from Batang, some from the Panchen Lama's area in Shigatse, and a few from other Tibetan areas in Kham and Qinghai). The rest were Mongols, Uygurs, Yi, Hui, and Han Chinese from border areas such as Gansu and Qinghai.

Our Chinese was too poor to allow us to enter even the preparatory class for the school, so my uncle arranged for us to study with a private tutor. Life in Nanjing was exciting, as there were always new things to experience. The school, for example, frequently showed propaganda films about the war with Japan, and the first time I saw one, I got frightened because I thought the guns and cannons I saw firing on the screen would actually hit me. At the same time, I was frustrated because I didn't understand much that they were saying in the films.

I worked very hard with my tutor and after a few months improved tremendously. Before long I was able to read simple novels. I remember being amused by a book about a Russian Eskimo who came to a big city for the first time and stared at all the cars and buildings. The story made me feel better because it gave me a little perspective. I laughed and laughed because I realized that that was just about what I had been like when I first came to Chongqing and Nanjing.

I wrote letters to my family, but I was not homesick and didn't mind that they did not send me letters in return. Every weekend, Tibetans in Nanjing got together at our house to eat, sing, and dance, so I was not totally cut off from my culture or food. After about seven months, my Chinese improved enough for me to be officially enrolled in a preparatory class.

The school was run in military fashion, and we were all treated like soldiers. We wore uniforms. (I thought they were very sharp.) And the teachers came to inspect our bedrooms every morning. We all had to make our beds with corners so tight and precise that they reminded me of the squares of tofu we bought in the market.

The Chinese government paid all our school expenses, and in addition they gave each of us a salary. I received eight yuan (Chinese dollars) per month for food and another two yuan for miscellaneous expenses. It was a good salary, and it was paid in silver *dayan* coins. The food was good, too. We got a special large tray with compartments for one vegetable dish with meat, one with no meat, and soup. We could also take a bowl and fill it with as much rice and steamed bread [ch. *mantou*] as we wanted.

The military aspects of the school carried over to the canteen as well. After we sat down with our trays, we had to wait to begin eating until a military official blew a whistle. Then after about ten minutes, he would blow the whistle again and we had to stop eating whether we were finished or not. (I remember there was a boy from Inner Mongolia who had bad teeth and couldn't eat meat, so he gave me his meat and I gave him my vegetable dish.) We ate quickly, but overall we ate very well.

We studied Chinese, math, history, and geography, and all the teaching was done in Chinese at a high level. It was wonderful. I felt fortunate to be there. I sometimes thought about my primary school in Batang and would laugh to myself at the difference. The Batang school taught very little compared to the one in Nanjing.

Sometimes when I thought about the differences between our simple village and Chiang Kaishek's academy in the capital of China, I was amazed at and proud of how far I had come. I was also thrilled when I got the chance to get a close look at Chiang Kaishek.

Every Monday morning, the students attended a meeting to commemorate Sun Yatsen, the father of the Chinese revolution against the Manchu dynasty. Everyone was required to attend, and high GMD Party officials would often come as well. Once Chiang spoke in person, and I got to see him and Madame Chiang from a distance of only a few feet. He had a narrow mustache and wore a large sword at his waist. I thought he was very handsome—even elegant.

I wasn't at the school long before the Japanese war began to close in on us. It wasn't something on a movie screen anymore. It was knocking at our door. In July 1937, the Japanese attacked Beijing, and then in August they attacked Shanghai. A few months later, Chiang ordered the Chinese government to move for safety to a temporary capital in Chongqing in the west, and our school moved as well. We didn't go directly to Chongqing, though. We moved westward gradually.

We stayed for a few months in Anhui Province, then moved to Jiangxi Province, and from there we relocated to Zhijiang, a city near Changsha.

While we were in transit, living conditions and, in particular, the food got much worse. However, we often had no classes, and the loose discipline and the relaxation of the structure provided by our military routine allowed students to have more time to meet and talk—and organize.

I experienced my first antigovernment criticism when some of the older student leaders complained that school officials were misusing the funds meant for us. They also spoke negatively about the state of the GMD government, arguing that most higher officials were interested only in getting rich and were doing so by means of rampant corruption, even though the government was losing the war to the Japanese and the majority of people were living in extremely poor conditions. As a result of the protests about conditions, the central government sent a special official to investigate and made some changes. This was my first exposure to political activism, and I was impressed. I agreed with everything the student leaders were saying, and I admired them for their courage and convictions.

Since we often didn't have formal classes, some of the student leaders taught us progressive songs that were not part of the GMD political curriculum. I still remember the words of one song, which said the "workers, farmers, soldiers, and traders should unite and save the country." This seems mild now, but at the time it was considered very progressive and revolutionary because it said that nongovernment elements were needed to save the country.

We were also deeply involved in opposing the Japanese oppression and exploitation of China. Although I was opposed to Liu Wenhui's rule in Kham, I felt patriotic about China in general. About this time I saw a wonderful Russian propaganda film about a daring young pilot. It was full of aerial dogfights and heroic deeds, and I suddenly got the idea that I could help the nation by joining the Chinese Air Force and going to fight against Japan. (My fantasy plan also included flying back to Kham and bombing the garrison of Liu Wenhui at Tartsedo, thereby striking a blow for Kham and the Bapas!)

My friend from Batang, Dawa—whose father had been executed by Liu Wenhui—had joined me at the school, and I quickly sold him on the idea of our both trying to become pilots. We were young and angry at the Japanese, and the times were so volatile and unsettled that almost anything seemed possible. As I think back about it now, it is amazing to think how far we actually got before we were finally stopped.

The first thing we did was write a letter to Zhang Zhezhong, the governor of Hunan Province. In it we said that we two were Tibetans who were outraged at what the Japanese were doing to China, and we wanted to become pilots so we could help in the fight against them. We were not sure whether the letter would reach him, so we also decided we should go to talk with him in person in Changsha. There was a problem, however.

Dawa and I had hardly any money, and at first we didn't know how we could afford to make the trip. Then Dawa came up with the solution. He was engaged to be married to Kesang Tsering's younger sister and had bought a gold engagement ring for her. We sold the ring for twenty-five yuan, borrowed a little money from some of the other Batang students, and eventually had enough for traveling expenses.

We got a leave of absence from the school by telling the administration that Dawa's fiancée had come to Hunan and that we needed to visit her. Because it was wartime and things were so up in the air that the school had little time to look closely into requests like ours, we got the permission to travel with no trouble. It was the beginning of a very exciting adventure!

The minute we had the school's permission, we took a train to Changsha and tried to meet Governor Zhang. We didn't succeed, but we were able to talk to his secretary. We knew we made a good impression on him because he invited us for a meal and praised us, saying, "It's amazing that border people like you two have so much courage and determination." He also wrote a letter of introduction for us to Mao Banchu, the commander-in-chief of the GMD air force, and sent a copy to Zhou Zhirong, who was the head of the GMD's Air Force Academy. Dawa and I waited eagerly in Changsha for an answer, but after two weeks we got nervous and decided that perhaps we should go ourselves and try to find Mao and Zhou at the air force complex in Wuhan.

By now we were running low on money. We looked well off and snappy in our fancy school uniforms, but appearances were deceiving. We scarcely had enough money to eat. Things were so bad that we decided to stay at a classy Wuhan hotel because the room charges there could be paid when you left rather than daily, as was the case at cheap inns. But we still had to pay for each meal, so we bought only ten or twenty cents worth of bread or the cheapest noodles on the street and went to a park and ate it. That way, we could maintain our cover by returning to the hotel still looking important and well off.

It took a lot of walking around before we found the air force school, and while we were searching, our money dwindled further. But during our walks I saw things that made a deep and lasting impression on me.

We passed expensive restaurants where the people with money ate, and sometimes I couldn't help stopping to stare at the food through the window. We were so hungry, and they had so much. We saw the other side of life as well. We often passed people who were terribly poor sleeping in the streets, and once we saw a woman still holding a dead child at her breast. I couldn't stop thinking about the contrast between the way the rich people lived and the life of the very poor. I felt a kinship with the people in the streets—Dawa's and my situation was really only a step away from theirs.

Things eventually became desperate financially, but we never thought of going back to school because we were convinced that an answer to our letter would come soon and we would start training to be pilots. By this time, we were so hungry that when we saw delicious food in restaurant windows, our mouths watered. Sometimes we had only one or two pieces of bread a day. So I wrote my uncle, who by now had moved to Chongqing, telling him we were trying to join the air force and asking him to send money. While we were waiting, the Chinese government convened a meeting in Wuhan that Kesang Tsering attended. My uncle forwarded money to me through him, and he sent his secretary to contact us.

Kesang Tsering invited us to meet him at a fine restaurant, and when we got there, we gorged ourselves. Hunger is the best sauce, and this was one of the best meals I have ever eaten. Kesang Tsering enjoyed watching us eat; then he got serious and scolded us roundly. He said we were irresponsible and shortsighted, and that there was no way he was going to allow us to join the air force. He wrote a letter to the head of the Air Force Academy telling him that we were not eligible to enlist because we were Tibetan minority students who had come to China to study, not to fight. He said that nothing good could come of our enlisting, because if we were injured in any way, the investment in us, the training and schooling, would be wasted. Moreover, if we were killed, the Tibetans would probably say that the Chinese were responsible. He wanted us to return to Chongqing with him, and that was that.

Dawa, who was engaged to his daughter, agreed, but I refused; he finally said that he would take Dawa with him and that I could just find my way back to school on my own. Ironically, the next day a letter arrived admitting us to pilot training school. We were to be treated as "exceptions" without having to take the entrance examination. But it was too late, and I took the money my uncle had sent and grudgingly returned to school, embarrassed because I had told everyone I was going to become a pilot and fight the Japanese.

Soon after I returned, it was time for exams, and of course I was completely unprepared. But I got a lucky break. My main teacher, Wang Xiaoxong, liked me, and he told me that instead of trying to take the exams, I could write an essay about the things I had seen in Wuhan. I jumped at the chance. My mind and imagination were full of the things I had just seen. I wrote about two of them. The first was the hardship that the Japanese invasion was causing the Chinese people. The second was the vast gulf between the way the rich and the poor lived in China, the tremendous difference between the wealthy people laughing in the restaurants and the poor people outside dying in the streets. I wrote about how moved I had been by seeing these things and how it had begun to change my thinking.

My teacher, it turned out, was sympathetic to socialist political ideas. Some of his friends were already members of the Communist Party, and he liked my essay very much. Without telling me, he corrected all the little mistakes and sent it to a newspaper in Zhijiang, and the paper actually published it. I didn't know anything about it until Mr. Wang called me over one day and gave me the ten yuan the paper had paid for my article and a copy in print. It was the first time I had earned anything by my writing. I was sixteen years old, and ten yuan was a lot at that time. It was enough to cover basic living expenses for a month. But the importance of the article was far greater than the money.

The trip to Wuhan had a major impact on my life. After the article was published, the other students suddenly began to notice me. I was no longer just the strange Tibetan who had said he was joining the air force, but an intellectual with something worth saying. They were surprised and pleased by my views, which they considered democratic. My thinking began to focus more sharply on social and political issues, and because my teacher and my fellow students took my ideas seriously, I became more eager to pursue them and to trust my instincts about what I thought and saw.

During this time, our school continued to move west, first to Guiyang, the capital of Guizhou Province, and then finally to Chongqing in late 1938. When we were in Nanjing, the school's administrators had watched what we read and controlled what we had access to. But the more we moved around, the more access we had to printed materials of all kinds, including communist publications. Chongqing had a much wider range of materials available than Nanjing because the Chinese Communist Party had offices there, as did the communists' Xinhua News Agency. I also discovered that I had an ally in my teacher, Mr. Wang.

Teacher Wang had been watching me ever since the publication of the essay. He told me he saw that my thinking was different from that of most of the other students, and he went out of his way to show me progressive and communist writings and newspapers, including articles and books by Stalin and Lenin. He was careful, though. Usually he would call me to his room in the evening on some pretext, so the other students wouldn't see. The first book he gave me was Stalin's *On Nationalities*. The next was a thin little book that had a tremendous impact on me. It was Lenin's brilliant *Concerning a Nationality's Right of Self-Determination*. Mr. Wang said he wasn't a member of the Communist Party himself, but he clearly had friends who were communist activists working for the Xinhua News Agency, and therefore I began to have access to a whole new set of ideas and social analyses. The things he gave me caused radical changes in the way I thought about things as a Tibetan.

What struck me immediately about the articles and books by Stalin and Lenin was that they were about things I knew. I had seen the terrible gap between the poor and the wealthy. I knew about how one group, like that led by the warlord Liu Wenhui, was oppressing and controlling other people—minorities—like our people in Batang and Kham. I hadn't known before that great minds like Lenin and Stalin had thought about issues like these.

I was especially impressed by Lenin's idea that individual nationalities should have the right to their own identity and freedom, that they should have the freedom to choose whether they would live free and separate or join in a union as equal partners with another country. I admired the Soviet Union, because all nationalities in the Soviet Union had equal rights and each nationality was a republic with its own government. And I understood what Lenin meant when he talked about the inevitable tension between the nationality that has power and the ones that do not. Having grown up in Batang and seen what I had seen, I understood the reality that the strong nationality would often use its power to oppress the smaller, weaker one, and that the smaller ones would fight bitterly against this. I felt sometimes as if Lenin knew exactly what I was thinking, what I cared about most. I also found exciting and persuasive the notion of the International, where communists would be represented as equals in a new political entity that transcended national boundaries. This introduction to communist ideology and theory influenced my thinking for the rest of my life. I became convinced that Tibet's problems would be solved by a communist revolution followed by Tibet (or Kham) joining the International as equals.

Because of my early success as a writer, in early 1939 I became the editor in charge of the school bulletin board on which news was posted weekly. Since I decided what articles to post, I was able to give special emphasis to issues I was interested in. One day, a Tibetan from Amdo (Labrang, in Gansu Province) named Kuncho Tashi (his Chinese name was Wu Zhengang) introduced himself to me. He was two grades higher, but he said he read the bulletin board often and liked my choices. Then he obliquely asked me if I had been reading any new books lately. I knew what he meant, and because he was Tibetan I felt I could trust him, so I said, "Yes, I have been." He asked what I liked and I told him. He said, "I am also quietly reading new books like this." After that, we became very good friends and shared ideas and readings.

Another Bapa, Ngawang Kesang, also joined our core group. He had been educated by the American missionaries in Batang and lived in their orphanage because his father had died when he was young and his mother was unable to raise him. After finishing primary school, the Americans sent him to a middle school in Chengdu together with two other Tibetan children. Ngawang Kesang told me that when the three of them first arrived in Chengdu the Chinese students thought they would be real bumpkins coming from a "backward" Tibetan area. He used to like to tell a funny story about this. When they were first shown around by their Chinese classmates, there was an organ in one room and the Chinese asked them whether they had ever seen anything like this, fully expecting the answer to be negative. Instead, Ngawang Kesang calmly walked over, sat down, and started playing it (he had learned this in missionary school). The Chinese students were shocked and said, "Well, these barbarian kids are capable."

After Chengdu, the Americans sent Ngawang to our school in Nanjing. He was nine years older than me, and smart—he knew Tibetan, Chinese, and some English and could sing all the Christian songs in Tibetan. He also had a deep desire to change our society and institutions, and we became close friends and comrades in Chongqing.

My formal studies continued, but I was now more and more absorbed in the informal reading and study of history and political ideology. A few close friends, like Kuncho Tashi, and I were deeply influenced by the idea of communism as we were learning to understand it. My teacher, Mr. Wang, helped us immensely by always giving us new things to read. For example, when he gave us a copy of Edgar Snow's book *Red Star over China,* we all read and discussed it, talking about Mao's life in Yan'an and what life had been like on the Long March.

This was our first opportunity to learn what was happening with the Chinese Communist Party, and we were very impressed. We passed the book around like hungry people sharing food. We also read an interesting book by a reporter about his trips to America and Russia. He wrote about introducing American workers to communist ideas, and was full of praise for Russia. One of the things that brought us together was having read and been influenced by Lenin's thoughts on nationalities. The things he said seemed to fit the needs of Tibetans exactly. We weren't sophisticated Marxists. We didn't really think much about landlords oppressing the common people or the fine points of class distinctions and class struggle. We focused on the things that seemed most directly related to our own lives.

The new ideas were exciting, and eventually, in 1939, a few of us decided that we should start a secret Tibetan Communist Party in the school. The name we gave it was the Tibetan Communist Revolutionary Group [tib. *bod rigs gung khran ring lugs gsar brje tshogs chung*]. At first there were only five members: Kuncho Tashi, Sherap (from Labrang), Maja Thundrup, Ngawang Kesang, and me [see figure 3]. We were very serious and earnest and pledged that for the rest of our lives we would work together for socialist causes, and especially for issues specifically related to questions of Tibetan nationality and self-rule.

In the early days, we met secretly, sometimes in parks and sometimes in the woods near the school. We would discuss and argue about Tibetan freedom and the need to oppose the oppression of people and unite all Tibetans. We frequently discussed what would be appropriate activities for us, and we undertook some simple tasks like translating the "Internationale" and the Chinese Communist Party's main songs into Tibetan. We also decided to send letters to Stalin and Mao Zedong informing them of the creation of our party, whose main purpose was to bring democracy and revolution to Kham and Tibet.

We thought a great deal about how to address the letters, since letter headings are important in Tibetan and Chinese culture. To Stalin we wrote, "Comrade Stalin, the great teacher and the great leader of the oppressed nationalities of the proletariat of the world" [tib. *'dzam gling yongs kyi 'byor med gral rim gyi gnya' gnon 'og tshod pa'i mi rigs kyi rlabs chen slob dpon dang rlabs chen gtso 'dzin blo mthun si ta ling*]. And to Mao Zedong we wrote, "Comrade Mao Zedong, the great leader of all the nationalities of the East" [tib. *shar phyogs mi rigs khag gyi rlabs chen gtso 'dzin blo mthun ma'o rtse tung*]. The reason for the difference in headings was that we felt the Soviet Union was extremely powerful and in the future would be the most powerful country in the world. By contrast, we thought that Mao Zedong would become the leader who established communism in Asia.

We also decided that we should try to influence the thinking of the other Tibetan students, so we organized a larger, more public group that was not explicitly communist. Kuncho Tashi and I argued that we Tibetans should form an organization to look after the interests of Tibetans. If we worked together, we might accomplish things for Tibetans at the school that we couldn't achieve as individuals. We pointed out that we were always together and did things together anyway, so why not make it official? Kuncho Tashi was the oldest of the students from Amdo and they all respected him. And the Bapas were willing to listen to me. I wasn't the oldest, but I was a strong personality, and they all took me seriously.

We talked about many ideas and problems we might try to address and finally settled on three basic issues: (1) we were opposed to any form of Han chauvinism by the GMD; (2) we were against the oppression of the people in Kham by GMD soldiers and officials; and (3) we asked for better treatment of the Tibetan students, and especially that the school improve conditions for teaching Tibetans. Kuncho Tashi and I recruited about twenty Tibetan students and gave this group the name the Sichuan Association of Tibetan Students from Various Regions [tib. *sa gnas khag gi bod pa gzhon nu zi khron bskyod pa'i slob grogs tshogs chung*].

In the spring of 1940, the Dalai Lama's Bureau Office in Chongqing threw a big party for all the Tibetans (and some Chinese) to celebrate the Fourteenth Dalai Lama's enthronement in Lhasa on February 22. We were invited and decided it would be a perfect time to formally announce the existence of our group. We had a picture taken of the members who were there, and then danced and sang for the rest of the night.

The first formal action we took was to petition the school authorities requesting action on the three points mentioned above, especially the need for more classes in the Tibetan language and better food. We felt that the food at the school in Nanjing had been a lot better than the food we were getting in Chongqing. A lot of the students from Batang were coming down with tuberculosis. We had heard that a better diet could help cure the disease, so we thought the school should improve our diet. Also, some of the Tibetan students had had to go home because they

Figure 3. Group picture of students in the Tibetan Communist Party and the Sichuan Organization of Tibetan Students, Chongqing, 1940. *Back row, from left*: Dawa *(first)*, Phünwang *(third)*, and Kuncho Tashi *(fourth)*. *Front row, from left*: Pema *(second)*, Kuncho Tashi's wife *(third)*, Ngawang Kesang *(fourth)*, Sherap *(fifth)*, and Chömpel *(sixth)*.

couldn't afford to stay. Besides these issues, we also wanted to make people aware of our group and to increase its influence and attract new members. (We did not sign individual names to the petition, only the general signature "A few Tibetan students.")

Our petition certainly got attention.

We soon learned that Gong Beicheng, the GMD Party secretary in our school, had been suspicious of us for some time and had already been asking the other students what the Tibetans were doing together all the time. He wasn't happy about our meeting together as a group so frequently for "social" activities. He suspected us and soon called Kuncho Tashi and me to his office.

"I want to know what you students are always getting together for," he said angrily. "If you keep it up, your studies are going to suffer. A student's job at this school is to study. It's not our custom to let students form organizations. In fact, this is a GMD school, and you are not allowed to form a separate organization."

Then he told us directly that we were not to meet together as a group anymore. As he spoke, he banged his fist on the table. It didn't frighten me, however. It made me angry, and I responded testily, "There is no contradiction between being a student and associating in a group like this! We made a proper request to the GMD government, and our organization isn't just Kuncho Tashi and me—not just two people—it involves all the Tibetan students. So even if you silence us, you can't silence all the students!"

"All right," he said, "if this involves all the students, then we will talk to all the students."

The larger meeting was even more contentious. Gong Beicheng began by lecturing us all about our duties as students. He reminded us that we had responsibilities and that there were a lot of things we were not permitted to do. He really worked himself up and pounded his fist on the table as he spoke to emphasize his points.

Some of the students were frightened by his anger, and a few began to cry from the tension. But I got just as angry and pounded my own fist on the table when I responded. "What do you think you're doing?" he roared.

"I am imitating you," I said. "You are our teacher, and I am following your example!" (He never forgave me for defying him in public like that.)

My action seemed to give the other students confidence, because we all spoke with one voice and said that we would not accept or obey his orders, and when he kept shouting at us, the Tibetan students all stood up and filed out of the room. We went back to our classrooms, where some of the students smashed the desks and chairs to vent their anger. It was invigorating to stand up to Gong and demand our rights.

After the meeting, Gong Beicheng again called Kuncho Tashi and me to his office and told us point blank that we could not continue to have a Tibetan association. We still refused to agree and told him that it was his behavior that was unacceptable, not ours. We said that we had come a long way to study here in China, living apart from our parents and enduring many hardships. Treating us this way amounted to oppression and we would not accept it. (I was only eighteen, but I had read a great deal and was confident in my knowledge and the legitimacy of my views.) Again we stalked out. At this point Gong reported the matter to Chiang Kaishek himself.

Chiang and a number of other high GMD officials came to the regular Monday meeting of the students and officials of the school. At first, the meeting went on more or less as usual, but just as it seemed to have ended and the students were all getting up to leave, an announcement was made that the students under the supervision of the Mongolian and Tibetan Affairs Commission school should stay.

When the room had cleared, we were told to come up and sit in the front. Then Chiang Kaishek rose and moved directly in front of us. He had a big sword hanging at his side, and he put his hand casually on the handle as he looked us over. You could see the anger in his eyes as he began to scold us.

"The central government has invested a lot of money to teach and train you," he said. "We have brought you here from far away so you can study and have the advantages of our teaching. And yet instead of studying you have been causing disturbances, challenging the authority of the school."

Because he was angry, his speaking style wasn't smooth. It was clipped and choppy as he emphasized each of the things we had done wrong. He pretended that he was talking about all of the students in general, but it was very clear that he was talking about the Tibetan students in particular. And when he was finished, he stood facing us, letting his eyes move from face to face, daring us to contradict him. I think he wanted to see what we would do, and as the silence continued, things began to get very tense. Then a Tibetan student named Pema [see figure 3] raised his hand and, in the formal way that all students used when they had something to say in a class, said, "Principal, I have something to report."

You could have heard a pin drop.

Chiang looked around to see who had spoken, and when he found him, he walked slowly over to him and had his assistant write down the name and number on his identification badge. *What* had we gotten ourselves into? We had heard terrible things about Chiang's temper. Supposedly, when he was principal of the Infantry School, some students who had made criticisms had been executed.

I thought it was over for us all then. But Pema, to our amazement, continued to speak. He looked right at Chiang and said, "You have said in your criticism that we are neglecting our studies and causing trouble, but we *are* studying hard and we are not causing trouble."

I think Chiang was surprised that any of us dared to speak. And although Pema was denying the truth of what Chiang had just said, he didn't do it in an aggressive or challenging way. Somehow he made it sound as if he was actually agreeing with him—that they were on the same side. He spoke simply. His Chinese was not good, and so he phrased things oddly. To our amazement, when he finished, the anger seemed to go out of Chiang. He actually nodded as if in agreement with Pema, and even seemed to be amused at the way Pema had phrased things. When the rest of us saw that Chiang's anger was abating, another student, who was known to be a bit of a sycophant, spoke up and said that he was also studying diligently. The tension eased perceptibly.

For the moment, Pema had saved the day. He was a very strange student, and when I asked him afterward why he had spoken up, he said that it was because the things that Chiang was saying were making him angry. But then when I asked him what he had hoped would happen, what he had had in mind by speaking, he said he didn't know—he had no idea.

If he hadn't spoken when and as he did, I really don't know how the meeting would have ended. The obvious thing would have been for the Tibetan students to apologize to Chiang and the school. But we didn't think of that until afterward, and we might not have done it. I don't know what might have happened then.

All of the Tibetan students were enormously relieved, and I was too, but at the same time Kuncho Tashi and I knew we were still in danger. The school knew that Kuncho and I were the ones behind the organization, and soon afterward they retaliated. It happened to Kuncho Tashi first.

According to the rules, students could not have their wives living with them, but Kuncho Tashi had brought his wife anyway, and eventually she got pregnant. The school now used that as an excuse for getting rid of him. He was told to take his wife back to Labrang (in Gansu) immediately, and because of the regulation, he had no choice. However, he was not permitted to return because the school secretly sent a letter to the GMD office in Labrang telling them not to allow him to do so. One day he was there and the next day he was gone. We didn't find out the details until later.

Soon after this, they eliminated me. One night, the head of the school summoned me to his office and informed me that I was to turn in all my badges and insignias and be officially separated the next morning. He may have said something about my not adhering to school rules and discipline, too, but I don't recall much from that night. I was too shocked and angry to register details.

When I got back to my room, I called some of my closest friends together to tell them what had happened. I said, "Kuncho Tashi has been sent home. I have also been expelled, so you will have to work hard to keep the work of our organization alive." I added, "I'm going to live at my uncle's house in Chongqing, so I will not be far away and will be able to keep in touch with you." This was the summer of 1940.

I was surprised and hurt by the expulsion. I had expected some kind of trouble or disciplinary action because of the disturbances we had caused, but nothing like this. At most, I thought they might send me home for a while.

I liked school and had never imagined not being a student. At first, I was simply numb. But I was young and full of the energy, hope, and resiliency of youth, and I got my balance back quickly. As I left the school grounds, I vowed not to slink away quietly. I started singing loudly, pretending that I didn't have a care in the world. I said to myself, "Well, you are just embarking on a new road. You have learned now that you will have to fight hard for your ideas and principles and that there are costs you will have to bear, but so be it."

PART II

The Tibetan Communist Party Era

CHAPTER 4

Planning Revolution

I was sad when I left the school, but I didn't regret what I had done. I felt we Tibetans were justified in organizing and protesting and that the school had no right to expel us. But I wasn't looking forward to telling my uncle.

"What did they expel you for?" he asked calmly.

When I told him about the association and the protests, he was sympathetic because he also had strong feelings about the treatment of Tibetans. All he said was that it was too bad that I had come so far to study only to have this happen. He had been hoping that the education I would get here would help me in the future.

He never said I had made a mistake by protesting, and in fact he and his wife both got very angry with the school because they thought the punishment was too harsh and unwarranted.

"No student from the Mongolian and Tibetan Affairs Commission school has ever been expelled," he said angrily. "If that's the kind of thing they're going to do now, I'm going to withdraw my daughter as well."

He did withdraw his daughter from the school, and I felt a little bad that I had caused all this trouble for him and my aunt. I tried to make them feel better by telling them that I would continue to study hard even though I was no longer in school—and I did so after my fashion.

Although I was staying with my aunt and uncle, they both worked during the day, so I was more or less on my own. They gave me enough money to buy food and have a little extra to travel in town, so it was easy to maintain contact with members of our organization who were still in school. All of my attention was now focused on what our organization's next step should be to implement our revolutionary ideas in Kham (and Tibet).

At about this time, Ngawang Kesang returned to Chongqing after finishing a postgraduate practical training program. He was receiving a small salary from the government and living at an inn. The inn was nearer our school than my uncle's house was, so he asked me to move in with him to make it easier to plan our next moves; for the next few months, I alternated between staying with him for three or four days and going home to spend a day or so with my aunt and uncle.

Ngawang and I discussed the future with Sherap, a member of our core group who was still enrolled in school, and decided that if we wanted to begin our operations in Kham, we should establish relations with other communist parties and seek their help. We decided to try the Soviets first because we admired the Russian communists from our reading of Lenin and Stalin, and because there was less risk of being caught by the GMD spies, who were looking for Chinese Communist Party agents but not Russians. So Ngawang Kesang and I went to the Soviet Embassy in Chongqing.

We found it by spotting the bright red Soviet flag with its hammer and sickle. We didn't go right up to the door and walk in, though. First we hung around outside watching carefully to try to see if anyone was following us. When we felt certain that no one was watching, we went in.

Nobody challenged us. Ngawang Kesang had on his good-looking school uniform, and I was dressed as respectably as I could. The first person we spoke to was a Russian woman who told us, in broken Chinese, to wait. After a few minutes, we spoke with someone who knew enough Chinese to understand what we wanted. "Come tomorrow," he said, "and then there will be someone to talk with you."

We came back the next day and met Fei Delin, a sinologist who spoke excellent Chinese and was the First Secretary of the Soviet Embassy. We told him we had started our own Tibetan Communist Party organization and that I had been expelled from school for trying to fight oppression and for having communist books and literature. We said that ultimately we wanted to go back to Kham and Tibet to start a socialist revolution and hoped that the Soviet Union would be willing to support our efforts. We also said that first we would like to go to Moscow to study and train. Fei Delin listened politely and was very encouraging. But he said that it would take time before he could let us know anything. Decisions about such matters would have to be made in Moscow, he said, and he would first have to send them a report. We should come back in a month or so and then he might have some news.

Three or four weeks passed, and we heard nothing. Ngawang Kesang had to be out of town on business, so I decided to go back to the embassy by myself. Fei talked to me again and once more was very kind and supportive, although he said that they hadn't heard anything from Moscow yet. "We don't know much about your situation," he said. "So why don't you write a brief report about the things you have been telling me, about your organization, the situation at school, and your thoughts about Tibet?"

I thought that was a good idea. Besides the things I had already told him about the school, our group, and being expelled, I wrote about the situation in Kham and our hopes of setting up a guerrilla base there after going to Moscow to get some training. I said we had studied guerrilla warfare from books and thought the tactics we had learned would be perfect for use in Kham and Tibet.

I found out later that one of the things going on while we were waiting was that Fei was doing a background check to see if we were who we said we were and if our story checked out. He must have been satisfied, because he continued to be very interested in me. We met several more times, and at these meetings we discussed in more detail most of the things I'd written about.

One day he asked me how I was managing financially. When I told him I was living with relatives who were giving me a little spending money, he smiled and said that the embassy would be glad to help me— and then he gave me one hundred yuan, and said he would do the same each month. I was startled by his generosity, since at that time one could eat for a month for only fourteen or fifteen yuan. When I went home to my uncle's, I was so excited about the money Fei had given me that without thinking I proudly told my uncle that I wouldn't need their help anymore (although I didn't tell them where the money had come from). My uncle looked a bit worried instead of happy, and I know he suspected that I was getting it from the Chinese Communist Party or from the Soviet Union. It could have caused real trouble for him with the GMD if they found out, but he never said anything about it to me directly.

With my new wealth, I bought more books than I had ever had before, and I began to study hard. My aunt and uncle ate dinner between six and seven in the evening, after which they played mahjong for a couple of hours with friends before going to bed. While they were playing mahjong, I went to sleep, and then around one or two o'clock in the morning, I got up and began to study. There was no electricity in those days, so I had to use candles. Eventually I made myself an oil lamp, but because I studied so close to the flame, the oily smoke used to make my nose black until I figured out a way to make a little chimney that would carry the smoke out the window but still allow me to get close enough to read. My aunt and uncle knew that I was getting up and studying, and they were very happy with me. I had come into some money, but I wasn't spending it foolishly in the bazaar. I lived the same kind of life I had been living before and was obviously studying hard.

Ngawang Kesang wasn't around much in those days. He had started working for Kesang Tsering and was off on trading trips for him, so I was left to wait for Moscow to respond to our request. I waited, at first expectantly and then patiently, but nothing happened. Weeks turned into months and there was no word from the embassy. So although the Chinese Communist Party was still weak after the Long March and the GMD was very powerful, I decided to try to make contact with the Chinese Communists and seek their assistance as well.

I knew a Chinese student named Liu Rensheng who had graduated from my school and was working for the well-known Chinese revolutionary writer and publisher Zhu Taofen. One day he told me that Zhou Enlai was going to give a lecture and invited me to come. Zhou talked for nearly three hours in a speech entitled "The War with Japan and International Circumstances." When he finished, the crowd cheered and sang songs about fighting against the Japanese and saving our nation.

I couldn't take my eyes off Zhou. To this day I still see him clearly and remember exactly what he was wearing. I wanted to shake his hand and tell him who I was and about my plans for Kham and Tibet, but the crowd pressed around him, and there was no way to get to him.

Afterward I told Liu that I needed to meet Zhou and asked if there was any way that it could be arranged. Liu thought for a while and then suggested that I write to Zhu Taofen and ask him to help set up a meeting. He and a friend of his helped me draft a letter in which I introduced myself and told him about the organization I had started and about my wish to go to Yan'an to meet Mao Zedong and study there. Of course, I explained that we later hoped to begin revolutionary guerrilla activities in Kham.

I didn't see Zhu in person, but I met his secretary, who was very helpful and seemed genuinely interested in my story. He told me that it was extremely dangerous to try to go to Yan'an at that time. "If ten people try to go to there," he said, "the GMD will catch them all. If a hundred people go, maybe two or three will get through." I told him I was not afraid. I still wanted to try. But, I added, before I went, I really wanted to meet Zhou Enlai.

He looked at me closely then. "How many of your people are going to go to Yan'an with you?" he asked.

I told him, "One. My friend Sherap." (Sherap wasn't politically sophisticated, but he wasn't afraid of anything. I thought he would be a good companion since Ngawang was now working as a trader.)

Then the secretary said, "We have been in contact with Zhou. He is at the office of our 8th Route Army in Chongqing." This was the bureau office of the Chinese Communist Party's army that was fighting against the Japanese in alliance with the GMD. He gave us directions to the office and told us to be careful because there were GMD spies in the area.

Sherap and I went the next day and sat for quite a while in a teahouse across the street, watching the entrance closely. When we were sure no one was watching us, we went in and were met by a young man who asked us who we were and what we wanted. We told him briefly, and before too long an officer named Ye Jianying came down from the second floor. Ye said that Zhou was writing an urgent document and that we couldn't see him just then. He added that he had come down to talk with us on Zhou's behalf and asked us to tell him our story.

In explaining our history and what we wanted, I didn't talk candidly about our hopes of getting to Moscow. I emphasized only the part about wanting to get to Yan'an. He seemed impressed, and when I finished he said, "It is good that young people like you two have such thoughts. I never imagined I would hear such things from Tibetans. However, it is quite difficult to get to Yan'an nowadays. Still, we will do everything we can to help you. But for today, I think it is best if you leave. We will meet again soon."

As we were leaving, he told us a better way to get into the headquarters the next time we came. We were very pleased with the way the meeting went and hopeful that something positive would develop from it.

Sherap and I went to the 8th Route Army office several more times and talked to Ye Jianying and sometimes others. On one visit, Ye suggested a plan: "We will try everything we can to help you," he said, "but it is very hard to go to Yan'an at this time. Therefore, we think you should go first to Xi'an, where we have an office and people who may be able to advise you. There won't be any problem getting there. You can get a ride on an army truck. The problem will be in getting to Yan'an. You will be on your own then; we can't help you after Xi'an. If you can't get to Yan'an, then we think you should go to Qinghai [Amdo] and start revolutionary organizing there. Later, when the situation loosens up, we can make contact and find a way to get you to Yan'an."

He looked at us and smiled. "When I was very young," he said, "I kept the revolutionary ideology in mind and stood on my own. Now it is time for you to do the same."

Sherap and I were excited and full of enthusiasm. We raised our hands and swore that we would be comrades for life and that we would never stop trying to achieve our revolutionary goals. We also decided that we had done enough waiting and resolved to try to get to Xi'an as soon as possible. Ye gave us each 450 yuan, an enormous sum of money for traveling, and soon we were on our way.

It was harder than we thought it was going to be. The first part of the journey went smoothly enough, but as we neared Xi'an, we reached a GMD checkpoint and were pulled over.

"Who are you?" a policeman asked.

"We are cousins on school vacation now and we are going to Xi'an and Xining to visit relatives."

It might have worked if we'd both had school uniforms, but of course I didn't have one, and the police noticed the difference right away.

"If you are both coming from school, where is your uniform?" they asked, looking sternly at me. I tried to tell them that I had simply decided not to wear my uniform, but the policeman got suspicious and said that Sherap could go on ahead if he wanted but I could not.

At that point we didn't know what to do. I finally told Sherap that he should go ahead. When he got to Xi'an, he could send his school uniform back and I would follow as soon as I could. And so I turned around and went back to Chongqing to wait for the uniform to arrive. But it was Sherap who returned instead. He told me that he had asked around in Xi'an, but from what he had heard it seemed impossible for us to get to Yan'an from there. It was very disappointing.

After I returned to Chongqing, I began meeting again with Fei Delin at the Soviet Embassy. During this time, I lived frugally so I could have more money for buying books. (When I went to a restaurant, I would eat simply, having only one dish and one or two steamed dumplings. I bought almost no clothes—only one shirt, which was sturdy because it was made from parachute-silk thread.) I shipped the books I bought to Tartsedo, where Ngawang Kesang was managing a store. I bribed one of the drivers of a military truck to take them to Chengdu, where I had a relative who reshipped them to Tartsedo. My plan was to have them ready for use when we began to expand our party's activities into Kham.

In my talks with Fei, I was careful not to mention my dealings with Ye Jianying, the Chinese Communist Party, or our attempt to go to Yan'an. Instead I continued to tell him that I wanted to go to Moscow and with Soviet assistance begin guerrilla operations in Kham and Tibet. I also kept in touch with the members of our organization who were still in the school, and some important things happened during that time. One was that our group wrote a letter denouncing Liu Wenhui for oppressing the people of Kham. Another was a radicalization of my thinking.

Kesang Tsering had formed an association of about twenty men from the Batang region who were living in Chongqing. They met for dinner, and after eating discussed political issues freely. One evening, Kesang Tsering invited me to join them. When the discussion began, there was a lot of complaining about Liu Wenhui's behavior in Kham, and much anger expressed at specific atrocities committed by the soldiers of his 24th Route Army. I listened for a while and then took a different tack because my ideas were changing.

I argued that this was too narrow a way to look at the situation in Kham. The enemy wasn't just Liu and his 24th Route Army, I said, the enemy was the GMD, whose orders the 24th Route Army followed! It was the Nationalist government of Chiang Kaishek that was oppressing us, and it was foolish not to see it as such!

I said I believed that Tibetans needed their own country, not just autonomy under China. An independent Tibet could be linked to the USSR and eventually perhaps to a communist China through the Communist International, but I thought that now we had to learn to think beyond our immediate and local problems in Batang and Kham. The people at the meeting were taken aback by my ideas because they were so different from what they were used to hearing, and so much more dangerous.

Then one day, I got a message from Fei Delin saying he wanted to talk to me. I immediately went to the Soviet Embassy, and I was not disappointed. After all this time, he said, he thought there might be a way I could get to Moscow by going through Xinjiang Province. He was very friendly, he seemed genuinely happy for me, and before I left he invited me for dinner at his house, which was outside the embassy compound.

When I arrived that evening, he smiled and said, "Sit down. I'm going to give you something special, something from the Black Sea that is eaten by the English kings and queens." It was the first time I had ever seen caviar.

He was in a cordial mood, and after dinner he got out some records and played them on his phonograph. One was the "Internationale." He asked me if I knew the song, and when I said I did, he said, "Why don't you sing it?" He was pleased that I knew the words and was able to sing it, and when I told him that the members of my association and I had translated the "Internationale" into Tibetan, he beamed, shook my hand, and called me "comrade." My hopes soared and I thought I would soon be in Moscow.

Unfortunately it didn't happen. Germany's invasion of the USSR on June 22, 1941, made any thought of travel there impossible. Fei and I then discussed what I might do next, and I told him that I thought the best thing for me would be to go back to Kham and begin the process of starting a revolutionary communist party there.

I also said that perhaps I would go to Tibet proper to start organizing there and that when that time came, I hoped that he and his country would support our guerrilla activities. I honestly didn't think the war with Germany would last very long, and I also believed that once I was in Tibet I could go to India, from where it might be possible for me to get to the USSR. Fei agreed and even gave me a secret code that he said I could use to contact him if I was able to get to the Soviet border. (When I made contact with the Red Army, I was to say to them, "I am a person from the Himalayas.") Fei was a good friend to me during these months, and when we parted, he gave me a great deal of money—about one thousand yuan, two hundred to three hundred U.S. dollars, and a similar amount in English pounds.

Once I made up my mind to go back to Kham, I acted quickly. Of course, I didn't tell my uncle about my revolutionary plans or my meetings with Fei. What I did tell him was that I was worried about staying in the Chongqing area because of the war and the Japanese bombings and would feel safer if I could go back to the Kham area, much closer to my home. My uncle, as always, was encouraging and helpful. My aunt was one of the people in charge of a new school built by the Education Ministry of the Nationalist government that was just opening in Derge, an important Tibetan principality in Kham, so it wasn't difficult for her to get me a position there teaching Chinese language and music. And so, at the end of 1941, I left Chongqing and headed west back to Kham— to teach school and begin a revolution.

As I was getting ready to leave, I learned that Kesang Tsering had died. Not many months after I had attended his dinner, he suddenly began spitting up blood, and before anything could be done to save him, he was gone. He was only forty-two. In the time before he died, he had begun to take me seriously as an adult, and we had had several long talks about politics. I remember him telling me, for instance, that he had changed some of his opinions since the early days and that he no longer had any animosity toward the Communist Party. But we still differed in our thinking. Like most of the people from Batang, Kesang was mainly interested in specific things happening in that region. He continued to see Kham and Batang as part of China, whereas it was clear to me that we had to think about larger questions concerning all Tibetans as a group, as a nationality. But it was sad to learn he had died at such a young age. I could still—I will always—remember Kesang Tsering, young, handsome, with fire in his eyes as he discharged his pistol in the air just after he had successfully driven the local Chinese army out of our town. Even as my thoughts returned to that childhood image, I realized that the road I was embarking on would be different and more complex. But I was eager to get started.

CHAPTER 5

Returning to Kham

It was early 1942 and I was twenty years old and full of optimism. The idea that our revolutionary work in Kham was about to begin was exhilarating, although I knew I had to be very careful. The first big decision I had to make was whether I should risk trying to take communist books and pamphlets with me to Derge. Chiang Kaishek's soldiers were on the lookout for communist agents and had set up checkpoints everywhere. I had heard stories about how people had been captured and executed for communist activities. In one case, I heard that a man was killed because he was caught with a copy of *A Dream of Red Mansions*, a classical novel that the soldiers mistakenly took for a communist book.

I decided to take the risk since I thought I needed these to make converts, but I took precautions. Since I was going in a truck convoy with my uncle's family and some officials from the Education Ministry, I packed the books in two boxes sealed with tape from the ministry and hid these under the many boxes containing the ministry's teaching supplies. When we were stopped, the soldiers never noticed them.

On the way to Derge, I stopped at Tartsedo and stayed long enough to launch our first revolutionary organization in Kham. We called it the Spark Association [tib. *me stag tshogs pa;* ch. *xing huo she*], based on Mao Zedong's famous comment that a single spark could set a whole prairie on fire. The original members were Ngawang Kesang (who was working in Tartsedo), myself, and two other Khampas from Batang, Topden and Dramdul.

Dramdul had served as a translator for the Red Army when it marched through Kham in 1935 but had left them to return home when they passed beyond the ethnic Tibetan zone. On his way home, however, he stopped in Chengdu, where he was seized and conscripted into the Nationalist army. I met him in Chongqing some years later, after he had been wounded in battle and discharged. We hit it off right away, and when I talked with him about my ideas for change and revolution in Tibet, he was very receptive. I sent him with a load of books to Chengdu, where he met and recruited Topden, who was working as a tailor at the time. I also contacted my former classmates (and party members) Kuncho Tashi and Sherap, who were in Labrang (in Gansu Province), and made arrangements to link our operation with them. Then I moved on to Derge with Dramdul and Topden, leaving Ngawang Kesang in charge in Tartsedo.

We planned to make Derge the hub of our new organization. It was one of the major centers of Tibetan culture and religion in Kham, as well as the home of a famous traditional Tibetan publishing house. Although nominally under the Chinese Nationalist government, Derge was ruled by its traditional Tibetan king and his government. The Chinese-appointed governor and small garrison that were located there did not normally interfere in local affairs, although the Chinese government's plan was to gradually expand their real power. The new school where I was going to teach was one step in that direction.

The school had been built and financed by the Education Ministry of the Chinese government and was scheduled to have about one hundred students who were to be selected through a tax system that required families to send one child to school. The students brought their own food, but the buildings, teachers' salaries, and other materials were paid for by the Chinese government. The younger students were about nine or ten years of age, the older ones twenty-five or so. As in Batang, students were taught both Tibetan and Chinese, but the Derge schools emphasized traditional Tibetan language and culture much more than those in Batang. I worked hard at being a good teacher, and not long after I started I was able to secure a position for Topden.

Having achieved this secure foothold, we were quickly able to turn to revolutionary work. How best to use our time and where we should direct our efforts were the questions that initially concerned us most. We all agreed that although we were Khampas, we had spent a good part of our lives in inland China and were too out of touch with the current political situation in our homeland to construct a detailed and precise plan for guerrilla operations. Therefore we decided to study the local society more fully: what were the realities of the current economic situation? How did people live, make money? What did they want? Need? What were they willing to fight for? And who were the local officials and elite?

At the same time, we began to seek out prospective members. To do so, however, we had to make some theoretical compromises, because although in theory communism was a movement of the "masses," we knew that it would be difficult—maybe even impossible—to "educate the Tibetan masses" in the way we had read about in Lenin's and Mao's writings. Tibet's peasants were conservative and heavily influenced by religion. They were not educated in the modern sense and would not be easy to recruit. In fact, we were afraid that if we tried to convert them, they might even turn us in, so we did not work with them at all.

Instead, we made our target population the youth of Kham, starting with the students in our school. They were to be the core of our communist party and guerrilla force. We worked cautiously, much like my teacher Wang had done with me, giving students whose thinking seemed progressive carefully selected materials to read and discuss.

We did not reveal our strong communist beliefs at first. I had learned my lesson earlier in Chongqing when one of my uncle's neighbors who worked in the Investigations Division of the Mongolian and Tibetan Affairs Commission found out I was reading communist newspapers. I don't know how he knew what I was doing, but one day he walked right into my uncle's house, took me aside, and told me to show him the newspapers. I was so surprised that I couldn't deny anything. He looked them over, read a few of them, said, "Thank you," and walked out without another word.

I was terrified and got a friend to help me get all the papers and magazines out of my uncle's house, and then I waited. Nothing happened, however, and I learned later that he had told some friends of my uncle's about it, saying only, "He is a young Tibetan, and he made a mistake. I just warned him this time." I never forgot that I had been too careless, and it made me especially conscious of the need for caution now.

Although we tried to keep a low profile, occasionally I let my true sentiments show, as I did one day when I came upon the monastery head [tib. *dgon dpon*] sitting at the side of the road watching a monk whipping a young girl. When I asked him why they were beating her, he said it was because she had made beer for the monks.

The Derge monks were different from monks elsewhere in Tibet because they drank beer. Every monk kept a pot filled with beer under his bed. Recently, the head of the monastery had tried to clean up this un-Buddhist practice by forbidding the beer-makers in Derge to sell beer to monks. Therefore, when they caught the girl selling beer, they decided to make an example of her. By the time I got there, they had ripped her dress from neck to waist and had begun to beat her. She was screaming and crying, and a crowd was forming. It made me angry because it was a perfect example of the hypocrisy and oppression the elite practiced against the ordinary people. Without even thinking about it, I grabbed the monk doing the whipping by the arm and yanked his whip away.

"What do you think you are doing?" he yelled.

I replied, "You people are acting unreasonably. Why victimize this poor girl who is just trying to make a living? Everyone knows that the monks in the Derge monastery drink beer. Why don't you punish them instead?"

More and more people started watching us. I could see they were shocked by my criticisms of the monks, but I wouldn't back down. Finally the monks left and I threw the whip away. People later said I was the only one who had ever stopped the monks from inflicting punishment and that I had humiliated the monastery head. Perhaps that was true, but I simply could not stand by and allow a simple Tibetan girl to suffer like this at the hands of these hypocritical monks. It was exactly that kind of behavior I had pledged my life to change.

As time passed, I began to develop a relationship with some of the more progressive members of the Derge aristocracy, since in the short run I felt they could be of the greatest assistance to our group. We had no illusions. We understood that while they might support throwing off the Chinese rule of the warlord Liu Wenhui, it wasn't likely that many of them would want to change the way society was organized. They had too great a stake in things the way they were. Still, they were more educated than the masses, and we felt we could talk to some of them about our ideas.

I began by developing a relationship with Chagö Tomden, one of the most famous aristocrats in Derge. He was a member of one of the wealthiest and most powerful families and a top minister in the Derge government. He had the ability to call up at a moment's notice an armed militia of hundreds, and he also had connections with the Chinese Communists that went back to 1935, when the Red Army marched through Kham. Chagö had initially fought against them but was defeated and taken prisoner. However, instead of killing or abusing him, the Red

Army treated him well, and he was grateful, adopting a soldier's children, who could not be taken further on the Long March.

Chagö and I met many times, and he became a good friend. I spoke with him often about my views on nationality issues and especially the need for Tibetan self-rule. I made the case that the current situation was unstable. There were really two power centers in Derge, I said, the official county government, which was backed by the GMD, and the Derge royal family, which headed the traditional government. At present, the Chinese (county) government wasn't strong and didn't interfere much in Derge affairs because other problems were occupying the GMD and Liu Wenhui. But, I said, appearances were deceiving, and the GMD would one day be able to turn its full attention here. When they did, I said, the power and scope of the Chinese county government would increase dramatically, and the Derge royal family's would decrease.

"If you wait until that occurs," I said, "it will be too late to do anything about it. The time to eliminate this threat is now, and the way to do it is to get rid of the Chinese county government and replace it with Tibetans."

"To do this," I continued, "you have to think beyond individual areas, like Derge or Batang. We need to model ourselves on Tibet proper, where there was a central government headed by the Dalai Lama. To be strong and secure self-rule, we have to establish a unified Tibetan government in the territory east of the Drichu River—a unified Kham." Chagö Tomden was smart, and he was receptive to this part of my thinking, but he disagreed strongly with my ideas about going further and creating a single greater Tibet that would comprise all Tibetans.

I believed strongly that we Khampas were members of the same ethnic group as the Tibetans west of the Drichu in Tibet proper, and that ultimately we should fight to create a greater Tibetan polity that included us all. At first, Chagö was just like Kesang Tsering. He liked to talk about us being Khampas, not Tibetans, or *pöpa* as we called them. He saw the two as different nationalities, or ethnic groups.

We argued a lot about this because I felt we Tibetans had to broaden our thinking. Tibetans were Tibetans, I argued, whether they lived in Central Tibet, Amdo, or Kham. It was wrong to see Kham as different and separate from Tibet or to think about freedom for Kham alone. Kham was part of a single, unitary Tibetan nationality, and we had to work for all Tibetans. I used Stalin's definition of a nationality (without using his name) as a group with a common language, culture, customs, and territory. So even though there were many different dialects in the

various regions of ethnic Tibet and slightly different local customs, there
was clearly a common culture and language that made us all Tibetans.

Chagö was not easy to convince. He hated the Lhasa soldiers and aristocrats because he felt they had oppressed the Khampa people when they
ruled there earlier in the century. I remember him looking at me and
smiling. "Phünwang," he said, "you know a lot about political theory,
but you don't know much about Tibetan aristocrats. When the Tibetan
government's soldiers came to Derge, the officers exacted heavy taxes
from the people. They whipped anyone who couldn't pay, and a lot of
people said that they were worse than the Chinese. The Chinese acted as
our lords, but they didn't steal things from the people." He gave me
many examples of the oppression of the Tibetan government soldiers
and officials. One, I recall, was especially shocking: a Tibetan official
found someone whose mount had good horseshoes, and he pulled out
the nails and took the horseshoes for himself.

I countered by arguing that although there were problems with the
laws of the Tibetan government and their past behavior in Kham, these
were problems *within* our nationality. Despite this, I said, only if we are
unified would we be able effectively to depose Liu Wenhui and form a
strong political entity that could hold its own against all outsiders. I
wrote a song at this time that spoke of this: "Don't differentiate between
the regions Ü-Tsang [Central Tibet] and Do-Kham [Amdo and
Kham] / We are all brothers of one nationality / We must be united as
one / We should advance with loyalty toward our nationality."[1] It was a
good song, but people like Chagö had a hard time understanding the importance of the idea of pan-Tibetan nationality.

The idea of a unified greater Tibet aside, Chagö had doubts about trying to dislodge the Chinese. While he agreed in general with my arguments on Khampa self-rule, he and his family had a lot to lose by trying
to expel the Nationalist troops and officials. He worried that if anything
were done to remove the Chinese county government, more Chinese
were sure to come into Kham, and what would he do then?

His response was a good example of some of the problems we faced
here and elsewhere. The people of Kham had lived for generations in
their remote valleys, more or less completely cut off from the rest of the
world. They didn't know anything about what was happening in the
world at large and thought things would be as they had always been. I

---

1. Tib. *dbus gtsang mdo khams ma phye, mi rigs gcig gi spun zla, nga tsho rdog rtsa
gcig sgril, rang rigs la rgya 'tsho dgos*—Goldstein, Sherap, and Siebenschuh

tried to explain that the GMD government of China was not unified or strong, and that the war against the Japanese was almost more than the Chinese government could handle. I told him that in Sichuan Province there were warlords who hated one another and whose wars among themselves made the whole region unstable. And then, I said, there was another factor. It was the Communist Party, which was growing in strength and importance and challenging the GMD. I was trying to get him to see that now might be a perfect time for Tibetans to take control of their homeland because China was weak and absorbed elsewhere.

We had many conversations like this. It was a strange, exciting, and dangerous time because I was leading a kind of double life. During the day, I taught at my school. Outside school, our organization continued to meet in secret. We would get together to make decisions about what our next moves and strategy should be, and then go back to our homes and workplaces to try to carry out our plans. We did everything by word of mouth because we were afraid that written documents might be discovered and used against us. Mostly what we did at this stage was just talk to people, find out what they were thinking, and try very carefully to educate them about what was going on in the world outside their own mountains and valleys.

For a while I felt we were making real progress, but soon my luck began to change. I was, of course, always in communication with Ngawang Kesang in Tartsedo, and one day I got an urgent message from him saying that I should be extremely careful now.

A Tibetan named Kesang Namgye, who worked in the GMD Party office in Tartsedo, had become suspicious of me. Some time earlier, when I had sent books to Tartsedo, he had confiscated a shipment. There was no identification on the package, so he didn't know who had sent it, but he suspected I was involved, so after I went to Derge, the GMD Party office in Tartsedo began to pay attention to me. Later I learned that they found out that I had been expelled from my school for being a communist. It was when Ngawang Kesang discovered they knew about this that he wrote to warn me that I might be in danger.

I was extremely upset when I heard this news. The GMD Party officials had their eye on me now, and nothing good was going to come of that. I had been in Derge for only four or five months. I had planned on staying for some time and using it as my base of operations. Now I had to rethink my plans, and even as I was going about my day-to-day activities as if nothing had happened, in the back of my mind I was working out plans for escape if it became necessary.

My escape plan was to go west across the Drichu River into Tibet proper. It was not an easy thing to do in those days because the Drichu was the border between Tibet and China, and only Tibetan traders could cross with ease. Everyone else was watched very closely. I had heard of cases where the Tibetan government's checkpoint guards turned back Chinese traders who had tried to disguise themselves as Tibetans. So it was likely that I would not able to cross the river, because I looked Chinese due to my short haircut and manner. However, I had taken steps to cover this eventuality while still in Chongqing.

Just before I left Chongqing, I visited the Dalai Lama's Bureau Office there. I told them that since I had to leave school, I was planning to go back to Kham and that I might eventually want to go to Tibet on a pilgrimage, and I asked them for their help. They seemed quite willing and said that there wouldn't be any problem. They must have been impressed by the things I did that got me expelled from school, because they said I was a good person who cared about Tibetans, and they gave me a letter of introduction to the governor-general in Chamdo, sealing it with their bureau seal. I still had that letter, and I hoped it would get me into Tibet if things continued to deteriorate in Derge.

Actually, I was suspicious about what their letter really said, so I secretly opened it, using heat to soften the wax seal. It turned out the letter was fine; it said I was a good youth who had strong loyalty to the Tibetan nationality. It went on to say that the Chinese government had falsely accused and expelled me from school. "But he is a good person," it concluded, "so if he later goes to Lhasa on pilgrimage, do not stop him anywhere on the road."

As it turned out, eventually I did need that letter. The GMD Party office in Tartsedo did not accuse me publicly of being a communist, but they began spreading rumors about me throughout the whole of Kham. This called more attention to me and made my work increasingly difficult— and finally, I felt, impossible. At the end of about six months, I decided that I couldn't stay there any longer, and so I began to plan my escape.

It wasn't a moment too soon.

Two things happened in the next few weeks. The first was that some Tibetan government soldiers dressed in civilian clothing came riding into Derge from across the Drichu. They said they were just there to do some shopping, but in fact it was pretty clear that they were spying on the Nationalist Chinese army in the area.

I found out where the soldiers were staying and invited them to visit me in my home. I served them beer and casually asked them what they were doing here. They said they were only trading, but I knew it was more than that, so during our conversation I told them about the number of Chinese troops in Ganze, Batang, Tartsedo, and so on. (They already knew this but seemed pleased that I was willing to pass this information on.) Then I casually asked them whether the Tibetan border guards would let a Tibetan pass if he had a letter of introduction from the Chongqing Bureau office. When the soldiers said yes, I asked them to pass a message to the officer at the Gamtok ferry crossing telling him that I had a friend who was traveling to Tibet with a letter from the Tibetan government and probably would be reaching the border soon. They agreed, and some time later, when they again visited Derge, I met them and asked if they had passed on the message. They assured me there would be no problem, so I started to make detailed preparations for the escape trip.

Not long after this, Chinese soldiers came riding into Derge. I immediately got suspicious. There was normally only a small force (about thirty soldiers) garrisoned here. Suddenly a company with more than a hundred troops showed up under a commander named Li, who quickly invited me to a banquet—in my honor! That was when I really feared I was in trouble.

One of the most traditional ways of getting rid of an enemy in China and Kham was to invite them to a banquet or special celebration and, when they came, to kill them or take them prisoner. I knew that Li must have heard all about me before coming here. (Why else would he invite me to dine with him? We didn't know each other.) I didn't know quite what to do. I finally decided that the only way was to pretend nothing was wrong and act as if I were delighted by the invitation.

On the night of the banquet, my heart was beating fast. Nothing happened at first. While we were eating, he was very cordial. (I think now that Li just wanted to feel me out. And I also think he was playing with me. I'm sure he knew what was going through my mind. Maybe it amused him to play this little game of false courtesy.) We talked about a number of subjects, and as the evening wore on and nothing happened to me, I grew bolder and decided to test him.

I told him I liked to hunt and asked him if he would lend me a rifle, because there were rabbits in the area and I wanted to do some rabbit hunting. It was a game, and we both knew it. It was also a test. Would he trust me with a rifle? Li smiled and said he would be happy to lend me a gun, which he did on the spot. I admired the weapon, thanked him, and after a couple of days I returned it to him, making a big point of dealing with him in good faith. We sometimes talked at length, and he asked me about my history and family. It was all very friendly, but I had no illusions about where it was headed eventually. Within days, my friend Dramdul told me how Li planned to arrest me.

Dramdul's father worked for the post office in Baiyü, a town located between Derge and Batang. He told me that Li was hesitant to make a big scene by arresting me in a large town like Derge, where even after a short time I had made a lot of friends. He didn't want to make a martyr of me or anyone else suspected of being a communist. I knew now that he was looking for a chance to take me when I was alone, and I decided to use the knowledge to my advantage.

The next time I talked with Li, I told him that it had been seven or eight years since I had been able to go back to Batang and see my family. I would be grateful, I said, if he would give me a permit so I could visit them. He agreed, and I knew exactly what he was thinking. I had to pass through Baiyü on the way to Batang, and that would be the perfect place for them to take me. I went to the Derge royal government, told them of my plans to go to Baiyü and then Batang, and asked them for three corvée horses. (I knew the word would get around about this and that it would help convince Li I was telling the truth.) I also told Dramdul to get a message to his father saying that I would be passing though Baiyü on my way to Batang and would like to spend the night with him if I might. I thought that Li would probably be confident he had me then.

Early in the morning a few days later, Topden and I left Derge with a villager the Derge government had sent to handle the corvée transport animals. Ngawang Kesang stayed behind in Tartsedo and Dramdul in Derge to continue our work. When Topden and I arrived at the Gamtok ferry site on the Drichu River, we stopped and told the herder looking after the animals that we wanted to eat there. It was a bit early, and he seemed surprised.

"Why do you want to eat here?" he asked suspiciously.

I said we liked the scenery and asked if there was a problem. "No," he grumbled and went to prepare the fire for us. When we were alone, I shouted across the river three times. That was the arrangement I had made in the letter I had previously sent to the Tibetan government's border checkpoint.

Everything happened like clockwork. On my signal, a boatman rowed a skin boat across the river, just as I had planned.

"What's going on here?" the man from Derge wanted to know. "Aren't you going to Baiyü?"

"Yes," I said. "But as long as we are here, I decided to go across the river and look at the scenery on the other side."

The Derge man looked dubious and became even more so when I finally told him to go back to Derge. But there was nothing he could do, and the boatman took Topden and me to the other side of the river. Once safely there, Topden and I headed west into the heart of Tibet—the kingdom of the Dalai Lama.

CHAPTER 6

To Lhasa

On the Tibetan side of the Drichu, we went to the checkpoint, where I showed my letter from the Dalai Lama's office to the Tibetan army officer in charge. We would not have been allowed to go a step further if he had not given us permission, but the letter seemed to impress him, and he told us we could go ahead.

Topden and I had been careful to bring gifts—bricks of tea and silk—for the various officials we would need to deal with. We gave two bricks of tea to the officer at the checkpoint, and he seemed pleased. In return, he served us some *tsampa* [roasted barley flour], dry meat, and barley beer, and then surprised me when he mixed the beer in with the tsampa. (We never do that in Kham, and I had never seen it done before.) When I told him I would rather have the tsampa with tea, he smiled, obliged, and simply said that he was happy to welcome us and had been pleased that I had contacted him and his soldiers ahead of time. Still smiling, he said we needn't worry, because he would give the gift we had just given him to the Tibetan government official in charge of tax collecting. I said that would not be necessary and that we had more tea, which we would send to the tax collector ourselves, and I sent Topden off with it immediately.

That afternoon, Topden and I were relaxing and having our dinner when we saw the tax collector's servant coming toward us carrying the two bricks of tea. I thought that must mean either that he was giving them back to us out of kindness or that he was a bit shy about accepting gifts. When he reached us, however, he held out the bricks accusingly and said, "The wrapping has been torn. Please give us two new ones."

We were young and inexperienced in dealing with Tibetan government officials and had never before seen anyone act as rudely as this.

"We gave you those bricks of tea as gifts," I said hotly. "We aren't selling them. It's not merchandise we have accepted money for. If you want them, take them. If not, leave them here and go on about your business." It was a standoff for a few seconds, but finally he turned and left with the torn bricks of tea. It would not be our last surprise of this kind.

Although the tax collector's behavior gave me a bad impression of Tibetan officials, the officer at the checkpoint had been very kind, and he continued to help us. On the second day, he sent us four horses and a servant to assist us on the next leg of our journey, and we set off for Jomda, the Tibetan regimental headquarters of General Mucha.

Two days of steady travel brought us to Jomda, where, as we passed the general's large, two-story house, the servant who had come with us from the ferry stop quickly told us that we had to dismount and walk when passing the general's house. Topden and I looked at each other because we had never heard of such a custom, but the servant, now nervous, told us again to dismount; if the general saw us on horseback while we were this near his house, he would punish us. The idea made no sense, but as we were unfamiliar with Tibetan government customs, we complied. Again we were very surprised.

Our next surprise occurred when we arrived at our inn. No sooner had we begun to unload our things than the innkeeper told us we needed to go see the general right away; otherwise he could be fined. It was getting late and we were tired, so we declined, telling him we would be sure to see the general early the next day. But the landlord pressed us, saying we should make a short visit now or at least go and tell the general's aide that we would make a formal visit tomorrow. We did the latter, spending the rest of the night wondering exactly what we were getting ourselves into.

The next morning, we got up early and presented ourselves at the general's house. We knew he was an aristocrat and a high official of the Tibetan government, so we took brick tea and a beautiful silk apron as gifts. We were met at the door by his aide, who told us to wait. When we had waited for more than two hours, I began to get angry. (I was, I learned later, just naïve. If I had given the aide a gift, we would have been admitted immediately.) I said to the aide, "I have come from China with a letter from the Dalai Lama's office. If I can't see the general, I am going to leave for Chamdo tomorrow." At this point, he realized he wasn't going to get anything from us, so he let us see him.

Though I had heard many stories about the arrogance of Tibetan aristocrats, this was the first time I had ever experienced it. We entered a room in which the general was sitting on cushions so high they were like a throne. He was dressed formally in a brocade gown. His hair was braided into two small, tight knots [called *bajo*] that stood out like little horns on the top of his head. Between them sat the small gold box that all high Tibetan lay officials wore [see figure 4]. His face was pockmarked and severe, and when he looked down at us, he acted like a king or high lama. I presented him with a ceremonial scarf and then nervously looked around for somewhere that Topden and I could sit while we talked with him. But there were no chairs; there were only a couple of very thin cushions on the floor. I couldn't imagine we were supposed to sit on them, and I didn't know what to do. Finally the aide caught my eye and with a steely look motioned toward the cushions, where we finally sat cross-legged, our heads well below the general's.

At first he asked a lot of questions about our plans: Where were we going? What did we intend to do? Then he said, "Since you came from China, I assume you have brought some porcelain cups." I said we had not, since the best Chinese porcelain-producing areas were occupied by the Japanese. "Really?" he said, and seemed genuinely surprised. He then asked some questions about the situation in China that began to make me wonder how cut off from the rest of the world he actually was. For example, at one point he asked, "Whose position is higher, Chiang Kaishek's or Liu Wenhui's?" For a minute I wasn't sure that he was serious. But he was, and I quickly told him Chiang's position was much higher than Liu's. I was stunned both by how completely out of touch he was with what was going on in the world and by the way he was treating us. He was, of course, wholly unaware of his own ignorance, and very condescending and patronizing. He made little effort to conceal the fact that he thought Topden and I were some sort of rude creatures from the Kham region—yokels who didn't know how to act. The more we talked, the more I wanted to get some horses from him and get out of there. But it wasn't that easy.

"You must have brought some brocade with you," he said, still searching, I think, to find something he could get out of us.

"Most Chinese brocade," I said politely, "is produced in Suzhou and Hangzhou, and they are also occupied by the Japanese."

We went on like this for a bit longer, and finally I said that if there was nothing else that he wanted to know, I wanted to leave. "Wait a minute," he said. "I heard that you have brought a letter from the Dalai Lama's office. Show me the letter."

When I gave it to him, he saw that it was sealed and said he was going to open it. I didn't want the seal broken because I didn't want anything to cause suspicion later about its legitimacy. So I quickly said, "You can't open it. It has the seal of the Dalai Lama's Bureau Office, and I have to present it sealed to the governor-general in Chamdo. If you open it, I will have to tell them how it was opened, and I will not be responsible."

It was true that I didn't want the letter opened. But he had also made me angry, and I was bluffing. It was tense for a moment or so, and then he smiled and handed me the letter unopened. Somehow or other I had earned his respect—how I will never know—but acting entirely on instinct, I pressed what I thought was my moment of advantage. "I am on my way to Chamdo," I said, "and I need horses." He smiled again and said that would be no problem; we could have what we needed. At that point, we were dismissed and took our leave.

Much later, after the Chamdo military campaign in 1950, I met the general once again when he was under detention in Chamdo. "I remember you," he said. "We are old friends, let us shake hands." He seemed to like me, and when he asked about my health and I told him I had been having some stomach trouble, he sent me some Tibetan medicine wrapped in silk and the gift of a fur hat. In the 1950 campaign, his army had fought bravely against the soldiers of the People's Liberation Army, and he had lost a lot of men. He was a courageous officer but not a thoughtful man. He was a good example of many of the Tibetan officials I would have to work among and around if I wanted to achieve my goals.

That afternoon, as Topden and I were having dinner, a maidservant of the general's wife came to our room carrying the silk apron we had given her. She told us the general's wife thought the apron was very beautiful and wondered if we had any more we could give her.

"If you need one, take it. Take whatever you want," Topden said angrily. But I intervened and told her that we had only two silk aprons. One we had given to her mistress and the other we had to give to the governor-general in Chamdo. The maidservant frowned and left.

The general sent us the horses he promised, and we made the trip to Chamdo in five or six days without any trouble. As soon as Topden and I were settled there, I went to see the governor-general, an aristocrat from the old and famous Yuthok family. He was one of the higher officials in the Lhasa government. It was a totally different experience from the meeting with General Mucha.

The aide took me directly to the meeting room, where I looked around for a throne but couldn't find one. All the seats were at the same height, and when I greeted Yuthok and presented him with a scarf, he greeted me warmly in return and asked me a lot of questions. He wasn't interested in whether I had brought porcelain or brocade, and he wasn't interested in playing the great man. He was instead very interested in my background. I trusted him instinctively, and after a short time I felt confident enough to go into detail in my answers. We talked for nearly two hours, and before we had finished for the day he asked me to come again the next day.

I was amazed at how easy it was to talk with him. The next day when I went to see him, he let me sit beside him, on an equal footing, and we had a long and very pleasant conversation. We were both sitting cross-legged, and because I wasn't used to it, after a while I became uncomfortable. He could see that something was bothering me and asked me what was the matter. When I told him and asked permission to stretch my legs out in front of me for a while, he just laughed and said, "Of course, go ahead." After we had talked for over three hours, he offered me dinner, and after dinner, when I wanted to leave, he asked if I could stay longer. It was dark by the time I went home.

Topden and I stayed in Chamdo for a full week, and every day I went to talk with Yuthok. At first what he wanted to know about was news from the outside world. I told him as much as I knew about the situation in China, the conflict between the Guomindang and the Communist Party—and as much as I could about Germany, Japan, and the Soviet Union. I also told him what I knew about the current status of the great world war. He was interested in everything I could remember.

He asked me what I knew about warfare. I said I had never been in battle but I had read books about it, especially about guerrilla warfare. I told him about some of the books and the theories of Mao and Zhu De. Eventually we got around to more specific issues. He asked me what I thought about the relative strength of Liu Wenhui and his possible vulnerability or intentions.

Basically, what I told him was that Liu Wenhui wasn't as strong as he looked. Although it might look like Chiang Kaishek and Liu Wenhui were working effectively together, I said they had different motives and agendas. Chiang was occupied on a number of fronts, and when he thought about Liu Wenhui at all, he thought about trying to keep Liu

Figure 4. Yuthok, Tashi Thondrup, Lhasa,
circa 1940s. (Photo courtesy of the Yuthok
family.)

weak. (Liu's power base was in Kham [Xikang] now, but it was much
poorer than Sichuan, where he had come from, so he was always trying
to find a way to get back there.) I told Yuthok that if he was considering
going to war with Liu, he didn't have to worry about immediate retalia-
tion from Chiang, and I reminded him about how Kesang Tsering had—
for a while at least—literally driven Liu Wenhui's troops out of the
Batang region and set up his own government. He was extremely interested when I told him these things, and I was excited because I realized
now that there were Tibetan aristocratic high officials I could talk to
who would take me seriously and value what I knew and had to say.

Still talking about the possibility of a war with China, I told Yuthok—
and I believed this increasingly strongly—that the way to win a war was
to develop a close relationship with the people. The way to do this, I said,
would be to lighten their taxes and other burdens, thereby establishing
a strong, loyal foundation. I said I didn't think you could win a war in

Kham or anywhere else if you tried to do it with an army alone. You had to have the people with you if possible, but at least not against you.

On one of the evenings we talked, Yuthok asked me to tell him my thoughts about the future of Tibet. Careful to steer clear of any specific mention of communism, I told him that I had strong feelings about the subject. The key to Tibet's future, I thought, was major reform of her political system—a change that at the very least would get rid of the abuses and inequalities of the current system. I also said I felt that we needed to change how we did things, in fundamental ways.

We needed to modernize, I said. We needed to build roads and factories and invest in modern machinery and methods of production. I gave him a lot of examples. When we make bowls by hand, the way we do now, I said, it takes several days to make one. If we had more modern methods and facilities, we might make dozens in the same amount of time. "The world is changing very quickly," I said with some heat. "I think if we do not reform ourselves, we will destroy ourselves. We won't have to worry about the Chinese or anyone else. We will be our own worst enemy."

This was strong stuff, but I was confident I could be candid and direct with Yuthok. He was not the tax collector or the general; he had been to India and had a much better sense of what was going on in the world. He agreed with everything I told him. But it was going to be very difficult, he said, to change the thinking of the people in power in Lhasa because their opinions were strongly held and deeply rooted in the old way of doing things. However, he agreed that something had to be done, that the old ways of thinking had to be changed somehow.

He asked me to stay in Chamdo. He said that if I wanted, he could find me a position, and I could help him train his army. "I like your advice," he said. "If Liu Wenhui attacks, you could help us defend ourselves. I think your ideas would work very well."

I was torn. I was gratified by his attitude and faith in me, and for the example he provided of a high aristocrat who could see Tibet's situation as I saw it and was willing to listen to new ideas. If we were to make any progress, he was the kind of person we would have to depend on. But I didn't see how I could accomplish much by staying in Chamdo. My larger purpose was to transform the Tibetan nation by helping to bring about major changes in the structure of society and by launching a guerrilla movement in Kham. My plans for securing support were still forming, and there was much I felt I still needed to

learn. But I was certain I had to go on to Lhasa and try to influence
the leaders of the Tibetan government, because if things were going to
change, it would have to begin there. Yuthok, however, had been so
kind that I couldn't bring myself to turn him down outright. So after
"thinking" about it for a day or so, I finally thanked him for his kind
offer but told him that I really wanted to see Lhasa before I did anything else.

I think he could see that my enthusiasm was genuine and respected
it. "All right," he said. "You should go to Lhasa." He paused, thought
for a moment, and then said, "When you arrive, you should meet with
some of the ministers of the Kashag [Council of Ministers]. Most of
them know very little about what is going on in the world. If you can
tell some of them the kinds of things you have been telling me, it might
open their eyes. The one you will want to talk with first is Surkhang. He
is young and educated and only recently appointed. I think he will be
very interested in what you have to say. If you have any trouble meeting him—or any other kind of difficulties—please look up my wife, who
lives in Lhasa. She will be glad to help you." (His wife, it turned out,
was Surkhang's sister.)

I was grateful to Yuthok for not insisting that I stay and for doing
everything he could to help Topden and me, including supplying horses
and corvée labor for the trip to Lhasa. The journey took about eighteen
days, and it gave me a chance to think about all the things that had been
happening and consider what they might mean for our cause.

One of the things I had been noticing was the situation of the villagers
and farmers on the Tibetan side of the river. We saw a lot of very poor
people and even some abandoned houses and fields. Because I had spent
so much time in China, I had not been aware of how much poverty there
was in Tibet. I was also struck by the way the aristocrats, the local officials, and the soldiers lorded it over the local people and oppressed them.
In some places, the people had to treat even the lowest government officials as if they were little kings.

The political situation was also more complex than I had thought.
Having been on both sides of the Drichu now, I could see that each area
was very different. Even though the Chinese were in control east of the
Drichu, they weren't a constant presence in each village. They sent significant numbers of troops only to areas where some kind of uprising occurred. Otherwise the troops stayed mainly in the garrison towns, like
Tartsedo and Batang. Moreover, the Chinese military and political officials were paid by the government and didn't depend on collecting their

salaries from the towns and provinces they occupied. Thus they weren't an immediate and oppressive presence in people's lives.

On the Tibetan side, it was different. The whole area was under the authority of the Tibetan government in Lhasa, but there were also local religious and lay lords who had enormous power. The people in the towns and villages, therefore, had two authorities to deal with, the national government's officials and the local lords. In addition, most of the Tibetan army troops stationed there were paid so badly that they commonly tried to get more income by exploiting the people. The same was true of many of the lower and local Tibetan government officials. Added together, all of these factors made the lives of ordinary Tibetans very hard. As we rode along each day, I did a lot of thinking about which side of the river might be the better place to begin our revolutionary activities. Where would we have the best chance of succeeding? What should our plan be?

When we reached Lhasa, I stopped thinking about these things, for a while at least. As we rode up the Lhasa Valley, the Potala, the palace of the Dalai Lama, rose majestically above the rooftops of the old city, taking my breath away. It was far beyond anything I had envisioned; this was one of the most exciting moments of my life.

For the people of the Kham region, Lhasa is the center of Tibetan culture and religion. Khampas try to go there at least once in their life. So in a sense, I too was just a Khampa pilgrim, and I was dazzled by the beauty of the temples and monasteries and by the sights and sounds: the nomads and pilgrims, the monks, nuns, and beggars side by side with aristocrats in their beautiful robes, the noise of the vendors and the smell of incense in the Barkor [the circular road around Lhasa's main temple, the Tsuglagang, that is both a major marketplace and a holy circumambulation path]. At first I didn't know which way to look, there were so many things to see.

I remembered from my childhood in Batang that people in my village were always saying that when a person arrives in Lhasa, he or she *must* visit the Jo [the statue of the Buddha in the Lhasa Tsuglagang temple, the most sacred statue in Tibet]. And one had to visit the Potala palace and the three great monasteries in Lhasa: Drepung, Ganden, and Sera. Drepung alone was said to hold nine thousand to ten thousand monks.

I wasted no time in visiting the Tsuglagang and other, smaller monasteries. Seeing the beautiful golden roofs of the temples and great monasteries, the huge statues of the Buddhas and Bodhisattvas, and the beautiful murals and religious paintings gave me a feeling of enormous pride in my Tibetan culture and history and increased my wish to do something for my people and civilization.

In one of our conversations, Yuthok had asked me if I was religious. I answered him honestly that, though I did not practice religion, I had not turned against it either. When I studied communism, I had not really paid much attention to Marx's ideas about religion. My friends and I concentrated on questions of nationality, equality, and democracy. I saw no contradiction between communism as I understood it then and religion.

In Batang, Tibetan opera performances were held annually in late summer, and I loved to watch them as I was growing up. Lhasa also has an annual opera festival that was just ending when we arrived, but there was still one performance to be held the next day at Sera monastery, three miles north of the city. It had been many years since I had seen a performance, so Topden and I went. As we reached the gates of the monastery, I heard the distinctive beat of the opera drums and could not stop tears from rising in my eyes. Although so far geographically from Kham and Batang, I was home again. It was as I told Chagö Tomden in Derge—we Tibetans all share a culture, language, and history.

I settled into life in Lhasa quickly and was surprised to discover that there were a lot of people from the Kham region living there, some of whom I actually knew. Sometimes it seemed that most of the people in Lhasa were actually from Kham. Then a few months later, at the end of 1943, my trusted comrade Ngawang Kesang arrived on business from Tartsedo, and soon afterward we decided to rename our revolutionary organization to better fit the situation in Lhasa. In fact, we gave it two names. For public consumption, we called it the Tibetan People's Unified Alliance [tib. *bod mi dmangs gcig sgril mna' mthun tshogs pa*]. For the inner circle of our organization, we used the name Tibetan Snowland Communist Revolutionary Association [tib. *gangs ljong bod rigs gung khran ring lugs gsar brje tshogs chung*].

As in Derge, we were always on the lookout for people to bring into our group. Our first ally among the Lhasa aristocrats was a young man from the Trendong family whose name was Tomjor Wangchuk. Everyone called him Trendong Sey ("son of the Trendong family"). Yuthok was close to forty, but Trendong was only a year older than I was, and, like Yuthok, he took my ideas seriously from the start.

When I first met him, he was studying Chinese and also trying to learn a little English. His Chinese language teacher's babysitter was from Batang, so I made contact with him through her. He was bright, wanted to know things, and was delighted when I showed him some new books we had brought with us. (One was a short Russian novel translated into Chinese, about an aristocratic girl who became a revolutionary.) Though his Chinese was still only so-so, he was smart and grasped main ideas quickly. He had democratic and reformist instincts and told us right away that there were a lot of things he deplored about the old Tibetan system.

The inner circle in Lhasa consisted of Topden, Ngawang Kesang, my brother Chömpel, myself, Trendong Sey, and a few other Khampas, like Phuntob and Norgye Lobsang. We also still had members elsewhere, like Sherap in Xining, Kuncho Tashi in Labrang, Tobgye in Yunnan, and Dramdul in Derge. We often had meetings at Trendong's house, but we took pains to keep them secret because the Tibetan government was as fearful of communism and revolution as the GMD. (Trendong would place his servant on notice to keep strangers and callers away when we were there.) We used to talk late into the night about Tibetan society and the country's future, and we talked frankly, holding nothing back. Trendong and I thought alike in many ways.

I gave Trendong as much information as I could. I told him about the history of the GMD and the Chinese Communist Party, about the major differences between the two, and about the CCP's policy toward minorities. He was interested in everything I had to say, and I tried to get him to see the possibilities that communism held. I told him that when the Red Army went through Kham in 1935, they established a brief government in which Tibetans had self-rule. I wanted to encourage him to see a connection between communist ideas and Tibetan independence.

Although he lived a privileged life himself, he believed the stories we told of the hard lives of the ordinary people, and he had no trouble accepting the fact that there was terrible oppression. He also agreed that Tibet was in great danger from without and within. On the outside, there were the British and the GMD, both waiting for a chance to increase their presence, power, and influence. And there was even greater danger from within, because Tibet was not unified. There was no sense of a common Tibetan people. The Kham and Amdo people did not trust the Tibetan government (in Lhasa), which in turn did not trust the officials of the Panchen Lama.

As we talked over weeks and then months, we began to get away from general theory and discuss a more specific, two-part plan of action for Tibet. The first part of our program was the reform of the current Tibetan government. We wanted to put a stop to the heavy taxes and the requirement of free corvée labor. We also wanted to change the structure of the government itself. We didn't want control of the government to remain in the hands of a few aristocratic families and monk officials from the central region. We thought it should be more representative of the whole of Tibet. If there were going to be aristocratic officials, then the government should also include representatives from among the Panchen Lama's officials in Tsang and from Kham and Amdo. We also thought the government should be more diverse and include other types of people, some scholars and perhaps traders. The main thing was that it should be more representative of all the Tibetan people. Maybe then, we thought, the government would be more receptive to modernizing and learning about new scientific discoveries and techniques for manufacture and farm production. I had been in Lhasa for six months now and had seen a lot of aristocrats. As a group, they reminded me of the Russian aristocrats I had read about in books: elegantly dressed, sophisticated socially, completely out of touch with the ordinary people, running the country blindly in the old way, ripe for revolution.

The second part of our plan was to begin guerrilla warfare in Kham, and we worked hard to devise a strategy to accomplish this. The GMD soldiers did not grow their own food; it was brought to them from China, so we believed that we could use the small villages around Batang as our base and cut off the Chinese supply of food and fuel. When the GMD sent small units of troops to investigate, we would overpower them and then just melt back into the villages. If they sent too many soldiers, we would retreat and wait for another chance. Avoiding major confrontations, we would systematically attack when the odds were in our favor and gradually weaken the GMD in Batang, so that finally we could drive them out.

The larger idea was to establish a new government, first in Batang, and then expand it to all of Kham. But I also ardently sought a unified Tibet, so the last part of our program was to merge the new Kham with Tibet proper, creating a single Tibet ready to join the modern world. We didn't have a specific timetable in mind at this point, but these were the things we talked about. However, we couldn't possibly accomplish any of them without economic and military support from the Tibetan government, so a major concern was how to approach them.

The Kashag, or Council of Ministers, was the supreme administrative office in the Tibetan government, and we carefully discussed the personality and views of each of the four ministers. Trendong quickly stated the obvious: that many of the ministers in the present government were extremely conservative, the head council minister actually being a monk official. They were comfortable with the present system of government and things as they were in general, and they were not likely to be receptive to any talk of reform. In the end, therefore, we decided that Surkhang was the one. (He was also the one Yuthok had suggested.)

Surkhang was young (only thirty-two) and had been a minister for just two years. He was educated and more aware than his colleagues of what the outside world was like, in part because his brother, with whom he was married polyandrously,[1] knew English well. He was the one we would try talking to, but the question then became how to approach him. Trendong said that it was out of the question for him to approach Surkhang. As he was a member of the government, such talk coming from him might frighten Surkhang and stop the process right there. Trendong said the one to do the talking should be me.

We decided it would look better if someone went with me, and we chose Ngawang Kesang. We felt that sending two people would give us more credibility—more of an impression that we were representatives of a group. Ngawang Kesang's ability to speak the Lhasa dialect did not equal mine, but I would do the talking, so we didn't think that would matter much. We also decided that it would be best to present our ideas in writing, as well as orally. Our two main points were the ones we had been discussing for months: the need for reform of the Kashag and our plan to begin guerrilla activities in Kham. Our specific request was for weapons. We decided we would ask the Kashag for five hundred British rifles and the bullets to go with them, and also for some wireless equipment.

Because of the radical nature of the request, we took a number of precautions to protect ourselves. Trendong wrote the initial draft of the letter because his Tibetan was the best. But if things went badly, we didn't want the Kashag to discover that he was the writer of the letter by tracing the handwriting (which was easy to do in Tibetan), so we had Phuntob copy the final draft, because his handwriting would be in the Khampa style. The heading of the petition read, "To the Kashag," but we didn't close with the name of our organization because we didn't want to frighten or bias them against us. We said we were individuals who had been in China and had recently come to Tibet, and that this represented our personal views. In the letter we closed with: "We submit this without deceit" (tib. *kha zhe gnyis med yin*). When we were satisfied with the draft, we took steps to arrange the meeting.

---

1. Fraternal polyandry—brothers jointly married to a wife—was a common form of marriage in Tibet.—*Goldstein, Sherap, and Siebenschuh*

When I left Chamdo, Yuthok told me that if I needed any help when I was in Lhasa, I should ask his wife. When I arrived at her house, she was busy overseeing the preparation of food for a lama whom she had invited to perform a religious ceremony. When she was finished, she was very gracious. I told her what Yuthok had said and about our meetings in Chamdo. She was interested in my life and asked questions about where I had come from and why I had gone to China. I told her my story in brief, and when I was finished she smiled warmly and asked, "While you were living in China for so many years, did you miss your parents?" I was surprised by the question but said truthfully that I had. She looked at me with concern and asked, "When you missed them the most, what did you do?" "When I missed my parents most," I said, "I always looked at their picture." Tears came to her eyes, and then she quickly called a servant and told him to bring me something to eat. I was extremely pleased by this gesture of inviting me to eat. It was unexpected. When I finished, I said I thought it was time to leave, and, as I had hoped, she asked if there was anything she could do for me. I said I would like to meet Minister Surkhang. She said her husband had already told her I might ask this, and it would be no trouble; she would ask her secretary to arrange it. A few days later, Surkhang's secretary sent a message calling me to the minister's house.

Ngawang Kesang and I presented a ceremonial scarf and some gifts to Surkhang when we entered the room where he received us. He stood up to greet us and was extremely polite, asking us immediately to sit down. There were two other officials present: his two brothers, *rimshi* [a lay official of the fourth rank who knew English] and *khenjung* [a monk official]. We sat carefully on a couch at one side of the room. All the seats were the same height.

He encouraged me to speak, and I began by telling him that Yuthok had suggested that I talk to him, and then briefly told him my story— about my boyhood in Kham and the time I had spent in school in China. I made much of our "patriotic" activities, stressing our activities on behalf of the Tibetan nation and downplaying the role that communist ideas had played. We went into detail about how the Khampas were suffering under Liu Wenhui and the GMD. And then—to see what he would say—I also talked a little about the way we saw Tibetans suffering on *this* side of the river from the onerous corvée labor demands and heavy taxes. I told him what I had seen on my journey to Lhasa. I waited for a reaction, but Surkhang didn't stop me or discourage me in any way, so I went on to say that I thought if things continued as they were, Tibet would be the cause of its own destruction. I said we wouldn't need the British or the Nationalist Chinese or anyone else to bring us down. We would do it to ourselves. Tibet had been a powerful and respected nation in the time of King Songtsen Gampo in the seventh century A.D.[2] We could be so again, I said, but only if we changed our ways.

When I told him about our organization, I said that we also had written new songs, and I noticed there was an organ in the corner of the room, so I asked if we should sing them for him. He said yes, and Ngawang Kesang played the music while I sang the following song [sung to the U.S. Civil War tune "Marching through Georgia"]:

Rise up, rise up, rise up,
Tibetan brothers.
The time for fighting has come but
Still haven't you awoken from sleep?
We can no longer bear to live
Under the oppression of powerful officials.

Rise up, rise up, rise up.
Tsampa eaters, rise up.
Seize control of your own land.
Seize political power.
Ü-Tsang [Central Tibet] and Do-Kham [Eastern Tibet] unite as one.
For the purpose of achieving development in a new Land of Snow [Tibet]
And for the people, fight to the end.
Spread happiness to all the people.
Spread happiness to all the people.
Spread it.

longs shog longs shog longs shog
nga tsho bod rigs spun zla rnams
'thabs 'dzing dus su bab kyang
da dung gnyid nas sad med bas
btsan dbang drag shugs dpon rigs dbang 'og
da ni bzod thabs med

longs shog longs shog longs shog
rtsam pa bza' mkhan rnams longs shog
rang sa rang bzung
rang dbang rang 'dzin dgos
dbus gtsang mdo khams yong su gcig tu sgril dgos
gangs ljongs gsar pa yar rgyas
dmangs gtso don la mthar phyin 'dzing

---

2. Songsten Gampo united Tibet in the seventh century and founded a royal dynasty that lasted until the middle of the ninth century. At its peak, it included much of today's Sichuan and Qinghai Provinces and parts of Xinjiang Province.—*Goldstein, Sherap, and Siebenschuh*

bde skyid 'tsho ba mi ser kun la khyab la dgos
bde skyid 'tsho ba mi ser kun la khyab la dgos
khyabs dgos

When Surkhang heard this, his eyes filled with tears, and he took a piece of silk from his pocket and wiped them. That this minister, one of the four most powerful people in Tibet, could be so genuinely moved by our Tibetan revolutionary song really surprised me. He had, I realized, a deep sympathy for the common people, a love of Tibet, and a concern for her well-being. It was this that gave me courage to go even farther.

I told him of our plan for reforming the current Tibetan government and making major changes in the structure of Tibetan society. And, of course, we told him about our plan to start a guerrilla war in Kham and eventually merge Kham with the rest of Tibet. We asked for weapons and economic aid. We also said that we realized that they might be nervous about giving five hundred rifles to relative strangers who were so young, and that therefore we were willing to have our parents brought to Lhasa to serve as hostages to ensure we kept our word.

If Surkhang was surprised by what we had to say, I think he was even more startled by how well we were able to speak about our ideas and how much thinking and knowledge they implied. We were young—I was just twenty-one years old—and we were Khampas, and they simply hadn't expected anything like this. (When they learned we could speak even a little English—I had studied some in China and Ngawang had gone to the American Mission school in Batang—they were astonished!) To his credit, though, instead of becoming defensive or dismissive, he took us seriously because he realized that what we were talking about deserved to be taken seriously.

When I finished, Surkhang asked me a lot of questions about events going on in the world outside Tibet. I used the occasion to tell him about the Soviet Union and the formation of the Chinese Communist Party, and I was able to bring up the subject of the communists' policies about minority nationalities. I stressed the difference between the way the communists treated minority peoples and the brutal ways of the GMD.

We also discussed the situation in Kham. He asked how many fighters we had and what our strategy would be. I had told all these things to Yuthok, and I knew Yuthok and Surkhang were very close, so I suspected he might have already heard some of this from Yuthok. I told him about the Chinese troops in Kham and Liu Wenhui. And I told him what I thought would happen if there was war. "If we can establish a government in Kham," I said, "in the future it will be good for creating a unified Tibet. But in the short term, if we establish guerrilla power in Kham, it will ease the burden of the Tibetan government as it prepares for war with China, because we will be between you and the Chinese. If we have one hundred to two hundred guerrilla fighters in Kham, you won't have to worry about the GMD invading Tibet, because they will be busy with us."

We must have talked for at least three hours on that first visit. Toward the end, Surkhang became thoughtful. "Your thoughts about the need for reforms in Tibet are very interesting," he said. "I agree with much of what you say. But I will have to explore it with the other ministers." Finally, at a lull in the conversation, Surkhang said, "That's enough for today," and we gave him our written statement and left.

Ngawang Kesang and I reported everything to our group. They thought that in general the meeting had gone extremely well and were encouraged by the genuine emotion Surkhang had shown when he heard about the suffering of the Tibetan people and listened to our song calling on Tibetans to unite and rise up against the Chinese. They did not see anything strange or amiss in the fact that Surkhang made no response to our request for weapons. His hesitation was certainly reasonable in light of the fact that we were young people who had almost literally come out of nowhere. It made sense that the Council of Ministers would have to discuss and think about it before moving forward. The consensus was that things were going as well as could be expected and that all we could do now was wait.

We went for a second meeting a few days later, and while it was also very cordial, Surkhang seemed a bit cooler. We discussed many of the issues that we had discussed before, and then Surkhang said—and it was true enough—that he couldn't make things happen by himself. He said the majority of the ministers were very conservative and it was going to be impossible to give a response to our requests in a short time. He said it was important to put this in the context of the current world war.

"America, Britain, Russia, and China will win the war," I said almost without thinking. "Germany, Italy, and Japan will lose."

Surkhang clearly disagreed. "The Germans have taken most of Russia," he said. "Over half of China is now occupied by Japan. If Germany and Japan win, the Council of Ministers feels that we don't have to worry much. The British will eventually have to withdraw from India, and their power will no longer be a direct threat to Tibet. And when Japan conquers China, they will leave Tibet alone. They are a Buddhist country, and we are very far away. They simply won't want to extend themselves this far."

I disagreed and tried to make it clear that I wasn't just voicing my own opinion. It was based on many things that I had been reading. "In fact," I said, "if Tibet was smart, it would be positioning itself on the side of the eventual winners as fast as it could. The Japanese are fighting in Burma right now. If the Council of Ministers sent troops to help fight against the Japanese there and supported the Americans, British, and Chinese, it might help them a great deal when the war is over."

I couldn't convince him. The meeting ended with Surkhang simply repeating that he couldn't give me an immediate answer. "At the moment," he said again, "the Council wants to wait and see what the outcome of the great world war will be." (Surkhang's opinion about how the majority of the Council was thinking was consistent with what Trendong heard. They genuinely believed, he said, that it was likely that Germany and Japan were going to win, and they thought that this would solve Tibet's greatest threat from China.) The third meeting was much the same. They would have to think about it; we would have to wait. It was extremely frustrating, and we finally decided we would have to try something else while we were waiting.

We had thought about the situation and the issues for a long time. We knew what we wanted to do, and we believed that we knew how to do it. But we needed weapons, and we couldn't act entirely on our own. So the group finally decided to pursue our earlier plan to go to India and see if the Indian Communist Party could help us get to the Soviet Union.

We left for India, using Ngawang Kesang's trading business as a cover. Ngawang was working for a large trading company that had branch stores in Kalimpong and Calcutta. The manager of the Calcutta store, a Chinese man called Zhou, was then in Lhasa and about to return to India. It was a perfect opportunity, and so we put a small caravan together. It consisted of myself, Ngawang Kesang, Zhou and his wife, and three or four servants. We also had a fair number of pack animals. (Money was not a problem because we still had most of what Fei Delin and the CCP had given us when we left Chongqing.) It didn't take long to get ready, and soon we were on our way through Tibet's southern mountains and valleys, heading for Kalimpong. I was excited to be getting to see India, and hopeful that there we would find someone to help us put our plans into effect.

CHAPTER 7

The Indian Communist Party

We took the well-traveled route south from Lhasa to Chushul and then south to Phari and Yadong, the Tibetan town on the border with Sikkim [see map 3]. This time I didn't need any letter or passport. We just crossed the Natöla Pass into Sikkim/India as if there were no border.

Before we left Lhasa, I had gone to see Yuthok's wife. She was very kind, as always, and gave me some dried meat and cheese for the trip. She also warned me to be careful when eating anything in Yadong and Sikkim, because there had been reports of people poisoning the food. I don't know whether these reports were true, but I couldn't get them out of my mind, so my friends and I were extremely watchful.

Nothing suspicious happened until we arrived at Gangtok, the capital of Sikkim. There we went to a restaurant where I had sweet tea [British-style tea made with milk and sugar] for the first time in my life. After I finished the first cup and was starting on the second, I noticed that there were bubbles in my glass, and I immediately suspected poison! I called the manager over and asked him what was wrong with tea; it had bubbles. I said it didn't seem clean.

"Why don't you think it is clean?" he asked.

I got angry and snapped, "If we get sick from drinking this, we know where to find you."

"This is ridiculous," he said, and threw up his arms and walked away.

I thought it was probably foolish to worry, but then the Chinese woman who was with us got sick to her stomach, and I was even more concerned. I didn't sleep very well that night, but the next day everyone was fine. I think the whole episode just goes to show how tense we were, always feeling that we had to be on our guard.

On the drive to Kalimpong, another incident surprised me. We had arranged to stay with the Sandutsangs, a well-known Khampa trader family, in Kalimpong, and they sent a car to pick us in Gangtok. The road from Gangtok snakes through the mountains, and was crowded with Indians driving cattle carts full of tangerines to market. Our driver was singing while he drove and not paying a lot of attention. Suddenly he sideswiped one of the carts, and it fell into a ditch, spilling the fruit in all directions. I was afraid there was going to be a fight, but instead of getting angry, the cart driver immediately looked at the sky and began to pray, repeating a phrase in a chant I couldn't understand.

I was amazed that he wasn't angry, since it was our fault. We waited there for about ten minutes, but he just kept praying and said nothing to us, so we finally drove quietly away. I was puzzled. To me it would have made sense for the man to shout and even threaten to fight. I would have done so. I wondered if his acceptance of what happened was the result of living long years under British rule and having to learn to accept harsh treatment and even humiliation. I had read a bit about Gandhi and his philosophy of nonviolence, and I also wondered if maybe that was what I was seeing. As the image of the driver looking at his cart in the ditch receded, I thought that kind of acceptance or nonaction would be a hard path for me to try to follow.

We went the rest of the way without incident, and when we reached Kalimpong, we stayed at Sandutsang's elegant house. When we had settled in, I began my effort to make contact with representatives of the Indian Communist Party.

It wasn't easy. The Communist Party was illegal, so it didn't have an office with a signboard. I had to be careful in inquiring, and it took me a month to learn that the man I needed to meet was an English doctor named Juedi (they called him "Juedi Babu," because in India all Englishmen are called "Babu" ["Babu" is a Hindi term of address equivalent to "Sir" or "Esquire"]).

Juedi Babu was about forty years old, and when I went to see him for the first time at his office, I brought a small Chinese-English dictionary with me. It was awkward to use, but I was eventually able to make clear where I was from and something about what I wanted. (I did a lot of talking with my hands. I pointed to my Tibetan dress to indicate where I was from, and I pointed often to a picture of Mao Zedong in his office

Figure 5. Phünwang *(left)* and Ngawang Kesang,
Kalimpong, 1944.

to try to make my political sympathies clear.) The newspapers were a big
help. He was very interested when I pointed to the picture of the chairman of the Indian Communist Party, and he wanted to know how I
knew him. I tried to tell him that we were "comrades," and also a little
about my experiences in China.

I wasn't sure how much of what I said got through, but he seemed
pleased with me. He shook my hand and asked me to come to his house
the next day. His wife, he said, knew some Tibetan and would translate
for us.

He had a home in a small village just outside the city. He said that we
needed to be careful, so he walked to his house first and I followed at a
fair distance, keeping him in sight but not appearing to be walking with
him. His wife was dressed in Nepalese fashion when I arrived. She knew
some Tibetan because her mother was Tibetan and had lived in Lhasa for
a while before marrying an Indian and coming here to live. She wasn't

fluent, but her Tibetan was good enough for her to serve as a translator, and through her I was able to give Juedi a much fuller and more accurate account of myself than I had the day before.

I told him about my experiences in Chongqing, seeing Zhou Enlai speak and meeting with Ye Jianying. I also told him that I had talked with Fei Delin of the Soviet Embassy and about my plans to seek support from the USSR. Finally, I asked him to inform the Communist Party of India that I was here and of my plans, because I was hoping they would be willing to help me get to the Soviet Union. He told me he understood and would see what he could do. I was to wait a couple of days, and then come back and see what he had learned.

A couple of days stretched into many. Juedi Babu worked in the afternoons at the hospital. He earned very little money, but he was friendly and quite generous to me. He was the head of a small group of party members in Kalimpong who held secret meetings once a week. At his invitation, I attended one of them, but since his wife wasn't there to translate, I couldn't understand what they were saying.

As the days passed, I worried that I was being put off the way I felt we had been in Lhasa, but finally Juedi told me that if I went to Calcutta, the Central Committee of the Indian Communist Party would talk with me.

Again there was a lot of secrecy involved. We would go by train in disguise. He told me to get rid of my Tibetan clothes and dress like an Indian. (I have a dark complexion and a large nose, and he said that would help me pass as an Indian.) And so, together with his wife and son, I left the next day for the train station in the Indian town of Siliguri. If anyone asked who I was, I was to tell them that I was a relative of his wife. (Before I left, they told me that I should not fight with anyone while I was traveling. I thought it was strange that they would be telling me this. Did I look like I would?)

We made it to Siliguri without incident, and from there took the train to Calcutta. We stayed in a third-class compartment, and when we boarded there were very few people in the car. Juedi's wife told me to stretch out if I wanted, and so I lay out full length, taking up at least two places. When I woke at midnight, I saw that the compartment was completely full of Indians, most of whom were standing. Embarrassed because I had monopolized so many seats, I immediately got up and offered my seat to the standers, but they flatly refused. They kept calling me "lama, lama," and told me to stay where I was. I was really surprised, because my experience in China had been completely different. There, I thought, they would have wakened me and told me I was taking someone else's seat! Here, they just said, "Lama, lama" and moved aside. I later learned that in this part of the country, the Indians call all Tibetans "lama" (so much for my disguise!). I also heard that when Tibetan traders take the train they sometimes produce a piece of beef and eat it very publicly to frighten the Indians away so they can sit alone in peace. I never saw that happen, though.

When I arrived in Calcutta, I found a strong Communist Party presence there. (The year was 1944—three years before India got her independence from Britain.) Here the party office was not hard to find. It was housed in a four-story building, and there was a red flag flying over it. I stayed there for the first few days. There were plenty of rooms, and since the climate was so warm, the sleeping arrangements were as basic as possible. At night, I simply put down a mat and slept.

Basu, the man I had to deal with, was in charge of the Communist Party in Calcutta. He spoke Chinese very well because he had been part of a medical team that the British/Indian Communist Party had sent to China early in the war. He told me that he had been a communist for a long time, and since we could speak and understand each other freely, he asked me how I had become a communist and about the details of my early life. I told him all about my experiences in China, why I had gone to Tibet, and that my goals, with his help, were to get to the Soviet Union to study and secure Soviet support to begin guerrilla activities in the ethnic Tibetan area east of the Drichu River. Basu listened carefully and, when I had finished, said what I was by now very used to being told. He would report everything I had told him to the Central Committee of the Indian Communist Party and see what their response was. Again I had to wait.

Since I could do nothing until Basu heard from the Central Committee, I occupied myself by seeing many of the sights in Calcutta—and complicated my life considerably by doing so. One day when I was out walking, I went to see a nearby bridge that had been camouflaged to protect it from discovery by enemy planes. On the road to the bridge I encountered a small boy begging for money. He was very winning and obviously in need, and in my situation I could easily sympathize with him, so I reached into my pocket and gave him a few coins from my wallet. I then put my wallet away and continued on, looking at the bridge and seeing what there was to see. Some time later I joined some friends and got into their car to go to another part of the city. When I sat down in the car, I could feel that my wallet was gone. I was stunned, and then remembered the last time I had taken it out—the charming little boy had stolen it quietly without my even knowing. My friends said this was not uncommon in Calcutta. In any case, because I was traveling so light, all the money I possessed had been in that wallet, and now it was gone. I didn't have a cent. It made life very difficult for me for the rest of the time I was there.

Not long after this, Basu told me that they needed to find another place for me to stay because if I stayed at the headquarters too long, the British police would almost surely notice me and begin to ask questions. I was told, therefore, that for the rest of the time it took to hear from the Central Committee, I would be staying at the home of a young Chinese named Bi Shuowang, who worked secretly for the Communist Party.

Basu took me to Bi Shuowang's flat in a multistory apartment building and introduced me vaguely, simply saying that I was a comrade from Tibet. He told Bi Shuowang that was all he needed to know, and that was the way it was between us from then on. He didn't ask me any questions, and I didn't try to find out anything more about him.

I stayed with Bi, his wife, and his older brother for a month. It was a hard time for me. I had nothing to do, no work or any other task to keep me occupied. And because I didn't have any money, I couldn't go anywhere or buy food to supplement the meals that Bi gave me. I hated being so dependent and feeling almost like a prisoner.

Everything about the situation was awkward, perhaps most so the sleeping arrangements. I slept in the living room, and since Bi's brother didn't come home from work till late at night, I had to stay up till he got home, no matter how late. Otherwise he would have had to walk over me on his way to bed. It was the same thing in the morning. I had to be up before the earliest riser in the household got up. Besides that, it was unbearably hot. So I didn't get much good sleep.

Finally, a message came from the Central Committee requesting that I meet them immediately. I was excited, both because I thought I would finally get out of Bi's house and because I hoped they would take me to what is now northern Pakistan, where I could cross over to Soviet Central Asia [Tajikistan]. However, instead of arranging for me to go to the Central Committee's main headquarters in Bombay, the Central Committee sent a representative to see me in Calcutta, and the news wasn't good.

Basu translated, and it was the same old story. The Central Committee thought that at this time my request was too dangerous. There were too many British troops in that area. I was likely to be caught. The risks were too great. Their view was, finally, that for the time being I should go back to Tibet, and later they would try to help me. They knew that I

Figure 6. *From left:* Bi Shuowang, Phünwang, Basu, and unknown, Beijing, 1982.

had no money, and so they gave me just enough for traveling. I was extremely discouraged.

I tried to think rationally and not let my disappointment color my assessment of the situation. Except for the time I had spent in Bi Shuowang's house with no money, I had been treated well in Calcutta. The Communist Party of India was poor, but the members were generally optimistic and upbeat, and not all my memories were bad.

I remember one gathering in Calcutta fondly. There were forty or so Indian communists and a few Englishmen who were British soldiers on their way to Burma. They all started singing revolutionary songs like the "Internationale," and then I volunteered to sing the "Internationale" in Tibetan for them. They were glad to hear this, as they had no idea it had been translated. I also sang a well-known Russian song, "If Tomorrow Brings War," in Chinese. It made us all very close and happy. I decided finally that on the whole I hadn't been treated badly. But in the end, I was back where I had started, and so I returned to Kalimpong. There I immediately told Ngawang Kesang the bad news. We were not going through India to the Soviet Union.

Although I tried to put things as positively as I could, he was, of course, also disappointed. I emphasized that we had at least made a good connection with the Communist Party of India. But after all was said, we had failed, and the question now was what to do next. We had spent seven or eight months in Calcutta and Kalimpong and were still no closer to implementing our ideas, either in Tibet or in the USSR.

We decided that we should go back to Lhasa. It was the end of 1944, and the war in Europe and the Pacific looked like it was drawing to a close. It seemed certain that the Germans were going to be defeated—just as I had predicted—so I thought it was time to go back to contact Surkhang and the Council of Ministers. They had told us that they wanted to wait to see how the war was going to turn out before they gave us an answer. Now was the time, we thought, to ask for that answer again.

We had an idea about returning to Lhasa that involved a man named Tharchin Babu. He was a fifty-five-year-old Tibetan from northern India who was producing the only Tibetan-language newspaper—*The Tibetan Mirror*—in Kalimpong. I was impressed by the possibilities a newspaper might open up for us and arranged to meet Tharchin through a mutual friend. Ngawang and I hit it off with him immediately, and we quickly became good friends. We had some very happy times with him, talking politics and singing together. Tharchin was a devout Christian and had an organ in his house, so Ngawang Kesang and he often sang popular Christian hymns in Tibetan while I accompanied them on the organ.

After deciding Tharchin had progressive views, we began to tell him a little bit about what we thought was wrong with the present Tibetan government and society and what kinds of changes ought to be made. It turned out that he shared a lot of our views, especially about the excesses of the traditional society. He was as critical as we were of the aristocrats living in luxury with their fine brocades and paying for it all by exploiting and oppressing the common people. We concealed our relationship with the Communist Party, but we took a chance and told him our ideas about seeking support to help establish guerrilla power on the eastern side of the Drichu to defeat Liu Wenhui. He liked our ideas and said he would help us.

We tried to persuade him to move his operation to Lhasa. This, we thought, would help us, because the newspaper was a perfect way to introduce new concepts and information that would eventually open the eyes of the people. But our idea clearly made him nervous, and he envisioned only problems. Basically, he said that it would be difficult to print the paper in Lhasa because it would be extremely expensive there, but I thought he might be worried more about the Tibetan government. In any case, he insisted that it would be best to continue to print it in Kalimpong and send it to Lhasa. Later, he said, when conditions were right, maybe he could come to Lhasa. (It wasn't clear what the conditions were that had to be right, but it *was* clear that we weren't going to get any further with the idea of bringing the paper with us now.)

Soon afterward, we left for Tibet. About halfway to Lhasa, we stopped in Tibet's third-largest town, Gyantse. Ngawang Kesang and I decided to rest the pack animals there for a day or so. We found some people we felt we could trust to watch our merchandise, and then decided to walk to Shigatse, the town where the Panchen Lama's great monastery, Tashilhunpo, was located.

My general impression of the state of things in this part of Tibet was that the people who lived there were no better off than the people of Kham. If anything, they suffered from worse injustice and oppression. I also felt that there were too many monks in Tibet who simply lived in monasteries and did not contribute directly to society. And of course, I felt more strongly than ever that the traditional system of estates and aristocrats was bad for Tibet. Although there were a few forward-thinking aristocrats, like Yuthok, Surkhang, and Trendong, who understood that there were serious problems with the old ways of doing things and were willing to consider change, as a group the aristocrats clearly seemed to put their own comfort and interests above those of the people or the Tibetan nation. I expressed these feelings in some of the songs I wrote at the time. In one I remember from that time, I wrote,

> Our Tibetan people
> Have existed for many thousands of years.
> At the time of heroes like Songtsen Gampo
> We became famous throughout the world.
> Now our nationality has declined
> And lost territory.
> Because of internal corruption
> The people are suffering greatly.
> Now is the time to decide whether to live or die.
> Whoever decides [to fight]
> Should unite as one
> And for the happiness of the people
> Strive until the last breath.

> *nga tsho gangs ljongs mi rigs*
> *lo stong mang po gzhis chags yod*
> *dpa' bo srong btsan sgam po'i dus*

skad grags 'dzam gling yongs su khyab
dengs mi rigs nyams
rgyal sa shor
nang rus mang bas
mi ser sdug ngal che
da ni shi gson dus bab
su sems thag bcad na gcig tu sgril
mi ser dmang bde' ba la
dbug ma chad bar du 'bad brtson byed

We sang this to the English tune "Deck the Halls."

When we finally arrived in Lhasa in early 1945, we told the rest of the inner group what had happened and that we were not going to be able to go to the Soviet Union. We discussed what to do, and they agreed with me that it was time to go back to Surkhang.

Getting to see him was no longer easy. His secretary said he was extremely busy, and it took me a while to get a chance to talk with him. When I did, he was not encouraging. Yes, he remembered what he had said about waiting till the outcome of the war seemed clear. Yes, it did look like Germany and Japan were going to lose. But the war wasn't actually over yet. Better to decide when it was over. He also intimated that the real problem was that it was difficult to get a decision from the older ministers about what we had discussed. We would have to wait.

He was stalling. I didn't know how many ministers he had talked to, if any. I didn't know what kinds of pressures and conflicts of interest he might have felt. But I knew immediately that he was just putting me off. Over the next few months I met him several more times, but each time it seemed like our hopes got slimmer and slimmer. The Council of Ministers, he said, was more concerned with the fate of Japan than of Germany, because Japan was much closer to Tibet. It still wasn't clear what was happening in the Japanese war. And so on. Finally he stopped seeing me. At that point, I knew it was time for us to return to Kham.

For a long time we had talked about what we might do if we returned, so when we got together to discuss specifics, a plan evolved almost naturally. Trendong, Phuntob, and another Khampa member, Lobsang Namgye, would stay on in Lhasa and continue to try to make contacts and get weapons we could use in our guerrilla activities. Ngawang Kesang, Topden, Tobgye, Trinley Nyima, my brother Chömpel, Amdo Tobgye, and I would go back to Chamdo and try to get Yuthok to help us.

I sent Yuthok a letter via traders saying that we would be returning soon to Chamdo. I told him that I had tried every means but received no help from the Council of Ministers and said I hoped he could help us. And so, determined that it was time for us to take matters into our own hands, we returned to Kham. We each carried a rifle and pistol, and we had some boxes of ammunition that Trendong had given us. We were determined to start doing armed revolution.

CHAPTER 8

On the Verge of Revolt

Everywhere we traveled on the road to Chamdo, we saw evidence of peasants' suffering. I still recall, for example, the day we arrived in Damshung, a nomad area north of Lhasa. As we passed the county headquarters, we saw freshly severed human ears hanging from its gate. This kind of barbaric punishment made us both sad and angry, so that evening we cut the ears down from the gate and hurled them against the county commissioner's window in angry protest. We also encountered many instances of bribery and extortion. It would have been easy enough to ignore behavior like this or just pretend not to see it, but I didn't want to turn my back on this kind of thing anymore. It was time to stop letting people who had power abuse it.

We arrived back in Chamdo in the summer of 1945. I told Yuthok about the meetings with Surkhang, our failure to secure weapons, and our trip to India, although I did not tell him anything about our contacts with the Indian Communist Party or our disappointment about not being able to go to the Soviet Union. Being a communist was not something one could admit, even to a good friend like Yuthok.

My talks with Yuthok were friendly. He understood what we were thinking and was sympathetic. "I believe what you have said about your intentions, and I think your ideas are sound. You and your friends have the courage to think about doing things that ordinary Tibetans would never even dream about. Establishing a guerrilla organization on the other side of the Drichu and wresting power from the Chinese will not be easy and will entail tremendous risks."

He paused for a moment, and then smiled. "Maybe," he said, "it is my karma that we met, but for whatever reason, I am glad we have. I only wish I could help you now, but, my friend, I really can't. If you wanted only a few guns," he said, "then I could help you, but if I try to give you more, word will get around. It's hard to conceal that kind of thing. And if word gets around, the Tibetan government will investigate, and it won't be just me who is in danger. It will be my whole family.

"I'm sorry," he said finally, "but for these reasons, I cannot give you the kind of help you want and need. I am the top civil and military officer in Tibet's Eastern Province, and there are certain things I must report to the government." He paused. "If there were suddenly a war between China and Tibet and thus a clear threat to this region, then I could justify giving you the weapons you want. But nothing like that is happening now, so I can't justify giving you the guns." Yuthok was a good man, and I appreciated his frankness. I assured him I understood his constraints, and I told him I would not make any trouble in his district.

Despite this setback, I was still eager to return to Batang. Our immediate goal was to begin guerrilla operations in Kham, and Batang was where we planned to start. During the two months we were in Chamdo, Germany had surrendered, and it was anticipated that Japan would soon be next (it wasn't until I got to Batang that I learned the United States had dropped two atom bombs on Japan and the war was over). The world was changing fast, and I felt we had to make our move.

Before I left for Batang, I asked Yuthok for two favors. The first was that if I got into serious trouble fighting with the Chinese Nationalist government, he would try to help me. The second and related request was for a written permit allowing me to return to Tibet if I ever needed to do so. He agreed and gave me a letter that was in essence an open-ended entry visa for Tibet. The letter was not sealed, so I read it after he gave it to me. It said, "Bapa Phünwang is my friend, and whenever he comes to cross the border, let him enter Tibet." I felt much better having that escape card in my pocket.

We traveled southeast from Chamdo via Trayab to the ferry port at Jisungang on the Tibetan side of the Drichu opposite Batang. I had been a boy of fourteen when I left. Now I was returning with a few guns and bullets and a commitment to mount a guerrilla attack against Liu Wenhui and the GMD. I was old enough now to feel the full weight of the risks we were taking and the seriousness of what we were committed to attempting, and I knew I had to be very careful.

The last time I had crossed the Drichu, it had been to escape to Tibet, and I had no idea what might be waiting for me in Batang when I returned.

I was unsure whether the Chinese were still on the lookout for me, so we stopped in Jisungang and I sent some of my comrades ahead to get the lay of the land. When they came back, they told me it seemed safe, but even then I took precautions. We were a group of eight, and we feared that that many strangers coming into Batang together might arouse suspicion, so we entered the city in groups of two or three at a time, spaced a few days apart. To our relief, nothing happened, and eventually we settled in safely.

I was surprised at how glad I was to be back in Batang. In some ways it was the same as I had visualized it, but it now seemed much smaller than I remembered. When I was a boy, it was the only town I knew, but I had since been to Nanjing, Chongqing, Lhasa, and some of the larger cities of India, like Calcutta, and the comparison was striking. My family was the same, though. My mother cried tears of joy when she saw me, and I have to admit that I was moved to be back with my family and relatives.

The GMD was another matter. After we had been there for a few days, we began to realize that the appearance of safety in Batang was a bit deceptive. When we arrived, the Chinese garrison commander, Fu Dequan, was not there, but I soon learned that although they did nothing at first, the GMD Party Committee was suspicious of me from the beginning, and they began asking questions immediately. Who was I? Where had I been? It had been two years since I had left Derge to go to Lhasa, and nobody in Batang had heard a word about me. What had I been up to?

There were people who knew that I was a suspected communist and that I had fled to Tibet. But fortunately no one knew what had happened after that, and I had engaged in no revolutionary activities in or around Batang the last time I had been here. Therefore I spread the word that I had gone with Ngawang Kesang to do business in Tibet and India, and because everybody knew he had a store in Kalimpong, the story sounded credible. So while the GMD officials had their suspicions, they had no evidence against me. But there were a lot of rumors about me, and my family was extremely nervous. I was also nervous and often stayed away from home, sometimes sleeping at relatives' houses, sometimes with friends at the monastery, and sometimes going back to Jisungang on the Tibetan side of the border. I moved around so much that my mother began to complain. I had been away for ten years, she said, and now that I was back I was staying away from home most of the time.

Then Fu Dequan returned and one day invited me to dinner. Why? I wondered. There was no obvious way to decline the invitation and stay in Batang, and even if I fled, it would have confirmed whatever suspicions Fu might have had. My friends were sure I was going to be arrested and told me not to go, but I didn't see how I could refuse.

My mind raced. What could he charge me with? What did he have on me? In the short time we had been in Batang, we had made contact with some of the students at the nearby teacher training school, but all we had done was sound them out by talking about our views in a general way. I didn't think anyone in Batang could have known about our activities in Tibet and India, or suspected our real plans. I thought the only compromising evidence against me that Fu Dequan might be able to produce was the fact that I had some books that would be considered revolutionary. It was not the sort of thing he was likely to make the basis of a big public arrest, though, so I was fairly confident that nothing was going to happen. I decided to go, but I went carrying my pistol.

I was young, and I think I let my emotions get away from me. My comrades and I discussed what our group should do if I were arrested, and I decided that if they tried to seize me, I would shoot Fu Dequan and kill as many soldiers as I could while my bullets lasted. I wasn't afraid to die, but when I entered the banquet room my heart was beating fast, and I was ready for anything.

It was a false alarm. When I got there, I discovered that the group included quite a few local businessmen. There were about a dozen people in all. I remained watchful and on the lookout for trouble, but it never came. When Fu Dequan came in after we were all seated, he looked at me and said nicely, "Oh my, look how big you have become." After that I calmed down, although I was still watchful. I think Fu must have enjoyed my nervous behavior. I think now that he was just sending a little message—not only to me but to some of the townspeople as well. He had his eye on me. He could pick me up any time.

Although I survived the banquet, things were still very tense. One day not long afterward, I got a message that I was definitely going to be arrested the next day. That night I tied felt on my horse's hooves, slipped out of town, and rode all the way to Jisungang, where I stayed till I got a message that it had been a false alarm again and it was safe to go back.

I was nervous as I returned to Batang that night. When I approached the village, I walked my horse with my sword drawn. At my parents' house, I threw a pebble against the shutter to wake them quietly. My father wasn't too worried to see me, but my mother was beside herself. She was certain that I was going to be arrested and that she would never see me again. The next morning, she invited a local lama to perform a ritual to give thanks for my safety so far and to protect me.

The message in all this was clear. It didn't make any sense for us to go on like this. We had to try to get weapons and start a revolt. Rather than sitting here worrying about arrest, we should be doing something concrete toward reaching our goals. We felt our best hope was to try to reestablish ties with the Chinese and Russian communists in Chongqing. With the war over, we thought, they would now be able to give us the weapons we needed. Ngawang Kesang and I were selected to go to Chongqing, but unexpectedly, just before we were to depart, our plan was changed by a chain of events just south of Batang in Yunnan Province.

The catalyst was Dramdul, my trusted comrade who had been with me in Derge. He had tried to join me in Lhasa but was turned back by the Tibetan army in Chamdo and deported to Deqen, an ethnic Khampa area in Yunnan. While there, he met a powerful leader named Gombo Tsering and talked with him about me, our group, and our plans for creating a new Kham ruled by Khampas. Gombo Tsering liked what he heard, and when he learned I was back in Batang, he sent word through Dramdul that he would like to talk to me about "important issues."

Gombo Tsering—his Chinese name was Hai Zhengtao—had been a part of the short-lived Tibetan Government [tib. *bod pa srid gzhung*] set up by the Red Army in Ganze when they crossed through the Kham region during the Long March. After that, he had been with Panda Tobgye for some years. Then, during the anti-Japanese war, the GMD had sent him back to Deqen with a supply of three hundred to four hundred guns and a mandate to establish a local Tibetan guerrilla force that would help protect against the Japanese, who were in control of nearby Burma. He was the commander of the militia force and literally the governor of the county. The local people called him "Commander Hai" [ch. *Hai Siling*].

We were interested in meeting him but also did not want to delay going to Chongqing, where we thought our future lay, so we decided to split up. Ngawang Kesang would take the direct route through Tartsedo to Chongqing, and I would first detour to Deqen to meet Gombo Tsering, and then join Ngawang in Chongqing.

The trip south to Deqen was on a main road and not difficult, and when I finally arrived and came face to face with Gombo Tsering, I was not disappointed. Gombo Tsering's thoughts about Tibetan nationalism and making a modern Tibet were similar to mine. We hit it off immediately. He was about forty years old. He wasn't highly educated, but he could write Tibetan and Chinese. We talked, and I told him quite a bit about myself, including my commitment to communist ideals and goals.

Figure 7. Gombo Tsering (Hai Zhengtao), Deqen,
1946.

I emphasized the need for the Tibetans of Kham to put aside their differences, unite, and drive out the GMD troops.

The more we talked, the clearer it became that Gombo Tsering and I
were in basic agreement on the important issues. Gombo Tsering agreed
that guerrilla action like the kind I was proposing was what was needed
and that it was militarily feasible. And, critically, he said he would provide guns and ammunition from his militia arsenal, so that we could
begin our operation in Batang.

Having reached a general agreement, I set off for Chongqing to meet
Ngawang Kesang, while Gombo Tsering went to Kunming, the capital
of Yunnan Province, to get up-to-date information on the situation in
China. We left it that when we finished our journeys we would meet
again in Deqen and finalize the details. I was twenty-four years old. After
so many failures, my dreams, I thought, were about to come true.

I was also excited about returning to Chongqing. I too wanted to find out what was going on in the post–World War II world and to talk with Soviet and Chinese Communist Party officials. Years ago, when we left Chongqing, they told us to go see what we could do in Kham and Tibet, and then report on our activities. Now it was time to reestablish contact.

Finding them, however, turned out to be a far bigger problem than we had thought. Ngawang Kesang and I searched for the old office of the CCP, but it was gone. We also tried going to the Russian Embassy, which was still there but nearly deserted. There was just a watchman who spoke only Russian. He kept saying, "Nanjing. Nanjing." We didn't understand what he meant at first. Finally we learned that the embassies and offices had been moved to Nanjing when the Nationalist government had reestablished its capital there. We spent more than a month in Chongqing but were unable to contact representatives of either party.

We thought perhaps we too should go to Nanjing to meet them, but we quickly learned that that also was problematic. The steamers that traveled the Yangtse River to Nanjing were sold out for the next five or six months. While we were contemplating whether to wait, we contacted Gombo Tsering in Kunming by letter (sent through traders we knew). We told him our situation, and he wrote back quickly, saying we should not try to go to Nanjing. He was emphatic that we should return to Deqen to finalize our plans.

What he said made sense. A trip to Nanjing would delay implementing our plan, and with no certain outcome even if we got there, we finally decided to go back to the Deqen area. Whatever we were going to do at this point, we would have to attempt it without the help of the other communist parties. We met up with Gombo Tsering in Sadam, in Yunnan, and from there traveled together to Deqen, where we discussed strategy and principles and drafted a charter for our new Tibetan political organization.

This document outlined our philosophy and major principles and laid out a set of rules for future members of our party. It also discussed the military strategy we would employ. We named our new group the Eastern Tibet People's Autonomous Alliance [tib. *bod shar rgyud mi dmangs rang skyong mna' mthun*]. Ngawang Kesang and I wrote the charter at night, when we had total privacy—mostly in Chinese but sometimes in Tibetan. During the day we would discuss the draft with Gombo Tsering, and then rewrite and revise. We had no plans to print or distribute it. We just wanted to express our ideas precisely and formally. When we were finished, we made only two copies.

We kept one in the house where we were staying, and we left one in Gombo Tsering's house. It made us feel good to write it because it reminded us that we were doing these things for higher reasons and trying to create something revolutionary for Tibetans that would last. I thought that this time we would certainly be able to change the Tibetan world.

The charter had several sections. [It is cited in full as appendix A at the end of the book.] Part 1 gave the name of the party, specifying that this name was provisional until it could be formally discussed at the first meeting of the representatives of the new alliance. Our aims were to establish a democratically elected government for all Tibetans of Eastern Tibet (Kham) and to abolish the corvée tax system, as well as other exorbitant taxes and levies. The new government would also work to rapidly improve the livelihood of Eastern Tibetans by utilizing resources, building roads, and improving farming.

The new government would be ruled by an assembly of representatives, who would, in turn, elect a central committee of ten to twelve members. From this, a standing committee of five to eight members would be appointed. Eastern Tibet would be divided into three administrative units: the Khampa regions of Xikang, the Khampa regions of Yunnan, and the Khampa regions of Chamdo [which was then part of political Tibet]. We further developed a set of rules for the operation of the government at lower levels [see appendix A].

We were not optimistic that we would be able to establish such a new government independent of Nationalist China. Chiang Kaishek seemed very powerful then. He had just defeated the Japanese, was supported by the United States, and controlled most of China. And though ultimately we thought that the Chinese Communists would be victorious because the Nationalists were so corrupt and oppressive, at that time the Chinese Communist Party held only a small area in the north. So we decided the best strategy was to avoid an open break with Nationalist China, while positioning ourselves for a Chinese Communist victory.

We did this in several ways. First, we explicitly stated in the document that our government would operate under the Three Principles of the People [ch. *sanmin zhuyi*] set forth by Sun Yatsen, the father of the Chinese revolution against the Manchu dynasty. Since both the GMD and CCP considered themselves to be Sun Yatsen's true heir, this positioned us within the mainstream of revolutionary Chinese political ideology.

Second, we decided to use the phrase "autonomous region" [ch. *zizhi qu*] rather than "independence" to describe our polity. We wanted to make it seem as if we were fighting against Liu Wenhui, not China per se.

And third, we related our actions to GMD policy by specifically referring to decisions it had made about Tibetans, e.g., the speech Chiang Kaishek made in August 1945 in which he stated that the GMD Party agreed to grant Tibet a high degree of autonomy or, at some point in the future, even independence.[1] We thought this would leave our options open and facilitate subsequent Chinese acceptance of our new government—no matter which side won the civil war.

As I look back on our charter, I am amazed by its boldness. At the time it was written, I had nothing but the clothes on my back and a pistol and rifle. But I believed that I (and my comrades) had the skill and the will and—with Gombo Tsering's guns—the means to change Tibet. I did not hesitate to dream great dreams. They seemed so real I could touch them.

Militarily we discussed whether we should initially include the Khampa areas that were part of Tibet proper, i.e., those west of the Drichu River, under the Tibetan governor-general in Chamdo. We agreed that it would definitely be useful for us to have a base in the Chamdo area so we could move back and forth if we had to, and we thought that the conditions were excellent for success there because the Tibetan government was oppressing the people badly through heavy taxes and extractions. However, we ultimately decided that it would be better to focus initially on setting up our new government in the Khampa areas then under China. We would develop only a secondary base west

---

1. In this speech, Chiang said:

As regards the political status of Tibet, the Sixth Kuomintang [Guomintang] Congress decided to grant it a very high degree of autonomy, to aid its political advancement and to improve the living conditions of the Tibetans. I solemnly declare that if the Tibetans should at this time express a wish for self-government, our Government would, in conformity with our sincere tradition, accord it a very high degree of autonomy. If in the future they fulfill the economic requirement for independence, the National Government will, as in the case of Outer Mongolia, help them to attain that status. But Tibet must give proof that it can consolidate its independent position and protect its continuity so as not to become another Korea. (Chinese Ministry of Information, "National Independence and Racial Equality," *The Collected Wartime Messages of Generalissimo Chiang Kai-shek, 1937–1945*, vol. 2 [1940–45] [New York: The John Day Company, 1946], p. 857)

—*Goldstein, Sherap, and Siebenschuh*

of the Drichu. As our power in the east increased, we would expand our activities in the west, and after Yuthok's term of office ended in 1948, we would rise up and take military and political control of Chamdo, merging it with the eastern part of Kham to create one large Khampa autonomous region. We also hoped that by this time we would be strong enough to overthrow the rest of Tibet or force the Tibetan government to accept democratic reforms. So while our document just used the name Eastern Tibet [tib. *shar bod*], our thinking was grander. Our long-term goal was to set up a new democratic government for all of Tibet.

We didn't talk in great detail about our proposed government's functions because until we expelled the Chinese from our area it seemed premature. It was enough to outline the general structure. We all agreed that we should start slowly and build our power step by step. The Deqen area would be our base of operations, since Gombo Tsering was already in control there and it was secure. Ngawang Kesang would stay there and begin recruiting members for our organization among students in the Deqen school. We also planned to take control of the GMD tax office in Deqen and use the money it collected to help finance our expanding organization. We didn't think any of this would be problematic, because there were no Chinese troops stationed there and Gombo Tsering was the de facto governor of the area!

In addition to this, we contacted other important Khampa leaders, like Panda Tobgye, Chagö Tomden, Ngawang Norbu (the administrative head of the Dargye monastery in Ganze), and members of several aristocratic families in Batang, like Bami Tseden and Sonam Lobsang. We explained to them generally what we were planning and sought their support. Because Panda Tobgye and Gombo Tsering were good friends and Chagö Tomden and I knew each other from the time I taught in Derge, it was easy to secure their general agreement. To others, we spread the word about our new organization through letters or through oral messages carried by traders we trusted. Our plan was to join with these local leaders only in the future. For the present, they would act outwardly as if we were not allied. We would fight openly, and they would support us from behind the scenes. Once our power increased, however, they would openly reveal their support for our alliance. They agreed with our plan.

My assignment was to take the first installment of forty or fifty guns and go north to Batang. I would establish myself in one of the small villages outside the city and make contact with the important families in the area and the older students. In our opinion, the people of Batang would not need much encouragement to go to war against the occupying Chinese armies. Since we had already contacted many young people, I was certain I could recruit several hundred fighters from among them.

We planned to organize in small groups at first and use the guerrilla tactics of Zhu De and Mao Zedong, which I had read about. Our strategy would be to strike at the GMD supply lines, disrupting the flow of their basic necessities while increasing our supply of weapons as we captured or destroyed small detachments of Chinese soldiers. As we accumulated weapons, we would increase the size of our force. We all believed that we could gather strength and momentum in this way, like an avalanche that starts with a few pebbles rolling downhill and eventually becomes an unstoppable force. [See appendix A.]

It was a different ball game now. Talking with people about our ideas, not revealing everything, trying to sound them out and find the sympathetic ones were one thing. Putting guns in people's hands was an act of war, and we had to be *extremely* careful. For one thing, we knew the villagers in Deqen would not like the idea that relative strangers were taking *their* guns to another area. And although not everyone would have known that we were communists, it would certainly have been clear that we were anti-GMD. The war between the Nationalists and the communists was being waged bitterly at the moment. Getting caught with a substantial number of weapons would be a death sentence.

To get the guns to Batang, our plan was to pretend that we were merchants, hide the weapons under some ordinary merchandise, like tea, porcelain cups, and brown sugar, and take them on a pack train. Gombo Tsering had given us some money to buy the supplies. But there were some surprises.

Our plan to hide the guns and ammunition among the goods was easier said than done. The bullets were easy enough to conceal, but the rifles were too long. They were good rifles, not the old one-shot kind but Chinese models that held three or four bullets each. But you couldn't hide them in standard pack-animal loads. They stuck out.

Eventually we decided to cut the wood stocks off the rifles and glue them back together when we reached Batang. Since there were always people visiting Gombo Tsering's house—where the guns were—we decided it would be prudent to move them to the house of a close associate of Gombo's named Drung Ashi. But the cutting took time. My brother Chömpel used a saw and did most of the work, but we decided he should work only at night, when there would be no possible interruptions. It was slow going, and we all were on pins and needles till he was finished because the longer it took, the more chance there was of someone discovering us. We felt we were very close to achieving our goal now; it was a tense but exciting period.

Then one evening, about two days before we planned to leave, Ngawang Kesang, Chömpel, and I were invited to dinner by Drung Ashi. We had just started eating when shots rang out. We stared at one another. For a moment, no one said a word, we just listened. When the sound of the first volley died away, Drung Ashi loaded a pistol, put it in his pocket, and left, saying he was going to check on what was going on. Just minutes after he had gone, another volley rang out, and he came back breathing heavily. "It's not good," he said. "I'm not sure what happened, but there apparently is a problem. You should hide at once."

Hands on our shoulders and pushing us ahead of him, he hurried us down the stairs to the ground floor, where all our goods were stored, and put us in a small storeroom way off at the back. It was empty, but there was a large Tibetan mastiff tied nearby. Drung closed the door, but we could see out through cracks in the wall boards.

We had no idea what was going on outside. We knew that there were no Nationalist troops in the area, so the shooting must be coming from the villagers. But why? Was it merely some trader testing a gun for a potential buyer, or was it related to us?

We stayed very quiet for a long time, listening and waiting. We could hear and see people rushing back and forth and talking, but no sounds were clear enough to identify. Then all at once, we heard a large crowd running into the courtyard of our house, we guessed maybe fifteen or twenty men. We could hear what they were saying now, and it was clear that they were looking for us. "Where are the Bapas?" they shouted. "Where are the Bapas?"

When they burst into the ground floor of the house, the first thing they saw was our packed loads. They ran to them and began ripping them open. When they found the guns, they shouted to others still outside, confirming that we had tried to take their guns and saying proudly that they had gotten them back. They were so excited that they began filing by the pack loads, each person taking one of the guns as he passed and then running outside.

All but two.

In spite of all the excitement, two of the villagers noticed the room where we were hiding. Paying no attention now to the shouts of their friends, they began to come closer. We could see them clearly through the cracks in the wall.

In the hour or so we had been alone, Ngawang Kesang and I had discussed what we were going to do if somebody found us. We didn't have any weapons—no guns, not even a knife. So we decided that if someone came to look in the room where we were hiding, I would pull the door open hard to surprise him. Then Ngawang Kesang would grab his feet and pull him down, Chömpel would grab his gun or knife, and we would have a weapon. Luckily we didn't have to try this.

As the two who were coming toward us got closer, the big mastiff bared his teeth, strained hard against the tether, and began to bark fiercely. They stopped and looked at each other. Then suddenly there were louder shouts from their comrades outside. They looked at the menacing dog, and after a few agonizing seconds, they turned and left.

Eventually they all left the courtyard, but we could still hear the shouts of the villagers, now far away, now closer. People were chanting things like "Gombo Tsering has sold our guns to the Bapa communists. He is terrible." We sat perfectly still, afraid to make a sound. Finally a servant girl from the household came to the room where we were hiding and in a frightened voice said, "They are looking for you everywhere. You had better get out of here as fast as you can."

We knew she was right. Our whole world was collapsing around us. We had to get out of the village before they found and killed us.

CHAPTER 9

Escape to Tibet

We decided we had to make a run for it. We quietly slipped out of the house into the courtyard to see where the villagers were. They were angry that they hadn't found us yet, and they were now trying to be more methodical. They carried torches, and the moving lights cast huge shadows—but this also let us know exactly where they were. We watched them carefully, and when they had gone to another part of the village, we sneaked out of the courtyard and into a stand of thorn bushes a ways behind the house. It was better than being boxed in the storeroom and was safe at night, but we knew we couldn't stay there long.

We were uncomfortable trying to move around without any weapons, so I suggested we contact a village woman originally from Batang whom I thought we could trust. We sent my brother Chömpel to her house because he dressed like a monk and the villagers didn't know he had anything to do with us. They weren't looking for *him*. He was gone for half an hour and then came back empty-handed. He reported that when he told her what we wanted, she got agitated and begged him to leave. "They will find out about it," she said, "and they will blame me later."

We knew we had to get out of Deqen, but we also had to find out what had really happened. So we sent Chömpel three times from our hiding place in the thorn bushes to see if he could get to Gombo Tsering's house or find Drung Ashi to learn the truth. We also told him to try to retrieve the copy of the "Alliance Manifesto" we had left with our things in Drung's home. Each time, however, he encountered too many people

and returned with no clear news. As dawn approached, we moved carefully to a wooded gully in front of a water mill, where we felt we would
be safe for a while. But we still didn't know exactly what had gone
wrong, so we sent Chömpel again to town.

We waited anxiously, and finally he returned. I can still see him walking quickly back to the gully where we were hiding, his shoulders sag-
ging, his hat carried loosely in his hand. The worst was true. Drung Ashi
told him that the villagers had killed Gombo Tsering. He said Drung had
hidden the document but begged us to leave as soon as possible because
they were searching for us everywhere. Chömpel told us that when our
host said this he held up his thumbs in a pleading gesture, the way beggars do. There was nothing to do now but get out immediately.

As we were leaving, Chömpel gave us more details. There was no
warning, he said. Gombo Tsering, his daughter, and his niece were shot
from ambush as they left their house. The gunfire came from a store just
across the street. Gombo Tsering was hit several times but managed to
stagger back inside. The shooters followed him into the house and found
him collapsed and bleeding on his bed, where they finished him off. (The
daughter and niece were both wounded in the attack but survived.)

We found out later that it was a Tibetan named Wang Wenjun who
had planned the attack. He and Gombo Tsering were relatives, but they
hated each other. Wang had been in charge of the local militia in the area
until the GMD brought Gombo Tsering back and made him the commander instead. Ngawang Kesang and I had worried about the possible
problems their bad feelings might cause and had tried several times to get
them to reconcile their differences, but to no avail. Wang would say,
"Yes, yes," but never did anything. And Gombo Tsering's main fault was
that he didn't pay attention to what others felt. He just gave orders. Ultimately, Wang Wenjun had rallied local people to his side by accusing
Gombo Tsering of making the area weak by giving away their weapons
to communists.[1]

We headed into the mountains. The books I had read about guerrilla
warfare always said that to avoid capture you had to keep away from
well-traveled roads and highways. So we climbed into the stony, snow-
covered terrain, where we hoped nobody would think to look for us.

---

1. Wang Wenjun's victory was short-lived. About a year after he shot Gombo Tsering,
Wang himself was killed in an ambush in Chamdo by a supporter of Gombo Tsering. Phünwang was glad when he heard the news, not only because Gombo Tsering had been
avenged, but also because he had heard rumors that Wang was still trying to kill him as
well. —Goldstein, Sherap, and Siebenschuh

It was hard going. The snows of November had begun, and we were poorly dressed for raw weather like this, as we had been able to take just the clothes on our backs. We also began to feel weak because we had consumed no food for over a day. And we had virtually no money. My brother had a few yuan on him when we fled, but Ngawang and I had not one cent.

Finally, after traveling for hours, we saw a sheepherder in the distance and motioned to him to come over. We didn't think he had any food, but we wanted to make sure of the road. It was no use, however. He took one look at us and fled. Going a little farther, we saw a small stone and mud-brick house with some plots of cultivated land on a mountain slope just across from us. There were three or four men collecting dung in the distant fields and a Tibetan woman cooking something at a small fire. They all stopped to look at us suspiciously, but at least they didn't run away.

We approached the woman and said we were muleteers working for a Tibetan trader from nearby Gyeltang and were searching for two lost mules. Had they seen any? (She was baking bread, and the smell and warmth of the fire almost overpowered us.) She said she hadn't seen any mules, and then we asked if we could buy some food from her, telling her we had left quickly without any. "First have some black tea," she said, and then she gave us some bread. When Chömpel tried to pay for what we had eaten, she refused our money, saying, "Oh, you don't need to do that." She did agree to let us buy a few more things to take, though. And then, with our bones warmed and our hunger satisfied, we went back out into the mountains.

Getting us where we were going was up to me. I liked geography. I used maps whenever I could, and wherever we were, I always tried to get acquainted with the lay of the land. I knew, therefore, that when we got to the mountains just ahead of us, we would cross the Thöndrupling Pass and descend to a village called Pangtsiwaka. From there on, we would be relatively safe. But that wasn't going to be easy. Though the mountain pass wasn't far as the crow flies, we were still staying away from the main roads and had to lead Ngawang Kesang because his eyesight was so bad. He held one end of a stick, and Chömpel and I took turns holding the other end.

Later that night, we finally reached the snow-covered Thöndrupling Pass and stopped to rest for a while at an empty way station. We ate snow to get fluids and then ate one of the pieces of bread we had bought at the cottage. But we didn't stop to sleep, because we were still afraid that the people from Deqen might be close behind. So we kept going in spite of the cold and our swollen feet. By the morning of the next day, we arrived exhausted at Pangtsiwaka, on the banks of the Drichu River, where we found a place to stay and got some much-needed rest. We continued to tell people that we were muleteers looking for some runaway mules. Our boss would be furious with us if we came back empty-handed, we said. We *had* to find them. The homeowner where we were staying was sympathetic and gave us some food for the trip.

On the other side of the river, the trail forked. If you went north, the trail took you to Batang and Derge, but if you went south, the trail went to Yunnan—to Gyeltang and Sadam. We had decided it was safer to head south, since they would be expecting us to head for Batang. However, to get to the other side you had to take a ferry, and we didn't have enough money. We decided to wait for other travelers to arrive. Luckily a wedding party soon arrived, and we blended in with them and crossed for free.

The cold and hunger were always with us. We continued to eat snow for water, and when we could find them, we would eat turnips that had been left in the fields. At one point, we thought we had gotten lucky. We came in sight of another wedding party and decided to follow them for a while. They stopped to eat, and when they left we eagerly went to search for leftover food. Unfortunately, all we could find was orange rinds, which we carefully collected and divided among ourselves. We were willing to eat almost anything. Later I wrote a poem about this difficult journey:

> At the time our revolutionary military force was established,
> Our comrades were killed secretly by evil people.
> I climbed a precipitous mountain
> And escaped from the mouth of the hungry wolf.

> At the pass of Thöndrupling,
> The snow was tastier than rice.
> When I looked at the great stars in the early morning,
> I forgot the difficulties of day and night.

> When we reached Pangtsiwaka,
> I became secure and happy.
> When I saw the blue water,
> My enthusiasm increased like fire burning.

> The rind of an orange on the trail
> Was food without equal;
> The [warmth of the] fire on my back
> Was bedding beyond compare.

> At the lake in Gyeltang,
> The cold air pierced my flesh and bones.

On a beautiful plain,
There were no sheep and no Tsering Tshomo [the heroine of a popular
    Khampa song].

When the rooster first crowed,
the moonbeams reached Sadam.
On the road in front of me, which twists and turns,
I will again take a new step forward.

gsar brje'i dmag dpung btsugs kar
blo mthun mi ngan lkog bsad

brag ri g.yang gsar 'dzegs te
spung ltogs kha nas thar song

don grub gling gi la kha'i
jha ba 'bras las zhim pa

spang rtsi wa khar slebs dus
blo bde sems skyid byung ba

g.yu chu sngon po mthong dus
snying stobs de bas rgyas song

lam thog tsha lu'i pags pa
'gran zla med pa'i gsol tshig

mtshan mo sgal pa me 'de
'gran zla med pa'i nyal zan

rgyal thang 'og ma'i mtsho khar
grang rlung sha rus brgyas pa

lung bde sa skyid thang la
lha lug mtsho mo ma mthong

bya skad dang po rgyag dus
zla 'od sa tham 'byor ba

mdun lam kyag kyog thog la
slar yang gom pa gsar spo

There was a mill outside Gyeltang where we were lucky enough to find a place to stay the night and get some tsampa. The next morning, we continued our flight, making a wide detour around the town to avoid the Nationalist Chinese troops stationed there. We traveled through a large pine forest that was so dense it was almost as dark as night.

After Gyeltang, we headed south to Sadam, but again we had to cross the river, which snaked back and forth. I approached the ferryman and asked him to please take us across. "We are traders who have been robbed," I said, "and we are just trying to get home." He gave us a long look and finally said, "All right. Wait till I have some other customers and you can ride across with them."

The fear, hunger, and lack of sleep had taken their toll on us all, and before long the tension began to build. Finally Ngawang Kesang could stand it no longer.

"What's the matter?" he said to the ferryman. "Why can't you just take us across and be done with it? I have been to Lhasa and to the great cities of China, and I have *never* seen anyone like you."

Then the ferryman got angry, and I thought we were going to lose any chance we might have, so I spent a lot of time calming him. I explained how tired and hungry we were. Eventually he took us across.

We continued moving fast, eating whatever we could find. Before too long, we reached a part of this mountain area where a minority people called the Lisu lived. We came upon a small village when it was almost dark, and went up to one of the houses to see if they would let us spend the night. Inside, we found several members of a family seated around the fireplace. The Lisu are a short people, and physically they all looked the same. All of them were smoking cigarettes through a special bamboo water pipe. When we asked if we could stay the night, they just stared at us.

We quickly realized that they didn't understand Chinese, and we certainly didn't understand their language. There was an awkward silence for a few minutes. They were cooking a meal of potatoes for themselves, but they made no motion for us to sit down or join them (even though what we wanted was obvious). Finally Chömpel took out one of the coins he still had and pushed it toward them. That got a response; they motioned us to sit and have some of the potatoes. They also let us stay the night.

We left very early the next morning, heading toward Sadam, a major town in Yunnan. We felt more comfortable using the regular roads and trails now. Still, when we saw merchants and traders approaching with their trains of mules, we avoided them if we could. Once, however, we simply couldn't avoid them, and they turned out to be a party of traders from the Batang region. It was very awkward because we knew one another!

They didn't recognize us at first because of our tattered clothes, but when they did we had to do some fast talking. We knew we couldn't use our old story about being muleteers, so we said that we were going to Sadam to do some trading and had been attacked by bandits, barely escaping with our lives. As they listened, they said nothing and looked back and forth at one another. We could tell that they were dubious. After telling them our story about what had happened, we said very little else. When it was time to leave, we said goodbye to one another and continued on our way, leaving them to think whatever they wanted to think.

Not long after that, we reached the outskirts of Sadam. It had taken twelve to thirteen days to get there (twice as long as normal). I had a relative living in Sadam, and I was sure we could stay with her family. But I wasn't willing to risk going directly into the town without checking first. We didn't make a move till it was dark.

The nationality living in this area are the Naxi, a people who controlled the southern part of traditional Kham. Long ago, the king of Sadam had sent one of his officials to Batang, and he took a Tibetan wife who happened to be my cousin. When we knocked at her door and she realized who I was, tears came to her eyes. Her reaction surprised me. I had been so afraid of detection, I hadn't paid much attention to the reaction of the traders from Batang or anyone else till now. But she stared at us and kept asking what had happened, and I finally understood. We must have been a sight. Our feet were badly swollen. We had lost weight, and our clothes were in rags.

I told her that we had been robbed and now were bankrupt, and I hoped they would let me stay with them for a while because my boss in Batang would be angry with me. I said I needed some time to decide what to do. I couldn't tell whether she believed me, but it didn't matter. Her willingness to help us was obvious.

She quickly found us a place to stay at the home of a member of her husband's family. Ironically, it was in a house very near to the governor of Sadam's—right under the nose of the government. But it turned out to be the perfect place to hide, because it was the last place that people would have thought to look for us. The house had a second floor where they stored grass for forage. We hid in the grass during the day and came down to the first floor at night.

Because we felt safe, we decided to take a chance and sent Chömpel back to Deqen to try again to retrieve the organization's charter we had left behind. He managed to find a few of our possessions and some documents and letters, but not the politically dangerous charter.

Not long after he left, a Tibetan trader named Huo Qichang (he went by his Chinese name) came through Sadam from Deqen. He told us they were looking for us high and low, and that the troops the Chinese sent to investigate the incident found a document with our names on it that contained references to our plan to establish a guerrilla force in Kham. The minute they learned this, the GMD formally issued a warrant for the arrest of Ngawang Kesang and myself. At that point, we knew we couldn't stay in Sadam much longer. We had to go back into Tibet proper, where the Chinese could not get us.

We decided that the best thing to do at that point was split up. Ngawang Kesang had relatives in Tartsedo who he felt would be willing to help him. Because of his bad eyes, he couldn't walk by himself and was slowing us down, so I borrowed money from our host and paid some traders to take him there. I didn't see him again for many years, but I learned later that in Tartsedo he told his story to Panda Tobgye, who helped him get safely to Chengdu. (I had told him that if he got as far as Chengdu, he should contact the Soviet representatives in the area, but instead he just kept on running and ended up in Hong Kong and then Shanghai. After the Liberation in 1949, he went to Beijing.)

My plan was to go in the opposite direction. I decided to work my way back to Chamdo, find Yuthok, and talk with him about what I ought to do next. To do this, I would need some money, and when Chömpel returned from Deqen, I sent him to Batang to get some for me. Here I had a stroke of good luck. Dawa, my boyhood friend, was a trader now and had come to Sadam on business. We were delighted to have found each other, and when he learned about my situation, he lent me half of the money he had brought with him for trade. Soon Chömpel came back from Batang with Trinley Nyima, and he also brought money. My family had borrowed against our land to help me. I was overcome with gratitude and more determined than ever to justify their trust in me.

When we were ready, Chömpel and I headed north to Batang. With the money they had brought, we bought guns and horses in Sadam for each of us, and I bought a long-haired wig to cut down the chances of anyone from Batang recognizing me, as the traders had earlier. We camped a little bit south of Batang and sent Chömpel into town to get word to my friends and family that I was hiding nearby.

Some old friends from the village came to see me. They told me not to cross the Drichu into Tibet because the Tibetan authorities would arrest me, but I told them I had to go. Of course, I knew I had the pass from

Figure 8. Sadam, 1947. *Back row, from left:* Trinley Nyima *(first)* and (Yeshe) Chömpel *(third)*. *Front row, from left:* Phünwang and Dawa.

Yuthok in my pocket. I asked them to continue recruiting in Kham, but my business lay elsewhere.

It was an emotional time for me because my father also came to see me. He was not educated, and the political theories that profoundly affected me would have meant little to him. But he didn't question me or my actions, and when I was in desperate straits he borrowed money against his land to help me.

We did most of our talking while walking in a farmer's field. I told him about what had happened to me in Deqen and about my plans to go to Chamdo and eventually continue the struggle. He put his hand on my shoulder and told me that if I wanted to be a real man, I should continue to fight for what I believed in. He then put his hands together and said a prayer for my safe journey. As soon as he did this, the image of Yuthok came to mind. When I was leaving Chamdo for Batang, Yuthok had put a ceremonial scarf on my neck and also put his hands together in prayer and prayed that no harm should come to me. I thought that in my life these were the only two who had ever prayed for me. I was moved by this thought.

The next day, my father went back to Batang, and it was time for us to move on. Because I had the letter from Yuthok, we had no trouble entering Tibet, although we had to stay in Jisungang for over a month because snow was blocking the pass to Chamdo. But we were out of China and out of danger of arrest by the Chinese. It was early in 1947.

CHAPTER 10

From Lhasa to Yunnan

Our trip to Chamdo was uneventful. My meeting with Yuthok, however, was not. We had done little more than greet each other when he smiled and said, "Well, Phünwang-la, so you are communist. You never said a thing to me about it."

"How did you know?" I asked, startled and a bit embarrassed.

"Word about the incident in Deqen and your escape has spread all the way to Chamdo."

For a minute I didn't know what to say. Finally I simply spoke the truth.

"I'm sorry," I said. "I never actually lied to you. You never asked me if I was a communist, so I never volunteered the information, because I was afraid that if I did, you wouldn't have been able to be my friend."

I waited for some reaction, but Yuthok said nothing, and so I continued. "We are trying to do something good for Tibetans. We want to free Kham from Chinese rule and reform Tibetan society. I want to see Tibet grow and prosper, like the other nations of the world."

Yuthok smiled again, and I could see that he was not angry.

"Whatever you are," he said, "I do not believe that you would ever do anything that would harm Tibetans." When I told him I wanted to go back to Lhasa, he paused, then said, "Between you and me, it won't be long before the news about Deqen gets there. When it does, it will spread quickly and make it very difficult and dangerous for you to stay in Lhasa. If I were you, I would get as far away as possible. Why don't you change your name and go to Dzayü [near the border with India; see map 2] and stay there for a couple of years till this all blows over? I can appoint you as the acting governor. I don't think the Lhasa government would even bother trying to go after you there."

"Thank you," I said. "Your offer is very kind, but I cannot accept. I must go to Lhasa. Even if the Kashag thinks I am a communist, they have no proof. They can't arrest me." Yuthok disagreed and continued trying to convince me that I would be taking too big a risk if I stayed. But I couldn't imagine going into hiding now—just dropping out of sight and wasting time. I didn't tell Yuthok, but I also had not given up my hope of contacting the Soviet Union through the Indian Communist Party. With World War II over, that seemed more plausible than ever. In any case, I was not going to give up. We had come so close in Deqen. We had the guns ready to take to Batang. I could still feel the excitement we all felt because we were about to *act*. I had to go on now, whatever the risks.

At last Yuthok was convinced nothing he could say would change my mind. "Okay, my friend. If you really want to go to Lhasa, I can't stop you," he said finally. "Is there anything you need? Anything I can do for you?"

When I told him I needed some money, he immediately offered fifty *dotse* (a Tibetan currency unit worth a great deal of money; at the time a yak cost less than one dotse). He was truly a good friend, and in about two weeks, when I left for Lhasa, I couldn't help thinking about his final warning. "Be very careful," he had said; "the government considers communists their mortal enemy, so there is great danger for you."

I arrived in Lhasa at the end of 1947 together with my brothers Chömpel and Thuwang (Thubden Wangchuk). This was not long after Reting, the former regent, had attempted a coup and failed. The Fourteenth Dalai Lama was only seven years old, and the government had been badly shaken by Reting's actions. It was not the most auspicious time I could have chosen for my return, since political tensions were high, and I had Yuthok's warning ringing in my ears. Fortunately, however, I was able to get settled quickly.

The uncle I had lived with in Nanjing and Chongqing now worked at the Chinese government's office in Lhasa. I knew I didn't have to explain myself or hide anything from him. He knew my political views because I had talked with him about them in Chongqing and tried to persuade him to join us. He had never criticized or disagreed with me, and he had promised me that he would never betray me or do anything to harm our group, so I went to him as soon as I arrived and told him the truth: that I had tried to establish a guerrilla force in Kham and that I had failed and had to run for my life.

As I expected, he wasn't shocked or angry. His reaction was practical. He wanted to get me a job teaching music at the Chinese government school in Lhasa. He thought this would dispel suspicions on the part of the Lhasa government, since I couldn't be much of a communist threat if the Guomindang in Lhasa was hiring me. But first he said he needed to put my situation in the best light to the Mongolian and Tibetan Affairs Commission in Nanjing, so we sent a telegram about the Yunnan incident to Nanjing under my uncle's name. It said that I was not a member of the Chinese Communist Party and that I had been trying to organize a military force in Kham to use against the oppressive warlord Liu Wenhui—not the Chinese central government (the Guomindang). He thought this would make it possible to work in the school—and he was right.

Very quickly I had some room to breathe. The Chinese government school, which had opened just a few years before, occupied the second floor of the Kyidöpa house, the Guomindang officials using the top floor. The school taught Chinese, Tibetan, and some English, and was to be a vehicle for building better relations between the Chinese and the Tibetans. The best students were to be sent to China to continue their education.

At this time there were forty or fifty students, some Tibetan, some Han Chinese, and some Chinese Muslims. Among the Tibetan students, some were the children of aristocrats. The teachers were a mixed group as well. There were two Tibetans from Batang, a few Chinese, and Tsadrü Rimpoche, a famous scholar in Lhasa who had many private students among the elite. (The Thirteenth Dalai Lama had sent him to Japan to study when he was young, and he was also very progressive in his views.)

It was an excellent situation. We were paid a good salary, had a comfortable place to live, and were among friends. My uncle knew a lot of people from Batang who lived in Lhasa and the surrounding area, many of them monks in Ganden, Sera, and Drepung monasteries. Most of the people in Lhasa who were from Kham already knew that the Guomindang had attempted to arrest me, so there was no awkward explaining to do.

From the beginning I looked at my teaching job not just as a convenience but as an opportunity, and we made the school our focus of activities. We moved slowly at first, trying to influence the thinking of students by teaching them revolutionary songs and talking about the issues and subjects the songs raised. As always, much of our message was conveyed through the words to our songs. We also sounded out other Khampas in Lhasa and friends from our previous stay, like the progressive local aristocrats Shökhang, Janglojen, and Kapshöpa Sey. Trendong Sey was out of Lhasa at this time. My uncle knew the Dalai Lama's family, so I also got to know the Dalai Lama's brother-in-law, Phüntso Tashi.

He was from Qinghai Province and was fluent in Chinese, and we had some good general conversations about reforming Tibetan society and uniting all Tibetans. I also tried to see Surkhang several times, but he always put me off, saying he was unavailable for one reason or another. (The end of the war had not made the Council of Ministers more interested in our plans).

Confident that we had settled in without problem, we decided it was time to try again to make contact with the Soviet Union, and so early in 1948 I sent my younger brother, Thuwang, to Kalimpong to try to renew our contacts with the Indian communists and with their help travel to the USSR. We hoped the Soviets would supply us with guns and ammunition via Xinjiang, as we had discussed some years before with Fei Delin. As always, though, things didn't go exactly as we planned.

Thuwang was able to make contact with the Indian communists in Kalimpong, and he seemed to have come at an opportune time. There was a split in the Indian Communist Party between those who wanted to gain power democratically through elections and those who wanted to take control by force. The communists in Kalimpong were for using force—and of course so were we. They had actually started actions in Siliguri, near Kalimpong.

Thuwang not only talked with the Kalimpong communists, but he also went to Calcutta and met Basu, as well as Joshi, the overall head of the Communist Party of India. After these meetings, he wrote me an enthusiastic letter explaining that the Kalimpong communists were going to help us militarily. They were getting ready to begin a guerrilla campaign of their own, he said, and would be willing to give us money to buy weapons if we helped them get guns. They knew that guns were easy to buy in Lhasa, so their idea was for Thuwang and some of their people to come back to Lhasa (with the Indians disguised as Nepalese traders). There they would buy rifles and pistols, and would let us keep the rifles if we helped them smuggle the pistols out of Lhasa to India.

This was not the news I expected, but it was good news nevertheless. I immediately began making plans for their visit, but when weeks went by, and then months, with no word from Thuwang, I began to fear the worst—that he had been arrested. Finally, however, we got word from him that the Kalimpong communists' cell had been discovered and many of the members arrested by the police. Fortunately, Thuwang was able to escape and hide for a while in the newspaper editor Tharchin's house. As soon as things quieted down, he slipped away unnoticed and returned to Lhasa. (It was, I think, at the end of 1948.) This was another crush-

Figure 9. Some members of the Tibetan Communist
Party, Lhasa, 1947. *Back row, from left:* Topden
(first) and (Yeshe) Chömpel *(second)*. *Second row,
from left:* Thuwang *(first)*, Phünwang *(second)*, and
Tobgye *(third)*. *Front row, from left:* Drug Chömpel, Amdo, and Trinley Nyima.

ing blow. Again our hopes had been raised and dashed. It was a difficult
time for me, and I began to wonder if we were ever going to succeed.

Meanwhile, my friend Yuthok's term as governor-general of Eastern
Tibet ended in 1948, and late that year he returned to Lhasa. He invited me
to his house soon after he arrived and greeted me with more disturbing
news. Just before he left Chamdo, he had attended a banquet to celebrate
the change in administrators. A Chinese official from the Mongolian and
Tibetan Affairs Commission was present, and at the first opportunity he approached Yuthok. "The head of the Tibetan Communist Party, Phünwang,
is in Tibet at this moment," he said slyly. "I hear that he is your friend, and
that when he was in Chamdo you frequently invited him to your house."

Yuthok said he was furious because this was said in front of the in-
coming Tibetan governor-general, Lhalu. But Tibetan aristocrats know
how to control their tempers, so though he was seething inside, he responded pleasantly, "I don't know whether Phünwang is the head of the
Tibetan Communist Party or not. He didn't have anything written on his
forehead saying he is a communist. I knew him as a student who ap-

Figure 10. Some former members of the Tibetan Communist Party, Lhasa, mid-1950s. *From left:* Topden, Phünwang, Lobsang Namgye, and Ngawang Kesang.

proached me with a letter of introduction from the Tibetan Government's bureau office in Chongqing. We became friends after the first meeting, and I did see him several times after that. I don't see why that is surprising. I never knew he was a communist. On the other hand, you knew he was a communist, but you also invited him to dinner many times. So how can you insinuate I did something improper when I didn't even know?"

Yuthok said they all smiled and went on to other topics. But he was worried for me now. "It is certain," he said seriously, "that this information will get back to Lhasa. And when the Council of Ministers hears about it, they will take it seriously. I advise you to leave for Kham as quickly as possible because you will be in danger of arrest if you stay. I tell you this as your friend," he said, and I knew his concern for me was sincere. He went on to say that he was also nervous for himself due to the Reting coup incident, when a bomb that was sent to the regent bore his name as the return addressee. He said he planned to leave soon for Kalimpong. The public reason would be that he was going to get treatment for his eyes, but when he got there, he said, he was going to drop out of sight for a while.

Yuthok's warning, following close upon the collapse of our hopes for support from India, made it clear that we were going to have to get out of Lhasa. Yuthok's suggestion that we return to Kham seemed a good idea, as I had read in a Chinese-language newspaper that came to Lhasa from Calcutta that some favorable changes had taken place in Kham. According to the articles I had read, some local members of the Chinese Communist Party had established a guerrilla presence in the Sadam area of Yunnan and were already in control of three counties there. We also heard that the nearby Burmese Communist Party had a strong force in the area. It was an obvious place for us to go.

We believed that any communist forces we met would be willing to back and assist us. We didn't have any sense that there were different communist parties with different agendas, as there are today. We thought everyone who belonged to a party that sang the "Internationale" was fundamentally the same, with the same goals and beliefs. If we could get there and make contact with these communist guerrilla forces, we thought they would support us, so that we could begin to establish our own power in Batang. So I sent my brother Thuwang, along with Topden's brother Tobgye, back to Kham overland to try to make preliminary contact with the communist groups in Sadam. We planned to leave and join them as soon as they made contact. (They left Lhasa in June 1949, disguised as monks with shaved heads.)

We began to make our own preparations for departure by borrowing money from some of our friends among the Khamba traders to buy trade goods, since we wanted to disguise ourselves as traders. There were nine of us in all; we all had pistols and intended to go armed.

As 1949 unfolded, the air in Lhasa grew full of excitement and tension. From the newspaper articles, it was becoming clearer that the Chinese communists were eventually going to win the war against Chiang Kaishek, and the Tibetan government was becoming increasingly nervous about the prospect that the atheist socialists would soon rule China. They even performed religious ceremonies to try to change the communists' luck. Meanwhile, we were ready to go. We were just waiting for word from Thuwang. But before a letter could come, the Tibetan government expelled us.

Our expulsion was public and without warning. One day in July 1949, I answered a knock at the door to find the lay official Changöpa together with another lay official, a monk official, and about nine or ten armed Tibetan soldiers. With the soldiers standing by and Changöpa, who had been to England, taking photographs, the monk official read a formal letter from the Council of Ministers stating that I was a member of the Communist Party and had to leave Lhasa within three days.

I was shocked and indignant. "Minister Surkhang knows who I am and what I am doing," I said angrily. (Later I found out that in fact Surkhang was one of the people who had participated in the decision to expel me.) I knew that there was nothing I could do about the expulsion order, but I was so furious that I wanted to have my say, as there was a large crowd gawking behind the troops.

"Lhasa isn't just a place for aristocrats," I shouted. "It is a place for all Tibetans. I have a right to stay here. And though you may expel me today, I will be back in Lhasa tomorrow!" I went on in this way for a while, criticizing the aristocracy and the government. The officials just listened, and then told me that I had to go back to Kham through India (not Tibet) and that they would send soldiers to accompany me. Angry as I was, I was glad that all the people and aristocrats who had gathered around had heard what I had to say. (From that day on, the Tibetan government posted several soldiers outside my door who followed me wherever I went. If I visited someone, they wouldn't go in with me, but would wait outside at the door.)

When I calmed down, I went to see a Tibetan from Tartsedo named Li, who worked as a translator at the Chinese government office. He was a friend of mine, and I thought he would be in a position at least to get permission for me and my friends to go back to Kham by way of Chamdo. Making us go through India was insulting and would be much more costly. But I was wrong. In fact, Li and the others in the Nationalist Government office had also been expelled and were preparing to leave themselves via India.

My own situation, meanwhile, was complicated by another factor. During the time I had been teaching in Lhasa, I had fallen in love with one of my students, a young woman named Tsilila [tib. *mdzes legs lags*]. She was a student from a Tibetan Muslim family who was in the highest grade I taught. Her family (whose name was Chumik Khangsar) sold animals and flour and was making a pretty good living in Lhasa. When I told Tsilila that the Tibetan government had ordered me to leave, she didn't hesitate for a second. She said she was going with me. I tried to dissuade her and suggested that we could arrange our affairs when I returned, but she said, "If I don't go with you now, we may never meet again." So we got married quickly, and she came with us. (Before we left Lhasa, I sent a letter to my parents telling them of my marriage, and I learned later that they were happy for me.)

Figure 11. Phünwang's first wife,
Tsilila, in Lhasa (date unknown).

On the night before the Guomindang officials were to leave Lhasa, the
Council of Ministers hosted a banquet for the officials at which they presented them with ceremonial scarves and generous travelling expenses.
We, in contrast, got no such treatment. Topden and I had already left
several days earlier accompanied by a dozen soldiers. We had our

weapons (the Tibetan government had not made any attempt to take them from us), and fearing they were going to assassinate us on the way to India, we made contingency plans to fight if needed. In fact, we were so concerned that we asked a big and very tough Tibetan friend from Amdo to travel with us. But it never came to that. The Tibetan soldiers simply wanted to be sure we left Tibet. The troops escorted us to the Indian border and then returned home.

When we arrived in Kalimpong, I went to see Yuthok immediately. "See," he said, pointing his finger at me, "I told you this might happen." I was happy to see him and readily admitted he had been right. When I explained what had happened, Yuthok took my hand in his and asked me if I had any financial problems. "If you do, please tell me and I can help you," he said. I thought I had enough money, so I declined, but I was grateful, as I knew he was serious about it. Then his eyes teared up and he told me to be careful on the journey. I said not to worry, and again said that I would return someday soon. He walked me to the road and waved as I departed.

In a day or so we left for Calcutta and from there went by plane first to a stopover in Burma and then on to Kunming in Yunnan Province. In Kunming, we could do little more than try to get a feel for what was generally going on in China and the world. I caught up on my reading and was surprised to learn of the success of communism in the postwar era. The creation of new socialist states in Hungary, Romania, Yugoslavia, Poland, North Korea, and Vietnam gave me confidence that the future of communism was great. I thought that we were seeing the creation of a large socialist family led by the Soviet Union, and I thought that ultimately, when the Chinese Communist Party replaced the GMD, China would join that family. Having failed to establish our own Tibetan socialist state, I was now determined to find the Chinese Communist Party and join their efforts.

We had left Lhasa before hearing anything definite from Thuwang, so we didn't know the real situation in the three counties in Yunnan we had heard were under Communist control. We weren't able to learn anything definite in Kunming, so we moved northwest about a hundred and fifty miles to a town called Dali. There we finally got confirmation that the communists did in fact control those counties, and we decided to go there immediately. We disguised ourselves as businessmen so we could join a large group of traders who were going to Sadam, and we arrived there on August 15, 1949.

In Sadam, we met Thuwang and a trader from Batang, who told us that a Communist Party organization called the Chinese Communist Party Committee of Western Yunnan had been established for the three liberated counties, which had been combined into one new prefecture. He told us that the communists' headquarters were located in a nearby town called Jianchuan. Excited, we set off for Jianchuan immediately.

We left early in the morning and arrived late the same afternoon. As we approached, we could hear the sound of gunfire, and we soon learned that this was a front-line area and that a battle was still in progress. I decided the best thing to do would be to find the commander of the communist forces as soon as I could. I located him without difficulty. His name was Ou Gen, and he was of the Bai nationality. He had a second in command, Wang Yizhong, who was a Han Chinese.

They gave us a simple meal, which we ate standing up because they had no furniture. When we had finished eating, I told them about our organization, emphasizing the length of time we had been in existence and the fact that we had established relations with communists in the Soviet Union and in the Chinese and Indian Communist Parties. Ou Gen seemed interested and told me that they had heard something about there being a Tibetan communist organization in Kham, but they had had no names or specific information.

Although they were very busy, they seemed glad enough to see us, and we soon got down to more practical business. They told us that they had in fact already liberated three counties here and suggested that we should go to Kham and begin guerrilla activities there. They hoped we could establish ourselves quickly in Batang and said they thought they would be able to support us with weapons in the near future.

The plan was for us to liberate the southern part of Kham while they continued to work in northwest Yunnan. That way our forces would be close enough to assist each other if necessary. Holding these territories back to back, we hoped to work from the center outward to eventually liberate all of northwest Yunnan and the rest of Kham, but if this was not possible, at least we would be able to hold this territory until the Communist Party liberated the rest of China. We all believed that our work might take two or three years and that the larger process of fully liberating China might take three or four, but we didn't doubt it would happen.

Amid all this, a troubling issue arose—the status of our Tibetan Communist Party. For Ou Gen, the situation was clear. He insisted we should join *his* organization. I disagreed strongly. Hadn't he just heard about our history? We had been in existence since 1939! We had been working for a decade. If we simply joined Ou Gen's group, that would relegate us to the status of brand new converts just now joining the Chinese Communist Party. I wanted some recognition for our years of revolutionary activity.

We argued about it, sometimes heatedly, but Ou would not budge. Finally Ou suggested that this was an issue that should be reported to the Central Committee of the Party, and after China was liberated, they would settle it. I could see this discussion was going nowhere, and I decided it was not worth holding up our joint guerrilla activities just because we could not agree about our status. I wasn't happy about it, but I eventually agreed that for the time being our group would be under theirs. I was convinced that we could sort it out fairly when I was able to make my case to higher officials. I did get one concession out of Ou: I got him to agree that when I joined his party, all of the members of our party would automatically be enrolled as members of the Chinese Communist Party.

We created a committee called the Chinese Communist Party of Kham and the Tibetan Border Area [ch. *Zhonggong Kangzang bianjing gongwei hu*]. I was the party secretary of this new committee, which consisted of myself and all the members of my party. Ou gave me the rank of Specially Appointed Member for Border Affairs of the Government of the Northwestern Parts of Yunnan. He told me that when I needed to make contact in the future, I should go to Sadam and contact He Wangbo, the leader of the Chinese Communist Party there. We also had a secret code with which I could communicate safely with Ou by telegram. Having agreed to all these things, we left for Sadam, where we began to prepare for our return to Batang.

So much was happening so quickly that it was hard to adjust to it all. Historically, change had always come so slowly to this part of the world that it could be measured in centuries. Now the realities we had to deal with seemed to change from week to week. For example, after World War II, Chiang Kaishek seemed very powerful and the Chinese communists seemed weak, but now the Guomindang was all but defeated, despite U.S. support. Similarly, earlier I had directed my efforts toward establishing a Tibetan Communist Party that would work toward the formation of a new kind of government that would unite all Tibetans (or at least all Khampas). I had dreamed that with the assistance of the Soviet and Chinese Communist Parties, we could attain self-rule as an independent communist Tibet that was linked to the Communist International. Now it was obvious that the best way to bring change to Kham and Tibet was by working within the Chinese Communist Party.

The Soviet and Chinese Communist Parties advocated the equality of nationalities and repudiated the subordination of smaller nationalities to a larger, dominant one. And they advocated the right of all nationalities to real regional autonomy. Thus we thought that being part of the Chinese Communist Party would lead to the restructuring of Kham, and possibly the whole Tibetan area on both sides of the Drichu River, as an autonomous republic that would function in a way similar to the autonomous socialist republics in the Soviet Union. It would be under the leadership of the Chinese Communist Party and under Chinese sovereignty, but it would be controlled by Tibetans.

As we set off to liberate Batang and the south of Kham, we were enthusiastic and committed. But at the same time, we all knew that we were no longer operating independently. We were now a part of the Chinese Communist Party.

PART III

The People's Republic of China

CHAPTER 11

The Return to Batang

Returning to Batang this time was a very different experience from my last visit. Then I had been a hunted man. There had been a warrant for my arrest and a price on my head. I had had to stay outside the town and secretly contact my parents and friends. Now everything had changed. Liu Wenhui had seen which way the wind was blowing and moved most of his troops to greater safety in Sichuan, and the troops of his that remained knew how badly the war against the communists was going and were demoralized. Moreover, Liu had appointed an uncle of mine as governor of Batang, so we faced much less danger than before. Nonetheless, the war wasn't over and the Chinese garrison in Batang was still there, so we decided to start our work covertly.

We began by contacting former members of our organization and secretly establishing a new organization we called the (Communist) Party Work Committee of the Kham-Tibetan Border Area [tib. *khams bod mtha' khul las don u yon lhan khang*]. The abbreviated name we used was the Batang Underground Party [tib. *'ba' thang gi gsang ba'i tang*]. We started with ten members; I was the party secretary. We saw our first task as building a base of dedicated support among the people, particularly the students. To facilitate this we also established the Democratic Youth League of Eastern Tibet [tib. *bod shar rgyud dmangs gtso gzhon nu mna' 'brel*], which was not secret and quickly swelled to forty or fifty members. I served as its head.

Organizing students and others was relatively easy because I had made contact with many of them in the past and they were aware of the growing strength of the Chinese communists. In fact, people saw the coming defeat of the Nationalists as an opportunity to take control of Batang, so it wasn't hard to bring people over to our side.

Encouraged by our initial success with students, we began to work on other fronts, such as the local militia, the monastery, and the hereditary local elite; many young monks joined our Youth League. Success bred success, and soon we were able to establish branch Youth Leagues in the towns of Derge, Litang, and Tartsedo.

The ultimate object of all our activities at this time was simple enough. We wanted to establish a Tibetan People's Government in Batang that would be under the leadership of the Chinese Communist Party. The major obstacle to accomplishing this was the Chinese garrison of about four hundred troops. We planned to move against them as soon as we believed we were strong enough.

One of the first converts I made when I came to Batang was a young telegraph operator from the telegraph office of the Nationalist Chinese government. With his help, I secretly sent a telegram to Ou Gen in Yunnan telling him that we were ready to start the armed insurrection and asking him to send us guns and ammunition. He agreed to send them at once, and we began finalizing our plan for taking control. We wanted to try to do this through guile, as Kesang Tsering and my uncle Lobsang Thundrup had, so we decided to call a meeting of all of the elite and government officials in Batang. We planned to seize the governor and the military commanders when they arrived, and then demand that the Chinese Nationalist troops surrender. If they did not, we were prepared to attack and drive them out of the area. (At the same time, I sent a telegram to Mao Zedong and Zhu De in Beijing giving them a brief history of the Tibetan Communist Party and its relations with the Chinese Communist Party in Chongqing, as well as an accurate picture of our current situation in Batang.)

However, just as we were about to launch our plan to take control of Batang, a telegram arrived telling us that Liu Wenhui had surrendered and the People's Liberation Army (PLA) was on its way here. With Xikang (Kham) now liberated, there was no point in continuing our revolt. It was just a matter of letting events take their course. Liu Wenhui's surrender meant that we could conduct our party activity openly now, and the first thing we did was take control of the Guomindang Party's office in Batang and make it our headquarters. My uncle simply turned it over to us. Then we held a meeting in the large hall of the American School (all the American missionaries had long since left).

I did the speaking. After explaining that there was a new People's Government in China, I assured them that this was a good thing for Tibetans by explaining that the Chinese communists and the PLA were completely different from the Guomindang. I remember saying, "The Guomindang were the ones who oppressed Tibetans; the PLA, the soldiers of the Chinese Communist Party, are the ones who will liberate Tibetans from the oppressors. You must distinguish clearly," I said, "between the new Chinese and the old Chinese. You may have heard all sorts of derogatory things about the communists, but they are untrue." Finally I explained about the USSR and its policies about nationalities. I said that this policy would be implemented in the new China.

When I was finished, we raised the new five-star national flag of the People's Republic of China and took pictures of ourselves standing under it. I was excited and proud. After so many close calls and disappointments, we at last had had success—and success beyond my wildest expectations. It seemed that a whole new era was about to begin for the Tibetans in Kham, and perhaps eventually for all Tibetans. I was twenty-eight years old.

After the meeting, we focused mainly on propaganda, especially on more fully explaining the new constitution of the People's Republic of China (actually what we had was the Common Programme, a precursor of the constitution that had been promulgated on September 29, 1949). We opened a center called the Home of New Culture, in which the communist books that I had bought over the years were made available to the people. We put up pictures of Mao, Stalin, Lenin, Zhu De, Marx, and Engels, and assembled the young people every evening to learn and sing revolutionary songs. It was a great time. Everyone was full of optimism and eager for change. The membership of the Democratic Youth League rapidly increased to over three hundred.

Then one day early in 1950, a telegram arrived from Beijing. Zhu De, the commander in chief of the People's Liberation Army, said that Chongqing had been liberated and instructed me to go there immediately and report our situation to Deng Xiaoping and Liu Bocheng. I was surprised. These were powerful men. Deng and Liu were the heads of the powerful Second Field Army and the Southwest Military and Administrative Bureau, whose jurisdiction included the provinces of Yunnan, Guizhou, Sichuan, and Xikang (Kham).

I was also surprised to learn that Chongqing had been liberated. Chiang Kaishek still had the backing of the United States, and I had assumed it might take another year or so for the Chinese Communist Party to gain

Figure 12. Members of the Batang Underground Party and the Democratic Youth League of Eastern Tibet, Batang, 1949. Phünwang is fifth from left in the top row.

control of Sichuan. At the same time, I was elated—we all were—that our efforts in Batang had gotten this kind of recognition from people at the highest levels of the new Chinese Communist government.

I arranged for my colleagues Topden and Chödrak to take charge of our organization while I was gone, and two days later I left with five comrades. We were all armed with rifles, and I disguised myself as a nomad by putting on a fleece-lined robe and wearing a wig to cover up my short, "modern" haircut. Even though Liu Wenhui had surrendered, there were still scattered bands of Nationalist soldiers at outposts along the way, and we could not be sure what they would do.

We were always on the alert, but we had no trouble until we approached the mountain pass leading to Tartsedo. There, in the distance, we saw a large group of what looked like soldiers coming in our direction from the pass. They were too far away to identify, so we concealed ourselves and sent two of our group on ahead to find out who they were and what they were doing there.

We soon learned that the people we thought were soldiers were actually Guomindang government officials. It turned out that although Liu Wenhui had surrendered, one of his commanders, Tian Zhungtian, had refused to yield and was continuing to fight. Having just lost a battle with the PLA, Tian Zhungtian had retreated to Tartsedo with about two thousand soldiers and had quickly taken control of the town. The people coming toward us were former Guomindang officials who had joined the communists. They were fleeing because they were afraid that Tian might arrest or kill them.

I also feared that Tian and his soldiers might stop or arrest us if we tried to pass directly through Tartsedo, so we immediately turned around and stayed at a place nearby that was safely off the main road. While we waited there, I met seven or eight other Khampas who had just fled from Tartsedo. It turned out that we knew one another, and they knew that I was a member of the Communist Party, so this made things freer and easier from the start.

We at once sent a message to our people in Batang instructing them to organize an armed force and join us, so that we could launch an attack on Tian Zhungtian as quickly as possible. I thought that it would also be smart to send someone to Derge to ask Chagö Tomden to send us his militia as well. Since I knew Chagö Tomden well, I left for Derge with a few companions.[1]

Events were moving swiftly once again. No sooner had we gotten to Derge and begun to plan the attack on Tartsedo than a telegram arrived instructing us to return immediately because a PLA force had defeated Tian Zhungtian and retaken Tartsedo. So that was that. By then, the troops from Batang had arrived, but now all I could do was send them back. I also told the Derge militia they could go home. That done, we left for Tartsedo immediately.

When we arrived, Tartsedo had been liberated for a few days. The PLA soldiers were still very much in evidence, and it was the first time I had seen mainline communist troops. I have to say that I was impressed,

---

1. It was interesting how quickly important local figures tried to curry favor with the new government. I later learned that when the PLA liberated Xining, Chagö Tomden, Panda Tobgye, Kesang Yeshe, and Tashi Namgye jointly wrote a letter to Commander in Chief Zhu De saying they wanted to meet him. (Tashi Namgye was the Guomindang official under Liu Wenhui who had discovered the load of communist books I had sent to Tartsedo.) Chagö Tomden's secretary, Wangye, secretly took the letter to Xining at roughly the same time that Liu Wenhui was surrendering to the PLA. When Wangye reached Lanzhou, the capital of Gansu Province, he met General Peng Dehuai and explained that he was sent by Chagö Tomden, who, he said, knew Zhu De from the time of the Long March. Peng immediately sent him to Beijing. When Chagö's secretary met top officials of the State Nationalities Affairs Commission in Beijing, the translator was Ngawang Kesang, my former Bapa comrade who was then working for that office. He later told me that the content of the letter was interesting because they were taking credit for our Eastern Tibet People's Autonomous Alliance in Deqen in order to seem "revolutionary," and had even attached a copy of our party's charter as their own. They got our document because the Guomindang central government had sent a copy of it to Tartsedo, and Tashi Namgye, who had worked for Liu Wenhui, knew of it. —*Phünwang*

especially by the discipline they maintained. There was no looting or abuse of the residents. The soldiers were extremely professional.

When we asked around, we learned that they were an advance force of the 52nd Division of the 18th Army, the army designated by the Southwest Bureau to liberate Tibet. Wu Zhong was the division's commander, and Yin Fatang (who in 1980 would become the head Party secretary in Tibet) was its political commissar. Tian Bao, a Tibetan who had joined the Red Army in 1935, was also with Wu. The 18th Army was part of the Second Field Army.

Wu and several other PLA officials came to visit me and asked a lot of questions about Tibet and also about the Indian Communist Party. I had heard that Wu Zhong was a famous military commander, and I was glad to get to meet him. He told me that the central government had instructed them to liberate Tibet and that at present they were on their way to set up bases in Ganze and Derge. (Not long after, his troops would attack Chamdo.)

I was excited to be in the thick of things, and I was extremely idealistic about the new "communist" Chinese, although I was a bit surprised when I saw some of them up close. I remember one particular episode, when Miao Hongshu, the head of the Communist Party in Tartsedo, got angry and began to shout and curse in a loud voice because something was not delivered on time. He reminded me of nothing so much as an arrogant GMD officer or an old-style Tibetan aristocrat. It would not be the last time that I would see a PLA or Communist high official lose his temper like this, but at the time I more or less dismissed it. I rationalized that the PLA was a relatively new extension of the people and that therefore it still contained a few individuals who harbored the old attitudes and ways.

I didn't have too much time to think about things like this, though, because I left a few days later escorted by about twenty soldiers. Our first major stop was at Ya'an, where I met Liao Zhigo and Liu Zhong, the new communist heads of the province. Indeed, they convened a meeting of several thousand people to welcome me. The power of events just kept sweeping me along, and I was enjoying the ride.

I learned in Ya'an that the plan was to fly me to Chongqing as soon as possible. However, the weather wasn't cooperating and it looked like it wouldn't be safe to fly for many more days, so it was decided that I would go by jeep to Chengdu and try to get a flight from there. Even that plan didn't work as smoothly as we had hoped, for when we got to Chengdu, we had to wait five or six days for an airplane. In a way, it became a small vacation. Like myself, the soldiers who accompanied me had been spending most of their time in rural areas, and so we all tried to enjoy ourselves and take advantage of some of the comforts of a much larger city. Every day they took me to good restaurants, where we ordered dozens of dishes and ate like kings—a fact that was soon to come back to haunt me.

When a plane finally came, I exchanged my Tibetan clothes for a PLA official's uniform. (The new uniform felt strange. I liked it, but it made me feel that my role was changing, and I wasn't sure exactly what that was going to mean.) Though the weather was better in Chengdu than it had been in Ya'an, it was still very bad. The plane shook badly and pitched sharply at times, and I was soon sicker than I ever wanted to be again. It was extremely embarrassing, because I got so sick that I finally had to throw up and could find nothing but my brand-new PLA cap in which to do so. Consequently, when I deplaned, I was unable to salute the PLA officials who greeted me because I couldn't put my hat back on. Other than that, however, everything was fine. Not long after we landed, I met Deng Xiaoping, Liu Bocheng, and He Long, the highest-ranking officials in the Southwest Bureau and the leaders in charge of the coming liberation of Tibet.

They wanted to know about my history, and I briefly recounted the story of my life from the time I had met Ye Jianying after being expelled from school so many years ago. I talked for at least an hour, and they were patient and listened intently. When I finished, they began to tell me about their immediate plans. They said that the central government had decided to send PLA troops to liberate Tibet, and that the Southwest Bureau's 18th Army would have primary responsibility for the liberation. (This was in March 1950.) They also told me that the government had decided to try to liberate Tibet peacefully, and they asked whether I thought a peaceful liberation would be possible. I told them I thought it was a much better strategy than trying to use military force. The use of force, I said, would be sure to cause deep hatred between Tibetans and Chinese. In addition, I said that if they tried to bring in large numbers of troops, there would almost certainly be problems feeding and supplying them because Tibet was a poor country and there were no roads capable of handling modern supply vehicles.

During my stay in Chongqing, I talked with Deng Xiaoping several times and often heard him speak. During one conversation, he and I decided that the name of our current regional committee—the Party Work Committee of the Kham-Tibetan Border Area—should be changed to the

Party Committee of Batang County. (I was appointed as its party secretary.) We also decided to change the name of our Democratic Youth League of Eastern Tibet to the China Democratic Youth League. I spent a lot of time reading and studying publications and documents dealing with the Communist Party's basic policies toward minority nationalities and was shown a number of internal documents—telegrams circulated just among higher party members. I also had several opportunities to talk candidly with other upper-level cadre about the current situation in the party and the PLA, and I attended several meetings of higher officials who were discussing issues specifically related to Tibet and the plans for its liberation. I was of course delighted to be included—so much so that I was amazed the first time I saw some high-ranking officers actually sleeping while Deng Xiaoping was speaking! (I remember thinking at the time that maybe some of the PLA officials were not as good as others.)

Then one day, Deng Xiaoping told me that since Tian Bao had never been to Tibet and had forgotten most of the Tibetan language he once knew, they were going to send me to Tibet with the 18th Army in his place. I would also replace him on the Southwest Bureau's Tibet Work Committee. It made sense, I thought, because I had good Tibetan and Chinese, and I also knew the area and many of the important people. Deng told me that my role would be pivotal: I would be responsible for winning the Tibetan upper classes over to the new Chinese policies, and in general for maintaining good relations between the Tibetans and the Chinese. To this end, I would also advise the PLA generals about Tibetan sensibilities and concerns of which they might be unaware. He Long and Liu Bocheng also told me that I would be responsible for finding Tibetan cadres who could serve as translators for the troops. They asked me to contact the bilingual members of my two Batang organizations and ask them to go to Tartsedo, where they would be organized and trained. I sent a telegram to Batang immediately, asking all the people who could serve as translators to meet me there.

The Central Committee's plan to liberate Tibet peacefully was predicated on the idea that the PLA would not harm the peasantry or badly disrupt their lives and culture. Discipline was to be the key. The soldiers were instructed not to take anything forcibly from the people and to respect symbols of the indigenous nationality, culture, and religion. Given the poverty of most of rural Tibet and the needs of an army of the size the communists were sending, I knew it was going to be hard just to supply the soldiers with food. Hungry soldiers are hard to discipline and control, so I suggested to Deng that they shouldn't depend on finding supplies as they went. They should bring the grain they needed from China. He agreed with my suggestion and immediately put He Long and another official, Li Da, in charge of producing a powdered food substitute. What they came up with was a mixture of egg, rice, peanuts, and beans that was light (and therefore easy to carry), nutritious, and easy to eat. All you had to do was add water. If you added boiling water, it made a kind of stew. It was, I thought, a brilliant solution.

In the process of getting me settled in my new position, Deng introduced me to Zhang Guohua, the commander of the 18th Army and the first secretary of the Southwest Bureau's Tibet Work Committee. Not long afterward, I took a plane to Chengdu with Zhang to work on the details of our part of the plan for liberation. From Chengdu, we went by car to the 18th Army headquarters at Xinjin.

The 18th Army had three divisions: the 52nd, 53rd, and 54th. The 52nd Division had already been sent to Kham via the northern road. Their advance troops had arrived in Ganze and were soon to move on to Derge. I was assigned to the 54th Division, which was going to be sent on the southern road to Batang. I was to be the Vice Party Secretary of the division.

I wanted to do well—the best job I could. To do it, I knew I would need some help. I had had no contact with the Chinese Communist Party for the past ten years, and I didn't know much about the current situation in either the party or the PLA. I didn't want to make foolish mistakes, so I asked Zhang Guohua if he could provide me with a secretary who was knowledgeable about current political affairs. Zhang searched carefully and finally sent me Cheng Jingbo, a member of the Party Committee of the 54th Division who was excellent in written Chinese. I was very pleased to get him, and now I felt I could take active steps with more confidence.

Since Deng Xiaoping had stressed the importance of building good relationships with the Tibetan upper classes, I bought gifts—Japanese swords, radios, brocade silk, and so on—to be distributed when appropriate. And when Zhang Guohua and I got back to Chengdu, I had thousands of silver *dayan* [coins] sent to Batang, because I knew the merchants and ordinary people would want to be paid for their goods and services in silver rather than paper money.

I was also responsible for organizing animal transportation for the army in Kham, so after buying the gifts in Chengdu, I went on to Tartsedo and invited all the important Khamba leaders—Chagö Tomden, Panda Tobgye, Yurubön, and others—to come to Tartsedo to discuss how best to handle the problem.

Figure 13. At Southwest Bureau headquarters, Chongqing, 1950. *From left, front row:* Wang Weizhou, Phünwang, and Zhang Guohua.

The PLA troops who were preparing to attack Chamdo were based mainly in Derge and Batang. We quickly decided that Chagö Tomden would take responsibility for transporting the supplies in the northern sector (Ganze to Derge), and I would be responsible for the southern sector (Litang to Batang). It was a big operation. I hired over a hundred thousand animals—mostly yaks—for transportation of goods to Batang alone. It wasn't hard to get them. Everyone was happy to supply animals because the PLA was paying in silver dollars. Many Tibetans made a lot of money from this. I later learned that there was also some skimming. The Tibetan transporters would often slide a thin knife into the rice bags and draw off a little from each. Had I known it at the time, I would have been angry with my countrymen, because I didn't want anything to spoil the success of the operation. But it was such a busy and exciting time that I didn't have time to think about much of anything but immediate problems.

We were trying to do two things at once. On the one hand, we were organizing for a military attack. On the other, we were doing what we could to persuade the Tibetan government to accept peaceful liberation. We sent religious leaders like Geda Trulku to Chamdo to talk with Lhalu, the governor-general who had succeeded Yuthok. And I went to see Panda Tobgye and persuaded his brother, Apo Raga, also to go to

Chamdo and try to influence Lhalu. We did everything we could to persuade Lhalu to help us convince the government in Lhasa to send representatives to discuss peaceful liberation. We made an honest effort to
bring this meeting about, but it simply was not to be. We got no official
response from Lhasa. We also knew that while we were making these efforts, the Tibetan government was sending officials like Shakabpa and
Changöpa to India to try to get help—including military help—from
other countries. Predictably, after a while, when the central government
saw which way the tide was running and became convinced it wasn't
going to change, it was decided to send the 18th Army across the Drichu
River.

The Tibetan soldiers fought bravely, but they were no match for the
superior numbers and better training of the battle-hardened PLA. The
Tibetans could not stop the forward thrust of the Chinese forces, and
within two weeks the entire Tibetan army in Chamdo [a total of about
ten thousand troops] had been captured, along with Ngabö, the new
governor-general [and council minister] who had just replaced Lhalu.

At this point, the battle for the eastern province of Tibet was over, and
I was soon on the way to Chamdo myself. The chance to be directly involved in events that might change the future of Tibet was something I
had been hoping and working for most of my life. Much had happened
that I had wished would happen, but the fact that many Tibetans had
been killed or wounded in the Chamdo campaign saddened me. Nevertheless, I believed that the Chinese Communist Party would create the
kind of society I had dreamed of for Tibet, and I was very much looking
forward to playing an important role in that process.

CHAPTER 12

The Seventeen-Point Agreement

I arrived in Chamdo thirteen days after it had officially been liberated by the 18th Army. It felt strange to enter the city as part of a victorious army. It felt even stranger, almost uncomfortable, when I learned that Wang Qimei, the fourth-ranking commander in the 18th Army, had arranged for me to stay in the spacious living quarters of Ngabö, the former Tibetan governor-general and council minister (where Wang himself had been staying). I told him immediately that I didn't need that much space and that I certainly didn't want to displace him. But he passed it off, saying that he wasn't sleeping well in the big apartment and that it would be more convenient for me as a Tibetan cadre, because there was a large meeting room close by. I thought he was just making an excuse to be polite, but I agreed because I didn't want to make an issue of it.

Even though the PLA had just taken Chamdo by force, the priority was still the peaceful liberation of the rest of Tibet. One of my most important assignments, therefore, was to try to win over the leading officials we had just captured, especially Ngabö. In particular, I was to try to persuade them that at this point it would be best for Tibet and Tibetans if Lhasa sent official representatives to Beijing to begin negotiating a peaceful settlement. I agreed with this, but it was not going to be easy, and I learned that my job had been made more difficult than it otherwise might have been because of some mistakes made by General Wu Zhong immediately after the victorious campaign.

Wu was a first-rate military commander, but he had no political subtlety and he had treated the captured Tibetans too much like defeated prisoners. For example, at the army's victory celebration, he and Wang Qimei sat at the center of the stage with all the captured weapons piled up like trophies on one side and Ngabö and the other officials under guard on the other side. The Chinese soldiers and officials in the audience were exultant and shouted slogans like "Knock down the imperialists!" This was, of course, a mistake, as we wanted to win them over, not humiliate them.

The next day, I took a ceremonial scarf, a new radio, and some fine brocade and went to see Ngabö. He was living in a modest one-story building on the same courtyard as the governor-general's residence. When I found him in his room, he was wearing ordinary Tibetan clothing and sitting on a very thin rug—a far cry from the regalia and ceremonial luxury he had been used to. Tsögo, his aristocratic aide and secretary, was also there. They seemed listless and defeated, and I felt strangely sorry for them.

I had my job to do, however, so I presented the gifts, introduced myself, and began the discussions. Ngabö was uncomfortable and distant, and after two days without making any real headway, I decided that if we were going to get anywhere, we had to begin to treat him with respect. So I went to see Wang Qimei and explained that the governor-general of Chamdo was a very prestigious position in the Tibetan government. When he traveled officially, he went in procession with five or six horsemen in front and the same number in back. In his office and residence, he had more than thirty servants hovering around him, and when he began and ended his day, a ceremonial cannon was fired. Ngabö, moreover, was also a council minister. Obviously things were very different now, but I urged that he be treated with more respect. He was not really our prisoner, but rather an important official in the Tibetan government whom we wanted to bring to the negotiating table. I suggested, for example, that we let him move back into his old quarters. (I said I would be happy to stay in a small room next to his.) Wang agreed, and so I was able to go back to Ngabö and insist that he take his old room back.

I also thought it would help if we invited him to eat with us in the rooms reserved for higher officers of the PLA. Until then, Ngabö had been eating in his room. We had three different canteens—a large one for ordinary soldiers, a medium-sized room for lower officials and officers, and a small one for the top-ranking personnel. (Not surprisingly, the food was much better in that one!) Wang agreed to this too, so Ngabö and his aide Tsögo began to eat with us. They were a little uncomfortable at first, but soon got used to the change.

Finally, I persuaded Wang to return the clothing of the thirty or so captured higher government officials from Lhasa. They looked poor and forlorn in the cheap clothing they had been given, and the effect on their morale was obvious. We needed to convince them, somehow, that we were not their enemy. By giving them back the clothes they were used to, we would be giving them back a bit of their dignity, which I thought was vital if we wanted them to see us in a positive light and help us.

Mainly what I did after making these changes was try to educate them about the new Chinese government. I spent many days and nights talking with Ngabö and Tsögo about the Soviet Union, communism, the current situation in China, and, most importantly, the Chinese Communist Party's policies on nationality, equality, and religious freedom.

I talked with them together, but I also spent time with Tsögo separately. He was close to Trendong Sey, a member of our Tibetan Communist Party in Lhasa, so he already knew a lot about me and from the start was friendlier to me than Ngabö was. I soon realized that Tsögo was quite progressive in his thinking about change and the future of Tibet, so I gave him more detailed information about the Chinese Communist Party. We sometimes talked late—till two or three in the morning—and Tsögo came over to our side more quickly than Ngabö.

In addition to spending a lot of time explaining the positive aspects of Chinese policies, I also did everything I could to emphasize how futile it would be for Tibet to try to resist China militarily. I remember being very blunt, pointedly quoting to Ngabö an old Chinese proverb: "Whether the rock hits the egg or the egg hits the rock, the result is always the same." The point was obviously that however a war started, it would be the Tibetans who would suffer. I knew that Ngabö understood what I meant because he had seen the strength of the PLA firsthand when they captured Chamdo. But I also knew that there were many other Tibetan leaders who knew almost nothing about the situation in China or the power of the PLA. I recall being amazed when I heard that some years earlier the monk official who was the head of the Council of Ministers had asked a member of a Tibetan delegation who had just returned from Nanjing, "Which city is bigger, Lhasa or Nanjing?"

As the efforts to improve relations with Ngabö and the other Lhasa officials began to bear fruit, we discussed an idea that we thought might persuade Lhasa to negotiate. Ngabö should write a letter to his colleagues on the Council of Ministers explaining what had happened to them and the realities and opportunities—and to urge that they agree to send representatives.

Ngabö agreed, and we considered the contents of the letter with great care. After Tsögo wrote a first draft, he, Ngabö, and I discussed and revised it several times. Then I took it to Wang Qimei, and he and Ngabö went over it carefully and revised it several more times. Finally Ngabö and all the other Tibetan officials signed it, and it was sent on its way to Lhasa.

The main point of the letter was that it would be much better if the Dalai Lama agreed to send a delegation to Beijing to discuss the terms of a peaceful liberation of Tibet because, if he chose to fight, there would almost certainly be much loss of life and the destruction of cultural and religious sites. We wanted him and his top officials to see that there would be much to gain by negotiating. The PLA had taken Chamdo by force, but they had treated its people and cultural and religious institutions with respect and restraint. The same would happen in Tibet. We wanted to send a message that would give the Council of Ministers in Lhasa confidence that the Chinese Communist Party members were reasonable people with whom they could talk. They were not wild monsters bent on destroying Tibetan religion and culture. We had two Tibetan officials captured in Chamdo take the letter because they could provide firsthand accounts of the way the Chinese troops had behaved and attest to the letter's genuineness.

Several months went by, however, and we got no reply. Since we had no communication with Lhasa, we had no idea what was going on, and the tension began to build. A new plan then emerged: Wang Qimei and Ngabö would go to Lhasa together with a small detachment of bodyguard troops to talk directly with the Council of Ministers. We were in the first stages of setting this plan in motion when we heard that the Tibetan Government had agreed to send a five-person delegation to Beijing.

The Tibetan delegation was to travel to Beijing in two separate parties. Two officials, Thubden Lengmön and Sampo Sey, were sent overland from Lhasa to Chamdo to join Ngabö and then travel from there to Beijing together. Two other officials, Commander in Chief Kheme and a monk official named Lhautara, were to go to the Chinese capital by sea via India. The Southwest Military and Administrative Bureau ordered me to accompany the Tibetan delegation leaving from Chamdo, so we assembled a group consisting of some translators, about thirty PLA soldiers, and the Tibetans—Ngabö and about ten other Tibetans, including his wife and a servant. We went on horseback to Ganze, where the main camp of the 18th Army was located, and from there we went by car to Chengdu. From Chengdu we flew to Chongqing, where, after a brief meeting with Deng Xiaoping and Liu Bocheng, we caught a flight to Beijing.

During the flight, there was a sudden change of plans; we were rerouted to Xi'an because Beijing was organizing a big welcoming ceremony for us and they needed an extra day to prepare this. In Xi'an, we were greeted at the airport by Wang Feng, the head of the Nationalities Affairs Commission of the Northwest Military and Administrative Bureau. That same evening, he hosted a banquet for the entire delegation. This was meant to be a gesture of respect and goodwill but nearly turned into a disaster.

The problem was Geshe Sherap Gyatso. Sherap Gyatso was a famous Tibetan monk-scholar who had taught Tibetan to Ngabö and many other Tibetan aristocrats when he lived in Lhasa. Wang Feng had invited him as a gesture of friendship to the members of the delegation. No doubt he thought they would appreciate the presence of an old friend. What he didn't know was that Sherap Gyatso disliked the Tibetan government intensely, particularly the aristocracy.

He was still bitter about an incident that took place in 1944, when he was working for the Guomindang. They sent him on a mission to Tibet with an entourage of about fifty Chinese whom he claimed were his students, and a large consignment of goods and money. When he and his entourage reached the northern border at Nagchuka, however, the Tibetan border troops stopped him. Ultimately, the Tibetan Council of Ministers decreed that Sherap Gyatso could enter Tibet, but insisted that his "students" and goods could not. Furious, he was forced to return to China. Then, in 1950, he was again stopped at Nagchuka when he went on behalf of the CCP to persuade Lhasa to negotiate. He never forgot how he had been treated by the "aristocrats," and when Wang Feng invited him to attend the banquet, he saw an opportunity to convey his feelings.

The evening began quietly enough with Wang Feng delivering a very gracious welcoming speech. Then, unplanned, Sherap Gyatso rose and said he would like to say a few words. At first he said some general things in Tibetan. Then, after telling the translator to not translate what he was about to say into Chinese, he launched into a tirade against the Tibetan government and the Lhasa aristocrats. Ngabö and the others were taken aback, but they maintained their poise and sat perfectly still, trying to pretend that nothing was wrong. Wang Feng didn't understand Tibetan, but he suspected something had happened from their expressions and because there was no translation into Chinese. After the banquet, he asked me what was said, and when I told him, he was genuinely upset and afraid Sherap Gyatso's insulting comments would prejudice the Tibetan delegation's attitude and that Wang Feng would be blamed for it by the higher-ups. We discussed the problem at length and finally decided that rather than run the risk of giving it greater importance by confronting it, the best thing to do was simply to ignore it and hope for the best.

The next day we boarded a train, and on the following day we arrived in Beijing, where we were greeted grandly. Premier Zhou Enlai himself was at the station, along with other top officials and about three hundred people of different nationalities, all of them there to welcome the Tibetan delegation. Even here, though, there were possibilities for mishap. There were short speeches and formal greetings, and I introduced the members of the Tibetan delegation to Zhou Enlai. But as we were walking from the station, I caught a quick movement out of the corner of my eye. Cholo, a Lhasa Tibetan who was working in the Nationalities Publishing House in Beijing (he had gone to China when the Guomindang was in power), secretly passed a note to Ngabö. I didn't say anything because I didn't want the Tibetan delegation to think I was spying on them, but several years later I asked Ngabö what the note said. Ngabö laughed and said it was a warning not to trust the communists' sweet-sounding rhetoric. Cholo told him that the Chinese Communist Party was no good and couldn't be trusted: not only did they not believe in religion but, even worse, they were committed to destroying it. The note, however, had no direct effect, and several days later, when the rest of the Tibetan delegation arrived, we began discussions about the content of what would eventually be called the Seventeen-Point Agreement for the Peaceful Liberation of Tibet.

We all stayed at the Beijing Hotel, and discussions began quickly. The head of the Chinese delegation was a senior official, Li Weihan. He was vice general secretary of the State Council, director of the United Front Work Department, and director of the State Nationalities Affairs Commission. For the Tibetan side it was Ngabö. However, when the Tibetans had private discussions, I felt that it was really Kheme who made the decisions. Even though Ngabö was a council minister and the official head of the delegation, Kheme was Surkhang's uncle and was also quite worldly, as he had already visited China in 1946 with a Tibetan delegation attending a Guomindang conference. He was also a member of the Tibetan search committee that discovered the Fourteenth Dalai Lama in

Qinghai Province. More recently, he had been with the Dalai Lama and the Council of Ministers at Yadong on the Indian border. Consequently, he was up to date with the current situation in India and the West, as well as with the thinking of Tibet's top leaders who were with the Dalai Lama. Beyond these things, we felt certain that Surkhang, the best informed of the Tibetan elite, must have talked with his uncle about what to do during the negotiations.

Ngabö, on the other hand, was, I thought, in a weakened position. There were popular rumors that he was in the pocket of the Chinese—that he had been bribed with gold or that, having been captured at Chamdo, he had been forced to change his loyalties. None of these things was true, but the suspicions existed, and I thought they must certainly have weakened his influence.

Not surprisingly, the discussions were difficult from the start, because both sides had very different conceptions of history, and those differences surfaced first in the language itself. For example, there was a disagreement about the terms for Tibet and China. The Tibetan delegation used the terms "Tibetan government" [tib. *bod gzhung*] and "Chinese government" [tib. *rgya gzhung*], which conveyed two equal political entities. Our side used the terms "central government" and "local government" because Tibet was considered a subunit within the larger entity of China.

Language was not the most serious problem, though. The first big argument occurred over the issue of sending PLA troops into Tibet. The central government insisted that it was necessary to send troops in order to drive the foreign imperialist forces out and then secure and defend the national borders. The Tibetan delegation objected strongly, insisting that since there were no foreign imperialist forces in Tibet, there was no need to send troops. If in the future foreign imperialist forces threatened Tibet, they said, they would immediately request assistance from the central government. Thus, stationing PLA troops in Tibet was not necessary. Arguments went back and forth, but in reality, the moving of the troops into Tibet was a foregone conclusion. The central government was committed to troops being stationed there. The Tibetan delegation argued long and hard but finally, under threat of the discussions collapsing and the PLA attacking, conceded. It was agreed, however, that a clause would be included in a secret codicil stating that in keeping with the special situation in Tibet, as few PLA troops as possible would be sent to Tibet.

Another big dispute arose over the relationship between the Dalai Lama and the Panchen Lama.

In 1924, after a long dispute with the Dalai Lama and the Tibetan government over taxation and politics, the Ninth Panchen Lama fled from Tibet to China. He lived in Qinghai Province with his top officials and developed close ties with the Chinese Nationalist government. Many of his top officials, like Che Jigme (see figure 18), spoke Chinese fluently and for decades before the Chinese Communist Party came to power had accepted that Tibet was a part of China. In 1937, the Ninth Panchen Lama died in Qinghai, and his officials set out to discover the next (Tenth) incarnation, as did the Tibetan government. When the late Panchen's followers identified his incarnation in a Tibetan area of China, the Tibetan government in Lhasa refused to recognize that boy as legitimate. They had identified several of their own candidates and proposed that the late Panchen Lama's officials send the candidate they had found to Lhasa for final determination of the rightful incarnation. The Panchen Lama's officials insisted their boy was the true Panchen Lama and refused to subject him to competition with other candidates in Lhasa. They then unilaterally acknowledged him as the new Tenth Panchen Lama.

Although that boy's status was not accepted in Lhasa, the Nationalist Chinese government accepted his legitimacy just before they fled the mainland for Taiwan. Thus, the Panchen Lama's officials and Chiang Kaishek's government recognized this boy as the Panchen. Nevertheless, since Tibetan tradition requires the Dalai Lama and the Panchen Lama each to confirm the legitimacy of the new incarnation of the other, the new Panchen Lama was not accepted by Lhasa.

The Chinese civil war changed the status quo. By fall 1949, the Nationalist forces were losing ground to the PLA in the northwest. When it looked like Qinghai Province was about to be liberated, the Tenth Panchen Lama (who was twelve years old) and his officials decided to withdraw from Xining, the capital of Qinghai, to a monastery at Xiangride in central Qinghai that had been given to the Sixth Panchen Lama in 1780 by the famous Qing dynasty emperor Qian Long. There they decided to contact the communists rather than immediately flee to Taiwan, so a representative was sent to find out what they were really like. When the representative reported favorably, they decided to remain in Qinghai and work with the Chinese Communist Party. On October 1, 1949, the founding day of the People's Republic of China, the Panchen Lama sent a congratulatory telegram to Beijing that expressed support for the coming liberation of Tibet. In return he received a cordial telegram from Mao Zedong and Zhu De. Consequently, by the time of the Seventeen-Point Agreement discussions, the Panchen Lama was already accepted by the Chinese central government as the proper incarnation and was fully in the camp of the Chinese Communist Party. — Goldstein, Sherap, and Siebenschuh

The central government knew that there was a history of conflict between the two lamas and that feelings ran very high on this issue. For example, when the Chinese government invited the Panchen Lama to the rostrum in Tiananmen Square on May 1, 1951 (Labor Day), the Tibetan delegation in Beijing attended the celebration, but Ngabö and the other Tibetan officials refused to meet the Panchen Lama officially because the Tibetan government still didn't recognize him. Ngabö gave Mao a ceremonial scarf that day, but did not present one to the Panchen Lama.

This was, therefore, a delicate situation for the central government because, although they had publicly accepted the Panchen Lama and were committed to returning him to his seat of power at Tashilhunpo, they wanted the agreement of the Tibetan government. All this was made more complex because it involved not just the Dalai Lama recognizing the incarnation, but also settling a variety of issues regarding taxes and other areas of authority. For a while, neither side was willing to give an inch. The Central Committee had decided they had to force the Tibetan government to accept this boy as the Panchen Lama and allow him to return to Tashilhunpo. But agreement did not come easily, as the Tibetan delegation flatly declared that they had no authority to recognize a lama, let alone the incarnation of the Panchen Lama. That was the prerogative of the Dalai Lama. The Chinese delegation countered by saying that the talks could not go forward without settling this issue. At that point, Ngabö sent a telegram to the Dalai Lama in Yadong, who replied (by telegram) that he accepted the boy as the Tenth Panchen Lama. The other issues were resolved by using vague language that avoided spelling out the details of their respective authority. A clause in the agreement simply said that the Panchen Lama could return and that both the Panchen and Dalai Lamas would retain the relative status they had had before the dispute arose.

Another issue that almost terminated the negotiations took place at the very end of the discussions. It concerned the central government's plan to establish a Military and Administrative Bureau [tib. *dmag srid u* yon lhan khang] in Tibet to oversee the implementation of the Seventeen-Point Agreement.

Before raising this issue at the formal meetings, Li Weihan invited Ngabö and me to his quarters. Li Weihan's thinking was that it would be useful to give Ngabö some time to think about the issue of the bureau and discuss it with his delegation. That night, Li Weihan began very smoothly. "Things are going well," he said. "We have been working very hard. Although we have had some disagreements, for the most part the problems have been solved and agreement reached. However, there is one last item we need to discuss." He paused. "There is a need for us to establish a Military and Administrative Bureau in Tibet. It will be an administrative office of the central government, but the Dalai Lama will serve as its head and a Chinese representative and the Panchen Lama will serve as vice directors." After he finished explaining this, Ngabö, who had listened in silence, politely excused himself. He and I walked back to our hotel. He did not say anything at all about Li's proposal, and so what happened next surprised us all.

Three days later, feeling he had given the Tibetan delegation plenty of time to digest the news, Li Weihan called a meeting. He began by discussing the proposal to establish a Military and Administrative Bureau in Tibet. When the Tibetan delegation heard the details, they erupted in surprise and anger.

The Tibetan delegation had liked the fact that the agreement as they understood it allowed the traditional government of the Dalai Lama to continue to function internally in Tibet. When the delegation heard about the new condition, they were angry because the idea of a Military and Administrative Bureau operating in Tibet seemed to undermine the traditional government's supremacy. It seemed as if what the Chinese side was giving them with one hand they were taking away with the other. While Li was explaining the details, I could hear Kheme whispering things like, "That's bizarre. These talks are never finished. This is not good."

It was obvious that it was the first time he or any of the others had heard the idea. And things went from bad to worse. I think Li was about to say something like "I'm sure Ngabö and you all have discussed this," but he was interrupted by Lhautara, a monk official, who was livid. He rolled up his sleeves and shook his fist in anger. "What is the matter with you people? Every day there is something new coming down from the central government. For weeks we have been arguing about a variety of topics, and now, when we thought things were just about finished, you propose something new like this!" Ngabö didn't say anything. He sat there silent. The other Tibetans were shocked by Li's proposal. After more angry comments from the Tibetan side, Li Weihan got angry and said, "If that's the way you feel, then you can all pack up your bedding and go home." The implication, of course, was that the PLA would liberate Tibet militarily.

Things seemed to be spinning out of control, and I decided to try to calm the situation. I rose and said, "Today at the meeting everyone has gotten angry. There have been lot of comments made and many misundertandings. Li Weihan has said we should return to the Beijing Hotel, so let's stop here for today. Later we can think and discuss the matter more calmly." I said this on my own to soften Li's ultimatum, making it sound as though he had meant for them to return to the *hotel,* not *Tibet.*

The Chinese delegation was caught off guard. They had not thought this was going to be a difficult issue, not only because it was presumed that Ngabö had already prepared the way but also because there were Military and Administrative Bureaus like this all over China. It was not something special it was going to impose in Tibet.[1]

Since we had heard nothing from the Tibetans about this after Li Weihan told Ngabö, we thought they had agreed. When we got back to the hotel, I went directly to the Tibetan delegation and tried to explain to them what the Chinese proposal actually meant. Kheme said to me, "Phünwang-la, this bureau makes no sense. It is just like adding a rider on the neck of a rider already on horseback." He was very upset and angry. I tried to provide a different interpretation. The first thing I emphasized was that the Military and Administrative Bureau was standard Chinese policy; it wasn't something invented just for Tibet. I explained that the central government had set up such committees in four large areas in the new People's Republic of China. In every case, they were intended to be temporary administrative structures that would represent the central government until more representative, permanent structures could be established. The bureau in Tibet would be just another of these temporary administrative structures and would not be above the Tibetan government. And, I reminded them, the Dalai Lama was to be the rider

1. The areas liberated in 1949 were administered by the People's Liberation Army, and initially the military was the controlling authority for the new government. At this time, China was divided into six large regions, four of which, the Northwest, Southwest, South-Central, and East, were administered by what were called Military and Administrative Bureaus. This military authority was a transitional phase that was to yield to civilian authority as soon as feasible. By 1954–1955, all four Military and Administrative Bureaus had been replaced by People's Governments. — *Goldstein, Sherap, and Siebenschuh*

of the horse—he would be the head of this bureau and would therefore be in charge. So they didn't have to fear this.

I also indirectly told Kheme and Lhautara that this issue didn't come out of the blue, but that Li Weihan had raised it with their side earlier. I didn't mention Ngabö specifically, though, as I thought that this would have been obvious to them. After we talked a while like this, Kheme and the monk official, Lhautara, said, "Oh, I see. Now we understand." Then I asked Kheme if he thought it would be acceptable to continue the meeting on this subject the next day. He said, "Yes. If it is like this, there is no problem."

While I was working hard to calm the fears of the Tibetan delegation, the Chinese government representatives were preparing for the worst. They genuinely believed that the Tibetan delegation would probably go home because of this issue, which would have been an enormous embarrassment. It would have meant war.

I immediately called Li Weihan and said I needed to meet with him. The first thing he asked was, "Are your people going to pack up their things and go back to Tibet?" I was glad to be able to tell him that they weren't. "Things are back on track," I said, "because I explained what the Military and Administrative Bureau really represented, and I convinced them that it would be temporary and would not negate the authority of the Dalai Lama's government." Li Weihan was surprised and a bit incredulous at first. "Really?" he asked. "Are you sure?" I told him it was true, and the next thing I knew he picked up the phone, called Mao, and said, "Phünwang has just told me that the problem has been solved. We can talk with the Tibetan delegation tomorrow." It was quiet in the room, and I could hear Mao's voice clearly. He was extremely pleased and so, obviously, was Li Weihan, who began to shake my hand enthusiastically. The next morning, with tempers cooled, both sides continued the discussion.

I never found out for sure why Ngabö did not tell the Tibetan delegation about the proposal ahead of time. I never discussed it with him, but I told Li Weihan my thinking when Li asked why they had been so startled when I raised this issue. I said I thought Ngabö kept the information to himself because he had been captured and there were many rumors that he had been bought off by the Chinese. He may have felt that if he indicated he was meeting separately with the Chinese side about an issue as volatile as this, it could add further fuel to these suspicions. After this last crisis, the talks were quickly concluded.

When all debate had ended and the parties had signed, the result was

Figure 14. Tibetan delegation writing the Tibetan
copy of the Seventeen-Point Agreement, Beijing,
1951. *From left:* Ngabö, Phünwang, Lhautara,
Phüntso Tashi, Sandutsang Rinchen, and Kheme.

the famous Seventeen-Point Agreement, about which so much has been
written and which even then seemed historic. From the beginning, I had
been highly conscious of what was at stake for Tibet, and I took my role
in the negotiations very seriously. I was in a special position because I
knew both sides very well, and I was convinced that it would be best for
Tibet to agree to a peaceful liberation. I knew that the central government would not hesitate to use force if it felt there was no alternative.
There was such a vast difference between China's economic and military
power and Tibet's that for the Tibetan delegation to make any decision
other than accepting peaceful liberation would have meant disaster.
Many Tibetans would have been killed outright, the economy would
have been devastated, and the chance for a peaceful evolution of the Tibetan way of life would have been lost. I felt I had to do whatever I could
to help achieve a peaceful outcome.

There was a big party after the signing, and for a brief time I felt like
a hero. Over three hundred people attended, including Zhu De, the com-
mander in chief of the PLA. Not long after the festivities were underway,
Li Weihan stood, raised his glass, and proposed a toast. "To comrade
Phünwang, for his important contribution toward the signing of the
Seventeen-Point Agreement."

The members of the Tibetan delegation were also happy with my efforts. By the end of the day, all had personally thanked me. Kheme, for
example, said, "Phünwang-la, when we came and learned you would be

part of the discussions, we were apprehensive because we knew that not long ago the Tibetan government had expelled you from Tibet. We didn't know what to expect. After a month of discussions, we have changed our minds. I know enough Chinese language to get by, and I know that when Li Weihan really told us to go home to Tibet, you told us to go to the hotel. We understand the effort you made to make the discussions work. You have made a major contribution to the friendship between Tibet and China."

CHAPTER 13

To Lhasa Again

The agreement was now signed and Tibet ready to be peacefully liberated. But a significant problem remained. The Dalai Lama and the top leaders of his government were still living in Yadong, on the Indian border, ready to flee into exile at a moment's notice. Since they did not know the details of the discussions in Beijing or the exact terms of the agreement, there was a real possibility that they would flee when they learned, for example, that Chinese troops would be entering Tibet as part of the agreement. The Tibetan delegation, in fact, was so worried that the Dalai Lama would leave that we had to add an item to the secret codicil saying that in essence it was permissible for the Dalai Lama to go to foreign lands and then return.

The central government, of course, wanted to make direct contact with the Dalai Lama as soon as possible and persuade him to return to Lhasa. It sent Zhang Jingwu [a Long March veteran who had worked in military and administrative positions for over twenty years] by plane via India to Yadong as its representative, with a copy of the agreement for the Dalai Lama. Li Weihan suggested I accompany him, but it was decided that this would not be a good idea because my previous involvement with the Indian Communist Party might cause problems. Therefore Alo Putrang was sent instead, and several members of the Tibetan negotiating delegation traveled with him. Ngabö and the original of the agreement were to return to Lhasa by land.

Zhang Jingwu's instructions were to go on to Lhasa with or without the Dalai Lama. However, when they met in Yadong, Zhang was pleased to learn that the Dalai Lama had already decided to return to Lhasa rather than flee into exile. Nevertheless, neither the Dalai Lama nor any other Tibetan official would explicitly indicate their acceptance of the agreement. The Tibetan leadership was adamant that they could not make a public statement until they met with Ngabö and examined the official copy.

There was, therefore, pressure to get Ngabö and the agreement to Lhasa as quickly as possible, so when Ngabö reached Chamdo, a small advance group of five hundred to six hundred troops under the command of Wang Qimei was organized and sent ahead with him. The main 18th Army force under the command of Zhang Guohua was to follow in about a month. I went with the advance group as a member of the Party Leaders Committee [ch. *gongwei*] along with fifteen or twenty Tibetan cadres from Batang. (My wife and infant son also accompanied me, my son tied on top of our saddlebags.)

How quickly the world had changed. Two years after being expelled, I was about to return as an important official in the new government of China. I was very optimistic about the future. I believed the new Communist Chinese government would usher in a golden era for minority nationalities, in which minorities would be treated as equals and would flourish. Tibet, I imagined, would gradually change and modernize as part of the PRC, yet would maintain its national identity, language, and culture. I had failed to bring change to Tibet through my own revolutionary activities but now felt I would be able to achieve my vision of a new Tibet under the umbrella of the CCP.

Since Zhang Jingwu was not accompanied by soldiers, our advance force would be the first PLA troops Tibetans in Lhasa encountered, so great care was taken to select the best soldiers from among the thousands of troops in the 18th Army. All the advance unit's troops were young and fit, well disciplined, and equipped with the finest weapons.

The Central Committee's goals for the PLA (which included troops and administrators) were really twofold: (1) to win the support of the Dalai Lama and the upper-strata people around him for the terms of the Seventeen-Point Agreement and secure them as loyal citizens of China, and (2) to establish a secure footing in Tibet with regard to supplies, communication, roads, and the like. Because of Tibet's influential religious history and institutions, and because there were no Chinese in Tibet who might be sympathetic to the CCP, work was to be undertaken in a slow and deliberate fashion [ch. *shen zhong wen jing*]. We were instructed clearly not to rush in and implement changes, and to avoid alienating the Tibetan elite at all costs. Change would come when the elite and the Tibetan people were ready for it, not before. Strict regulations were issued instructing soldiers to respect Tibetan culture and traditions, even though they might seem strange and possibly even repugnant. And everyone was ordered to be careful regarding even the smallest actions. For example, when solders visited a temple, monastery, or other religious site, they were instructed to go around the religious site clockwise because that was Tibetan custom. And, critically, we were not to get involved in internal Tibetan political affairs. Regulations such as these gave me confidence in the party's nationalities policy and the future.

However, I quickly began to learn that real people and real life were not quite the same as principles written on a page or pronouncements at meetings. Virtually everything that I knew about communism and the Chinese Communist Party was from books, not firsthand interaction with officials in the field. My education was about to broaden. Wang Qimei, for example, did things that shocked me. He had been through many battles and was known as a very skillful and brave soldier. But he was a strict disciplinarian, had a short temper, and was exceptionally suspicious. I had some bizarre and, in retrospect, portentous experiences with his suspiciousness on our trip to Lhasa.

Wang Qimei, I soon found out, did not trust Ngabö and the Tibetan government. Before we departed Chamdo, Ngabö and I decided where we would stop each night on the trail. That way, we could travel at different speeds during the day but meet every evening. (We traveled a bit slower than Ngabö because our troops were all on foot.) One day, however, Wang Qimei's horse suddenly got sick and died, apparently because it ate some poison grass. This delayed us, so Wang told the troops to set up camp where we were and stop there for the night. Ngabö was ahead of us. The following morning when we arrived at the previous night's scheduled trail stop, we found a note from Ngabö saying he had left to cross the next mountain pass that evening because the grass and water for his horses weren't good at the trail stop. He wrote that he would wait for us on the other side at a place called Tsachuka.

When I translated this to Wang Qimei, he became agitated and said that Ngabö had intentionally gone ahead to make contact with the Tibetan army and ambush us at the pass. Wang immediately called a meeting of the leaders group and heatedly conveyed his suspicions. I insisted that Ngabö would not do that, but Wang refused to listen and said we should stop where we were because it was too dangerous to move forward.

I thought that was ridiculous and told him that Ngabö had no reason to try to ambush us. He was committed to peaceful liberation, I said, and we knew that Zhang Jingwu, Chairman Mao's representative, had already arrived in Lhasa and nothing untoward had happened. If the Tibetan government wanted to create an incident, they could easily have done so with Zhang, since he had no troops with him. So why, I asked, would they suddenly want to attack us now? Moreover, even if the Tibetan soldiers wanted to ambush us, they couldn't just sit on the top of the mountain pass waiting. These mountains were already covered with snow, and there was no place one could wait in ambush. Even wild animals like deer couldn't survive up there. I used many such arguments to calm Wang, but he just got angrier. Finally, out of exasperation, I suggested that if he didn't believe me, he should send me with some soldiers across the mountain pass to see whether Ngabö was waiting at the village on the other side. Wang didn't like this alternative either, saying that if something happened to me, the group's only Tibetan cadre, he would get in trouble in Beijing. It was all very strange. Finally, after much argument, Xu Danlu, the head of our intelligence operations, supported my view and Wang grudgingly agreed to proceed. When we reached Tsachuka, we found Ngabö not only waiting for us, but waiting with grain. He had sent his staff to secure grain for the troops, as we were having difficulty buying supplies on the road.

I was somewhat bemused but also a bit shocked by this incident. Wang, though a top-level People's Liberation Army commander and schooled in the CCP's nationalities policy for Tibet, simply had no feel for Tibetans or their culture. I recall thinking that maybe this kind of hyper-suspiciousness resulted from having fought so many battles. It was puzzling.

Despite being wrong about this incident, Wang continued to be irrationally suspicious of Ngabö. Another example occurred about three days later, soon after we stopped for the night at Ngabö's manorial estate near Giamda. The manor house was a grand stone building that was three stories high. There was a plain in front of the house where we camped in tents. However, our situation made Wang uneasy. There were mountains close by on the left and the right, and he was afraid that the Tibetan army was hiding in them, waiting to suddenly pounce on his troops. I said that this was silly, that they would never attack us, especially when one of the highest Tibetan government officials was with us. If they attacked here, Ngabö would literally be our hostage. But he didn't listen and stationed guards on high alert.

Ngabö, following traditional Tibetan etiquette, invited the officers to have dinner at his manor house. When Wang heard this, his suspicions skyrocketed. He now said he was sure Ngabö was going to poison the food, and refused to attend the dinner. Again I was astonished. I told him that although there was vague talk about people in this part of Tibet having a custom of poisoning travelers to capture their "luck," those stories were not true. In any case, Ngabö was a Lhasa aristocrat and a top Tibetan official, not a local peasant. "Besides," I said, "if you are nervous, you can always eat only the things that Ngabö himself eats." Wang would not listen and insisted he was not going, so we had another big argument, during which I insisted that it would be totally inappropriate for him not to attend. We were trying hard, I said, to develop good relations with Ngabö and win him over to our side. When we got to Lhasa, we would depend on his help for many things. "There is no choice," I said. "You must go; otherwise our future work will be harmed. It would be extremely insulting if the head of the PLA army didn't go to his banquet, especially since he made a special effort to invite us to a meal at his home."

Wang reluctantly agreed to go, but I know that Ngabö was aware of his suspicions. After he had a few drinks of Tibetan beer, Ngabö said, "Commander Wang, if one soldier dies before we cross the next pass [i.e., while still in his area], I will cut off my head and give it to you." I assumed he noticed that Wang Qimei was playing with his food rather than eating it. Wang smiled but didn't say anything.

Looking back, I think that my later conflicts with the Chinese Communist Party started with incidents and arguments like these, although even earlier, there had been some suspicions and tensions. For example, before we left Chamdo, the young Tibetans who had come from Batang to help the PLA held a day-long party. Each person contributed money, and everyone ate Batang food and sang songs. I wasn't able to go to the party during the daytime, as I had meetings, but at night I went.

The next day, an intelligence officer of the 18th Army wrote in his report, "Last night Bapa Phünwang and all the Tibetan officials in Chamdo held a meeting, the content of which is not known." Later that day, Wang Qimei asked, "What kind of a meeting did you people hold?" I didn't know of the report then, so I asked him what he was talking about. When he told me that there was news of a meeting held last night,

I almost burst out laughing. I told him it wasn't a meeting; it was a party, and it wasn't just for Tibetans; there were some Chinese officials there as well.

Another example also occurred in Chamdo. We usually had an official meeting once a week to discuss our own work and lives and comment on other officials. In one of these meetings, Cheng Jingbo, the Chinese official assigned to me as a secretary/aide, first praised me and then said, "However, it is necessary to investigate the political line [ideology] of the Tibet Communist Party in Batang in the future." I didn't respond one way or the other, but I thought that he must have some criticism of me if he was talking like this, and that maybe he was not just my personal secretary, but had another spying agenda as well. However, the other people there did not pay much attention to his comment, and no one else said that our former organization should be investigated. Later, I learned that he had actually investigated our underground party and youth league in Batang, and was especially suspicious of some of our songs—for example, the one I wrote that begins, "Rise up, rise up, Tibetan brothers, rise up," and then says that we (Tibetans) should fight to the end to establish a new Tibetan people's government.

I also learned that Wang made a report to the higher authorities about me. He gave this report to a Chinese official to copy, but that official was busy and gave the job to a Tibetan staff worker from Batang named Tarchin. Tarchin came to me that night and told me that Wang had written, "While Phünwang does excellent work and has high prestige among the Tibetan cadres, most of the Tibetan cadres obey only him, not us. From this it is clear that even though all the Tibetans are party members, there is a nationalistic contradiction between Tibetans and Chinese."

I didn't get angry at these incidents, but I remember thinking I should be a bit careful. I didn't consider these incidents to be a preview of future problems between Chinese and Tibetans; I thought they were mostly caused by Wang Qimei's personality. In retrospect, perhaps there was more to it. Later, when I was in prison, I thought hard about what had caused my incarceration, and all these seemingly small incidents came to mind as forewarnings that I had underestimated. At the time, though, they were more irritating than threatening. And they did not deter me from speaking my mind.

For the PLA officials, going to Tibet was, in a sense, just like going to another Chinese province, like Yunnan or Guizhou, because they believed that Tibet had been part of China for a long period of time. They didn't understand the long-standing and deep-seated Tibetan notion of there being two distinct countries linked as "priest-patron." And even those who understood this didn't seem to pay attention to it. Despite the Central Committee's emphasis on respecting and showing deference to the customs and traditions of the different nationalities and the special characteristics and status of Tibet in China, the PLA often did not really understand the way Tibetans looked at things. I saw this as a potential problem and felt pressured to try to bridge the gap by conveying the Tibetan perspective to my Chinese colleagues.

When we reached the outskirts of Lhasa in early September, we stopped to rest and clean up a bit. Alo Putrang, the Chinese cadre who had accompanied Zhang Jingwu, came to meet us and report on their journey and the situation in Lhasa. He told us that the Dalai Lama had returned a few weeks earlier [on 17 August] and that Zhang and he were staying in the Trimön House. They had not, he said, started any real work.

At the same time, this was still the old society, and the Council of Ministers informed Ngabö that he could not enter Lhasa without the two ceremonial hair knots, called *bajo*. Since Ngabö had cut his long hair when he went to China, he now had to arrange for a false hairpiece, and we had to wait until this was completed.

The advance troops finally entered Lhasa on September 9 and were billeted in what was called the "new military camp" [tib. *dmag sgar gsar pa*] in the southeast part of Lhasa. The Tibetan Council of Ministers sent two high officials, Liushar (Thubden Tharpa) and Kheme, to be liaison officers in charge of our arrangements. We entered Lhasa in a grand way. Carrying huge pictures of Mao and Zhu De, Wang Qimei and I marched around the Barkor at the front of the troops. I was wearing my PLA uniform, and this was one reason why Lhasa people started saying that I had brought the Chinese troops to Lhasa.

There were thousands of Tibetans watching us, and I recall being surprised to hear one lady say, "These are the communist solders we heard so much about, but they are nothing special—they are still Chinese." They had heard that the communist solders were different from the Nationalist troops, and thought they would look physically different.

After we marched through the streets to our quarters, Wang Qimei and I went to see Zhang Jingwu and reported on our journey. From then on, we took orders from him. Because the main army force under General Zhang Guohua was not scheduled to arrive for another month or so, we did not have much day-to-day administrative work to do. Our immediate priorities were to establish cordial relations with the Tibetan government and the elite. We tried hard to show our respect for Tibetan culture and religion; for example, we gave alms to every one of the twenty thousand monks in Lhasa's three great monastic centers. We also had to develop the infrastructure to build roads linking Lhasa with inner China, and establish garrisons in key locations along the borders, but that work would start in earnest only when the main force arrived. All thoughts of socialist reform, therefore, were put on the back burner, and we did not pay any attention to propagandizing the masses about them, let alone issues of class struggle and exploitation.

Initially, we visited all the more senior members of the Tibetan government. These were simple courtesy calls and were not intended to involve serious discussions of CCP policies (although we did talk generally about the Seventeen-Point Agreement). We presented each official with gifts befitting his rank (tea, silk, brocade, and so on), and most aristocrats responded to our visits in the very polite and proper manner of the Tibetan aristocracy. They were cordial and gracious, but most were also careful and did not reveal their own views and attitudes.

But not all. When Wang Qimei, a few other officials, and I visited Lukangwa, the acting prime minister, we got a real surprise. Wang Qimei first said something innocuous like "The Seventeen-Point Agreement between the central government and the Tibet local government has been signed, and today we have come to visit you. We would like to present you with these gifts." Lukangwa immediately responded with an angry tirade, the gist of which was that because China and Tibet in the past had been in a priest-patron relationship, there were now two governments, one Tibetan and one Chinese. "You Chinese seized our territory in the Tartsedo area in the past, and now you have brazenly attacked us by force and, under the name of 'liberation,' seized our territory in Chamdo. Wang Qimei," he said, pointing, "during the Chamdo war, you were one of the military officials. People called you 'Vice Political Commissar Wang.' Now, after you have defeated our troops, you have arrived in Lhasa promoted to 'Commander Wang.' But we here will not be easy to suppress. Leaving everything else aside, the grain for your soldiers will not last." Lukangwa was highly emotional.

I was shocked. This outburst went completely beyond any norm of acceptable Tibetan aristocratic behavior. The Lhasa elite did not confront one another directly in this manner. Even bitter enemies would talk politely, as if they were old friends.

Ironically, Wang never understood the full impact of what was said because our interpreter, Tarchin, took it upon himself to mistranslate so as not to provoke Wang. Consequently, he translated Lukangwa's use of the terms "China" and "Tibet" as "central government" and "local government" and toned down his verbal attacks. Later, when we returned home, I told Tarchin that in the future he should not change what people said; he had to translate exactly. Tarchin said he knew that he should do that, but feared that if he had translated correctly, both of them might have gotten very angry, and it might have created a serious incident. It didn't matter, I said. It was his responsibility to translate accurately.

Even though Wang Qimei did not know exactly what Lukangwa had said, he realized from his expression that it was a criticism. I recall that Wang's face became red as he listened. It was a tense moment for this first visit, but it would have been much worse had Tarchin done his job correctly.

Afterward Wang asked me what Lukangwa had said, and I told him without softening the message. He responded, "That man is really a reactionary. However, at least he is honest and says what he thinks. Those other aristocrats always say good things to your face, but you never know what they are really thinking." I had to admit he was right.

An amusing incident illustrating this occurred soon after, at a party hosted by Ragashar, one of the council ministers. When I entered the house, I was surprised to see that he had a nicely framed picture of Chairman Mao hung on a wall. Ragashar was not at all known as a "progressive" aristocrat, so having a photo of Chairman Mao was somewhat strange. Consequently, I was not surprised later when that picture accidentally fell to the floor, revealing a picture of Chiang Kaishek behind Mao's. Minister Ragashar got very nervous about that mishap, and I had a good laugh to myself.

Actually, when I heard Lukangwa's tirade, I could understand why he said what he did. There were many historical reasons for it. But it was very hard for me to convey these effectively to Wang and the other Chinese because they completely accepted that Tibet had been part of China for hundreds of years. Still, I told Wang, "You should not think that what Lukangwa argued is so very strange, because Tibetans have considered China and Tibet separate, priest-patron countries, since long ago." He said nothing in reply.

The Lukangwa incident also was a wake-up call that made me realize just how difficult it was going to be to build real trust between the Tibetan government and the central government. There was an enormous gap in their views and perspectives. It also made me realize that it would

take a long time to change ideas and establish a new, socialist Tibet—
although I still believed this ultimately had to and would happen.

Lhasa had not changed in the two years I had been gone. The Potala
Palace still glittered on its imposing hill, and the city was filled with a mix
of Tibetan residents, monks, and pilgrims. But a new era had begun.

CHAPTER 14

With the PLA in Lhasa

The main force of the 18th Army arrived in Lhasa on October 26, 1951, under the command of Zhang Guohua. As Zhang was the senior commander of the PLA forces in Tibet, one of his first tasks was to pay a courtesy call on the Dalai Lama in Norbulingka Palace (Zhang Jingwu had already done so at Yadong). Tibetans placed great significance on such ceremonial events, so I wanted it to be done correctly. We needed to make sure that the Dalai Lama and his entourage felt we were showing him and the Tibetan government proper respect. I also knew that Mao Zedong felt the same, because Li Weihan had told me that when Zhang Guohua was about to leave Beijing, Mao told him at a private meeting that he should prostrate himself before the Dalai Lama three times in accordance with Tibetan custom. Zhang apparently did not like the idea, because he asked whether Chairman Mao didn't think a salute would be good enough. Mao got a bit angry at this response and said sharply, "Zhang Guohua, you have sweated and shed blood for the revolution. What is so important about prostrating yourself three times before the Dalai Lama?" Zhang didn't answer, but as it turned out, he was not convinced.

The PLA leaders in Lhasa had numerous discussions about the ceremony, as well as meetings about protocol with the Dalai Lama's lord chamberlain. Zhang wanted to show respect but did not want to prostrate himself, so he suggested that I, as the leading Tibetan cadre, should prostrate myself instead. I had no problem with this because it was part

Figure 15. Leaders of the Tibet Work Committee visiting the Dalai Lama at Norbulingka Palace, Lhasa, November 1951. *From left:* Jigyab Khembo, Ngawang Namgye, Li Jue, Wang Qimei, Zhang Guohua, the Dalai Lama, Zhang Jingwu, Tan Guansan, Liu Zhengguo, and Phünwang.

of our Tibetan culture, and it was finally agreed that Zhang Guohua would lead our procession and present the Dalai Lama with a ceremonial scarf and the ceremonial offering, the *mendre densum* [which consisted of a statue of the Buddha, a book of religious scriptures, and a stupa]. I would follow immediately behind him wearing Tibetan clothing (instead of my PLA uniform) and prostrate myself three times. The other Chinese officials would follow me and present ceremonial scarves.

The Tibetan government approved our plan, and I heard later that they were pleasantly surprised at a Communist Party official like me prostrating myself. Later I teased Zhang about not obeying Mao's order and told him that I would tell Mao when I next got the opportunity. Zhang got nervous and said, "No, no, don't tell anyone else."[1]

1. The Dalai Lama later wrote of this event:

When they came for an audience, they were accompanied by a Tibetan in national costume and fur hat. As they entered the room, this man made three formal prostrations. I thought this rather strange as he was evidently a member of the Chinese delegation. It turned out that he was the interpreter, and a loyal supporter of the Communists. When I later asked why he was not wearing the same

The arrival of Zhang Guohua's force, however, was not the end of the troop movements into Tibet. Another sizable unit—about one thousand troops—under the command of Fan Ming arrived from the Northwest Military and Administrative Bureau in Gansu and Qinghai Provinces on December 1. We now had troops and officials from both the Northwest and Southwest Bureaus, and our first real task was to merge the two sets of troops and their officers and officials.

Some tension arose between the two bureau forces even before the Northwest's troops arrived in Lhasa. As Fan Ming neared Lhasa, he sent one of his officials, Bai Yufeng, ahead to meet with Zhang Jingwu and Zhang Guohua regarding arrangements. Fan Ming had definite ideas about his arrival; he wanted his troops to march in a grand procession around the Barkor. When Bai told us this, Zhang Guohua immediately said that this would be a bad idea. "For one thing," he said, "your animals and soldiers will be tired after their long journey, and therefore they will not make a good impression. For another thing, when our main force entered Lhasa, there was an elaborate ceremony in which the council ministers and the Tibetan army participated, so it is really not appropriate to do this again." Then Zhang introduced him to me, saying, "This is Phünwang. He is the top official among Tibetans and a committee member of the Southwest Bureau. We should ask his opinion."

I was put on the spot, but I expressed my feelings honestly. "I agree with Comrade Zhang's reservations," I said. "And in addition to his concerns, I think that if you bring your troops into the city, it will be difficult to find enough grass to feed the hundreds of horses and camels you have." I added that having another grand procession of troops would be an unnecessary flaunting of Chinese military power. "We are trying hard," I said, "to give Tibetans the impression that we are friends, not conquerors." So Zhang told Bai Yufeng to tell Fan Ming not to risk offending the Tibetans by marching around the Barkor. Fan Ming, however, ignored Zhang Guohua's instructions and did exactly what he wanted. Looking back, this incident was a precursor to the serious conflict of views that developed within the party leadership in Tibet throughout the 1950s.

Mao suits as his companions, he replied good-naturedly that I must not make the mistake of thinking that the Revolution was a revolution in dress; it was a revolution of ideas. (*Freedom in Exile: The Autobiography of the Dalai Lama* [New York: Harper Perennial, 1990], p. 72)

—*Goldstein, Sherap, and Siebenschuh*

Fan Ming's arrival in Lhasa also created problems with the Tibetan government because Fan was angry about the manner in which they received him. We had suggested to the Council of Ministers that they should send officials to receive Fan outside the city in accordance with Tibetan custom. They agreed. However, they sent a delegation headed by only a mid-level fourth-rank official. From our side also, our top leaders, Zhang Jingwu and Zhang Guohua, failed to attend. Instead we sent lower officials—Alo Putrang, Xu Danlu, Cheng Jingbo, and myself.

None of these decisions was lost on Fan Ming. He was so furious with the Tibetans that when the head of the Tibetan welcoming delegation stepped toward him to present him with a ceremonial scarf, or *khata* [tib. *kha btags*], he angrily pushed it away, treating the gesture with contempt. We were all shocked by his behavior. I overheard the Tibetan officials expressing disbelief at what they were seeing, and I had to admit that I agreed with them. I could not imagine what Fan was thinking. He should have been treating the representatives of the Tibetan government with respect, not disdain. His behavior made a powerful negative impression on me, and certainly on the Tibetan officials.

Although incidents like this were regrettable, our mandate from Beijing was to forge a good working relationship between the Southwest and Northwest Bureau units. Since each had its own administrative office for Tibet (called the Tibet Work Committee [ch. *Xizang gongwei,* tib. *bod las don u yon lhan khang*]), we set out to merge the two sets of officials into a new, unified Tibet Work Committee that would discuss and decide on all important Tibetan affairs for the Chinese side. Zhang Jingwu became the head of the new Tibet Work Committee, with Zhang Guohua and Fan Ming, respectively, the first and second deputy heads. Zhang Guohua was also appointed head of the new, unified military command. At age twenty-nine, I was the Tibet Work Committee's only Tibetan member.

Altogether, the new committee consisted of eleven officials, eight from the Southwest Bureau and three from the Northwest Bureau. However, the Northwest Bureau officials were given important posts and ended up having substantial power in day-to-day work activities. Fan Ming, for example, was appointed director of the United Front Work Department, a critical office because it was responsible for managing relations with Tibetans. Mu Shenzhong and Ya Hanzhang, the other two senior Northwest officers, were given important positions as well.

With the influx of all these officials, we realized we had to have more space, so I was assigned the task of renting one or more houses. Since all the good property in the center of Lhasa was owned by aristocrats and the monasteries, it wasn't easy to find suitable quarters. Fortunately, I was able to rent my old friend Yuthok's house. It was centrally located and large enough to accommodate Zhang Guohua, myself, and most other newly arrived officials, with enough room left over to store some of our grain. Zhang Jingwu remained in the Trimön House.

Not long after this, we decided we needed even more space, and concluded that it would be better for us to buy rather than rent a house, so I again spent a lot of time visiting and negotiating with the families who owned suitable buildings. I didn't have to search long before I was able to purchase a handsome house owned by the Sandutsang family, the Khampa traders I had stayed with in Kalimpong in 1943–1944. It became the formal office building for the Tibet Work Committee. (Since the building was a private house, we did not need to get the Tibetan government's permission to buy it. We simply paid the owner the selling price, and he gave us a certificate of ownership.) In all our dealings we paid in Chinese silver *dayan* coins, as Tibetans did not accept Chinese paper currency.

During this time, I thought very little about socialist reforms. For the present, our strategy was to win over the Dalai Lama and his officials, and through them gradually reform the traditional society. I was as committed to reforming the old Tibetan system as I had ever been, because I knew that common Tibetans were still suffering under its oppressive system. But I agreed with the Central Committee's approach of going very slowly and patiently, as I also knew that there was much opposition to change in Tibet.

The majority of Tibetan officials had a poor understanding of the new realities they faced. Even Ngabö, our closest supporter, still used the terms "China" and "Tibet" in his speech as late as 1955 rather than the new terms—the "central" and "local" governments. Some aristocrats, like Shökhang, Janglojen, Kapshöpa Sey, Chapa Kesang Wangdü, and Trendong, were progressives who felt this was a great opportunity for Tibet to move into the modern world, but they were relatively few and not influential.

Another segment of the elite, led by the acting Prime Minister, Lukangwa, and the Lhasa monastic/religious leadership, opposed the Chinese presence completely. They were deeply committed to retaining the old system just as it was. We therefore saw no likelihood of winning them over.

The majority of Tibetan officials were conservative but appeared less hostile, at least on the surface. They seemed to accept the new situation in their speech and behavior, and were generally friendly to us, but they also were clearly not interested in quickly changing the old feudal system. They appeared resigned to the need for change, but seemed to be striving to prolong the old system as long as they could. Therefore, we saw our task as isolating the anti-China elite, supporting the progressives, and winning over the majority in the middle. But this obviously was not going to be easy or quick, so the issue of reforms in Tibet was not something I actively thought about at this time.

The problem wasn't just the Tibetans, though. There were some problems on our side, too. There were disagreements between the Northwest and Southwest Bureau officials about how we should do our work. And some of Fan Ming's troops acted with less discipline than I thought PLA troops should display.

Fan and his soldiers often behaved very arrogantly toward Tibetans. For example, early in 1952, Fan Ming's jeep caused an incident in the Barkor. Fan Ming was driving a jeep he had brought with him from Qinghai (dismantled). It was the only vehicle in Lhasa other than the Dalai Lama's (who never used his), so seeing a car in Lhasa was very unusual. While Fan was driving through the crowded Barkor market, the noise of the engine terrified some of the vendors' donkeys, which were tied to the merchandise tables. They bolted and pulled down the tables and the canopies above them, trampling and damaging some of the merchandise. The Tibetan vendors were furious and responded by throwing stones at the jeep, a few of which actually hit Fan Ming and his bodyguard. Fan was livid and arrested some of the Tibetans on the spot.

I knew nothing of this until a few days later, when an aunt of mine came by and told me about the incident, which she had witnessed firsthand. She said that the merchants not only were arrested but were accused of having been deliberately sent by the Tibetan government to throw stones at Fan. She also heard that they were badly beaten that night. She came to me because she felt that what happened to them was unfair. The whole incident, she said, was the fault of the Chinese. It was their jeep that had frightened the donkeys and caused them to damage the merchants' goods. That's why people got angry and threw the stones. And she insisted over and over that she knew these people personally and they had not been sent by the Tibetan government. She finally asked my assistance in freeing the Tibetans who were still being held.

The next day, I went to Zhang Guohua and reported what I had heard from my aunt. I told him I thought she was right about everything, except that I doubted the Tibetans had been beaten while in custody. I didn't believe that soldiers of the PLA would do such a thing to local people. "No, it is true," Zhang said. "Fan Ming did beat them. He reported to us that the Tibetan government had intentionally sent these people to throw stones at him. We didn't challenge that, but still we criticized him and told him he should not have acted like that." I was surprised and told Zhang that if high PLA officials like Fan Ming beat the people, it would have a negative influence on Tibetans' opinions, and I strongly urged him to free the Tibetans immediately. Zhang agreed and, at a party meeting, criticized Fan Ming, saying, "Our only Tibetan member, Phünwang, also disagrees with your action." Soon afterward, Fan Ming released the Tibetans.

Unfortunately, the affair in the Barkor was not an isolated incident. On another occasion, when I was riding with my colleague Alo Putrang, we saw horses from Fan Ming's cavalry grazing in some Tibetan farmers' barley fields. We had strict rules prohibiting this, as we knew it was likely to cause trouble. And sure enough, we soon saw Tibetan farmers throwing stones at the horses to drive them away. What surprised us, though, was that then we saw some Northwest Bureau soldiers come over and grab and threaten the farmers.

Alo Putrang was a longtime member of the Communist Party with impeccable revolutionary credentials. He also had great idealism about how the CCP should treat minority nationalities. Without talking to me, he angrily rode over and confronted the soldiers, telling them they were acting in complete violation of the policies of the CCP and should stop immediately. I didn't say anything, because my colleague had said it all. Alo later reported this to Zhang Jingwu.

Numerous other occasions like this bothered me. For example, Mu Shenzhong often would gallop his horse through the market areas, making Tibetans jump aside to avoid being hit. I thought this was arrogant and uncalled for. Thus, from the beginning I was disappointed by some of the Northwest Bureau's attitudes, and I worried that this kind of behavior could endanger our overall goals if it became more common.

It was a difficult problem to deal with because on the surface we all got along quite well. During the New Year's holiday period [of 1952], I played a lot of mahjong and Chinese chess with Zhang Jingwu, Zhang Guohua, and Fan Ming, so I got to know them well. We were comfortable with one another, and they treated me with respect. The problem as I saw it was that although they were very talented and experienced in combat and also clever about politics within the Communist Party, many

Figure 16. Phünwang playing Chinese chess with Zhang Jingwu, Lhasa, circa 1952. Zhang Guohua is watching.

of them had limited broader knowledge of the world. They had joined the party early, and many had not had the opportunity to go to school. (Zhang Guohua himself had joined the PLA at age twelve and had never finished primary school.) Few if any had studied Lenin's and Stalin's writings, and therefore they were not well educated about the Communist Party's policy toward nationalities. Even though the party declared that all nationalities should be treated equally, there were remnants of the Guomindang attitude of Han superiority—what we call in communist jargon "Great Han Chauvinism" [ch. *da Hanzu zhuyi*], especially among the elements within the Fan Ming contingent.

The realization that this existed bothered me. When I saw some of Fan Ming's troops acting arrogantly, I felt both angry and sad. I genuinely believed that all nationalities must have equal rights in the new China and that we had to prevent the ugly head of Great Han Chauvinism from reappearing. One could not talk about Marxism and democracy if one nationality, such as the Tibetans, was subordinate to another nationality, such as the Han. I had thought this attitude had ended with the de-

feat of Chiang Kaishek and his Nationalists, but I was beginning to realize that perhaps I had been a bit too naïve.

I was very busy at this time and seldom had much time to meet and talk
with my close comrades, like Ngawang Kesang and Topden, but on the few
occasions when we did get together, this issue came up and they expressed
similar uneasiness. Nevertheless, we were all still highly optimistic. These
small mistakes did not affect the party's main nationalities policy. Although
the Communist Party's plan for Tibet's future had not been clearly spelled
out at the time, I believed Tibet would ultimately be administered as a
highly autonomous ethnic political entity, similar to the Soviet republics,
and I thought I could play a role to ensure the best outcome for Tibetans.

Truthfully, however, I did not have much time to think about the future of Tibet, especially since it seemed a distant problem. The Tibetan
government was still in power, and there was no talk of changing it. Despite some growing uneasiness, especially about the attitude of Fan Ming
and the Northwest troops, I was pleased with the way things were going.

CHAPTER 15

A Year of Problems

In 1952, we experienced serious conflict on two fronts—with Tibetans in Lhasa and within the Communist Party in Tibet. But we also made significant progress in beginning to create new, modern institutions in Tibet.

At the beginning of 1952, we were suddenly confronted by organized opposition in the form of the so-called Tibetan People's Party, a group that began hanging posters in the market saying the presence of so many Chinese troops was causing inflation and hardship for the people and that they should go back to China. The Tibet Work Committee thought that the brains behind this organization was Acting Prime Minister Lukangwa, who was using the People's Party as an indirect way to attack the Seventeen-Point Agreement and our presence in Tibet.

However, to be honest, the sudden presence of thousands of our troops and officials in Lhasa had indeed led to serious inflation and shortages of foodstuffs and fuel. We had anticipated it might and urged the Tibetan government to organize the flow of food for us, since we knew that the real problem was not a shortage of grain in Tibet per se, but rather the lack of an efficient system for getting surplus grain from the countryside to Lhasa and selling it in an orderly manner. This was the Tibetan government's obligation under the terms of the Seventeen-Point Agreement, but for the first few months we were unsuccessful in getting them to take charge—due, we thought, to Lukangwa's dominant position. So at this time, we did what we could ourselves. Many aristocrats and monasteries had huge stores of grain at their estates in the countryside, which we tried to persuade them to sell to us. We also cut rations for our troops, dispersed many of our soldiers to other parts of Tibet, arranged to buy rice from India, and got permission from the Council of Ministers to open new fields in the western suburbs of Lhasa.

At the same time as the Tibetan People's Party issue arose, we noticed that the Tibetan army carried a "snow lion" flag in its drills and ceremonial appearances rather than the national flag of China. (They also continued to wear their own uniforms.) Some of our leaders, especially Fan Ming, believed this was not appropriate; it made it seem that Tibet was still not part of China. This led to heated arguments at the time the Tibet Military Area Headquarters was established in February 1952.

The Tibet Military Area Headquarters was the new office that would be in charge of all PLA troops in Tibet, including, in the future, the Tibetan troops. The Tibetan army was slated for eventual integration into the PLA, but in 1951 and 1952 it continued to function independently under its traditional leadership. Many of our cadre, like Fan Ming, disapproved, but this had been agreed upon in the Beijing negotiations. However, the central government also thought it was important symbolically to show that the new Military Headquarters was for both Chinese and Tibetan troops and had stipulated (in the secret codicil to the Seventeen-Point Agreement) that two senior Tibetan officials would serve as its vice commanders. The Tibetan government complied and selected Ragashar and Ngabö for this. Both wore PLA uniforms at the inauguration ceremony. However, the Tibetan army troops who participated in the ceremony continued to carry their own snow lion flag. This infuriated Fan Ming and others in the PLA, who insisted that since Tibet was not a country it could not have its own national flag. Fan felt that we should force the Tibetan government to stop what he considered blatantly reactionary and "separatist" activities.

Serious arguments occurred over the use of this flag, but Acting Prime Minister Lukangwa refused to yield. His position was that this was not a national flag at all, but rather the flag of the Tibetan military. As evidence for this, he stated that this flag had never been flown on any Tibetan government buildings, and technically he was correct. I wasn't involved in this issue, so I don't have a clear recollection of the whole chain of events and the many arguments, but to be honest, I could understand how seeing the Tibetan army carrying their snow lion flag made many PLA troops and commanders unhappy.

Zhang Guohua and Zhang Jingwu opposed Fan Ming on this issue. The 18th Army's basic instructions from Chairman Mao and the central

Figure 17. Tibetan army with its snow lion flag, Lhasa, 1952.

government clearly said we must go slowly and make every effort to win over the Dalai Lama and the elite. Holding this as the prime directive, Zhang Jingwu and Zhang Guohua believed that forcing the Tibetans to stop using their military flag would be counterproductive. They felt it was a minor symbolic issue that was not worth an acrimonious fight. I supported their view at the Tibet Work Committee leaders' meetings since I knew better than the others that it was essential for our side to advance cautiously and focus on our long-term goals. We needed to convince the Tibetan elite that we were not their lords or enemies if we were to eventually persuade them to begin making changes themselves. Of course, Fan Ming strongly disagreed. For him, I thought, the flag was not the real issue. He wanted to end the independence of the Tibetan army and government altogether, regardless of the consequences for Tibetan-Chinese relations, so he insisted that we should not let such behavior go unpunished. I used to joke with some of my Tibetan colleagues that Fan Ming's personality was like that of a brash Khampa who was aggressive and always ready to fight, whereas the Southwest Bureau officials were more like the cautious and calculating Lhasans.

Fortunately, the views of Zhang Jingwu and Zhang Guohua carried the day, and the Tibet Work Committee did not push on this issue. Actually, as late as 1958, when I last left Lhasa, the Tibetan army was still carrying their military flag, although by then they were carrying the national flag as well. This flag issue was the first big difference of opinion that occurred *within* the Tibet Work Committee. It would not be the last.

Soon after the inauguration of the Tibet Area Military Headquarters, the Tibetan People's Party conflict came to a head. Despite our urgings, the Tibetan government had not curtailed the party's political agitation. The People's Party started to organize demonstrations, and ultimately gave us a petition in the name of the "Tibetan people" asking us to leave only a handful of officials and troops in Lhasa, much as had been done during the Qing Dynasty. By April 1952, the situation became so tense that we began sandbagging buildings in preparation for war. Many Chinese officials thought that the People's Party was about to launch a full-scale military attack (in collaboration with Lukangwa and the Tibetan army). We were prepared to fight back if attacked, but we had clear orders from Mao Zedong that we were not to fire the first shot. We convened many meetings with the Council of Ministers urging them to restrain the dissidents, but they basically said their hands were tied because Lukangwa stood between them and the Dalai Lama. We finally concluded that we had to appeal directly to the Dalai Lama and persuade him that things were getting out of control.

The Tibet Work Committee contacted the central government, asking permission to demand that the Dalai Lama dismiss Lukangwa (and his co-acting prime minister, Lobsang Tashi). Beijing sent a telegram instructing Zhang Jingwu to do this, but told him to first ascertain the "Tibetan" view by asking me and Che Jigme, the head of the Panchen Lama's officials. When Zhang showed me Beijing's telegram, I told him that I agreed that the two acting prime ministers had to be dismissed. I then passed the telegram to Che Jigme, who surprised me by giving it back to me and asking me what it said. Since he spoke fluent Chinese, I assumed he could also read and write Chinese, but when I said, "Why don't you read it yourself?" he told me he did not know how to read Chinese. Later I learned that when he took notes at meetings he used Tibetan letters to record the Chinese pronunciations. I read the telegram to him, and he said he also agreed that the acting prime ministers had to be dismissed.

Zhang Jingwu, as the head of the Tibet Work Committee, ultimately sent the Dalai Lama three letters, but nothing happened. Finally, when the tension was soaring and the danger of violence imminent, he personally went to see the Dalai Lama to explain our views and insist that he dismiss the prime ministers.

Fortunately for both sides, the Dalai Lama was, I think, already aware of the problem. I recall being at a meeting where Lukangwa was arguing vehemently; the Dalai Lama caught my eye and smiled, tapping his temple with his finger to indicate Lukangwa was hardheaded. In any case, the Dalai Lama quickly removed Lukangwa and banned the People's Party. The tension in Lhasa diffused, and life returned to normal. In my opinion, a major disaster had been narrowly averted.

The removal of Lukangwa restored the Council of Ministers to its pre-1950 role as the highest office in the Tibetan government (under the Dalai Lama). The impact was almost immediate. The council ministers were moderate in their views and generally sought to avoid confrontation and conflict. In this more cordial atmosphere, we began a number of exciting new initiatives with the approval of the Tibetan government.

One of the most important of these was an initiative to stabilize the supply and price of grain and end the spiraling inflation. We decided that the key was to create a system in which grain stored in other parts of Tibet could be systematically obtained. To accomplish this, we proposed to the Tibet government that we establish a new joint grain authority. The head of the board of directors for the grain authority/storage facility was my old friend Surkhang, the council minister. Ngabö, Langdün, and I were the vice directors.

We held many meetings to work out the details. I knew the customs of the Tibetan upper class, so I made sure that during the meetings we served sweet [English] tea and biscuits. Our meetings became popular, and most of government officials associated with the enterprise actually attended them. People in Lhasa started joking that now the Tibetan government offices were empty since most officials were attending the grain authority meetings.

We bought grain from distant estates of aristocrats and monasteries, and then used the Tibetan government's corvée transportation network to move it to Lhasa to be stored and sold. The central government provided us with a hundred thousand silver dollars *(dayan)* as capital for this. I was glad to be given this important responsibility from our side, and with the Tibetan government's help, we were able to quickly accomplish our goal. Starting this grain authority also had a secondary benefit because it enabled us to persuade the Tibetan government to allow a number of progressive former Tibetans officials, like Janglojen Kung and Kumbela, to rejoin as full Tibetan officials working for us.

Figure 18. Council Minister Surkhang, Kheme, and Che Jigme, Lhasa, 1952.

One of the things that I felt strongly about was the need for modern education in Lhasa. The Tibetan government had tried to open public schools in the 1920s and 1940s but had been forced to close them almost immediately due to the threat of violence from the monasteries. Now the situation had changed, and from early on, we in the Tibet Work Committee discussed the need to start providing public education. I was given responsibility for finding a site for the school and organizing the staff. In early 1952, I was able to buy a suitable house from the Dalai Lama's family and set up a board of directors. We named it the Seshin School after the family whose house it was. Zhang Guohua was nominally the director. Tsarong Dzasa, a senior aristocratic official, and I were the vice directors.

I thought it was important to make this not just the Tibet Work Committee's school but to involve important Tibetans at all levels. The first principal of the school, therefore, was the eminent Trijang Rimpoche, one of the Dalai Lama's two senior tutors. I went to see him many times and finally secured his agreement after the Dalai Lama had given him permission (although Trijang Rimpoche didn't actually do the day-to-

day work of a principal). Janglojen Kung was the vice principal. We recruited a number of well-known Tibetan scholars like Tsadrü Rimpoche
as teachers, and my wife also was a teacher. The school taught Tibetan,
Chinese, and mathematics and was popular with students from the beginning. The central government paid all the initial expenses and salaries
for teachers and students. I believed the school would be the foundation
for educating progressive young Tibetans. This was the first step toward
creating a new and modern Tibet.

After this, we founded the Lhasa Youth Association, headed by a progressive young aristocratic official named Shökhang. Many youths from
aristocratic and business families joined the association; initially there
were forty or fifty members. At association meetings, we explained the
central government's policies but mostly taught new socialist and revolutionary songs and organized the members to perform singing and
dancing. Shökhang was very talented in music and dancing and made the
meetings entertaining and very popular. Prior to this, there had been no
venue for young people to come together and mix.

I also headed a new research committee that translated news and di-
rectives into Tibetan. This meant inventing new terms in Tibetan, so I
brought some of the best-known Tibetan intellectuals into this committee, men like Janglojen Kung, Tsadrü Rimpoche, Geshe Chödrag, Demo
Rimpoche, and Kheme Dzasa. We rented a house from Kapshöpa Sey, an
aristocrat, and worked together translating materials from the central
government. In the beginning, once a week we posted a "newspaper" in
Tibetan on the walls of the Barkor. We initially called it "Brief Commu-
nications in Tibetan" [tib. *bod yig bsdus 'phrin*]. Then we mimeographed
the newspaper and distributed it once a week, then once every three days,
and finally once a day. A few years later this officially became the *Lhasa
Daily*.

All this was very time-consuming and left me little free time, but it was
also rewarding. These were the kinds of changes I had long hoped for in
Tibet. In the past, I had hoped the Tibetan government would do things
like this, but they hadn't. Now, with the new circumstances, it was finally
beginning.

While all of this was happening in Lhasa, the Panchen Lama was still
waiting to return to Tibet. The terms of the Seventeen-Point Agreement
specified that he and his officials were free to return. An advance group
of his officials, led by Che Jigme, had arrived with Fan Ming in Lhasa in
December 1951 and had discussed arrangements for him to meet the
Dalai Lama in Lhasa before continuing on to his home base in Shigatse.

Figure 19. Lhasans reading the proto-Tibetan "newspaper" in the Barkor near the Tsuglagang, Lhasa, 1952. *From right:* Phünwang, Kapshöpa, and Tsadrü Rimpoche.

In June 1952, twenty-six years after his previous incarnation had fled to exile in China, the Tenth Panchen Lama arrived in Shigatse and his home monastery of Tashilhunpo. He was accompanied by the Northwest Bureau officials Fan Ming and Ya Hanzhang.

Despite his return, there were still bad feelings between the officials of the two lamas, and the core issues that had led to the previous Panchen Lama's flight to exile had not been resolved. The two sides had very different views on their relative status, and this spilled over into our Tibet Work Committee.

The Panchen Lama's officials believed that they were equal to and independent from the government of the Dalai Lama, while the Dalai Lama's side considered the Lhasa government to govern all of Tibet, including the Panchen Lama. It saw the Panchen Lama's government as no different in structure than the estates and administrations of other lamas and feudal lords. This became a major bone of contention within the Tibet

Work Committee because Fan Ming, Zhang Guohua, and Zhang Jingwu also had very different thoughts on this subject. In a word, Fan Ming (and the Northwest Bureau) supported the Panchen Lama, and the Southwest Bureau officials supported the Dalai Lama's position.

Fan Ming felt strongly about this. He had studied Qing dynasty history in preparation for the liberation of Tibet and found that the Qing government commonly used the term "Back Tibet" (ch. huo zang) for the Panchen's areas in Tsang Province (around Shigatse), contrasting it with "Front Tibet" (ch. qian zang) for the Dalai Lama's areas. This, he felt, supported the Panchen Lama's insistence that he was not under the Dalai Lama but rather was autonomous. Because Fan Ming considered the Panchen Lama's side as historically autonomous, patriotic to China, and supportive of socialist reforms, Fan and the other officials from the Northwest Bureau believed that the Chinese government should strongly support the Panchen Lama and his interests. Doing so, they felt, would make Tibet more stable and secure for China. Conversely, they opposed Beijing's policy of considering the Dalai Lama to be the main figure in Tibet, and sought to institute a new policy that favored the Panchen Lama or at least treated them both as equals. Fan Ming actually favored creating two autonomous regions in Tibet, one headed by the Dalai Lama and the other by the Panchen Lama. This would have been the contemporary incarnation of the Manchu dynasty's "Front" and "Back" Tibet policy.—Goldstein, Sherap, and Siebenschuh

Fan Ming's views on the Panchen Lama were not shared by Mao Zedong, Zhou Enlai, or the cadres from the Southwest Bureau in Lhasa, like Zhang Guohua. They believed Tibet had been ruled by the Dalai Lama and his government, and agreed with the central government's policy of giving priority to him. I also agreed with this: I knew that politically all of Tibet was (and had been) under the Tibetan government in Lhasa. There were many districts in Tsang (the so-called Back Tibet) that were under the Lhasa government, many others had to pay taxes to both the Panchen Lama and Lhasa, and the entire area was under the authority of a governor appointed from Lhasa. The Manchu notion of a "Front" and "Back" Tibet was simply a myth.

The question of the status of Tsang vis-à-vis Tibet was secondary to the differences in opinion about when to start socialist reforms. Fan Ming believed that the best thing for China was to implement reforms in Tibet quickly. He felt trying to win over the Dalai Lama was not useful because he and his officials were hopelessly reactionary and feudal. The

Panchen Lama, however, was progressive, and if he were given control over his own region, he would certainly start trial reforms there. These could be used to get the peasants in the Dalai Lama's region to demand the same reforms. Despite Mao Zedong's stricture that the PLA should go very slowly in Tibet, Fan wanted to move quickly to reform Tibet, and he saw the Panchen Lama as a vehicle to do so.

While Fan Ming was still in Shigatse (with the Panchen Lama), the Tibet Work Committee in Lhasa received a telegram from him out of the blue, suggesting that we establish an autonomous administration in the Tsang area under the Panchen Lama. Zhang Jingwu and Zhang Guohua were shocked by this proposal and immediately convened the Tibet Work Committee (in Lhasa) to discuss the telegram in detail. Most totally opposed the suggestion. The feeling was that it would exacerbate the existing conflict between the Dalai and Panchen Lamas, alienate the Tibetan government, and produce intense hatred of us among Tibetans in Lhasa. Most importantly, it would totally undermine Mao's gradualist strategy and make the long-term goal of winning over the Tibetan elite impossible.

As the only Tibetan cadre in the leadership group, I, of course, was asked my view. I felt strongly that giving the Panchen Lama a separate autonomous region not only was politically a terrible idea, but also was based on *bad* history. Historically, the Panchen Lama's government was clearly subordinate to the Dalai Lama. Moreover, creating two autonomous regions violated the Seventeen-Point Agreement, which stated that in the future we would establish *one* autonomous administration in Tibet. The agreement did not say anything about *two* autonomous administrations in Tibet. The Tibet Work Committee, therefore, totally rejected Fan Ming's proposal.

Both sides then sent reports directly to the Central Committee in Beijing, and Li Weihan convened a major meeting in Beijing in 1953 to examine the issues. After several months of heated debate and argument (I was not present), Mao Zedong himself settled the issue by deciding that in Tibet the Dalai Lama was the superior and the Panchen Lama the subordinate. Mao demonstrated this visually by holding his forefinger and middle finger out level (with the remaining fingers in a fist) and saying the Dalai and Panchen are not like this. Then he rotated his hand so one finger was on top of the other and said, they are like this. In other words, the Dalai Lama is above the Panchen Lama. So Chairman Mao determined that there would be a unified Tibet, with the Dalai Lama at the head.

Fortunately, Fan Ming's approach did not prevail, but his strong views and the split in the party in Tibet made me think about how to best transform Tibet, and about my Han Chinese comrades. There seemed to be a significant difference between my way of thinking and theirs. Of course, we were all communists and cadres, but I was also a Tibetan, so the issue of nationalities in Marxism was particularly salient for me. Most of the Han cadres had real courage and were determined to do revolutionary work, and they had lots of practical experience. But most really did not have much in-depth knowledge about Marxist theory. In their mind, destroying the local tyrants and dividing the land was communism.

Superficially, they knew and accepted the doctrine of the equality of all nationalities, but they did not know what equality of all nationalities really meant. For example, if someone says to you that you may eat a fruit, you still could not eat a fruit because "fruit" is an empty concept. One has to move to a more specific level and talk about apples, bananas, pineapples, and so on. Similarly, the equality of nationalities is an empty concept unless it specifically includes the equality of politics, economy, language, and so on. So I thought my Chinese comrades really had not gone beyond overall concepts in their thinking. As I came to have more contact with them, I began to realize that this lack of clarity was a problem, and that implicitly there were two routes for reforming Tibet.

One approach was to reform from the top down, with Tibetans conducting reforms by following the orders of the Communist Party. I did not like this approach because I did not think it was compatible with true communism. I also did not think it would win over Tibetans to the new society.

The other approach was for Tibetan themselves to conduct the reforms and become, so to speak, the owner of their own home. In this method, the Tibetans were the commander and the CCP was the consultant to the commander. Tibet needed to reform itself, but the new socialist Tibet should be created by Tibetans themselves.

I now realized that Fan Ming and his Northwest Bureau supporters had the former, top-down approach in mind, and this worried me. The Zhang Jingwu/Zhang Guohua faction differed from them on the Panchen-Dalai Lama issue, and their views had prevailed, but I also had nagging fears that deep down they too had a top-down mentality. So for me it was a bit unsettling. Not only did many leading Han officials have only a simplistic understanding of communist nationality ideology, but many, if not most, seemed to have accepted the top-down model.

By the end of 1952, however, I was satisfied with the progress. The extremist views on both sides were blocked—Lukangwa and the anti-Chinese People's Association had been disbanded and Fan Ming's attempt had been denied. Our relations with the Tibetan government had improved tremendously, and a number of important initiatives had been started, such as the primary school and the youth group. I thought we were back on track to gradually "winning over" the Tibetan elite and amicably inducing them to eventually begin reforms.

CHAPTER 16

An Interlude in Beijing

In 1953, my life took a sudden turn when I was sent to Beijing with a delegation of Tibetan religious leaders attending the inaugural meeting of the Buddhist Association of China. Fan Ming, as director of the Tibet United Front Work Department, was in charge of organizing the delegation, and suggested I accompany them because this was an important delegation and I was the leading Tibetan cadre. (Zhang Jingwu and Zhang Guohua thought that made sense, and so did I.) The delegation included important religious figures like Kundeling Dzasa, Dünjom Rimpoche, and abbots and lamas from all sects. This visit afforded the central government an excellent opportunity to make a good impression on these influential religious leaders, and it was decided to send them on a tour of a number of Chinese cities so that they could get a better idea of what the nation was like. I of course accompanied them. It was interesting for all of us, and before I knew it, eight months had passed and it was time to return home. Everyone, including me, was looking forward to this, but I never got to go.

Just before we were going to depart, two senior cadres from the State Nationalities Affairs Commission, Wang Feng and Liu Geping, informed me that it had been suggested—I assumed in Tibet—that I remain in Beijing. They said that most of the party's real work in Tibet had not yet started, so this was a good time for me to get training in the capital. Working in a department of the central government, they said, would hone my leadership skills and allow me to get to know all the main players dealing with nationalities affairs. Thus I was sent to work in the State Nationalities Affairs Commission as vice chief of the Politics and Law Department and vice editor-in-chief for the Nationalities Publishing House. I was also director of the Chinese People's Association for Friendship with Foreign Countries.[1]

In fact, I found it useful being in Beijing and having an opportunity to see how things worked. I met all the officials who dealt with minority nationalities in general and Tibet in particular, and I was frequently asked to attend discussions and meetings dealing with Tibetan affairs, as well as sometimes translating for Tibetan delegations. I was also the main liaison person for the offices of the Dalai and Panchen Lamas in Beijing, so I was quite busy.

I was probably somewhat naïve, but I took all this at face value. Some years later, however, I discovered that the decision to keep me in Beijing had been politically manipulated by Fan Ming. He wanted me out of Lhasa because my presence there was cramping his style and hindering his agenda. When the party leaders discussed major issues, my views were often solicited. Since I was the only Tibetan on the leaders committee, my comments counted for more than my age, rank, and experience would otherwise have allowed, and since I disagreed with Fan Ming on most key issues, like the autonomy of the Panchen Lama, Fan felt his power and influence in Tibet would be enhanced if I were gone. Consequently, not only did he suggest I accompany the Buddhist delegation to Beijing, but he also suggested that I be kept there for "training." At the time, however, I had no inkling of this, and in our face-to-face encounters, Fan Ming and I were very friendly and collegial.

Being in Beijing allayed the fears I had had in Lhasa about Han-Tibetan nationality relations. I was genuinely impressed by the atmosphere at the State Nationalities Affairs Commission. It had many high officials from different nationalities, and there was no feeling of a top-down, Han-dominated approach. I was also impressed by the way the central government paid attention to minority affairs and minority

1. In the PRC, the basic governmental organs that deal with nationalities issues are the United Front Work Department, the State Nationalities Affairs Commission, and the Nationalities Affairs Committee. The United Front Work Department is directly under the Central Committee of the Party, so it is most directly linked to China's top leaders. It is a high-level policy- and strategy-formulating organ. The State Nationalities Affairs Commission is under the State Council, which in turn is under the Central Committee. It is concerned with government policy and official dealings with minority nationalities. The Nationalities Committee is under the National People's Congress and is the least powerful of the three. It is a venue for the expression of nationality opinions. — Goldstein, Sherap, and Siebenschuh

cadres. Most members of the Tibetan elite were known by the central government, and when a Tibetan holiday was celebrated in Beijing by Tibetans, top Chinese leaders like Chairman Mao, Premier Zhou, and Politburo member Liu Shaoqi came in person.

Two major events occurred in China in 1954 that affected my life: the inaugural meeting of the National People's Congress and its approval of China's first constitution, and the Dalai Lama's first visit to inland China.

Both the Dalai Lama and the Panchen Lama were invited to participate in the National People's Congress, and both accepted, the Dalai Lama serving as its vice chairman. Since I was working in Beijing, I became deeply involved in their visit, as well as in helping to translate the constitution into Tibetan. I also attended the first National People's Congress as a delegate.

The Dalai Lama's visit to China was very important to the central government because it would be the Dalai Lama's first view of the country. Everyone was concerned that all aspects of his trip go well, and great care was given to the arrangements. Although the relative positions of the two lamas had been settled by Mao at the Beijing meeting the previous year, the central government had not made its decision public. It decided to take the opportunity of the joint visit to do so in a way that would overtly resolve all confusion and contradictions among the party leaders and cadres in Tibet. A document laying out the guidelines for how the two lamas should be received—called "The Central Government's Instructions Regarding the Reception of the Dalai and Panchen" [ch. *Zhongyang guanyu jiedai Dalai Banchan de youguan zhishi*]—was drafted by Li Weihan and modified and approved by Mao himself. It stated unambiguously that wherever the two lamas went and whatever activities they participated in, the Dalai Lama should be treated as chief [ch. *zheng*] and the Panchen should be treated as vice or subordinate [ch. *fu*].

The Dalai Lama and the other deputies from the Tibetan government traveled to Beijing via the southern route through Chengdu. Zhang Jingwu accompanied them. Fan Ming accompanied the Panchen Lama and his deputies on the northwest route via Xi'an. While they were en route, a copy of this document was sent to party leaders in all relevant provinces and Tibet, as well as to the party leaders accompanying the lamas.

The two sides' response to the document revealed their different views. Zhang Jingwu responded that the solution was completely correct and in accordance with the situation in Tibet. He said he would follow the guidelines one hundred percent. Fan Ming's reply was more equivocal. His telegram said some comrades, like Liang Xiangxian (the head of the Shigatse branch of the Tibet Work Committee and secretary to the Panchen Lama), disagreed with the decision. I got to see these telegrams because of my position in the State Nationalities Affairs Commission in Beijing. I immediately knew it was really Fan Ming who disagreed, because Liang Xiangxian was from the Northwest Bureau and would do whatever Fan Ming told him. I told Liu Geping and other leaders my opinion about Fan's telegram, and they agreed but said it didn't matter because Mao himself had authorized these guidelines. So we prepared the reception exactly according to the reception document.

So important was this visit that every aspect of the arrangements was monitored carefully by top leaders. For example, both Xi Zhongxun and Deng Xiaoping personally came to inspect the arrangements for the two lamas' residences. Xi was originally from the Northwest Bureau and was close to the Panchen Lama's group. He shook his head when he saw the different level of arrangements for the Panchen Lama but did not say anything. On the other hand, Deng Xiaoping—from the Southwest Bureau—praised us and said everything had been arranged perfectly.

Meanwhile, I was delegated to go to Chengdu and Xi'an to present ceremonial scarves to each of the lamas on behalf of the State Nationalities Affairs Commission. I went to Chengdu first and presented a beautiful scarf to the Dalai Lama, and then to Xi'an and presented a similar scarf to the Panchen Lama. Later Zhou Enlai sent his private plane to take the Dalai Lama from Chengdu to Xi'an so that he and the Panchen Lama could make the final leg of the trip to Beijing together (by train). After the Dalai Lama arrived in Xi'an, I went back to Beijing on Zhou Enlai's plane. It was the first time I had seen a plane with a bed, and I was amazed.

As the time approached for the Dalai and Panchen Lamas to arrive in Beijing, a disagreement arose regarding who should receive them at the train station. Within the State Nationalities Affairs Commission, three of us were responsible for handling the reception: Zhao Fan, personal secretary to Li Weihan, the commission's director; Peng Sika, a Mongol who was vice director of the General Office of the Nationalities Affairs Commission; and me. We were informed that the higher authorities had decided that Zhou Enlai would receive them. I was unhappy with that plan and said in our subcommittee that this was not appropriate. When Ngabö had come to Beijing in 1951 for the Seventeen-Point Agreement negotiations, Zhou Enlai went to receive him, but in Tibetan society, Ngabö was only a council minister and was subordinate to the Dalai Lama. If only Zhou Enlai now came to receive the Dalai Lama, it would appear to Tibetan officials (who were highly attuned to etiquette) to show a lack of proper respect for the Dalai Lama. We all agreed, and Zhao Fan reported this to our superior, Li Weihan. Li responded that Premier Zhou Enlai was the top leader in the State Council and was also one of the most senior figures in the party. If Zhou received the lamas, he said, it would be perfectly acceptable. But, he concluded, since our views differed, "I will tell Mao and Zhou and let them decide."

The next morning, Li called us to his office and told us that the Central Committee agreed with us and had decided to also send Zhu De to the train station. Zhu De was commander in chief of the PLA and a member of the Standing Committee of the Politburo. At that time, his was one of the two pictures hanging on the walls of almost all offices—the other one was Mao's. This was perfect to show the central government's special respect for the Dalai and Panchen Lamas, and the reception was very well received by Tibetans.

Three or four days after the Dalai Lama arrived, a major meeting was arranged for the Dalai Lama and the Panchen Lama with the top leaders of China—Mao, Liu Shaoqi, Zhou Enlai, Zhu De, and Deng Xiaoping; I was to be the translator. It was the first time the Dalai Lama had met China's top leaders, and they him. Interestingly, only Mao spoke. Mao told the Dalai Lama that he and the central government were very happy about the Dalai Lama's first visit to Beijing and they welcomed him. The relationship between Chinese and Tibetans, he said, was very important, and in the future the central government would expend great effort to support the development of Tibet.

The Dalai Lama in turn told Mao that he was happy to have come to Beijing. Previously, he said, he had not known the real situation in China, so he had gone to Yadong on the Indian border and had thought about seeking asylum abroad. But, he said, since Zhang Jingwu had come, he had gradually come to learn more about the overall situation, and now he was very happy to have an opportunity to meet Mao and the other leaders.

The Dalai Lama was impressive. He was only nineteen years old, but he spoke well, without exhibiting any signs of nervousness. Mao was friendly and forthcoming. He did not act like the great ruler he was, but spoke informally, like a friend. Several times during the conversation, Mao pointed at me and told the Dalai Lama that I was a good person

Figure 20. Chairman Mao and other leaders of the central government officially meeting with the Dalai Lama and the Panchen Lama, Beijing, 1954.
From left: Lobsang Samden (the Dalai Lama's brother), Liu Geping, Li Weihan, Deng Xiaoping, Liu Shaoqi, the Dalai Lama, Mao Zedong, the Panchen
Lama, Zhou Enlai, Zhang Jingwu, Xi Zhongxun, Fan Ming, Nangmagang Ta-
lama (a leading official of the Panchen Lama), Wang Feng, and Phünwang.

among Tibetans. I was translating everything both said in their conversation, but I did not translate this part to the Dalai Lama. It was too embarrassing. Once Mao also used me as an example and said, "For example, Phünwang is from Chamdo. . . ." This, of course, was wrong, but
I did not point out the mistake and just substituted Batang for Chamdo.

Deng Xiaoping was sharp and noticed this mistake. Later that afternoon when he relayed the contents of this meeting to the ministerial-level
officials, he said that everything had gone very well that morning except
that Chairman Mao had made a small mistake, but fortunately, Phünwang had been there and had not translated it. Liu Geping later told me
this, and after I explained what the mistake was, he also said I had done
the right thing.

The conversation lasted about an hour. Mao and the other leaders
then accompanied the Dalai Lama out of the house, and Mao personally
opened the car door for him. Mao seemed quite happy about the meeting. He shook the Dalai Lama's hand and told him, "Your coming to Bei-

jing is like coming back to your own home. Whenever you want to meet me, please call me. You can come to my place whenever you want to. Don't be shy. If you need anything, you just tell me directly." When the Dalai Lama and I were seated in our car going back to our quarters, the Dalai Lama was also very happy. He was so excited he hugged me and said, "Phünwang-la, today things went extremely well. Mao is a great person who is unlike others." I also was very pleased that this critical first meeting went so well. My hopes for Tibet, in a sense, rested on this.

The central government had organized a small party leaders group in Beijing for the Dalai Lama's visit. It was headed by Zhang Jingwu, and I was a member. Every day, the group had the responsibility of reporting the activities of the Dalai Lama and the Panchen Lama to the central government, and my main task was to visit the Dalai Lama and his officials to see what they were thinking and what suggestions they had. I also occasionally visited the Panchen Lama and Che Jigme, but my main task was the Dalai Lama. Every day I called on him, and when he attended social events or traveled to other places, I accompanied him. For example, often there were dance parties in the evening, and occasionally the two lamas attended. It was common at these for girls from the state dance troupe to go up to the guests and invite them to dance (the foxtrot). However, we had strict instructions from Zhou Enlai not to let the lamas dance even if they wanted to. I think Zhou was concerned about doing anything to damage the lamas' stature as religious figures.

The Dalai Lama was extremely alert, and he liked to observe people and size them up. He noticed right away that Zhou was a very good dancer and told me that the way Zhou danced made him appear youthful. "Zhou dances like a twenty- or thirty-year-old," he said. By contrast, when Mao and Zhu De danced, they looked their age. The Dalai Lama also frequently told me things he had observed about other people's character, including Chairman Mao. For example, the Dalai Lama was careful with his own appearance and once commented to me after a meeting with Mao that he was surprised to see that the cuff of Mao's sleeve was frayed. He was quite correct that Mao was not fastidious about his clothing.

I had met the Dalai Lama many times in Lhasa at meetings and ceremonies, but we never had had a chance to meet alone and talk freely. Tibetan court etiquette prohibited that. But in Beijing, where I visited him every day, we were often alone and had many opportunities to talk freely. We became friends. The Dalai Lama kept a diary about important events, and sometimes he asked me to go to his quarters so he could check whether some of the words he had attributed to Mao or others were correct. Often I ate with him, and after a while, whenever he had meals, he asked his lord chamberlain to prepare an extra pair of chopsticks for me because I might come to visit him. He told me that while it was impossible for us to eat together in Lhasa, here in inland China we two could do this.

During our many conversations, I told him about how I had become involved in revolutionary activities and what my goals were. I also explained to him about the Communist Party and the reforms that were taking place in inland China. He was extremely interested, asked many questions, and openly agreed that the Tibetan nation was backward and had to be reformed. Without reforms, he said, there was no hope for Tibetans to progress. It was wonderful to get to see and know the real Dalai Lama—the person behind the pomp and ceremony—and from these conversations, my own hopes for the future were bolstered. I really came to believe that under the Dalai Lama's leadership, Tibet would be able to reform and improve with a Tibetan flavor. The Dalai Lama was the unquestioned leader of the Tibetan people, and as such did not need to fight or scheme to keep his high position. He could unilaterally put into practice his good thoughts about Tibet's future.[2]

In the course of these conversations, the Dalai Lama talked about many things, including the characters of the different council ministers

---

2. The Dalai Lama wrote in *Freedom in Exile* (pp. 86–87) of Phünwang in Beijing:

In due course I became good friends with Phuntsog Wangyal. . . . Phuntsog Wangyal turned out to be a very able man, calm and wise; a good thinker too. He was also very sincere and honest, and I enjoyed his company a great deal. Evidently, he felt very happy in his assignment as my official interpreter, not the least because of the access it gave him to Chairman Mao, whom he idolized. However, his feelings toward me were equally strong. Once when we were talking about Tibet, he said he was full of optimism for the future as he considered that I was very open-minded. He told me how many years ago he had been to a public audience at the Norbulingka and seen a small boy on a throne. "And now you are a small boy no longer, here with me in Peking." This thought moved him very much and he wept openly. After several minutes he continued, now speaking as a true Communist. He told me that the Dalai Lama should not rely on astrology as a tool with which to govern the country. He also said that religion was not a reliable thing to base one's life on. Because of his obvious sincerity, I listened carefully. On the subject of what he called superstitious practices, I explained the Buddha's emphasis on the need for thorough investigation before accepting something as true or false. I also told him that I was convinced that religion is essential, especially for those engaged in politics. At the end of our conversation I felt that we had a high regard for one another. Such differences as we had were personal matters, so there was no basis for conflict. In the final analysis, we were both Tibetans thinking deeply about the future of our country.

—Goldstein, Sherap, and Siebenschuh

in Lhasa, and even about his own family members. He also told me that when Ngabö had visited him after he returned to Tibet from signing the Seventeen-Point Agreement, Ngabö had cried when talking about the difficulties he had endured and the lies and rumors being spread about him—for example, that he was in the pay of the Chinese. I was surprised to hear this. The central government and I had always thought that Ngabö was completely on our side, but when the Dalai Lama told me about their meeting, I realized that Ngabö still stood on their side. I thought about this a lot, and after a while decided I could understand it.

Ngabö was an aristocrat and a council minister, so it was not unreasonable that his attitude and his loyalty were still on the side of the Tibetan government. I did not think that this was wrong. I was on the side of the central government and a member of the Chinese Communist Party, but I also had my own thoughts deriving from being a Tibetan. Because of my background, there was a difference between my attitudes and those of the ordinary Chinese cadres. At that time, although Ngabö had a close relationship with the central government, I also understood that this was not because he was versed in the Communist Party's ideology and believed in it. He had a close relationship with the central government because he felt it was futile to fight the PLA. I had to concede that his reaction was understandable, but it was surprising nevertheless.

Meeting often with the Dalai Lama made me realize that he was not in good physical condition. In fact, his physical condition worried me enough that I suggested he start doing exercises to radio music every morning. Talking with the Dalai Lama about his life and food really surprised me. Although he was the ruler of Tibet, he lived a very Spartan life. His daily diet in Lhasa was tsampa, butter tea, dried meat, noodles, meat dumplings, and one or two simple vegetable dishes. He had never, for example, tasted sweet tea until he was in flight to the Indian border in 1950. Compared to the standard of living of the larger aristocratic families, who had cooks specializing in Chinese cuisine, the Dalai Lama followed a simple lifestyle. He was admired by his people as a god, but in some respects, the quality of his life was poor. He was, in a sense, a prisoner of tradition, and his officials would not permit any changes. Not surprisingly, he was amazed by the variety of foods he received in inland China, where he had scores of different dishes to choose from, most of which he had never seen or heard of before. I got the impression that when he compared his own and other Tibetans' style of living with that of the Chinese, he understood that the standard of living in Tibet needed to be improved, and he became committed to reform the old Tibetan society.

In our discussions, the Dalai Lama was very curious about new things. He wanted to learn about everything. Sometimes I was afraid that I could not answer all his questions correctly; for example, when we went to the Beijing opera, I was not familiar with this art form and had to ask others for help.

One day, Mao unexpectedly came to visit the Dalai Lama at his residence at about 8 P.M. During their conversation, Mao suddenly said, "I heard that you have a national flag, do you? They do not want you to carry it, isn't that right?" After I translated Mao's words, the Dalai Lama asked me, "Who does he mean by 'they?'" Although I knew who he meant, I translated this back to Mao, who responded frankly that "they" meant Zhang Jingwu, Zhang Guohua, and Fan Ming.

Since Mao asked this with no warning that the topic was to be discussed, the Dalai Lama just replied, "We have an army flag." I thought that was a shrewd answer because it didn't say whether Tibet had a national flag. Mao perceived that the Dalai Lama was concerned by his question and immediately told him, "That is no problem. You may keep your national flag." Mao definitely said "national" flag [tib. *rgyal dar*]. "In the future," he said, "we can also let Xinjiang have their own flag, and Inner Mongolia, too. Would it be okay to carry the national flag of the People's Republic of China in addition to that flag? Would that be all right?" The Dalai Lama nodded his head yes. This was the most important thing that Mao told the Dalai Lama, and I was amazed to hear it.

My mind was racing. I didn't know whether Mao had discussed this with other leaders in the Politburo or whether he mentioned it on his own. As I had always paid great attention to the Soviet Union's nationality model, I was excited because I took Mao's comment that Tibet could use its own flag to mean that China was contemplating adopting the Soviet Union's "republic" model, at least for these three large minority nationalities. That's why I thought it was something new and very important.

That night, I went to see Zhang Jingwu to tell him about this. Zhang Jingwu listened, and then asked me, "When Chairman Mao said 'they,' who was he talking about?" I responded, "He explicitly said you, Zhang Guohua, and Fan Ming." Then he asked me whether he had said anything else in addition to mentioning their names. I said he hadn't. Just the names. It struck me as odd that Zhang had paid more attention to the people mentioned by Mao than to the issue.

Some time later, I mentioned Mao's comment informally to Liu Geping. He understood the significance right away and responded the same way I did. He did not pay attention to who the "they" referred to; instead he was interested in the issue. He said, "According to this, it is possible that in the future some nationalities, like Tibet, Xinjiang, and Inner Mongolia, could get the same system as that of the Soviet Union, while the other, smaller ones would get 'autonomy.' " He thought that would be wonderful. We both thought that the central government must have this idea if Mao had said that. In subsequent years, I searched for written mention of this conversation about the flag in party documents, but I have never seen it mentioned.

Many years later, when I was in prison, my mind wandered back to Mao's remarks, and I became extremely anxious to leave a record of his conversation. At the time—it was 1974 or 1975—I recognized that I might never be released, the Dalai Lama was in a foreign country, and Mao was very old. I became obsessed with preserving a record of this encounter, and I wrote it down.

After the People's Congress meetings finished, the Dalai and Panchen Lamas went on tour to other Chinese cities. Liu Geping and I accompanied the Dalai Lama, and Liu Chun, a vice director from the State Nationalities Affairs Commission, accompanied the Panchen Lama. Most of the time, the Dalai and Panchen Lamas toured separately.

Liu Geping was an important official who was a member of the Hui (Muslim) minority group. He also had been an activist member of the CCP since the early days. We discussed the coming tour and both felt this was a great opportunity to inform the Dalai Lama about the history of the Chinese Communist Party and its policies. Since Liu Geping was a longtime party member, we decided he should talk to the Dalai Lama about the party's history. I would explain to him the Soviet Union's nationality polices and Marxism-Leninism. The Dalai Lama was very eager to learn about all aspects of communism, and I think we had an effect on his thinking. Even now, he sometimes says that he is half Buddhist and half Marxist. But he was also realistic, and understood that in practice things are sometimes different from theory, just as not every Buddhist follows the Buddha's words in the same way.

At another meeting at which I translated, Mao asked about the Dalai Lama's impressions of China from his sightseeing in other cities, and said that if the Dalai Lama had any thoughts on Tibetan affairs in the future, he could tell the central government directly. Then he said, "We sent Zhang Jingwu and Zhang Guohua to Tibet, but if you do not like either of them, I will change them. We sent Chinese cadres to Tibet to help Tibetans, not to order them around and gain high positions in Tibet. So whoever you do not like, I will change them." I thought this too was a very important comment.

The Dalai Lama told Mao his impressions of the trip, stressing that he now understood clearly the need for Tibet to reform and develop in the future, and was committed to doing this. At the end of the conversation, Mao shook hands with the Dalai Lama's relatives, his teacher, and all the other council ministers and left the Dalai Lama's quarters. I should mention that I have heard that the Dalai Lama's autobiography says that Mao told the Dalai Lama that from the Communist Party's point of view religion is the opium of the people. I wasn't translating on that occasion, so while I don't doubt Mao said that, I have no firsthand knowledge of it.[3]

In February 1955, the Dalai Lama and the Panchen Lama jointly hosted a celebration of the Tibetan New Year. Before the event, Mao, who was going to attend, asked me about how to do the ritual of *chemar*. This is our traditional New Year's custom: a small rectangular wooden container with two compartments, one with tsampa and one with wheat, is offered to a person, who takes a pinch from each and throws it into the air as an offering to the gods. Mao was going to be presented with this box, so I explained to him what to do. He understood, but when he actually performed the *chemar* offering, he didn't do it correctly. He threw a bit of tsampa to the sky and then threw some to the ground and joked that he threw it into the sky for the deities and to the earth for the ghosts. Everyone laughed.

At the time of the New Year, Mao asked the Dalai Lama if he would welcome the government sending me back to Tibet. The Dalai Lama answered that he definitely would and said some words of praise for me. Mao then asked the Panchen Lama, and when he too agreed, Mao called

---

3. The Dalai Lama wrote in *Freedom in Exile* (p. 99) about this:

[Mao said to me] "Religion is poison. . . ." At this I felt a violent burning sensation all over my face and I was suddenly very afraid. "So," I thought, "you are the destroyer of the Dharma after all." . . . I hoped he would not sense the horror I felt: it might have broken his trust in me. Luckily, Phuntsog Wangyal [Phünwang] was not, for some reason, interpreting between us on this occasion. Had he done so, I am sure that he would have discovered my thoughts—especially as we invariably discussed everything together afterwards.

—*Goldstein, Sherap, and Siebenschuh*

Wang Feng over and told him to make arrangements to send me back to Tibet.

I reported all this to my boss, Li Weihan, but told him that I preferred to stay in Beijing and attend the high-level Central Party School for a year to learn more about communist theory. I had read lots of books on communism but never had had a chance to study it with experts. I knew that several Soviet scholars were teaching communist theory, and I was very eager to study with them, although I wanted to go back to Tibet after finishing my studies at the Central Party School. Li said he agreed with my request, but I needed to get permission from the director of the Organization Department of the Central Committee, which I did without difficulty.

While the Dalai Lama was in Beijing, he did not discuss important political issues with Mao, leader-to-leader. I had expected him, as the head of Tibet, to raise issues he was concerned about, but he did not. Perhaps it was because he was young—nineteen years old. In any case, the real conversations about important political issues were conducted by the council ministers, headed by Surkhang. There were two major issues— the establishment of a Military and Administrative Bureau for Tibet and the historic dispute between the Tibetan government and the Panchen Lama's "government."

The creation of a Military and Administrative Bureau for Tibet was a sensitive issue. It was specified in the Seventeen-Point Agreement, but the central government knew that previously the Tibetans had been opposed to it. Consequently, since these bureaus were being replaced with people's governments in other parts of China, the central government suggested during the Dalai Lama's visit that it would be okay to omit that step and instead establish a preparatory committee for the creation of a Tibet Autonomous Region with the Dalai Lama as its head. The regular Tibetan government would continue to function until the Tibet Autonomous Region was actually created. This was received well on the Tibetan side and agreed to.

The central government also felt strongly that it was important for the Dalai Lama and the Panchen Lama to resolve their differences, so it encouraged them to use this opportunity to discuss the outstanding issues. But it also decided that it would be a mistake to try to force a solution. Instead the government told both sides to work out their own solution, which they did.

At this time, I had many opportunities to talk with Surkhang because we were both staying at the Beijing Hotel. He treated me like an old friend and often came to visit me. Once, I recall, he told me, "Phünwang-la, now things are over [meaning the old society]. When you first came to meet me, I was still sleeping. You told me several very important things that I was unable to do. That was my mistake, and I regret it. However, at that time it was difficult to do anything. Now, all that is over. But we are still good friends."

I was interested in learning more about Tibetan history, so I asked him many questions about it. He had a superb knowledge of Tibetan history, and he offered to write up something for me about the major events from King Songtsen Gampo in the seventh century A.D. to the current Dalai Lama's government. Several months later, just before he went back to Tibet, he gave me a handwritten manuscript. I kept that small book for a long time but lost it when I was put in prison. I still regret that. Surkhang's Tibetan was exceptional, and in general he was extremely intelligent.

Every day after dinner, there was dancing, and Surkhang liked to attend. One evening while on the way, he told the driver he wanted to see a certain shop. The driver had to drive the wrong way on a one-way street to get there and was stopped by a policeman. Surkhang, who did not speak Chinese, immediately got out of the car and untied his long hair (from the top of his head, as Tibetan officials wear it) and showed it in his hand, saying to the police in Chinese, "Sorry, sorry" [ch. *dui bu qi, dui bu qi*]. When the policeman saw the long hair, he knew he was a Tibetan and let him go. Such things happened several times, and the Chinese liaison staff were surprised that Surkhang was so smart and could so easily figure out how to solve problems. They said that compared to Surkhang, the other Tibetan officials were like villagers.

Surkhang actually almost died in Beijing. One day he suddenly got very sick and was diagnosed with appendicitis. We wanted to take him to the hospital, but the other council ministers said they had to meet to discuss it. They met several times about what to do because most of them felt that the appendicitis was a bad omen and it was not good to have an operation in China. One actually suggested that they needed to do a divination to decide what course of action to take. Surkhang was in excruciating pain, so we reported this to the Central Committee. That night, at around eight or nine o'clock, Zhou Enlai sent an order saying there was no need to do divination and that we should take Surkhang to Beijing Hospital immediately. He ordered me to accompany Surkhang and stay with him in the hospital from beginning to end. We told the other Tibetan council ministers of the government's decision and took Surkhang to the hospital. The hospital called in the best doctors to perform the operation, and I stayed right beside him. When the operation was finished, the doctor told me that it had gone well and I could leave the room. I immediately called Zhou Enlai with the good news. "Did you stay there from beginning to end?" he asked. I told him, "Yes, I did." Surkhang stayed in the hospital for three days.

At first, when the Tibetan delegation came to Beijing, they had all kinds of worries about what would happen to them. They were especially concerned about how the Dalai Lama would be treated. But the central government had prepared well, and after the many meetings and tours, most of them were pleased. They were delighted and relieved that Mao and the other top leaders had treated them with great respect. In particular, the older officials (like the Dalai Lama's lord chamberlain and tutors) were pleased that Mao, in their eyes "the emperor of China," had gone in person to visit the Dalai Lama in his quarters. This was the first time in Tibetan history that such a thing had happened.

Even though they did not openly say it, I knew that many members of the Tibetan delegation were worried about the Dalai Lama staying too long in inland China. They were especially worried that his attitude and opinions might undergo changes. Ngabö and Surkhang did not worry about that, but the others did, and there was pressure on him to return to Lhasa as quickly as possible, so in April 1955, the Dalai Lama left Beijing.

The Dalai Lama and the Panchen Lama went back through the northwest, stopping at Labrang monastery (in Gansu), where they carried out a religious ceremony attended by over ten thousand Tibetans. After this, the Panchen Lama went back via the northern route, and the Dalai Lama went on to Chengdu in Sichuan. There an awkward and unpleasant incident occurred.

When the Dalai Lama went to a Chinese city, the first party secretary and the governor almost always received him. However, in Chengdu, Sichuan's first party secretary, Li Jingquan, did not show up.[4] Moreover, although Li Dazhang, the governor, came to visit the Dalai Lama, he

---

4. Li Jingquan was known in the Chinese Communist Party for being ultraleftist. It was assumed he was absent because he did not want to have to show respect to the Dalai Lama—someone he presumably saw as a religious reactionary (or worse). Less than a year later, Li Jingquan would start socialist reforms in the Tibetan areas of Kham under his control.—Goldstein, Sherap, and Siebenschuh

had his coat draped over his shoulders in a style that was considered disrespectful.

The Dalai Lama, as I said, was observant and noticed things, including the fact that Li Jingquan did not show up. He asked me and the Chinese officials who were responsible for the reception where Li was, but we passed it off by saying that Li probably was out of town. The Dalai Lama, however, did not seem to believe what we told him. Later, when he again asked us about Li, we told him another story, but the Dalai Lama seemed to know we were not telling him the truth.

As it happened, we were in Chengdu for the May First celebration, and the Dalai Lama was invited. When we got there, he was surprised to see Li Jingquan. Li continued to insult the Dalai Lama by first shaking hands with some specialists from the Soviet Union and only then with the Dalai Lama. I thought that was terrible. We had tried to cover for his not coming to receive the Dalai Lama, but now when he finally showed up his rudeness was too much. I thought something must be wrong with him, and the Dalai Lama was clearly not pleased.

The Dalai Lama had not planned to stay long in Chengdu, but an earthquake in Kham temporarily cut off the road to Tartsedo and Lhasa. An unexpected result of this was that he was able to spend some time with Zhou Enlai.

Zhou and another top leader, Chen Yi, had attended the Bandung Conference in Jakarta and stopped in Chengdu on their way back to Beijing. Publicly, the government said that Zhou and Chen were simply taking a rest in Chengdu, but in fact, Zhou knew that the Dalai Lama was there and stopped especially to meet him.

When we learned they were coming, the Dalai Lama told us that he wanted go to the airport to greet them. We said, yes, of course, but this led to an argument between Xu Danlu (in our group) and Li Jingquan regarding who would be the first person in the reception line at the airport. Li Jingquan wanted to be first, but Xu Danlu said that the Dalai Lama was not just the head of Tibet but also the vice chairman of the Standing Committee of the National People's Congress. No agreement was reached.

The next morning, the Dalai Lama and I went to the airport. We waited for about an hour in one room while Li Jingquan waited in another. When Zhou's plane arrived, we went out to receive him, and so did Li. Li did not say anything to us nor we to him. Li, however, was closer to the disembarkation stairs and tried to shake hands with Zhou first. However, as soon as the plane door opened, Zhou Enlai saw the

Dalai Lama and waved to him. Zhou then walked directly to him, shook his hand, and asked about his health. Only after this did he pay any attention to Li Jingquan. Later people told me that Zhou knew and disapproved of Li's attitude toward the Dalai Lama and had criticized Li in private.

The next day, a meeting was convened to allow Zhou Enlai and Chen Yi to apprise us of the events that had transpired at Bandung. Zhou invited the Dalai Lama to attend the meeting, and when we got to the meeting hall, the Dalai Lama was seated in the front row of the auditorium. Only Li Jingquan was seated on the platform with Zhou Enlai and Chen Yi. However, when Zhou and Chen entered the meeting hall, Zhou said loudly, "Vice Chairman Dalai Lama, please come up and sit here." So the Dalai Lama and I went to sit on the platform, and the Dalai Lama was very pleased.

Zhou and Chen stayed in Chengdu for three days and had several conversations with the Dalai Lama. One day, I recall, Zhou made a special visit to the Dalai Lama and talked with him for more than two hours. The Dalai Lama told Zhou that everything had gone very well on his trip to China and all officials, especially Mao, had treated him very well. In addition, he said, he was pleased with the discussions about establishing the Preparatory Committee for the Tibet Autonomous Region instead of the Military and Administrative Bureau. And he said that he was inspired by his visits to other cities and by seeing what was happening in China. Tibet, he said, was backward and its people poor. He said he now understood clearly that there was a large gap between Tibet and China and that Tibet needed to gradually reform. Zhou replied, "Mao and I clearly know that all Tibetans believe in the Dalai Lama and respect him greatly. And your thinking is correct. However, when you go back to Tibet, it would be better not to do reforms immediately." I thought that Zhou felt that the Dalai Lama was young and impressionable, and so might act too precipitously and alienate the conservative religious and lay officials in Lhasa. The Dalai Lama responded, "Yes, that is true. We Dalai Lamas are believed in and respected because our position was determined by history. But your position was achieved in a different way. You have worked hard and sacrificed for many years to finally reach your high position." I thought that was a very astute comment on his part, as did Zhou Enlai.

At their second meeting, Zhou expanded on what he had said to the Dalai Lama. "Regarding implementing reforms in Tibet," he said, "you need to think very carefully. The Central Committee's policy is that sta-

Figure 21. During Zhou Enlai and Chen Yi's stop in Chengdu, 1955, after
attending the Asian-African conference in Bandung. *From left:* Xu Danlu, Liu
Geping, Li Dazhang (governor of Sichuan), the Dalai Lama, Zhou Enlai, Chen
Yi, and Phünwang.

bility is the priority. Now you have seen firsthand that China has un-
dergone tremendous changes, and that by comparison, Tibet is backward. However, in Tibet the conditions for carrying out reforms are not
yet sufficient. Therefore, things should be done carefully. If there is a big
gap between the leaders' thoughts and the masses' thoughts, the reforms
will not be successful. Only after the thoughts of the leaders and the
masses are matched can reforms be gradually carried out." Although
Zhou said "masses' thoughts," I understood that he really meant the
upper circles. The real masses would have been happy if the reforms
ended the tax and corvée labor of the old society, but the aristocrats and
monasteries would not be happy, and might oppose reforms and create
chaos in Tibet.

The faith of Tibetans in the Dalai Lama was brought home to me
again on this trip by my own family. My father heard that the Dalai
Lama would be going back to Tibet through Chengdu, so he came to
Chengdu to try to see him. The Dalai Lama very graciously agreed to
give an audience to my father, who prostrated himself and presented a
ceremonial scarf. My father was thrilled and stayed a few days with me.

On the evening of the May First celebration there was a fireworks display, and the other staff invited my father to the eighth floor to watch. I had other work and was not there. My father liked to drink and got so drunk that he had trouble walking down the stairs to our room. The Dalai Lama actually held his hand and helped him walk to our room, but by then my father was so inebriated that he did not recognize him. Later, when he found out that the Dalai Lama had helped him to walk downstairs, he was afraid I would be angry and asked the others to keep that a secret from me. However, he was enormously proud that the Dalai Lama had helped him, and when he went back to Batang, I heard that he told people, "Come here to touch my hand. My hand can bless you because it was held by the Dalai Lama." When he was about to leave Chengdu for home, he was very happy and told me, "After meeting the Dalai Lama, my life is complete."

The Dalai Lama then prepared to leave for Tibet. I hadn't mentioned I would be returning to Beijing until just before he left Chengdu. At this time, I told him that I would stay in Beijing to attend the Central Party School for a year and then I would return to Tibet. He told me to return quickly.

CHAPTER 17

Beginning Reforms

My year in the Central Party School in Beijing flew by. It was exciting for me, and I learned a great deal. Then, just before my graduation, Wang Feng called and told me that Vice Premier Chen Yi needed a Tibetan cadre to accompany him to Lhasa, where he was going to represent the central government at the inauguration of the Preparatory Committee for the Tibet Autonomous Region. "We decided you should go as his special consultant," he said. I was happy to go and, together with Zhang Jingwu and Wang Feng, became vice head of the delegation (which consisted of about sixty people from different nationalities plus about eight hundred staff, performers, etc.). We left Beijing in mid-March 1956.

Along the way, we stopped in Xi'an and held a meeting of the entire delegation. Zhang Jingwu and Wang Feng gave speeches about the central government's policy toward Tibet and nationalities in general, and I gave a speech on understanding nationality and religion in Tibet.

It was somewhat irritating for me to hear both Zhang and Wang say basically that since Tibetans did not know anything, the delegation should direct the work in Tibet. It must have also irritated Chen Yi, because after we finished he spoke, criticizing Zhang and Wang indirectly by saying that when they got to Tibet they should consider themselves students and guests, not teachers and higher authorities of the central government. "We don't really know about Tibet's situation," he said, "so we should learn from Tibetans instead of ordering them around. We should be careful not to adopt the attitude that we Chinese are the big nationality and Tibetans are the small minority nationality." It was wonderful for me to hear a top-level official saying this.

At our next stop, in Xining, the capital of Qinghai Province, we received the stunning news that Chairman Khrushchev had issued "a secret report" in which he severely criticized Stalin. The Chinese central government ordered the content of the report distributed to higher officials, and in Xining we attended a meeting at which most provincial level officials were present. There was great surprise and consternation. Most of us could not believe that Stalin had done the horrendous things Khrushchev said he had. Stalin was like a god to us, and some shed tears. I didn't like this criticism of Stalin at all.

At the end of the meeting, Chen Yi said, "Under the leadership of Stalin, the Soviet Union has had great achievements; however, it is also possible that Stalin made mistakes. But since Stalin was like a teacher, it is okay for a student to say that his teacher has made a mistake. However, comparing Stalin's achievements to his mistakes, his achievements are clearly more important." Chen Yi did not actually say Khrushchev was wrong, but from his words I thought he believed so. All the officials liked Chen Yi's contextualization.

We then broke up into smaller discussion groups, and at my meeting, I said, "This report did not say anything about Khrushchev's own mistakes. He made no self-criticism. Khrushchev was a coal miner before Stalin raised him to his present position. If Khrushchev says Stalin was a butcher, then he was the person who took orders from the butcher. And since Khrushchev held many posts in the Soviet Union under Stalin, he also had responsibility for wrongdoing. Moreover, Khrushchev's speech at Stalin's funeral talked of Stalin as a father and teacher and highly praised his achievements, but now, after Stalin's death, he has accused him of being a butcher. Such behavior does not make sense to me." I thought Khrushchev was not telling the whole story.

From Xining, we took cars and on April 17, 1956, arrived in Lhasa. Just before arriving, Chen asked me to sit with him in his car. As we drove through the city together, Chen was stunned by the majesty and grandeur of the Potala Palace. "You Tibetans," he said, "are a great nationality. It is amazing that over a thousand years ago you were able to build such a magnificent building." Chen was also an army marshal; I found it interesting that he sized up Lhasa quickly, and said, "If one holds the hills where the Potala and the Jagpori Medical School are, one controls Lhasa."

Then we began a whirlwind of meetings and celebrations. Chen Yi presided over the ceremonies opening the Preparatory Committee for the Tibet Autonomous Region and held meetings with the Dalai Lama, the Panchen Lama, and other high Tibetan officials. The political goal of establishing the Preparatory Committee of the TAR was to gradually replace the traditional Tibetan government and feudal society. We did not say that in public, but most people knew it. Nevertheless, many Tibetans thought the autonomous region was acceptable because the Dalai Lama was its head.

In Xining, Chen had asked me to write a memo for him about what kinds of questions Tibetan lay people and monks would ask him. I wrote that most questions would relate to nationalities policy, Chinese-Tibetan relations, and reforms, particularly since reforms were being started in the Tibetan areas of Sichuan Province (in Kham). He therefore had time to think about what to say and spoke carefully and thoughtfully.

He did not say that reforms were imminent, but he didn't say they would be postponed indefinitely, either. Rather, he stated clearly that reforms would be carried out in Tibet at some point because without them Tibet would not be able to develop and improve its standard of living. But he also left it vague as to when this would occur, and emphasized that reforms would be carried out only after discussions with both the upper circles and the masses. Moreover, he said, the reforms would be implemented so as to be beneficial to both. He assured the elite that they need not worry about their standard of living because the reforms would not reduce the upper circle's income. "The central government," he said, "has a policy of reimbursement that will actually improve your living standard. So you do not need to be afraid when you hear the term 'reform.'" I agreed. In all his comments, he strongly emphasized that if we rushed and forced people to reform, it would bring an undesirable result.

Interestingly, at a meeting of the Tibet Work Committee, Chen Yi pointed to a map and said that in the future it would be good if Lhasa became the center of a Tibet Autonomous Region that included all the ethnic Tibetan areas, including those now in other provinces. This would be good for the friendship of Chinese and Tibetans, and it would also be good for Tibet's development. This had also been proposed in 1953 by Derge Sey (Kesang Wangdü) and other Khampa representatives at a meeting in Beijing, but had not been followed up on. I thought a lot about this after Chen Yi made his comment, and felt that doing this would make reforming Tibet much easier; but to be honest, I could not

Figure 22. Inspecting PLA troops at ceremonies marking the establishment of the Preparatory Committee for the Tibet Autonomous Region, Lhasa, 1956. *Front row, from left:* Phünwang, the Dalai Lama, Chen Yi, and the Panchen Lama.

tell whether these were his own views or ones that had been discussed by the Central Committee of the party.

Despite Chen Yi's moderate comments and reassurances about reforms, and his expressions of respect and admiration for Tibetan culture, the atmosphere within the Tibet Work Committee was more extreme than when I had left in 1953. Returning to Lhasa after a lapse of three years, I found a heightened eagerness among the Tibet Work Committee cadres for starting reforms quickly. Trial reforms were already being discussed for later that year, and the Panchen Lama said at the Preparatory Committee meeting that he wanted to carry out trial reforms in his area.

Of course, it was not just Lhasa that was changing. During the summer of 1955, Chairman Mao moved to the left, criticizing the party and the government for moving too slowly to implement socialism in China, meaning agricultural collectives. This precipitated the socialist transformation campaign, in which officials throughout China rushed to set up communes. This leftist surge created conflicting strategies in Tibet. On the one hand, the central government had repeatedly said that reforms in Tibet should not be rushed and that implementation required the agreement of the upper circles. On the other hand, Chairman Mao was now saying that China was lagging behind and must implement socialist reforms quickly. These were not incompatible views, and Chairman Mao might not have meant to include Tibet, but because he had not clarified the issue, there was ambiguity. In Lhasa, Fan Ming had been eager to start reforms from the beginning, so he took the new socialist transformation as a signal to push for their rapid implementation. At this time, Fan was the dominant leader in Tibet, since both Zhang Jingwu and Zhang Guohua were often away. Zhang Guohua had heart problems and insomnia in Tibet and did not stay there for long periods, and Zhang Jingwu had other responsibilities in Beijing, so the day-to-day operations were controlled by Fan and his lieutenants from the Northwest Bureau. The call from Chairman Mao to transform China gave him, he thought, the sanction from the top to move toward implementing reforms in Tibet, especially since Li Jingquan, the head party secretary in Sichuan, had begun reforms there (in the Tibetan areas as well as the Han), as had Gao Feng in Qinghai.

Under the leadership of Fan Ming, therefore, plans were made to start trial reforms in Tibet later in 1956, and Fan set about creating the needed infrastructure for implementing full reforms by recruiting many thousands of Chinese cadres from inland China. (I heard that most of the Chinese cadres were from areas under the old Northwest Bureau, such as Gansu and Shanxi.) He also started to recruit and train thousands of local Tibetans to be ready to serve as local cadres. But he made no formal announcement of his plans. He did everything quietly, within the Tibet Work Committee.

The influx of so many Han cadres into Tibet created an acute shortage of housing, so Fan went on a spree buying houses, mostly from the aristocratic elite. In Lhasa, most aristocrats were landowners, their wealth deriving mainly from their manorial estates. With the exception of a few trader aristocrats, they did not have much money because they were not in business. But when Fan bought houses from them, he inadvertently transformed many into capitalist aristocrats, because they used this money to do business with India. People told me that there were thousands of mules carrying cargo every day between Kalimpong and Yadong. And during that period, ten to fifteen government trucks loaded with silver coins came to Lhasa each day from inland China. I actually heard that most of the silver coinage in Chinese banks was brought to Tibet (and most of this ultimately flowed into India through Nepal,

Sikkim, and Bhutan). Later on, this made it easier for the elite to flee into exile in India.

I was not happy with this turn of events, and I soon had a chance to do something about it. I had planned to return to Beijing with Chen Yi to participate in the National People's Congress meeting, which was scheduled to start in mid-September 1956. However, just before we were to leave, Zhang Guohua, Zhang Jingwu, and Wang Feng told me that Li Jingquan's implementation of socialist reforms in Kham had encountered some problems, and they wanted me to return to Beijing via Kham to assess the situation. They had recently sent an investigation group from Lhasa to Kham, but they thought that since I could talk frankly with both local cadres and the leading local figures, I could obtain a better sense of what Tibetans there really felt about these reforms and what had actually happened. I was instructed to go on to Beijing from Kham and report my results directly to the central government.

Chen Yi returned to Beijing on May 31, and soon afterward I left by car for Tartsedo. Along the way, I met with many leaders and important figures, such as my old friends Chagö Tomden and Panda Tobgye. Everyone told me the same story—that the reforms in Kham had been done poorly and in a rush. There was inadequate planning and no careful discussions with upper-strata Tibetans. In Tartsedo, I also discussed this with Tibetan cadres, most of whom were my former subordinates from Batang. They reported the same thing. Finally I met Zhang Xiaoming, the Han Chinese who headed the investigation group sent from Lhasa. He not only reinforced verbally what I had found but gave me lots of detailed materials about the reforms that revealed how this had led to some revolts. It seemed clear that the leaders in Tartsedo had simply ordered people to implement the reforms. All of this was disturbing. For the first time, I started thinking seriously that there was something wrong with the way the party was pursuing its nationality policy for Tibetans.

When I arrived in Beijing in late June, Wang Feng arranged for me to report my findings to Li Weihan (then the head of the United Front Work Department) and Ulanhu (the head of the State Nationalities Affairs Commission). I thought a lot about how best to do this, and decided that it would be most effective for me to present the results primarily as Zhang Xiaoming's findings, because he was a Han Chinese and the head of the special investigation group. I feared that if I gave a negative report on my own, they might think that my judgment was colored by my being Tibetan. I gave my comments verbally and then gave them Zhang's written report. I emphasized strongly that when we conducted reforms in

Tibet in the future, we should first plan well according to the local people's needs and, critically, discuss the reforms carefully with the upper circles. Li Weihan and Ulanhu said my comments were valuable and would be reported to the higher authorities. Later, I was happy to learn that both Mao and Zhou Enlai had signed the summary document made of my report, indicating they had actually read it.

After the National People's Congress meetings, Zhou Enlai invited all the Tibetan deputies to a meeting on September 20, together with the Tibetan delegates who had just attended the meetings of the People's Political Consultative Conference. He said that the reforms in Kham had encountered many problems, and the central government was paying special attention to the problem by sending Liu Geping, a senior official in the State Nationalities Affairs Commission, to investigate the situation and correct any mistakes. Zhou Enlai also said that as for Tibet, the reforms had not yet started and would not be started for at least another six years. "And when we start reforms there in the future," he said, "they will not be conducted in the rushed manner of Kham, but instead we will consult with both higher and lower circles and make sure that they are carried out in a 'gentle' way." Therefore, he said, "you delegates should not be alarmed by the events in Kham." I was instructed to go to Tibet to report this to the Dalai Lama and the other officials of the Lhasa government. Che Jigme was sent to do this for the Panchen Lama.

In November 1956, I went back to Tibet. Although we could not eliminate the harm done in Kham, I thought Zhou Enlai's response was good. On the way, I stopped in Tartsedo, and there met with a much colder reception than when I had passed through on my way to Beijing. The party secretary was now saying that Tian Bao and I were opposed to reforms. I rejected that completely and said clearly that I did not oppose reforms. They were definitely necessary, I said, but how and when to do them were critical, and they had been incorrectly implemented here.

After I arrived in Lhasa, it became my main responsibility to propagate the central government's instructions and views to people outside the party, particularly the Dalai Lama and the higher Tibetan officials. I also called together the many Khampa traders in Lhasa to explain this. It was not easy, because the situation was tense. Liu Geping's investigation criticized the way reforms had been started in Kham, and this led to some changes in their implementation, but the central government decided not to stop the reforms. It accepted that there had been mistakes but instructed only that these should be improved or corrected. Consequently, there was one nationality in China—Tibetans—with two nationality policies: one for Tibet and one for Kham/Amdo. The reforms continued, and this led to the serious uprising in 1958–1959.

It was frustrating for me because the central government did not seem to understand the relationship between Kham and Tibet. While it was true that the Seventeen-Point Agreement was enacted for Tibet proper, not for the ethnic Tibetan areas of Kham and Amdo, Tibetans in all three were of the same nationality, with the same religion, identity, and language. Therefore, whatever happened on the eastern side of the Drichu River would inevitably have a major impact on the western side. Even though the central government said that the reforms would be delayed in Tibet, the way they conducted the reforms and handled the situation in the eastern Tibetan areas affected the attitude of Tibetans in Tibet, who worried that the same thing would happen to them. If you kill a sheep on one side of the pen, it will certainly scare the sheep on the other side. When the central government carried out two different policies for one nationality, it caused the problems of the late 1950s. I still firmly believed that reforms were necessary, but it was very sad to see them being done in a way that was producing such a negative effect on Tibetans in Lhasa. Despite this, I never dreamed that this trouble in Kham would soon spread to the whole of Tibet, and that in two and a half years, it would lead to the uprising of 1959.

PART IV

Incarceration

CHAPTER 18

Tension in Lhasa

In 1956, the Indian government invited the Dalai and Panchen Lamas to India to participate in the Buddhajayanti, the celebration of the 2,500th anniversary of the birth of the Buddha. The Tibet Work Committee did not think giving the Dalai Lama permission to leave the country was a good idea, but they were overridden by the central government, which instructed them to allow the lamas to decide for themselves whether they wanted to go. When they both chose to attend, the Tibet Work Committee discussed the possibility of my accompanying the Dalai Lama, but in the end it was decided that it would be inappropriate, because to do so would look like we did not trust him.

The Dalai Lama arrived in New Delhi on December 5, 1956, and began a four-month stay that was more than just a religious visit. The implementation of reforms in Kham earlier that year had precipitated a rebellion there that in turn had brought the United States Central Intelligence Agency into the picture.

One of the Dalai Lama's brothers, Gyalo Thondup, was a leader of an anticommunist Tibetan group in Kalimpong that urged the Dalai Lama to go into exile and fight the Chinese with U.S. assistance. Another brother, Taktse Rimpoche, came from America and also tried to persuade him not to return to China. At the same time, others, like Ngabö, questioned this advice and challenged those advocating that the Dalai Lama stay in exile to show evidence that the U.S. was really willing to help Tibet.

While this was unfolding in India, Zhou Enlai stopped twice in New Delhi (on a trip to Nepal) and talked with the Dalai Lama about this, urging him to return to Lhasa. He brought a guarantee from Mao Zedong that there would be no reforms in Tibet for at least the next six years, and that there could be a further postponement after that if conditions were not appropriate. Prime Minister Nehru also advised the Dalai Lama to return. — Goldstein, Sherap, and Siebenschuh

Before the Dalai Lama made his final decision, Ngabö returned to Tibet, using as a pretext the fact that his wife (who had accompanied him) was close to giving birth. I was in Lhasa when he arrived, so I heard firsthand his account of what was going on in India. He obviously thought that things were serious because he requested two things from Tan Guansan, then the top-ranking cadre in Lhasa. The first was that he be allowed to join the Communist Party. This was first time that he had asked this.

The second request was even more surprising. He said that if things came to a point where the Communist Party and the PLA were not able to remain in Tibet, he wanted the PLA to take him and his family with them. I was genuinely amazed because it meant that he thought there was a reasonable chance that the Tibetan government would actually drive out the PLA. He must have thought the claims of support from the United States were plausible, but if Ngabö believed that the central government might be pushed out of Tibet, what must the other Tibetan officials be thinking? It didn't speak well for future stability in Tibet.

Ngabö's two requests were reported to the higher authorities in Beijing, although Tan Guansan assured Ngabö that he didn't have to worry about leaving because there would never be a time when the PLA would not be in Tibet. To the party's great relief, all of this became moot when the Dalai Lama decided to return rather than live in exile. He arrived in Lhasa on April 1, 1957.

In the summer of 1957, I returned to Beijing to attend that year's session of the National People's Congress. Not long after I arrived, Wang Feng invited me to meet with him and asked me about the situation in Tibet. He started off by flattering me: "You are not only the highest Tibetan cadre in the party but also a Tibetan leader who has won the trust and respect of Mao Zedong, Zhou Enlai, and other top leaders, like Chen Yi and Li Weihan. Harmony among leaders is important, and at present there seems to be a problem concerning the relationships among the party leaders in Tibet. As the only Tibetan in the Leadership Committee," he said, "tell me honestly what you think about the party leaders in Tibet and any problems you see there. I will report your thoughts and suggestions to the central government."

Such a politically sensitive question about my superiors was unexpected and put me in an awkward position. However, I had a good impression of Wang from past contacts, and since he was the deputy director of the State Nationalities Affairs Commission, he seemed the right person to be asking questions like this. I decided to speak freely. "To tell you the truth," I said, "Zhang Jingwu and Zhang Guohua are working in accordance with the central government's nationality policy, but Fan Ming is doing things that seem to contradict it." I elaborated, and then said that I thought if the central government did not keep a close eye on what Fan Ming was doing, more problems were likely to occur in Tibet in the future. Wang paid close attention, but it was hard to tell exactly what he was thinking. When I finished speaking, he thanked me and said, "You are right. Fan Ming worked under me in the past. As I remember, I thought he was flashy, without substance."

I was relieved to hear this, and immediately felt more comfortable about what I had just said. Moreover, I was impressed at how well informed the leaders from the central government seemed to be about what was happening in Tibet. Later I would learn that saying this was the worst thing I could have done.

That year's National People's Congress meetings were not especially eventful until the end, when Wang Feng told the minority delegates that the central government was going to convene a special meeting to discuss our concerns at Qingdao, a resort area not far from Beijing. He urged us to share our thoughts frankly, saying, "If you have any suggestions, you can tell us your true thoughts. These will assist us in improving our work in minority areas. You don't need to worry; your suggestions will not be put into your records."

The Qingdao meeting began in July 1957. It was attended by the minority nationality delegates to the National People's Congress, as well as those attending the Political Consultative Conference. Everyone met first in a plenary session and then in smaller groupings. Tibetans comprised one such group, although within it there were also subgroups, like the group of Tibetan Communist Party members.

At the first plenary session, there were many complaints that all the power in minority areas was in the hands of the Han Chinese cadres, although minority officials often had impressive titles. One delegate, for example, complained that in his area the head of a rural township walked, while his subordinate accountant, a Han Chinese, rode.

The delegates from Xinjiang thought that the answer to this problem was to make major changes. They argued forcefully that the current structure of minority autonomous regions needed revision, and called on the Central Committee to establish a system of minority "republics" [ch. *lianbang*] analogous to that of the "socialist republics" in the Soviet Union. This would give greater autonomy and power to the minority cadres and their governments vis-à-vis the Han. Intellectually I agreed, but strategically I thought that such a system would be very difficult to achieve in Tibet. Not only would there be opposition from Han cadres, but on the Tibetan side there were many problems that would have to be solved, for example, the relationship among the subethnic regions of Amdo, Kham, and Central Tibet, as well as the relations between the Tibetan government and the Panchen Lama's government. But the idea created a lot of excitement.

The Tibetan delegates did not raise any big issues like this at the plenary sessions. However, at the smaller, all-Tibetan session, Derge Sey suggested that the central government should transfer four counties (Gönchen, Beiyül, Dengko, and Seshü) from Derge (in Sichuan) to Chamdo (in Tibet). He argued that this made sense because the queen of Derge was already a deputy director of the Liberation Committee of Chamdo, and Jomda County—which was historically part of Derge—was administratively under Chamdo.

I knew immediately that this wasn't going to be a popular idea with the government. In fact, I thought it was a ploy by the Derge delegates to avoid having to undergo the socialist reform process that was in progress in Kham, so I said quickly, "This will never happen. If our group suggests moving Derge administratively to Tibet/Chamdo, other Khampa areas in Sichuan will request the same kind of treatment. Consequently, I doubt that the central government will want to set a precedent by agreeing to shift Derge." Ngabö and most other Tibetans agreed with my opinion, and the idea was dropped. We then discussed other minor suggestions. During these discussions, a Chinese official from the United Front Work Department was taking minutes of our group's conversations. I did not pay attention to him, but in retrospect, I should have.

The next day, we had a small meeting of Tibetan Communist Party members. The head of our group was Tian Bao (the governor of Tartsedo). He had not been present the previous day, and immediately he came to me and said, "I don't understand you people. Why on earth did you decide to suggest shifting Derge to Chamdo?" Confused, I asked what he meant. He said, "I saw in the report of yesterday's meeting that your group recommended that the central government should move Derge. Your name," he said pointedly, "was specifically listed among those who made this suggestion." I was startled and quickly explained how the discussion had actually gone. "The person taking the minutes of the meeting must have gotten confused," I assured him. But I was troubled about the way things had been misrepresented and added, "As the head of the Tibetan party members' group, would you please explain what really happened to Ulanhu and Wang Feng?" Tian Bao promised he would, but I decided not to leave things to him, and went to explain what happened myself.

I didn't think this confusion about what we had suggested was deliberate. As I thought back over the events of our meeting, I remembered that after we discussed the shifting of Derge, Ngabö suggested that before the democratic reforms began in Derge we should ask the central government to take special care of a very important Red Hat sect (Nyingmapa) monastery there. We all agreed on this point, and I guessed that the person taking the minutes must have confused this approval with our reaction to the earlier discussion. Still, I decided to follow my instincts and tell the higher-ups the truth myself.

When I found them, they were busy playing mahjong, so at first I simply watched and said nothing. (When one person dropped out of the game, they invited me to take his place, but they were using a complex Chinese scoring system, so I declined.) I was impatient to set the record straight, but they were engrossed in the game, having a good time, and it didn't feel like the right moment to interrupt them with a business matter. I waited and watched for a while longer, hoping they would stop. They didn't, however, and I finally decided that my telling Tian Bao was enough and left.

The next day, I got a message that Zhou Enlai had arrived in Qingdao and wanted to meet with Ngabö and me. When we arrived, Zhou didn't waste any time. "There are several things I want to discuss with you," he said. "First, it is not appropriate to consider changing the border of Tibet." At first I wasn't sure what he was getting at, so when Ngabö asked me to translate what Zhou had said, I didn't know exactly what to tell him. Then it suddenly came to me that Zhou must be referring to our meeting, and I asked him if he meant the administrative change for Derge. When he said yes, I quickly told him about the mistake and explained that I had already told Tian Bao what really happened. "Okay, okay," he said. "It must be the recorder who made the mistake. Let's just forget about it." He then went on to talk with us about a plan to tap a major geothermal energy source in northern Tibet, and I assumed that the record had now been set straight once and for all. I would later learn it had not.

Soon after this meeting, Ngabö and I took a military airplane back to Lhasa, where I quickly became involved in an interesting incident and forgot about the misunderstanding in Beijing. What happened was this. The previous year a young Tibetan peasant named Wangye Phüntso had attended a training class for implementing democratic reforms in Gyantse against the orders of his lord, who wanted him to do corvée work and not go to school. When Wangye ignored his lord, the local headman whipped him for his disobedience.

On the face of it, the incident seemed both ordinary and unimportant. A serf being whipped by his lord was a common occurrence at that time. However, Fan Ming saw the incident as an opportunity to attack the Tibetan government and its traditional institutions. First he published an account of the whipping in the *Tibet Daily* newspaper, which was under his control. Then he called a meeting of the Tibet Work Committee, where he strongly urged that the Tibetan lord be punished to prevent future incidents like this. He argued that if Tibetan officials or lords were allowed to persecute common Tibetans who wanted to serve us as cadres, local Tibetans would be afraid to work for us in the future. I became directly involved in this when Fan Ming suggested that I should be sent to settle the problem.

It was not a simple issue. The Tibetan government still retained judicial authority over Tibetans, so any intervention by us to settle a conflict between a lord and his serf would constitute a direct challenge to their authority. I thought that must be why Fan Ming suggested that I should be sent. He wanted a Tibetan to be the one to challenge the Tibetan government.

I, however, did not want to undermine the Tibetan government's authority. I was still committed to fostering change in Tibet gradually through the Dalai Lama and the Tibetan elite, so I decided to settle this issue by mutual agreement rather than force. I thought the incident was minor and should not be treated more seriously than it deserved. I also thought it was a bit unfair, since when Fan Ming's soldiers did similar things to the local Tibetans, he did not treat their transgressions seriously.

I brought a number of Tibetan government officials (who were also part of the Preparatory Committee for the Tibet Autonomous Region) with me to investigate the incident. We began by asking Wangye Phüntso and the local headman who whipped him to explain exactly what had happened and why. After sifting through their testimony and other accounts, we decided to follow Tibetan custom and try to arrange a compromise. We asked the headman to apologize, and we gave some money to Wangye Phüntso to help him "recover" from his beating. As we expected, they both accepted our decision, and the matter was closed.

When I returned to Lhasa and made my report to the Tibet Work Committee, Fan Ming was not pleased, because he had wanted us to act unilaterally, thereby setting a precedent for subsequent interventions. However, although I had been able to block Fan Ming's plan, in one sense even what I did broke new ground. This incident should have been settled entirely by the Tibetan government, so this joint investigation/settlement represented the first time that the Preparatory Committee for the Tibet Autonomous Region had exercised limited authority. It was also the first time an official had apologized to a serf.

Meanwhile, in the larger world around us, tensions were rapidly rising. Although Mao had said clearly that there would be no reforms conducted in Tibet, he did not extend that policy to Eastern Tibetans living in Qinghai, Gansu, Sichuan, and Yunnan. Socialist reforms, therefore, continued to be implemented in these areas, and many Tibetans rose up in a series of bloody rebellions. The PLA was able to suppress them, but in the process many rebels fled to Tibet proper. In 1957 and early 1958, a stream of armed Khampa refugees (often with their families) came to Lhasa, bringing firsthand accounts of what had happened in their areas. It was a public-relations disaster for us. I remember one case personally.

In late 1957 (or perhaps it was early 1958), Chanju-la, a prominent woman from my hometown of Batang, fled to Lhasa in a truck and went to stay with her uncle, the council minister Surkhang. I was living next door to Surkhang at the time, and learned of this early one morning when I was having my breakfast and she suddenly showed up at my door. I was surprised to see her, especially looking so poor. She was from one of the biggest aristocratic families in Batang, but she now wore shabby clothing. "Phünwang," she said, "look at me, I have become a beggar." Genuinely surprised, I asked her what had happened. She said that after democratic reforms began in Batang there was an uprising, and the Chöde monastery was bombed by airplanes. She said her husband's sister-in-law had been so severely beaten at public "struggle" meetings that she eventually committed suicide by jumping into the river. She said she also had been struggled against, and all her property had been confiscated with no compensation. Overnight, she said, she had become penniless. She told me a host of painful details about how she had suffered and asked me to help her get medical treatment in Lhasa. Taken aback by what I had just heard, I urged her to join me for breakfast and promised to help.

While we were eating, she told me more stories about how the democratic reforms had been implemented in Kham. Because I was a party member and cadre, I knew she was probably moderating what she said, but I was sure that she would hold nothing back when she talked with Surkhang. As I listened to her, it was easy to imagine the effect such stories were going to have. For a long time, we had been assuring people that reforms would be postponed for six or more years, and that when they were eventually implemented, the livelihood of the upper circles would be improved, not reduced. Now I realized that while we were confidently saying these things, people like her were pouring in from Kham and telling their relatives and friends a very different story. How could someone like Surkhang believe our promises when his cousin was telling him her real experiences?

As more and more armed Khampas poured into Lhasa, rumors arose that they and the Tibetan government were planning to attack the PLA militarily. Many Han cadres became extremely suspicious. Chen Mengyi, the commander of the PLA in Lhasa, for example, one day reported to Zhang Jingwu that the Tibetan government was gathering armed people from all parts of Tibet in the vicinity of Lhasa. I was skeptical, but I said nothing until a few days later, when Chen reported to Zhang Jingwu that five hundred or six hundred horsemen had arrived in the Lhamön area below Ganden monastery.

I knew Chen's main concern was that if the Tibetan government was preparing for war, then the PLA should also prepare for war. But I was sure that this was unnecessary, so in front of Zhang Jingwu, I told Chen that his information could not possibly be accurate. I was familiar with Lhamön, and so was Zhang Jingwu. In 1951, he and I had ridden horses to Ganden monastery to give alms to the monks, and we had passed Lhamön on the way. There were only a few households in the village, and there was no possible way the people there could feed five hundred to six hundred horses and soldiers. So I warned that misleading information such as this was dangerous and could exacerbate tension between the PLA and the Tibetan government. As the village was nearby, I suggested that Zhang should drive there with some Tibetan cadres and find out what was really happening. Zhang thought for a moment and then agreed. "Without hard evidence," he said, "we should not change the PLA's status and needlessly frighten the Tibetan government."

The next day, an official party went to Lhamön. When they returned, they reported that they had not found any horsemen there. Instead, they had found animals that villagers had brought back from their mountain pastures and had left outside to graze. When Chen's source had seen these animals at night, he obviously thought they were armed horsemen. It was a close call. The tension and suspicion on both sides had risen so high that I honestly think that if I had not been in Tibet at the time, Zhang Jingwu would have listened to Chen. The PLA would then have started to prepare for war, and this in turn could have moved the Tibetan government to retaliatory action.

Everyone was on edge now and ready to find danger in even the slightest incidents. One day Phüntso Tashi, a translator for Zhang Jingwu in Lhasa, told me that a cat had sneaked into his apartment the previous night and woken him up. He didn't pay any attention to it himself, but the next morning a Chinese couple who shared the apartment with him said that when they heard the noise (made by the cat) they thought the Tibetan government's soldiers (who guarded the house because it was owned by the Dalai Lama) were quietly trying to enter the apartment. They told Phüntso Tashi that they were so frightened they stood beside their door with guns for the rest of the night.

On the Tibetan government's side there were also incendiary rumors flying about—for example, rumors that reforms would be carried out soon and the estates and properties of the aristocracy and monasteries would be confiscated. Some aristocrats quietly started to move their wealth to India. Even progressives, like my old friend Chagö Tomden of Derge, did the same. He had a close relationship with the CCP and was serving as an official in Sichuan, so he had no trouble borrowing three trucks from the PLA by telling them that his grandson Namgye Dorje and his daughter wanted to go to Lhasa on a pilgrimage. They did, but actually he sent his most important valuables with them and then secretly had the valuables transported to India.

One day Chen Mengyi came to see me about the grandson and said, "We lent our old friends Chagö Tomden and Namgye Dorje 150,000 silver dollars [*dayan*] to buy grain from Shigatse. However, several months have passed, and he has not yet given us the grain. You are good friends with the family; please ask him to give us the grain as soon as possible." I spoke with Namgye Dorje immediately about the whereabouts of the promised grain. "Don't try to get cute," I told him frankly. "Remember that your grandfather is still in Tartsedo in the grasp of the Chinese." He knew exactly what I meant and assured me that he would produce the grain soon, but I don't recall if he ever did. Later I learned that soon after this he became a general in Chushigandrug, the Tibetan guerrilla army that Khampas started in Lhasa in 1958.

Not long after this, a strange event occurred that further exacerbated the general tension. A Han Chinese soldier who was about to be transferred from Lhasa to inland China wanted to see the Potala before he went back. When he tried to enter the palace, he was stopped by two Tibetan guards, who told him he needed a letter from the Tibetan government's army office [tib. *dmag spyi khang*]. He argued that he was leaving soon and didn't have time to get the necessary permit, but the guards refused to let him enter, and when he kept insisting and acting strangely, they arrested him. That's when they found he was carrying two hand grenades. (Nobody ever found out for sure why.) The guards suspected that he might have been planning to kill the Dalai Lama, so they detained him and ultimately gave him a whipping. This in turn caused an uproar in the ranks of the PLA and the Tibet Work Committee, because the Tibetan government did not have the authority to apprehend or punish PLA soldiers.

Chen Mengyi asked me to try to secure the soldier's release, and I went to see the Dalai Lama's brother-in-law, General Phüntso Tashi. He explained exactly what had happened and why the soldier had been detained and punished. "Phünwang-la," he said, "this is not just a casual incident." When I told Chen Mengyi the details, including the fact of the two grenades, he was genuinely surprised. He said he had no idea what the soldier could have been thinking, and I believed him. Among other reasons, I was sure that if the PLA had any designs on the Dalai Lama, they certainly wouldn't act in such a clumsy or haphazard way. And I was certain that they meant the Dalai Lama no harm. When I met again with Phüntso Tashi, I told him that our military headquarters knew nothing about the incident and there was absolutely no plan to harm the Dalai Lama. My advice was that the Tibetan side should release the misguided soldier immediately and let him go back to China. He agreed, and ten or fifteen days later the PLA soldier was released.

My life during these months was as full of movement and change as the times themselves. In the midst of the volatility and political tension caused by the Khampas collecting in Lhasa, I went to Beijing to attend the 1958 session of the National People's Congress. It was the time of the "Antirightist" campaign, and I recall that Wang Feng made a speech at the Political Consultative Congress meeting in which he said forcefully that we had to oppose local nationalism.[1]

Only a year earlier, in 1957, Mao had said we had to oppose local nationalism *and* Great Han Chauvinism. Wang Feng, however, didn't mention Great Han Chauvinism at all. I was bothered by this. "Why is he changing things now?" I wondered. But I didn't have much time to think about it, because soon I was on the way back to Lhasa. Or so I thought.

There was nothing out of the ordinary about the first part of the trip. I stopped in Chengdu to visit my two sons, who were enrolled in the 18th Army's kindergarten boarding school. Then, just as I was about to leave for Lhasa, I received a phone call from Zhang Jingwu in Beijing asking me to return immediately. He was a little vague about why. There were various things to do, he said. Loose ends to tie up. I suspected nothing and returned as he requested. I would not leave Beijing again for twenty-two years.

---

1. "Local nationalism" (ch. *difang minzu zhuyi*) refers to a complex of characteristics including placing the interests of one's local nationality above the interests of the nation, being hostile to other nationalities, and, in the extreme, advocating nationality separatism. — *Goldstein, Sherap, and Siebenschuh*

CHAPTER 19

Labeled a Local Nationalist

I returned to Beijing in April 1958. When I asked Zhang Jingwu what they wanted me to do, he said the Central Committee was going to make a change in my work assignment, but Deng Xiaoping and Politburo member Peng Zhen were away from Beijing, so I would have to wait to hear. I had no sense that there was anything wrong. I actually thought they might want me to take on additional responsibilities in Tibet. I didn't get suspicious until days went by with Zhang refusing to say anything at all about the change in my assignment. I started to wonder why he was avoiding the subject.

After days of waiting, I was finally told to go to a meeting at which I would learn the Central Committee's decision. When I arrived, Zhang Jingwu and Zhang Guohua were already there. Wang Feng was unable to attend and had sent Liu Chun (vice director of the State Nationalities Affairs Commission) in his place. Zhang Jingwu spoke first.

"As you know well," he said, "we are opposed to local nationalism. You have said and done things that suggest that you harbor thoughts of local nationalism. Because you are the leading Tibetan cadre, the Central Committee has decided it is better to stop your work in Tibet and bring you to Beijing instead. Your new work assignment will be as deputy director of the Nationalities Institute at the Chinese Academy of Social Sciences." Then he dropped the real bombshell. "However, you should consider that now you have two tasks. The first is to do your job. *The second is to cleanse your thinking.*"

I was stunned. I had worked side by side with Zhang Jingwu and Zhang Guohua for nearly eight years, and I never dreamed that they thought of me as someone who needed to *cleanse* his thinking. To be honest, I wasn't even sure exactly what it was about my thinking they were referring to. "Local nationalism thought," I said, "is a very general term. If you could be more specific, it would help me know what things about my thinking I need to cleanse." No one said anything at first. After what seemed like minutes, Zhang Jingwu said, "Phünwang, at last year's Qingdao meeting, you agreed that Derge should become part of Chamdo. This is one of the important things you should consider."

This was insane. I couldn't believe my ears. It was hard to believe this was actually happening. "This makes no sense at all," I said. Then I told them what had really happened. "Ask Ngabö," I said. "He was at the meeting where the discussion of Derge took place. I have already clarified this issue with Zhou Enlai." I could feel myself becoming both excited and frustrated. I wanted answers. "Is there anything besides this?" I asked pointedly. "Phünwang," Zhang Guohua said slowly, "when the PLA marched into Tibet, you brought many books with you. Among those, you had Lenin's *On Nationality Self-Determination.* You need to think about that, too."

This was even more ridiculous. How could a communist's reading Lenin be wrong? I was really angry now, and my mind was racing. I had never expected something like this to happen to *me*, but I knew how things worked. They had obviously made up their minds, and it would be useless to argue with them at the moment. I turned to Liu Chun to see what criticism *he* had, and he said vaguely, "Phünwang, there are things I could say about when you worked in the State Nationalities Affairs Commission." I had no idea what he was referring to, and when I pressed him for specifics, he would say no more. I realized then that, at least for now, there was nothing more I could do.

I left the meeting as quickly as I could, trying hard not to reveal how angry I was—and how depressed. While I understood clearly that I was being accused, I still didn't understand what I was being accused of. And it hurt that the people who were accusing me were officials like Zhang Guohua and Zhang Jingwu, with whom I had worked closely for so many years. How could they possibly believe that my thinking needed cleansing? Deep down, I still thought the whole thing must be a misunderstanding that would soon be resolved. How naïve I was!

Since Wang Feng was not present at the meeting, I went to see him. Earlier, when I had worked at the State Nationalities Affairs Commission, Wang Feng and I had been very friendly, visiting each other often.

But when I tried to talk with him now, I could tell that things had changed. Suddenly it was much harder for me to see him. He made one excuse after another. I later learned that Wang was the one who had started the nationwide campaign against minority cadres, the so-called local nationalism campaign of 1957. He was behind the whole thing, and when he wanted to accuse me, Zhang Jingwu and Zhang Guohua agreed to support him.

Eventually I got to see him, and he didn't mince words. "Among the Tibetan cadres," he said, "there are three leaders whom we have been watching closely: you, Tian Bao, and Tashi Wangchuk. Tashi Wangchuk is the worst in terms of his support for local nationalism. We discussed him many times with the leaders of Qinghai and finally decided to relieve him of his position as deputy party secretary and also to lower him two ranks. We will only allow him to continue as a deputy in the National People's Congress.

"You are the second most serious problem. You know your mistakes, and you need to clean them up. We are removing you from all your positions in Tibet. Your assignment now will be to work here in Beijing in the Chinese Academy of Social Sciences and at the same time clean up your thoughts.

"Tian Bao has also made mistakes. He will continue to work where he is and at the same time clean up his thoughts. I want you to understand," he said finally, "that the party is protecting you while you go through the ordeal of rectifying your nationality thinking [ch. bao hu guo guan]. We could have expelled you from the party. Instead we are giving you a chance."

When he had finished, there was nothing for me to say. The full seriousness of my situation was clear. It was not just a simple misunderstanding. Although they said Tashi Wangchuk had the biggest problem, they allowed him to continue working in Qinghai. Yet in my case, they took all my positions away and transferred me to Beijing. How bad was it going to get?

My situation in Beijing was hard to get used to. On the one hand, I was not under arrest. I continued to receive a salary. They did not send anyone to follow me or restrict my freedom of movement. My office had to report my activities to the higher authorities, but I could go wherever I wanted. On the other hand, I really had no work to do and was alone with my thoughts much of the time. Because I had been accused of things I knew I hadn't done or said, and things that for other reasons made no sense to me, I had no idea how to confront the problem.

After they told me to clean up my mistakes, no one spoke to me about my so-called incorrect thoughts. In fact, no one from the higher author-ities paid any attention to me at all. Logically, I thought, if they felt I had made mistakes, they should have told me what they were and helped me correct them. But they never did. They just ignored me. Whenever they asked me to attend meetings, I went and listened but did not participate. I thought about what was going on all the time, and I finally concluded that perhaps they had transferred me to Beijing and put me in an unim-portant position because they just wanted to keep me out of Lhasa.

When my father learned what had happened, he made a special trip to Beijing to visit and try to comfort me. He told me a moving story that I never forgot. "Most Chinese," he said, "are not very good. But there are some really excellent individuals. I saw a Chinese platoon leader who treated his solders very well and the soldiers liked him. When the higher officials treated him and his men badly, he took about sixty soldiers with him and fled. They were good people, and while they were on the run they did not take food from the local people, even though they were hun-gry. Eventually they were captured, the leader was tied up, and his sol-ders were ordered to stab him. The soldiers were told that if they did not obey, they would be killed on the spot. When the platoon leader heard this, he told his men that they should do as they were told and not worry about him. 'You have parents and wives and children,' he said. 'You need to think about them. I am finished, so stab me, stab me.' The soldiers wept as they carried out their orders. (Ironically, they were all killed any-way.) The platoon leader was a real hero." I was moved and strength-ened by that story. I thought that a man should act like that Chinese pla-toon leader. One has to be brave whatever happens. Later, when I was in prison, I often thought about this story, and it gave me the courage to survive.

Unlike the brave platoon leader, however, I had no clear-cut "enemy" or situation to face. Try as I might, I still could not understand what I had done. I wondered if the real problem was the position I had taken regarding the pace of the reforms in Kham. But the vague charges they made against me seemed on the one hand so wrongheaded and on the other so trivial that I didn't see any point in trying to write letters of rebuttal or calling people to explain. For example, Zhang Guohua made what seemed clearly to be an accusation that I had brought Lenin's *On Nationality Self-Determination* into Tibet. But Lenin's works were one of the main sources of communist doctrine, and Lenin was considered one of the most important teachers in the Communist Party. As a student, I had read the "teacher's" [Lenin's] book, and I believed there was nothing wrong with doing that. What was I supposed to say? That I was sorry I read and appreciated Lenin? When they put a label on me like this, I felt they must have other motives. But I had no idea what they were.

In the past, I had always thought that the Communist Party was an enlightened and truthful party. Since 1949, I had seen a number of things that had bothered me, for example, the views of some officials, like Fan Ming, but these seemed isolated and idiosyncratic. Now, with the Antirightist campaign and the attacks on minority cadres like myself, I started to see a dark and unjust side within the party.

At the same time that my problems were causing me to rethink my views, I was appalled by another campaign of the central government—the Great Leap Forward. It proclaimed that within a short period of time China was going to surpass Britain and catch up to the United States in industrial production. Offices and people were encouraged to melt metal into steel. (They in fact produced mostly junk.) The whole thing was unreal—like a child's game of make-believe.

There were no meetings in Beijing to criticize me, but Lhasa was a different story. There the Tibet Work Committee gathered all Tibetan cadres for a meeting at which they informed them of my "mistakes." (I learned later that when Zhang Guohua and Zhang Jingwu went back to Lhasa, they told the Dalai Lama that I had problems regarding my thinking on nationality and nationalism and that they had arranged for me to work in a institute in Beijing while I rectified my thinking.) My secretary Kesang called me from Lhasa and told me about the Lhasa accusation meeting.

Most Tibetan cadres, Kesang said, were shocked at what the leaders said about me. In their hearts, he said, they didn't believe the accusations and so said nothing, although some jumped on the bandwagon and invented things to say about me. One from Amdo, for example, claimed I was recruiting a dangerous faction within the party. But most kept silent, and after the meeting criticized the party among themselves. They said that when the Chinese arrived in Lhasa, most of them spent their time playing mahjong and poker and generally doing nothing. "Phünwang," they said, "was like a jack-of-all-trades and used to do all sorts of things, like buying houses, establishing schools, and helping both sides understand each other better. He worked very hard. Now he is repaid with accusations of mistakes in his thinking." These accusations also had a powerful effect on many aristocrats in Lhasa. Some thought, "If the Chinese are accusing Phünwang of having mistaken thoughts, then what future do we have?"[1]

When I learned that some Tibetan cadres had attacked me at the meeting, I was shocked and hurt because I thought they were my friends. How could someone who knew me well accuse me of recruiting a faction within the party? These were the kinds of things I couldn't understand—or stop thinking about.

After I had been in Beijing for a few months, it occurred to me to call my secretary Kesang in Lhasa and have him separate my private papers from those related to the office and send them to me. I was too late. Officials of the Tibet Work Committee had already come to my office several times, he said, to search through my things, and had taken away all the documents, private as well as official. Kesang went to see the official in charge to insist that he return my private documents, and eventually he did. When these arrived in Beijing, I went over them carefully to try to see what they might be using against me. It didn't take long. As soon as I saw the letter I had written to Ngawang Kesang in 1940, I knew they would be very suspicious of it. Ngawang Kesang had had an idea that we should win over Tibetan leaders like Aba Alo in Labrang (a major Tibetan area in Gansu) and use their power to help start our revolution there. In the letter, I told him that we should make friends with Aba Alo and people like him. I cautioned, however, that we should not pin our hopes on such people. Expecting them to help us, I said, was like expecting a pig to fly—by which I meant, of course, that it was hopeless. "On the contrary," I said, "we should rely on those young Tibetans who have advanced thinking and new ideas. Now that we have an organization in our school, when we expand into the Tibetan areas, we should try to fan the small fire that is our organization into a blaze." Our Tibetan Communist Party, I wrote, could directly affiliate with the Third

1. Phünwang's detention also had an impact on the Dalai Lama, who later wrote in *Freedom in Exile* (pp. 111–12):

I always felt that so long as Phuntsog Wangyal [Phünwang] retained the confidence of Chairman Mao, there was hope for Tibet. . . . At the end of 1957, a Chinese official informed me that Phuntsog Wangyal would no longer be coming to Tibet because he was a dangerous man. . . . I was amazed to hear this, as I knew that Chairman Mao thought highly of him. . . . I was . . . even more sad when I heard, the following year, that my old friend had been stripped of office and detained. Eventually he went to jail. . . . All this despite his being a sincere and dedicated Communist, as anyone could see. It made me realise that the Chinese leadership was not truly Marxist, dedicated to a better world for all, but really highly nationalistic.

—*Goldstein, Sherap, and Siebenschuh*

Communist International (led by the Soviet Union), or it could affiliate with the Chinese Communist Party as a suborganization, or it could continue as an independent party. Whichever we ended up doing didn't really matter. What was important was that through *our* Tibetan Communist Party we would organize young Tibetan students and intellectuals to start *our own* revolution. Zhang Jingwu and Zhang Guohua, I was sure, felt this letter showed that I not only had thoughts of local nationalism, but also entertained the idea of being independent of the Chinese Communist Party.

Another document that worried me was a report I had written that detailed our plan for establishing a guerrilla force in the Kham area. It had been written in 1943 to give to Surkhang and the Council of Ministers if they expressed interest in supporting us with weapons. Its purpose was to convince them that we were serious, and it had a well-thought-out plan for launching a guerrilla war in Kham. (I thought I had destroyed it after liberation, but obviously I had not.) In the report, I used a lot of Mao's now well-known guerrilla strategies, for example, "The enemy advances, we retreat; the enemy camps, we harass; the enemy tires, we attack; and the enemy retreats, we pursue."

They also found a nationalistic song I had written just after I left Chongqing. I often had used songs rather than essays to convey our ideology because I felt they were the most effective means to reach Tibetans and spread our thinking. In this song I had said, "Our Tibetan nation with thousands of years of culture / had become outstanding during the time of the hero Songtsen Gampo [in the seventh century A.D.]. / Now our nation has become degenerate and people suffer from oppression. The time to decide whether to live or die has come. / Whoever decides should unite as one. / From the bottom of our hearts [we] should unify as one. / To achieve the people's happiness, we swear to fight until death." (Many people in Kham and Amdo can still sing this and other songs.) In light of what had just happened to me, I could see how documents like these might have fueled suspicions. And as if these materials weren't enough, there was an article in Tibetan published in Kalimpong in June 1958 in the *Tibetan Mirror* newspaper that praised me as a Tibetan nationalist.

I learned about this late one night when a Tibetan friend named Lowang stopped by to visit. He told me that after Tharchin Babu, the editor of the *Tibetan Mirror,* had learned I was being kept in Beijing, he published an article about me with my picture. It said:

The two friends, Ngawang Kesang and Phünwang, [previously, in 1943,] talked a lot to me about opposing the old and new Chinese governments for the purpose of achieving Tibetans' independence. I never forgot those discussions, but at that time I didn't know that you two were spies of the Reds. Later, you led the Reds and handed over your cherished homeland and the whole of Tibet to the enemy. Thinking about those events, I felt disheartened, but I thought that probably you had acted like that as a tactical method. But I also was not sure whether it was like that or not.

Recently, I heard that Phünwang was demoted because he was loyal to Tibet. . . . I heard . . . that he was demoted because he talked very strongly [in support of] Tibet at a Chinese meeting. I am not sure if that is true or not. . . . I felt sad after hearing that he got demoted. If that news is true, I praise him from the bottom of my heart. These are the ignorant words of your old friend. [*The Tibetan Mirror*, June 1958]

Lowang, who had been working for the Chinese government's Office of Industry and Commerce in Kalimpong, told me that when his bosses saw the article, they considered it important and sent the newspaper to the State Ministry of Foreign Affairs. He said that the article seemed to make his superiors suspicious of him too, and before long, they quietly recalled him and his wife to Beijing.

Despite all of these materials, I was not especially worried because when I was organizing our Tibetan Communist Party and talking negatively about China, I was talking about the *old*, Guomindang China, not the CCP and the new People's Republic of China. Had not the CCP also criticized and opposed Chiang Kaishek's Guomindang? I thought they would come to accept this. In retrospect, it was wishful thinking that this distinction would save me.

Strangely, in Beijing the government never publicly declared that I was accused of having "thoughts of local nationalism." When I met Chinese and Tibetan cadres who knew me, it was awkward. They frequently asked me why I was in Beijing instead of in Tibet. I didn't know who knew what, and so all I told them was that I did what the party wanted and that it was not my choice. Some said they thought it was odd, given the tensions and problems in Tibet, that I was here and not there. Some were kind enough to say that they thought Tibet needed people and leaders like me. However, knowledge of my problem gradually spread among the people who knew me in Beijing. (Many Tibetans in Beijing knew my problem from the beginning, because they received information from Lhasa.) It wasn't too bad at first, because at that time, many officials in my institute were being accused as rightists and so on, so my case did not seem unusual. But as the news spread, fewer and fewer people came to visit me. I guessed they were afraid that if they did, they might also be accused or have problems later. So I was gradually more and more isolated.

In 1959, I picked up the newspaper and was stunned to read that a major uprising had occurred in Tibet, which the paper claimed had been planned in advance by the Tibetan government. I couldn't imagine how it could have happened, and there was no way for me to find out, until a few months later, in May 1959, when Tibet sent a delegation to Beijing headed by my old friend Tsögo. I met him and asked him frankly what exactly had happened. "Phünwang-la," he said, "I swear to God [tib. *cho rombo*] the uprising was not planned in advance, and it was not organized. I have relatives and friends in Lhasa who participated, so I know the situation very well." Then he gave me some examples. "Shasur [a powerful aristocrat who was a council minister] is my close relative. His wife's valuable gold amulet box and headdress, together with all their cash, were wrapped in a cloth package but left on the table because they fled so suddenly. If the uprising had been well planned and well organized, a council minister like Shasur would not have left his family's most valuable things behind. Similarly, Lord Chamberlain Phala also left many gold watches when he fled. And the Dalai Lama not only left behind a collection of watches but also his personal diary." Tsögo had many similar examples. He said finally that he was sure the decision to flee was made suddenly, which certainly made more sense to me than the newspaper's account.

The news of the uprising in Tibet was unsettling, to say the least. But things were quickly going from bad to worse in Beijing, too. The Nationalities Institute became more involved in the terrible nationwide Antirightist campaign, and every institute in Beijing started to attack and criticize its own leaders. Indeed, each institute was given a target number—a certain percentage of people—who were to be labeled as rightists. Bao Erhan, the head of our institute, was usually not around day to day, so that left five people, including me, who were the actual leaders. It was our job to discuss who should be labeled rightists in our group. It was not acceptable to find no one guilty.

Labeling rightists was supposed to start within the party, and in my unit there were three party leaders, including myself. That meant that we had to label one of us. It was not really appropriate to label me, because I had worked at the institute for only a short time. Moreover, I had already been labeled and told to clean up my thinking. Wang Libing was the real head of our institute, so he would not put the rightist label on himself. That left the third leader, who was a deputy director. By default, we put the rightist label on him. It was insanity. It was not a matter of whether he had made mistakes or not; we chose him in order to reach the target for our institute. I was bitterly disappointed that this was how things were being done within the Communist Party. I wondered where our socialist ideals of justice had gone. I didn't know it at the time, but as bad as things seemed then, they were about to get worse.

CHAPTER 20

To Prison

At the beginning of 1960, I was told to write a detailed history of my life from the time I was eight years old. I had written many shorter histories, but this one, they said, had to be detailed because it was going to be used in a formal political investigation. In our system, those were ominous words, and from the time I was told to begin writing, they sent people to watch me whenever I went out.

I produced a document of more than twenty pages. It did not to go into great detail about the years before 1949 because I was afraid my contacts with Soviet and Indian communists would be misinterpreted. For those days, I concentrated on surface details—where I went and what I did—saying as little as possible about what my thoughts had been. When I got to the period after 1949, I felt I could go into more detail. I mentioned, for example, that I had had good relations with the leaders of the Tibet Work Committee. I also said that I had had differences with Fan Ming because I thought many of the things he had done were not in keeping with party ideology.

When I had finished, I submitted the report and waited. For two months, there was no response, and of course I had no idea what the silence meant. Then one day in late August 1960, at about six o'clock, a person I knew came to my house and told me—without explanation—that I was expected to be at a meeting at the institute that evening.

When I arrived, I was greeted by a subordinate of mine, who surprised me by acting as if he were my superior. I began to feel that something bad was coming, and I didn't have to wait long to find out. He got right to the point. The leading party group of the State Nationalities Affairs Commission, he said, had decided that from now on I was to be isolated from the outside world [ch. *ge li*]. "You will be confined to the institute," he said. "The isolation is to begin immediately. You will not be allowed to go home." I was to be kept in a room with two party members, my guards, who would go with me everywhere, even to the toilet.

When I heard the party's decision, I went numb. It was true that during the current Antirightist campaign many people were being arrested or detained. I knew from experience that such things could happen to almost anyone—like our third leader at the institute, whom we had recently labeled a rightist by default. But it is one thing to be aware of what might happen and another to hear the sentence pronounced on oneself. I had not imagined that something this extreme would happen to me, and as soon as I began to think more clearly, my thoughts ran immediately to my children.

After I had been told to remain in Beijing in 1958, my two younger sons, who were in kindergarten in Chengdu, were sent to live with me. Since it seemed that I might be assigned to Beijing for some time, my wife, Tsilila, also sent my oldest son from Lhasa. She then tried to change her own work assignment to Beijing, and while the process of petitioning for reassignment dragged on, she sent our daughter to Beijing as well. My children were together for the first time in years, but it was a strange and complicated situation. The two boys from Chengdu knew virtually no Tibetan, and the two children from Lhasa knew no Chinese. My mother-in-law, who was living with us, didn't know a word of Chinese, and the babysitter knew no Tibetan. I had to translate among them all, and as I sat helpless in detention at the institute on that first night, I couldn't sleep for worrying about them.

The next morning, as soon as possible, I tried to tell the officials about the situation with my family and pleaded with them to allow me to go home—under guard, of course—so I could give my children the keys and make arrangements for someone to help look after them. They refused, and so I asked if they would allow my oldest son, Phüngang, to come to the institute so I could give him the keys and tell him what to do about taking care of his younger brothers and sister. They agreed but would not let me meet him when he came. Through a window, all I saw was his back as he was leaving. It would be the last time I would see any of my children for a decade.

For the next ten days or so, no one spoke to me about why I was being kept in isolation, and I finally asked a leader at the institute to ask the central government to clarify their reasons for holding me. Three days later, he told me that the leading party group of the State Nationalities

Affairs Commission had met and determined that I had been involved in major national and international political events and had not been honest about this. "Now," he said, "you must make a clear and detailed confession."

I had no idea what events they were referring to, and I immediately wrote a short but strong letter telling them that I had not been involved in any "national and international events." I said I had already fully explained everything I had done in the past; there was nothing more to confess. "Consequently," I concluded, "if there are 'major national and international events' that I have not told you about before, I take full responsibility for them, but I am not aware of what they might be." For the moment, I felt good. I thought that when they read my letter they would investigate, and when they found there was no basis to this accusation, my isolation would end.

Two weeks went by with no response. I was puzzled and began to get depressed. I was allowed to talk with the people from the institute who were guarding me, but I was usually not in the mood to chat. However, one day, when the other guards went to the bathroom, I was left alone with Yu Guang, a Chinese staff member who was a former revolutionary cadre from the Northwest Bureau. He asked me if I had said anything about any disagreement or unhappiness with other leaders when I reported my history to the party. I said I had, and when he asked me to explain, I told him that I had told Wang Feng that Fan Ming was not doing a good job in Tibet and was acting contrary to the central government's policies.

"You made a big mistake," he said.

"How?" I asked.

"Fan Ming is Wang Feng's right-hand man [ch. *gan jiang*] from the Northwest Bureau. You made a *big* mistake," he said again, shaking his head.

So now I knew. While Wang Feng smiled and acted friendly when we met face to face, behind the scenes he and Fan Ming had been undermining me and pulling me down. I was angry at how naïve I had been, but it was too late to do anything about it now. I was clearly in trouble. However, I did not think the situation was hopeless. I knew I had done nothing wrong, and so I believed that gradually I would be able to persuade the leaders that they were making a mistake. Much later I learned that when the State Nationalities Commission made its report to the central government, it said that I had a serious political problem and needed to be isolated and investigated. Mao read the report himself and on the final version wrote that "the matter should be investigated thoroughly," and that even if I had a "sky-size" [very serious] problem, they should make every attempt to win me over. (I had no idea at the time that my "crimes" were considered so serious.)

I was kept in a room on the second floor and allowed to leave only to go to the bathroom. When I did so, I had to pass a door that was always closed. I assumed there must be somebody staying in the room, and one day when the door was ajar, I saw four or five people, none of whom belonged to my institute. When they realized I could see them, they quickly closed the door. The way they looked at me was strange, and I suspected that they were from the Public Security Bureau. Later that day, when I went to spit out my window, I saw two people standing just outside, as if to prevent me from trying to escape. It was then I began to realize that I was not an ordinary "isolated" person and that my situation was much worse than I had thought. It was extremely frustrating. I wanted to be able to explain how wrong all this was, that they were making a terrible mistake. But there was no one to tell.

On August 31, six men suddenly entered my room, handcuffed me, and showed me a letter signed by Xie Fuzhi, the director of the Ministry of Public Security. It said, "Phünwang is suspected of counterrevolutionary acts and should be arrested immediately."

For a few seconds, it was hard to get my breath. The world was upside down. Everything seemed the reverse of what it should be. I had devoted my life to communism and change for Tibet. Now the party was arresting me for *counterrevolutionary* acts, an extremely serious crime, and there was not a thing I could do about it. I could barely think or believe that it was happening. But the handcuffs were real enough, the people were there, and they said I had to sign the letter. (For some reason, I looked at my watch and noted that it was 4:30 P.M. I have never forgotten that.) I took a deep breath and signed the order carefully. "I am a loyal party member," I kept thinking. "What can they be talking about?"

After I signed, they walked me outside. Two policemen held my arms. Two walked in front and two in back. (I did not see any of my colleagues, and later found out that they had all been sent to plant trees outside the institute.) There were three cars waiting for us. I was put in the middle car, and we left immediately. My particular institute was located on the campus of the Institute of Central Nationalities, and as we drove through the grounds, I saw that some students were watching from their windows. I was thirty-eight years old. I had no inkling that I would spend the next eighteen years in solitary confinement.

Everything that was happening was ominous and forbidding. We drove for at least an hour after leaving Beijing. I remember some details vividly. There was a thunderstorm with lightning and heavy rain. I couldn't remember ever seeing such a heavy downpour. I couldn't see anything but rain through the car window.

When we arrived at the prison, I was taken to a waiting room and turned over to the prison staff. The guards told me to take off my wristwatch and all my clothes, and they gave me a prison uniform. It was still raining hard. The peals of thunder were so loud that I felt they might actually tear down the walls of the prison.

When we got inside the prison block, the guard led me through several gates. When we reached my cell, he opened the door and told me to enter. I still remember that first glimpse. The door was framed by metal. It was thick and heavy, and the guard had to strain to push it open. At the bottom was a small hinged window for passing food in and out, and higher up was a peephole, which allowed the guards to look in. Immediately behind the heavy door was a lighter, barred door. The sound of the heavy door slamming shut behind me was like a gunshot.

The room itself was bare and depressing. It was about nine feet wide and seven paces (about twenty-one feet) long. Fixed to the floor on the right wall toward the back was a low bed with a very thin mattress and a pillow. Behind the door on the right was a walled-in area containing a cement toilet, a washbasin, a cup, a bar of poor-quality soap, a toothbrush, and toothpaste. The ceiling was high, with a single hanging light bulb that I could not reach or turn off. It was on all the time. There was a tiny window that was open during summer and closed in winter, but it was so high I could not reach it or see out. The walls were white, and I noticed that there were no sharp edges on the door, bed, basin, or toilet. I thought they were afraid that prisoners might commit suicide. It was extremely depressing.

I couldn't sleep that first night because the thunder was still rolling and my mind was full of painful and conflicting thoughts. I tried to make sense of what was happening. For ten years, I had devoted all my efforts to the success of the Chinese Communist Party. The Guomindang had not been able to catch me, and the Tibetan government had expelled me from Tibet for "communist activities." Now it was the same Communist Party I had spent all those years trying to help that had put me in prison.

I felt utterly powerless. Tears came to my eyes, and, alone with my thoughts, I composed a poem in Chinese about that night:

> The mountains and valleys are shaking with heavy thunder
> It is hard to know whether to laugh or cry.
> It seems a dream, but it is true.
> It seems true, but it is a dream.
> The sky and earth are dark
> And the cell is circling around.
> My heart hurts and feels like it will burst
> My tears are flowing down.

I did not know it at the time, but the prison I was in was called the Isolation and Introspection Institute for the Central Government's Senior Cadres [ch. *Zhongyang gaoji ganbu geli fan xin suo*]. In everyday language, it was called Qingchen Number One [ch. *Qingchen yi hao*]. It was the main prison for political prisoners. Ironically, later, during the Cultural Revolution, Zhang Jingwu also spent seven or eight years in this prison, as did his wife, Yang Gang. He died, and she went crazy after three years—drank her own urine and took off all her clothes. Later, after her release, she told me that she was unable to find out how her husband had died there. The only thing she found was an x-ray picture from the hospital, from which she learned that both his arms had been broken and there was no food in his intestines. It is said that Fan Ming was also kept in the same prison for two to three years, as were Xu Danlu, my compatriot Ngawang Kesang, and my brother Thuwang (who spent fourteen years there). Liu Shaoqi's wife, Wang Guangmei, was imprisoned there for twelve years. Among all the prisoners held in this prison, I spent the longest time—eighteen years.

Prison was hard to adjust to. Except for a brief time on the third day when they came to my cell and shaved my head, I spent all the time in my cell alone. None of the soldiers or guards would talk to me. Even on the rare occasions when I was taken to a hospital to see a doctor, the guard and the doctor never said more than a word or two. I thought there must be a rule for people who worked with prisoners. Even if I spoke to them, they just listened without saying a word. Whenever they ordered me to do something, they used very simple and short words, as if they were giving commands to an animal.

At the time of my arrest in 1960, prison conditions were very poor because China was facing severe economic hardship. For the first two years, the prison diet was the same—two pitifully small meals per day.

In the early morning, they provided only a cup of hot water. The first meal, at 10 A.M., consisted of three pieces of steamed cornbread and one bowl of vegetables made without cooking oil or meat. We ate again at about 4 P.M., a meal that usually consisted of two bowls of noodles mixed with some vegetables. Sometimes they gave us last year's rotten sweet potatoes, which smelled terrible. There was never enough food. My living conditions had fallen from the sky to the earth, as we say in Chinese.

I was hungry all the time and became so thin I could see the bones of my cheeks. When the prison guard brought meals in their metal containers, I could hear the rattle made by the metal, and I came to find the sound pleasant and even soothing. I constantly fantasized about food. I would become furious when I had to pick stones out of my bread because it meant I had lost some of what would have been food, and I sometimes dreamed that the steamed cornbread grew bigger. I was so hungry that I often thought about asking the guards to give me the melon peels that were thrown on the ground in Beijing, but I finally decided that if I did they might treat me even worse. Fortunately, beginning in 1963, the prison improved the quality of the food and provided three meals a day. From then on, though the food was still terrible, there was enough so that I was not hungry all the time.

After one or two months, the guards occasionally allowed me to exercise in a small yard for at most an hour. On the walk from my cell to the yard, a soldier stood guard every five or six feet. When I reached each soldier, he would say, "Arrived," and then tell me, "Go," and so on with the next soldier. When I arrived in the yard, they would close the door behind me. In the yard, several soldiers watched me from the top of the wall, but there on the ground I was always alone. I had no contact with any other prisoner. When I walked or exercised, all I could see was sky, clouds, and occasionally a bird. At first, I was allowed to exercise only once or twice a week. Later they increased it to two or three times a week, but they kept me off balance. Sometimes, for reasons I never understood, they let me go to the yard only two or three times a month.

The prison had its routines. On May 1, they provided me a set of summer clothes made of coarse cloth. In November, they gave me a set of cotton-padded winter clothing. Every two weeks, I was allowed to take a shower. Sometimes they deliberately left an almost worn-out pair of shoes with very thin soles in the shower room. I took this to mean that if I did not tell them what they wanted, I would end up like these shoes, worn out by spending all my life in prison. During the first two years, I was allowed nothing to read, so I just sat in my cell all day. I would walk around the cell in circles until I was too tired to walk anymore, and then I sat on the bed. I used to sing Chinese and Tibetan songs to pass the time, and sometimes I would dance and sing. I also composed poems in my mind. They used many means to hurt my feelings and break my spirit. I have forgotten most of them by now, but they taught me a powerful lesson—the real value of freedom.

The questioning began almost immediately. One afternoon a week or so after I arrived, two guards came to my cell and took me to another room, where there were four men seated behind a long table. I was told to sit on a hard wooden stool in front of them.

"What is your name?" one of them asked.

"You know what my name is," I said hotly. "Otherwise I would not be here." I was angry about everything that had happened and was not about to act like a humble, frightened prisoner. I felt I had nothing to fear because I had done nothing wrong.

"What did you do to be brought here?"

"I didn't do anything. You people brought me here."

"There is a reason for your being here."

"What is the reason?" I asked. "I know of no reason to be here."

"If there was no reason, you would not be here!"

We went back and forth like this for a while, both sides getting increasingly angry, until finally my interrogator had had enough.

"From now on you may not use your name anymore," he said. "Your cell number is 0689. Henceforth that will be your name." With that he pushed a button to call the guards. "Take him back to his cell," he said angrily. And from that day on, they never used my real name. Only the cell number.

After several days, they called me in for questioning again and asked me the same questions. I answered the same way as before. And so it went.

As I thought and thought about what was really happening, I came to the conclusion that since the Chinese as a race were very suspicious, they must be on some sort of fishing expedition to try to find out if there was something bad hidden in my history. I genuinely believed that after a few weeks of this, they would realize there was nothing to find and release me. But they didn't, and after a few months had passed, they said something that changed my thinking about my incarceration. At the end of a session, the lead interrogator told me I had to tell them truthfully what I had done. "You know," he said ominously, "you were not put in this prison for nothing." As soon as I heard those words, I knew this was not a fishing expedition. I knew I would not easily get my life back.

Solitary Confinement

The interrogations continued for the next two years. The questioners focused specifically on the activities of our Tibetan Communist Party, and during this time they tried to break my spirit in a number of ways. For example, because they knew I was worried about my children, they sometimes let a baby cry outside my cell window late at night. The sound was like a knife piercing my heart. Sometimes they sent a woman to my cell around seven or eight o'clock at night, her face nicely made up and heavily perfumed. I never knew when she was coming. When she did, she would open the cell door, ask a few questions designed to provoke me, and then leave. The perfume always lingered in the air.

Another cruel tactic they used involved my food, which was served through the small opening in the cell door. Sometimes a young soldier would wait outside for the food to be delivered, and spit on it through the bars of the inner door before I could get to it. I hated it when they did this, and so after a while, when I heard the delivery coming I would run to the opening to cover the food with my hands.

The idea that they would even consider doing this made me furious, and I would sometimes point to the red star on the soldiers' caps and say, "You are an insult to that star. Do you know what it symbolizes? It symbolizes the countless people who gave their lives for the revolution. You are a disgrace to those brave men and women." Sometimes I even spat back at them. Eventually, however, I decided that they were just trying to make me angry and sap my mental strength and will. When I realized this, I decided that if I controlled myself, it would be a victory for me. Gradually I learned to ignore whatever they were doing.

The interrogations continued, sometimes once a week, sometimes once every two or three weeks, and sometimes intensively for nine or ten hours a day. Most of the time, they asked me questions about my life, sometimes telling me to write about a particular event, sometimes asking broader questions. Usually, three or four days after questioning, they brought me the transcript of the session and asked me to read it. If I disagreed with things in it, we would argue, and sometimes they would make changes. But ultimately I had to sign a final transcript and place my fingerprint on it.

We spent lot of time arguing about absurdly minor details. For example, during one interrogation I told them that when I was in Chongqing, I went to the Chinese Communist Party's office, where I saw Chairman Mao's picture and noticed that he did not have his upper button properly fastened. (I think I must have noticed such a thing because I was a student at the Guomindang School at the time, and the dress codes there were extremely strict.) This was one of the things they chose to argue about. They told me that there was no picture of Mao in that office. I insisted there was, and said that if it was not in that particular office, then it must have been in another office. I remember that at this session the leader sat with crossed legs, smoking beside the interrogator's table, and after several arguments like the one about Mao's picture, he said angrily, "Phünwang, you should think carefully and then answer the question." When I heard him call me "Phünwang," I remembered that was my name. For almost two years they had called me only by my cell number, and I think I had temporarily forgotten who I was and what my name sounded like. When I realized this, I began to cry. The tears welled up from deep inside and streamed uncontrollably down my cheeks.

The interrogation process was continuous and never conclusive. They said they wanted me to confess my crimes but spoke of them only in general, so I never knew exactly what they were accusing me of. There was no fixed term to my sentence; the burden was on me to confess if I wanted my confinement to end. But I believed I had not done anything wrong, so I was always trying to guess exactly what it was they thought I had done. When I asked them directly, they said nothing. It was extremely frustrating. And since nothing I said seemed to make any difference, after some years I stopped arguing over little points and signed whatever they brought me.

The formal interrogations weren't all I had to endure during these first few years. Sometimes, without warning, men would come to my cell at night and beat me. They never gave me a reason; it was simply one of the things they did to break my spirit. They didn't beat me often, but I never knew when it might happen. I still recall one day when several guards came and twisted my arms behind my back so far I thought they would snap. Then they took off their shoes and beat me on the head with the heels. "You like to argue," they said, "well, go ahead and argue." I still have scars on my head from this and similar beatings. Sometimes they would get angry with me and lock me in a filthy, terrible-smelling room for hours or even days.

When they couldn't get the answers they needed by means of beatings and interrogations, they tried other methods. One day, I started to hear a high-pitched buzzing sound—like a cicada chirping shrilly in my ear—and wondered what it was. At the same time, I noticed that there was often a yellow residue in the cup in which they gave me my hot drinking water in the morning. I tasted some of it and thought it tasted like a vitamin, and at first I thought they were secretly doing things to strengthen my health. I thought that since they were still the representatives of the Communist Party, they did not want my health to suffer too badly. I guessed, therefore, that while on the one hand they were treating me very badly, on the other hand, they still had some compassion.

After a month or so, I noticed that sometimes there was more yellow residue, sometimes only a little, and sometimes nothing. I also noticed that when there was more, the sound in my ears got worse and I felt very nervous. When there was less, the sound in my ears decreased. Gradually I became convinced that this residue was not a vitamin, and I secretly tried to save some of the yellow substance, so that if I got released in the future, I could test it in a laboratory and find out what it really was. However, they must have been watching me carefully, because whenever I tried to hide it, they always found it and took it away.

I also noticed that whenever they intended to question me the next morning, I became very nervous and could not sleep the night before. I had to put cold water on my chest repeatedly to ease the tension. I knew they were giving me something to cause this but never knew what. When I was released from prison, I questioned friends who had also been in prison, and they told me they were given the same kind of substance, which had the same result. To this day, I do not know exactly what it was.

The worst torture they used on me was something that produced inaudible electric sound waves that gave me terrible headaches. I don't know how they did it, but sometimes the pain was so great it felt as if my skull would split. At that point, I would frantically kick the metal food window on my door and scream at them to stop. I kicked so hard once that I cut my foot and got so angry that I soaked my finger in my own blood and wrote on a copy of the *Communist Party Manifesto*: "Chairman Mao, Premier Zhou, fascism, and Great Han Chauvinism are the main irreconcilable enemies of all the Tibetan people." Later, when I returned the book to the guards, I had the satisfaction of knowing that they must have seen my blood-written words.

They used this sound-wave torture regularly for more than three years. There were only about ten or fifteen days per month when they did not send the waves. I know because it was so painful that after a while, each time it started I made a little cut on my finger and used my blood to write on the wall "First time," "Second time," and so on. Each time I wrote the two characters. By the end I was up to about the 550th time.

One day, I read in a newspaper about some Chinese reporters who had been arrested in Brazil and who had gone on a hunger strike that led to their release. I thought this might be a way to stop my tormentors from sending the sound waves, so I told them that unless they stopped, I would eat only one meal a day. Then I said I would fast for a day or two. The waves kept coming, and finally one day, I was so desperate that I told them that from then on I would not eat at all. In the beginning, they brought delicious food to tempt me, leaving it outside the door and using a fan to blow the aroma into my cell. When they saw that this did not work, they made several delicious meals and left them on my bed. I didn't touch them.

On the sixth day of my hunger strike, they took me to the interrogation room, where they held my arms and legs tightly and tried to inject something into my leg. However, I struggled so wildly that they were unable to give me the injection. Then they tried pouring milk into my mouth, but I closed my mouth as tightly as I could. Even when they used a screwdriver to pry apart my teeth (and actually broke one of them), they were still unsuccessful.

The next day, they again took me to the questioning room, but this time they tied me tightly on the floor. Then they put a thin plastic pipe through my nose, and through this tube they sent milk into my stomach. Someone was pumping beside me, and I could feel the cold liquid enter my stomach. After that, one of them smiled at me and said, "You see, we have ways to deal with you."

I said, "Yes, you fascists do have a shameless way of treating me, and I cannot stop this. So from now on, I will start to eat. If you bring me food, I will eat it. However, I still do not surrender to you." I was taken back to my cell, swaying as I walked. That afternoon, they gave me some rice soup to begin the process of helping me regain my strength.

All of the things they did were hard to deal with, but the total isolation was the hardest. I was not allowed to have newspapers for the first two years and never a radio, and I had no one to speak to. I found it unbearable. A day seemed like a month, and a month like a year. Whenever they called me for questioning, I had to go, but otherwise I just sat alone looking at the walls. I would often hallucinate that the wall on the other side of the cell was coming toward me. It was terrifying. I believe this is the reason I nearly went crazy, and why many people actually did.[1]

To hang onto my sanity, I would close my eyes and recall visions of my early life in the beautiful hills of Batang. I would try to visualize crossing mountain passes and streams I knew well, and finally arriving in familiar places with good associations. Sometimes I would focus on my parents' house, calling to mind each piece of furniture and thinking how I would redesign and arrange them in a better way. Sometimes I would pull some straws from my mattress and put them on my bed to design an ideal house for them. I tried to focus my mind like this to ease the terror of the walls closing in on me. To keep myself from complete depression, I always comforted myself and encouraged myself. When thoughts of regret at my failures arose, I would tell myself that those didn't matter, that there was no use thinking about such things. I forced myself to stop thinking about why I did or didn't do this or that.

To calm myself and keep my bearings, I also danced and sang, and I even composed poems and songs in my head in both Tibetan and Chinese. One of these was about Batang:

Going up and up, on a trail brightened by the dawn,
Crossing a mountain pass, sweat dripping,
I reach a huge meadow behind the mountain.
Lovely meadow flowers in bloom
I go down and down through the beautiful meadow,
My feeling of happiness getting larger and larger.

1. It is hard to measure the impact of such incarceration, but a casual comment made to Goldstein one day is revealing:

I was sitting in Phünwang's house in Beijing in July 2001, sipping coffee and making small talk. I described a visit I had made that morning to a large market where hundreds of birds of all sizes and shapes were on sale. Phünwang's wife, Tseden-la, nodded and said she knew the market well and had actually gone there once looking to buy a bird. She liked birds, she said, but ended up not buying one because Phünwang absolutely refused to have them. After prison, the idea of a bird in a cage was too painful, she said softly. I looked at Phünwang. He nodded, and then, with a smile and a twinkle in his eyes, said that a few years earlier when he was visiting relatives in Switzerland, he was so disturbed by their caged birds that one day when they were out of the house, he opened the cage and set the birds free.

A turquoise river sits at the far edge of the meadow,
And a mountain forest rises behind the blue river.
Mountain birds are singing happy songs in the forest,
Rabbits are dancing happily on the river.

lam skya po di nas yar yar 'gro
dka' rngul chu bzag bzhin la la rgyab
la phar rgyab spang chen gcig la slebs
snying rje po'i spang rgyan me tog shar
nga mdzes pa'i spang la mar mar 'gro
nga'i sems pa dkyil nas yar yar skyid
spang sgno po'i mtha' la gyu chus bkor
chu sngon po'i rgyab la nags ris bkor
nags kyi gseb la ri byas skyid glu len
chu'i sgang la ri bong dga' bro brdung

After I was released from prison, I read some books that said that between the enemy and oneself, it was harder to overcome oneself than the
enemy. I thought that was extremely perceptive. It took several years to
adjust to the harsh conditions of my imprisonment, if one can ever be
said to adjust to utterly solitary confinement. It was never easy, but eventually small changes made my life at least a bit more bearable. For example, after the second year they allowed me to read newspapers like
The People's Daily and *New Observation,* and after that gradually they
lent me selections from the works of Marx, Engels, Lenin, Hegel, and
Stalin. As soon as I finished one volume, I could ask for the next. Since
they never lent me any entertaining books, I read and reread the socialist books just to keep my mind as sharp as I could.

During the daytime, I spent most of the time reading, as the light in my
cell was much better then. At night, when the light was poor, I sang and
danced for two to three hours. The floor of my cell was almost worn out
with my dancing. After they rang a bell to announce it was time for sleep,
they did not allow me to sing or dance. They never turned off the light at
night, and I knew they were always watching, but my life eased after they
began to allow me to read, and gradually I adjusted better and learned to
control my anger and frustration. I was also able to keep track of time.

In another concession that lightened my burden, eventually they allowed me to weave straw hats. I loved this work so much that I tried to
slow down the process because I was afraid that after I had finished one
hat they would not give me more straw. If they asked me to finish the job
in three days, I made it last for four or five. Unfortunately, the weaving
ended as suddenly as it had begun. I hated having no physical work to do.

Years later, after being released from the prison, I met Wang Guangmei, Chairman Liu Shaoqi's wife, and we shared prison experiences. When she complained that she had been forced to perform menial tasks, such as cleaning windows and washing prisoners' bedding, I could only think how lucky she had been. If they had given me such work, I would have been happy indeed. I recall that often while sitting or pacing in my cell, I would watch the ants on the floor and the spiders on the walls. The ants were busy carrying things back and forth and the spiders spinning webs, and I envied them.

I had no such kind thoughts about the mosquitoes. During the summer, there were swarms of them in my cell. Because the guards would not give me a net, I had a terrible time sleeping. The bites and itching were terrible. When I got up in the early morning, there were thousands of mosquitoes on the wall, and I set out eagerly to kill them. Soon the tiny bloodstains covered the walls, and I deliberately left them in plain sight to protest my inhumane treatment.

Although my situation improved slightly after a few years, the questioning never stopped. Eventually, after many years, my interrogators got more specific in their accusations. At one session, they asked about some of the songs I had composed. At first I wasn't sure which ones they meant, because I had written and translated many revolutionary songs like the "Internationale." They said they wanted me to tell them the lyrics of the "guerrilla songs" I had composed, which I did. I learned later that one aspect of my so-called big political mistake was related to the *Tibetan Mirror* articles Tharchin had published in Kalimpong. He had printed some of our organization's songs, including one that originally had been a Chinese "guerrilla song." I had kept the Chinese words of the first part but replaced the second part with Tibetan words to convey my feelings about the situation in Kham in the early 1940s. My interrogators were really only interested in this song, which called on Tibetans to rise up and take revenge against the Chinese. The Tibetan words were:

> Look out, look out, you uncivilized [lit. wild] Chinese.
> You were shameless not one time, not two times, not three times.
> First, you killed four Yangchen people,
> Second, you stabbed Sheyngo Kunchog to death.
> Third, you beat Atri to death with a stick,
> Fourth, you used Nyarong Chime Drolma as a target and killed her.
> And you committed serious crimes, stealing the wealth of the people.
> We have never seen such cruel behavior.
> No love and no compassion,
> Treating us Tibetans as animals.

No love and no compassion,
You evil and savage Chinese bully the soft and avoid the tough [literally:
    slip on hard soil and sink in soft earth].
Your usual food is Tibetans' blood and pus.
Now if we do not take revenge,
We will no longer tie our belts like real men.

sgug dang sgug dang rgya rgod tsho
kha rong ham pa gcig dang min, gnyis dang min; gsum dang min
dang po yangs can mi bzhi bsad
gnyis pa zhal ngo dkon mchog gri tshab bskul
gsum pa a khrid dbyugs pas bsad
bzhi pa nya rong 'chi med sgrol ma sbib ['ben] gtsab skul
mi ser rgyu 'phrog nag che la
de 'dra' spyod pa ngan po mthong ma myong
sha tsha med, snying rje med
nged bod rigs dud 'gro' khungs la bzhag
sha tsha med, snying rje med
khyod rgya rgod rigs ngan rnams
sra sar 'dred snyi sa zug
nam rgyun bza' rgyu thams cad bod kyi khrag dang rnag
da ni dgra sha ma lon na
pho chen sked rag mi 'ching ngo

The next day, they brought me back and said the words of the song I had given them were not complete. I thought they were, and we argued until one of the interrogators, Wu Yu, asked me in Tibetan to tell them the original words for the line "You evil and savage Chinese bully the soft and avoid the tough [tib. *sra sar 'dred snyi sa zug*]." I couldn't remember any other words, and after some time Wu Yu said, "Wasn't the original phrase 'You evil and savage Chinese shit in restaurants' [tib. *za khang nang la skyag pa btang*]?" In Khampa slang, the expression "to shit in a restaurant" means to be ungrateful, the thrust of the words being "Not only did they take our land and benefit from it, but they shit on us by oppressing and mistreating us."

I was astonished, not just by the question but also by the fact that Wu Yu spoke and understood Tibetan. (After my release, I learned that he was from the Nationalities Publishing House and had been attached to a special group the government had set up for the interrogation and examination of my case.) As soon as he said the words, I recalled the phrase. He was correct. It was the original lyric. But at some point we had decided to change it. My mind was racing. I couldn't imagine how they could have known details like these, which I myself had completely forgotten. They could only have learned about them from someone in our organization, and I immediately suspected that it must have been Ngawang Kesang, because he had been with me during most of time when I wrote those songs. So they must have arrested him, I thought. Then I also remembered that when Chömpel came back to Lhasa from India in 1948, he told me that Tharchin had published some of my songs in his newspaper. I realized now that this might be the reason they were accusing me of having "a big international political problem." Based on the lyrics of this song, they were accusing me of encouraging Tibetans to rise up against the Chinese and take revenge. This was why they were saying that I was a "complete nationalist," whose thoughts contained no sense of socialism and communism, just loyalty to my own nationality.

Now that I knew what I was accused of having done, I argued forcefully, using the Chinese Communist Party's Marxist ideology. "You are confusing two different historical periods," I said. "In the old society, every nationality and class had the right to fight against its oppressors because the system then was exploitative. At the time these songs were written, the relations between Chinese and Tibetans [in Kham] was one of oppressor and oppressed. The oppressor was the Guomindang—actually the 24th Route Army of the warlord Liu Wenhui. The incidents mentioned in that song referred to atrocities committed by Liu Wenhui's officers—the regiment commander Ma Dehang, who killed four Yangchen people, the commander Fu Dequan, who stabbed Sheyngo Kunchog to death, and Zhang Han, who shot Nyarong Chime Drolma. There is no way one can extrapolate from these to the Chinese people as a whole. Liu Wenhui was part of the Guomindang counterrevolutionary army that ruled and oppressed China. They are the same counterrevolutionary force that the Chinese Communist Party was fighting, so it is wrong to accuse me of inciting Tibetans against Chinese on the basis of this. If I am a counterrevolutionary because I fought against the warlord Liu Wenhui and the Guomindang, then the Chinese Communist Party should also be treated as counterrevolutionary because it too bitterly opposed the Guomindang and spent many years fighting it. However, once the new society began, I became a member of the Chinese Communist Party and worked energetically to achieve its goals. I engaged in no counterrevolutionary activities and did not try to stir up Tibetans against Chinese. There is nothing in that song, or any other of our revolutionary songs, that indicates I opposed the Chinese Communist Party or the Chinese people as a nationality in the new society." I was pleased because I thought that distinction was so clear that even they would understand and accept it. But that was not what happened.

They didn't know how to refute my arguments, but they did not accept my points, and for about a month we continued arguing. Then one day, Wu Yu asked me to review the notes of the most recent interrogations. "Whatever you may say to us now," he said harshly, "we know that your real goal was 'independence' for Tibetans [tib. *rang dbang rang btsan*]." He was so angry that he was literally gnashing his teeth and spit was coming out of his mouth. Surprised by the level of his anger, I became angry myself. Nothing I said had made any impact on their thinking. It was infuriating.

"When did I ever say 'independence'?" I snapped. "You are just making things up. You are disgusting. Chiang Kaishek's government—the Communist Party's enemy—issued a wanted poster to arrest me, but they couldn't catch me. Now you people have arrested me. You wear the mask of the Chinese Communist Party, but actually *you* are doing counterrevolutionary work. You are doing the work of the Guomindang. If the Guomindang government on Taiwan knew this, they would reward you. You are a bloody butcher," I said. "You do not have a soul. If you were in Japan, you would serve Japan loyally, and if you were in Taiwan, you would be loyal to the Guomindang. You are only serving the Communist Party because you happen to be here. You do not have a soul." I signed the interrogation note but was so angry that I deliberately sang the "guerrilla song" as loudly as I could as I was being taken back to my cell.

It was the time of the Cultural Revolution, and I was able to read about it in the newspapers. I was shocked by what I read. I was not only angry at how unjustly I was being treated, but also angry at what was happening in China in the name of communism. When I saw pictures of thousands of people holding Mao's small red book to ask for instructions in the morning and report their actions in the evening, I believed they must have lost their minds. I remembered the ancient Tibetan yogi Milarepa's words, "The world sees Mila as crazy, but Mila sees the world as crazy" [tib. *'khor bas bltas na mi la smyo, mi las bltas na 'khor ba smyo*]. It was an accurate description of how I perceived my situation as I sat helpless in prison watching the madness rage outside.

As I became aware of the insanity of the Cultural Revolution, my hope of getting out of prison dimmed, so I decided that at present I needed to focus on something else, and concentrated on studying logic. I thought that Mao and others were conducting a badly flawed political campaign because their logic was confused. So I read and reread the works of Hegel and Marx and Lenin. According to Hegel, everything in the world was constantly changing, and these changes followed certain laws. I wanted to find out what these laws were.

From the start, I had a strong desire to make notes about my thoughts, and I repeatedly asked the guards to give me pen and paper and ink. They never responded, so I invented ways to make my own. When I washed my clothes, I saved the colored water (produced when the dye leached out) in an extra washbasin. After the color became dark through evaporation, I painted it on newspapers to darken them completely. Then I chipped white paint from the walls, dissolved it in a bowl, and used it as ink. Using straw from the mattress as a pen, I began writing down my thoughts. I wrote about ten thousand characters in this way. Unfortunately, I soon learned that the notes I wrote on newspaper did not last long because the white color faded quickly. I had to find another way to write.

For my next attempt, I tore off the blank edges of the newspapers and used rice gruel to stick them together to make pieces of paper. On this, I used the dye concentrate as ink. I secretly pulled a metal wire from the heating installation and sharpened it to a point on the floor to turn it into a pen. In order to conserve paper, I wrote in extremely small letters. But because there was so much I wanted to say, I didn't have enough of the paper I had been making this way. I finally got the idea of using toilet paper for writing paper. I remembered that people in India cleaned themselves with their hand and water after they defecated; by borrowing their custom, I could save the toilet paper for writing. I carefully smoothed the rough straw surface of the toilet paper and found that it worked relatively well. I wrote several hundred thousand characters using this system.

Although I was allowed to keep my notes, I could not keep personal belongings in my cell. I remember that one day, when they let me out for exercise, I found a small, shiny black pea on the ground. It had probably been carried into the prison yard by the wind. Because it was beautiful, I picked it up and secretly kept it. It became a precious personal possession for me, a victory over the system, and I made every effort to hide it from the guards. Sometimes I hid it in my palm and sometimes under my tongue if I had to go out of the cell. Amazingly, I succeeded in keeping it for three or four years, and was happy and even proud that I had been able to hide something from their constant searching. Eventually, however, they found the pea and took it away. I was heartbroken and blamed myself. In retrospect, I know it was foolish to blame myself, but at the time I wasn't really in my right mind.

Time passed. Year succeeded year, and before I knew it, nine years had passed. I had read a tremendous amount about Marxism and socialism and dialectical materialism, but I had had no contact with any other prisoners or with the outside. I did not know what had happened to my children, my wife, my parents, or my friends. It was as if I had been surgically removed from society, gone without a trace, entombed alive in a sealed crypt.

Then one day, out of the blue, my tormentors finally told me the real charge against me.

CHAPTER 22

A Vow of Silence

One day in 1969, nine years after my arrest, I was taken to the interrogation room, where an official said, "For many years, you have been asking the reason for being kept in this prison. Today you will get your answer."

I had been in prison too long to trust them. All I could think was that it must be some kind of trick, another attempt to break me down. I wondered frantically what lies they were going to tell me now. What game were they playing? I was thinking so many things at once that I had to force myself to concentrate on whatever it was the official was about to tell me. I wanted to hear *exactly* what he had to say.

What I heard shocked and infuriated me. "In 1955," he said, "while the Dalai Lama was in Beijing, he had a very important *black* [evil/secret] meeting that you attended. This is the reason that you were arrested and kept in prison. Please tell us about this meeting."

As prepared as I thought I was for anything they might try to throw at me, I was astounded at the charge. It was ridiculous. There had been no such meeting. I felt like screaming at the sheer stupidity of the whole idea. I concentrated hard to keep control so I could respond.

"Today," I said, as calmly as I could, "you have told me clearly what I am charged with. I will give you an equally clear response. First, however, let me ask a question or two—just to establish some facts. You know that the Dalai Lama did not come to Beijing alone. He came with other officials from the Tibetan government. The Dalai Lama was never completely alone, so he and I could not have held such a secret meeting by ourselves. There would have been others attending. Isn't that correct?"

"Yes," he said, "there were others also who attended the meeting."

"Did Surkhang attend the meeting?"

"Yes, he was at the meeting."

"What about Ngabö?" I asked.

"He was also at the meeting."

"And the Dalai Lama's lord chamberlain, Phala, council minister Liushar, and several other Tibetan officials?"

"They all were at the same meeting."

"Who else was at the meeting?"

"Tian Bao," he replied, "and Huang Zhenqing [Aba Alo of Gansu]."

I paused for a moment, thinking now I could easily rebut their accusation. "You have finally told me the reason I have been in prison for nine years. I am glad to hear what the accusation is, because it is easy for me to refute. This charge is totally and absolutely untrue. This secret '*black* meeting' to plot counterrevolutionary activities never happened. You people have all the power, and you can kill me or do whatever you like with me, but let me tell you how ludicrous this charge is.

"First, when the Dalai Lama came to Beijing, Xu Danlu from the Tibet Work Committee accompanied him day and night and made a daily written report to Zhang Jingwu, who reviewed it and then sent it to the central government. So it was impossible for me and other Tibetans to have held a secret '*black* meeting' with the Dalai Lama without the central government's knowledge!

"Second, if we say hypothetically that such a meeting did occur, then why am I in prison while others who attended are in high positions? I don't know where Huang Zhenqing is now because I haven't seen his name in the newspapers, but among those you say attended the meeting, Ngabö is now a vice chairman of the Standing Committee of the National People's Congress, and Tian Bao is a vice director of the leading group of the Revolutionary Committee of Sichuan Province. If the meeting you say we all attended was such a *black* meeting, then why were Ngabö and Tian Bao, who also attended, promoted while I was imprisoned? And why wait fourteen years to raise the issue?

"So all this talk about a secret *black* meeting is nonsense. There was no such meeting. And it is easy to check—go and ask Ngabö and Tian Bao about it."

While I was speaking, I suddenly realized what they were trying to do. Throughout the years of interrogation, they had focused on my activities in the pre-1949 period, when the Tibetan Communist Party was opposing Liu Wenhui and the Guomindang and striving for Tibetan freedom from their rule. The song lyrics, guerrilla warfare plans, and so on were all from that period. There was no question about this. I accepted that we were trying to overthrow them, and I insisted I was justified in doing this, just as the Chinese Communist Party was justified in opposing the Guomindang. These were not counterrevolutionary activities, they were revolutionary activities. And while they might not like that the lyrics said we were seeking Tibetan independence, none of this was relevant to my activities and thinking after 1949, when I joined the Chinese Communist Party. They had nothing to charge me with after China became the People's Republic of China and I was an official in the Chinese Communist Party. I realized now that by trumping up this ridiculous accusation that I had participated in a secret meeting with the Dalai Lama in 1955, they were trying to get me to confess that I had played a major role in fomenting the Tibetan rebellion in Kham that began in 1956. (Many years later, I learned that when the interrogation team reported that they had found no evidence of any wrongdoing by me in the post-1949 period, they were ordered to continue to investigate, that is, to find something. The "*black* meeting" was their attempt to do this.)

It was madness. To be told suddenly that they had kept me in prison and tortured me for nine years on a baseless charge was almost too much to bear. It was evil and cruel. They were destroying my life for nothing, and I decided that I was not going to accept it any longer.

"After the new China began in 1949," I said as calmly as I could, "I did everything according to the policies of the Central Committee. In addition to not saying a single word against it, I made important contributions to the success of the central government's liberation of Tibet. This charge is ridiculous and so easy to disprove that you must already know it. Therefore, this is all a sham, and from now on, I will have nothing more to say to you." Then I took a Khampa oath. "Whatever you want to do to me, you can do it. I can't stop you," I said angrily. "But from now on, if I speak another word to you, I will not consider myself a man."

I signed the transcript of the interrogation without reading it, deliberately putting thumbprints all over the paper to make what I said more emphatic. I really didn't care what they did to me anymore. I understood now that I was powerless to change their mad views. They were not interested in the truth. But I could control my own actions, and I swore I would from that moment on. I would never again participate in this sham. They looked at each other, astonished, and then had me taken back to my cell.

They brought me to the interrogation room many times after that day, but I refused to speak a single word. For a long time, they didn't seem to tire of trying to get me to talk, but nothing worked. No matter what they did, I just shook my head and said nothing. They would stare at me, and I would stare at them.

Eventually they gave up trying and stopped coming to my cell, and I felt I had won a great victory. But I had paid a terrible price. I was now totally cut off from human interaction and, I thought, from all hope as well. Because I was no longer speaking, even the slight possibility of persuading my tormentors of my innocence was gone, and I now had to adjust to something even worse than solitary confinement: total silence. My prison experience had already taught me that silence and isolation could affect my sanity. To try to keep a grip on reality, I threw myself into the study of dialectics and logic. I had thought that Chairman Mao and the other leaders of China were conducting the insane and terribly destructive Cultural Revolution campaign because they misunderstood the lessons of Marxist dialectics and logic, so I focused on the laws of change. I read and read Hegel and others. Hours became days, days months, and eventually I spent years thinking about how the laws worked and how to convey my thoughts symbolically in a diagram. I tried thousands and thousands of sketches and figures, but was never satisfied with the results. Then one day, after four years of trying, suddenly I folded a piece of paper and through the folded lines, I saw and then drew a diagram that allowed me to understand the relationship among the ideas I had been trying so long to understand.

When I realized what had happened, I was so happy that I laughed loudly and wildly. When they heard the noise, the guards thought I must either be causing trouble or had gone crazy. They came rushing into my cell and put handcuffs on me, and left them for fourteen hours. (The cuffs were so tight that they left deep marks on my hands, which did not disappear for several years.) After that outburst, they left me alone again. Then one day in 1975 (during my fifteenth year in prison), several officials came to my cell and said that I had lost my sanity. They took me from the prison to a hospital where prisoners with mental problems were treated.

They may have been right. I might have lost my grip on sanity for a while. After my release, I read that solitary confinement was a technique first used by the British. Later it was found that keeping a prisoner in solitary confinement for several months could drive him or her crazy, so in many countries the courts no longer allowed it. In those countries, prisons could use solitary confinement as a punishment for only a few days. I also read stories about other people's experiences in prison. Nehru, Gandhi, and Mandela each spent over twenty years in prison, but with the exception of Mandela, they did not serve all twenty years at one time. They were confined for four or five years, released, and then arrested and thrown into prison for another four or five years. Moreover, they were allowed to read and talk with other prisoners. For example, Mandela's twenty-six years in prison were spent on an island where he did stonework with other people with whom he could talk. I was kept alone in a tiny cell, unable to talk with anyone and eventually bound by my own oath of silence.

If it was hard to keep track of time in the prison, it was even harder to do so in the mental hospital. The days blurred together with little to distinguish one from another. However, at some point, an official from the Public Security Bureau came to my room. He asked if I missed my children and said I could see them if I wanted. I missed them very much, but I didn't trust him and simply made a noncommittal gesture. The next day, however, they did bring my children into the hospital and actually let us talk for twenty to thirty minutes.

I had not spoken to anyone for six years. I had not seen my children for fifteen years. I scarcely recognized them at first, because they had grown so much. When they saw me, they burst into tears, and I also cried. I found it physically hard to speak because I had not used my vocal cords or formed words for so long. I had become like a dumb person, and I was unable to prevent myself from drooling.

My brother Thuwang was with them and a girl they said was a relative (she was my wife's older brother's daughter, who had become our adopted daughter while I was in prison). When we got our emotions under control, my children told me stories about their successes—how they had graduated from high school and college. It was all lies. They wanted to tell me comforting things, because they were afraid if they told me how hard their lives had been, it would make me worse. My brother didn't even tell me about his years in prison. When I asked the children where their mother was, they told me she had gone to Lhasa. But they seemed uncomfortable with the subject and acted so strangely that I knew I wasn't getting the truth. After I was released, I learned that she had died a terrible death during my ninth year in prison.

In conversation with Melvyn Goldstein, Phünwang's son Pengjing recalled this first meeting with his father:

One day people from the Public Security Bureau told us that we could meet our father but that he had mental problems and was talking nonsense. It was the first time since he disappeared in 1960 that we were told that he was alive and in custody.

He was in the Anding Psychiatric Hospital on Anding Road. When you entered, you saw all kinds of insane people. In the building, all side corridors from the first floor to the fifth floor were blocked so that you could get to the fifth floor only from the inside. When we got there, there was a huge iron gate. People from the Public Security Bureau opened the gate and then took us to our father.

My siblings and I were very happy to learn that our father was still alive, but we were also very sad because he was in terrible shape. It seemed like he was in a stupor. He could not control his movements and saliva kept dribbling from his mouth.

We didn't talk much because of his condition, but as difficult as it was for him to talk, I remember vividly my father haltingly telling us two things. First, he said he had done nothing wrong. He had done nothing harmful to the party, to the people, or to the country. Second, he told us proudly that he had created a new theoretical dialectical system. We had no idea what he meant.

Meeting my father was painful, but not as shocking as it might have been, because I had a friend whose mother had been imprisoned for seven years. She was normal when she entered but was mentally ill when she was released. During those years, it was not unusual for prisoners to lose their sanity. But while Father was in such bad shape that today people would regard him as crazy, for us it was enough to know that he was still alive.

After my release from prison, I learned what had actually happened to my family. After my arrest, my wife, Tsilila, came to Beijing. For a time she worked in an office, and she and her mother looked after the children. My children had a hard time. They didn't take to the streets or get involved in criminal activities, but their schooling suffered badly. Among my sons, Phüngang was able to finish only two years of senior high school, Pengjing only middle school, and Pengang only primary school. My daughter, Pengnyi, finished high school.

The family had a hard time socially and politically as well. Immediately after my arrest, our Chinese neighbors began treating them badly, calling them names and ostracizing them. One day, for example, a neighbor's wife said to my wife, "You Tibetans are bad. You are trying to separate from the motherland." My wife got angry and retorted, "What do you mean, calling us separatists? Until the Chinese arrived, Tibet was united. So who separated what from whom? We Tibetans didn't invite the Chinese to come to our country, so how can we be separatists?" The angry neighbor immediately told the officials that my wife was advocating Tibetan independence, and they organized a big "struggle session" against her that was attended by several thousand people.

During the Cultural Revolution, my family suffered even more. Party officials accused my wife of being from a high family and of ridiculous things like having a drum and other ritual implements made from human skins, as well as having implements for inflicting whippings and corporal punishment. They also said she had a machine for sending telegraphs, and they ordered her to turn all these things over to them. Since she did not have any of these things, she couldn't comply with the order, and she had to undergo many vicious struggle meetings, at which she was attacked and beaten.

Finally, one day, as had happened to me, they kept her isolated in the office where she worked, the Measuring and Standards Bureau [ch. *Cehui Ju*], and didn't let her go home. They locked her in a filthy, windowless basement. They took her out of that room only to hold a struggle session against her, and then immediately put her back in the basement. On March 10, 1969, she died in that basement.

They say she committed suicide, but I am not sure. Strangely, my close comrade Topden also died in prison at nearly the same time—March 1969—in Chengdu. They say he committed suicide by cutting his wrists. I am suspicious, because it all seems too coincidental. And the authorities now refuse to give me the official photos they took of my wife's body.

Phünwang's son Pengjing recalled these same events:

At first I knew nothing because they simply called my father for a meeting and he never came home. There was no news about him after the meeting. He was not labeled an enemy or a counterrevolutionary or anything. It was as if he had been erased from this world. No one knew where he was, and no one knew whether his disappearance was the result of something good or bad. Of course, we wondered why he did not come back. My older brother might have had a deeper understanding than the younger children, but I was just six years old, and I knew nothing.

We felt some difficulty at that time compared with other children of the same age. First, we were Tibetan. We were the only Tibetan family in the neighborhood. And at that time, our neighbors knew little about us. They just referred to us as serf owners. I remember that when I was young, I was quite shy. When I walked, I always kept aside and bowed my head. I seldom talked to others.

At that time, my mother didn't work in the same place as my father. Soon after he disappeared, my mother developed a bad temper. Now we are old enough to understand. She was young at that time, and the pressure was too much for her. It was hard for her to manage five children. We just saw that our mother smoked a lot and had a bad temper.

*Our mother had some money, so we did not feel too much financial
pressure. The difficulties we had were from pressure on our minds. We children were okay because we were so small. But it was different for our
mother, who had grown up in Tibet. She had nobody to talk with. At that
time, most of her relatives were not in Beijing. My mother was a frank and
straightforward person. During the Great Cultural Revolution, she had a
quarrel with one of our neighbors. She was criticized because of something
she said during that quarrel.*

*As I mentioned, we were pretty well off during the early 1960s, until the
beginning of Great Cultural Revolution in 1966. After the Great Cultural
Revolution, the situation became worse and worse. I still recall the first
confiscation of our property. I remember that it happened in the summer
of 1966. I was twelve and had just come back from school. Suddenly a lot
of people from the work unit arrived. They belonged to the revolt faction of
the revolutionary organization, and they began to search our home. I didn't
quarrel with them, but my sister did. She shouted at them and tried to stop
them. But it was useless. They paid no attention to her. They opened up all
the suitcases and confiscated all the money and valuable things we had.
That was the first confiscation.*

*You ask how I felt. I felt different than the others, who were angry. It
was strange. I felt that we were destined to suffer this, that it was natural
because we lived in such an environment. The problems had already existed
before my father vanished in 1960. This suffering just seemed to be delayed
for several years. At that time, I just felt that such a thing would happen to
us sooner or later.*

*After confiscation, we had nothing left, and life was extremely hard for
us. I remember that my mother started to smoke the worst-quality cigarettes. And her temper got worse. If she had had a more flexible personality, things might have been different. But she was firm and unyielding. I remember when we were small that she told us to stride proudly when we
walked. When she did things, she always tried to do them cleanly and perfectly. That is to say, no matter what the situation in our family, when we
walked out, we should act proud. I think that if she could have been more
flexible, she might be alive today. But she was hard and unyielding, and she
could not bear the suffering.*

*After the first confiscation, they returned some stuff to us and some
money so we could live. I remember that at that time my mother worried
about the same thing happening again, so she began to secretly stockpile
food and some other things. At that time, she dared not do such shopping
openly, so she would leave the house quietly with only a small bag. Each
time, she brought back a few things, like sausages, oil, salt, and corned
beef, etc. I remember that my older brother had a classmate who lived close
to our home, and he helped us. Our storage room had quite a lot of food at
that time, and these proved useful later.*

*The second confiscation happened in 1967, the second year of the Cul-
tural Revolution. This time, they confiscated all our meat, and we lived on
our stored food. There were a lot of people living in our neighborhood who*

kept an eye on us. When we went out, they would ask what we were going to do and report our activities.

My mother was a Communist Party member, but she was not an important official, and one day they came to our home and took her away. We were all at home, but there was nothing we could do. They just said, "Wrap up your things and come with us." So she went. She died fifteen days later.

I knew that she was detained in the basement of her work unit. There were several people detained there. I tried to bring her some food, but I wasn't allowed to see her. Then one morning, four or five people from her office came to our home. My younger sister and I were the only ones there. (My older brother had been sent to prison, my youngest brother had been sent back to Kham, and I don't remember where my older sister was.) They asked the two of us to go with them to the office.

When we got there, we were taken to a small room in the basement. Since my sister was very young (only nine years old), they only let me enter the room. I remember there was a bed with a sheet, which they lifted to let me see Mother's face. I was stunned when I saw her. I stared blankly and did not know what to say. After letting me see her face, they showed me her wrist, which looked like it had been cut by a piece of glass or the edge of the radiator, which was rough and had sharp edges.

I was fifteen at the time.

The news of the death first of Zhou Enlai in January, and then of Chairman Mao in September 1976, extinguished the last ember of hope I had. No matter what happened, I had clung stubbornly to the belief that someday the details of my case would reach people at the highest levels. I knew Mao Zedong and Zhou Enlai personally, and I believed that Wang Feng and others had lied to them about what I had done and what was happening to me. I hoped against hope that one day Mao and Zhou would realize that I was innocent and order my release. Now that hope was gone, and it seemed that my isolation and solitary confinement might simply continue indefinitely.

One day in 1978, I wrote a poem to convey my feelings of sadness and defiance:

At dawn a beam of sunlight shines through the window.
[At dusk] the last light shines on the iron door.
Heavily locked, in my terrible cell
I have passed eighteen years alone facing only the wall.
Summers, winters came and went.
But spring flowers and autumn moons never reached this place.
Here I discovered how many cruel punishments exist,
For suffering has always been [the fate] of intellectuals.
For this adversity, I am grateful
[Because] my diligent reading and thinking has brought me understanding

About the self and other,
And I learned the true nature of all things that exist.
I searched for happiness in the suffering,
And happiness won out.
So from that suffering, I obtained a happy result.
Freedom, I lost you in pursuit of you,
Though without you, I still feel free [in my heart].

nyi gzhon 'od thig lcags phra'i gseb nas 'phros
mdangs kyi lhag ma lcags sgo'i ngogs su gsal
nyam nga'i btson khang sgo lcags mdo shug mnan
gcig pur gyang la mi lo bco brgyad bltas
tsha gdung grang ngar myangs zin slar yang myong
dpyid kyi me tog ston gyi zla ba rnams
lcags ri mthon po'i phyi rol pha gir yod
gling 'dir khrims gcod gtong thabs rnam grangs mang
blo ldan rnams la sngar nas gnod cing 'tshe
sdug yul las ngan bdag la bka' drin che
thos bsam 'bad pa bskyed pas go rtogs brnyed
de yis rang gzhan gnyis kar rgyus yod dang
dngos po kun gyi ji lta'i gnas lugs shes
sdug bsngal khrod nas bde ba 'tshol nas su
bde ba'i sems kyis sdug bsngal gzhom par byed
bka' yang skyid pa'i 'bras bu lag tu lon
nga ni rang dbang ched du rang dbang shor
rang dbang med kyang rang dbang yin par tshor

Some months later, guards came to my cell and took me to an office
in the mental prison. They didn't say a word, and I had no idea what was
happening. An official I had not seen before ordered me to take off my
prison uniform and put on civilian clothes, which they provided. I did
what they said without speaking, but my mind was racing. What were
they up to now? They continued to say nothing, but next the official returned the clothing I had been wearing when I was first arrested. (It had
turned yellow after eighteen years in a box.) He also gave me my watch,
whose band had become brittle with age. I was so confused about what
was happening that I never thought to check to see whether the watch
was working.

"You will be taken outside," the official said.

I wasn't sure what he meant. He didn't say I would be released or
become a free man, just that I would be taken outside. Then he added,
"You will be taken to a nice place. Your two children will be with
you."

I tried not to get my hopes up. It looked like I was being released, but
after all their attempts to break me, I did not trust them and still thought

this might be just another trick. Perhaps I was simply to be transported to another prison and the raising of my hopes was just a cruel joke. They gave me some pills to take, but I secretly threw them away.

It was the end of April 1978. When we got outside, they put me in a car. We drove off, and I never looked back.

PART V

After Prison

CHAPTER 23

Release from Prison

Nobody told me where we were going. After about an hour's drive into the heart of the city, we pulled into the Beijing Rail Station, and I saw that my children were waiting for me.

It was a difficult and confusing moment. I was numb. I don't know how to explain it, but I seemed to have lost the ability to respond emotionally. I recognized my children, but I felt no joy. They cried when they met me, but I could not return their emotion. Because of the years of self-imposed silence, when I wanted to say something, the words did not come easily, and I drooled uncontrollably. The years in prison had taught me to be suspicious of everything, and I could only think that this might be a trick and that they planned to put us all in prison.

We didn't have much time to talk before the train came, and the discussion about what to do was hurried. My children had been told that I was to be taken to Sichuan and that we would stay in a nice cottage formerly used by Guomindang army officers. The officials wanted my whole family to go with me, but my children thought it might be a ploy to get them all out of Beijing, so they suggested that only my sons Pengjing and Pengang accompany me for now. The others would follow when they were sure it was safe. While they explained this to me, I was in a daze. All I could say was "yes, yes" in Tibetan.

I boarded the train with my two sons and some officials from the Beijing Public Security Bureau office, without knowing what we were doing, and for the first part of the journey I was confused and disoriented. I felt like I had been taken from a world I knew to another planet. I had been in solitary confinement for years and was accustomed to having no communication with anyone. Now suddenly I was shoulder to shoulder with hundreds of noisy passengers milling about. For a while I became almost a zombie.

Eventually I began to collect myself a bit, but that only brought worries of a different kind. When I was able to focus better and think more clearly, I became troubled because I realized that I didn't know for sure what my status was. Although they hadn't put handcuffs and leg irons on me, they had never told me I was free. The police who accompanied me at the station and on the train told me I had to go to Zigong County in Sichuan Province. That was all. If I were free, I thought, wouldn't someone have come to shake my hand and officially tell me so? I began to fear that this was a trick and I was headed for an even worse prison than the one I had just been in. I had terrible stomach pains and could not sleep. Pengjing had brought a guitar with him, and they told him to play it to soothe me. He played beautifully, but the songs reminded me of happier times and ended up making me feel even worse. It was hard to understand. Here I was, out of solitary confinement and apparently entering human life again, and yet all I could feel was fear and depression.

When we arrived at the train station in Zigong County, some local officials took us to our new quarters, which consisted of two tiny, dilapidated rooms and a kitchen. When they saw it, my sons said, "We have been duped. They told us that we would be staying in a lovely house, and they have put us in an old shack." I felt even more suspicious and depressed. I learned later that the central government's policy was to send released prisoners who had had serious "political problems" to areas where they could not have a big impact or influence, that is, to not allow them to live in large cities or along main highways. In retrospect, it was to be expected that we would be placed in a location like this. But I didn't know that at the time.

The day after we arrived, we had a meeting with the Beijing Public Security Bureau officials who had accompanied me. At that meeting, they formally declared that I was released from prison and handed me a paper to sign. Although I was still in a somewhat dazed state, I could understand what I read, and when I examined the paper carefully, I noticed that it said I had been imprisoned for seeking independence for the Tibetan nationality [ch. *gao zangzu duli*] without specifying whether they were talking about before or after 1949. It said that even though my case had been an example of a contradiction between the enemy (me) and the people/Communist Party, they would treat it now only as a contradiction *within* the people (a much less serious label). It also said that my salary would be 120 yuan per month, about half what I had been earning before I was put in prison, and that from now on my salary would be paid by the People's Political Consultative Conference of Zigong County, a body comprised of former elites and non–Communist Party members. There was no talk of reinstating me into the Communist Party or giving me a serious position.

What it all meant was that I had been released from prison but not declared rehabilitated. As I looked at the document, I understood that I had no choice but to sign it, but when I did so, I wrote on the paper, "These statements do not correspond to the real facts of my situation, so I plan to make an appeal to the Central Committee to rectify this." The local Chinese officials looked surprised. They had been told I was crazy, but obviously I was not as "disconnected from reality" as they had thought.

After I had signed, they gave me a box that contained personal documents confiscated at the time of my arrest. The box contained things like letters, my bankbooks, and photographs. They told me the box contained everything, but I realized immediately that it didn't. They did not return the brief history of Tibet that Surkhang had written for me, nor did they return any of the things I had written in prison. I wasn't angry, though. I actually felt lucky to have gotten all the photographs back.

It took me a long time to adjust to being with my family again and being in the outside world. When I signed what they wanted and accepted my personal things, my life as a free man officially began, but I didn't really feel free. Although there were no guards or bars and I wasn't locked up in my cell at night, I was angry because I felt they were still falsely accusing me. They had needlessly taken eighteen years of my life, and I wanted them to admit that it had been a mistake.

I think when people saw me in those days, they must have thought I was insane. If someone had said I wasn't human, he would have been wrong, because I was breathing and walking. But if, conversely, someone said I *was* human, would he have been correct? I was confused and couldn't think or speak well. Even though I was living with two of my sons, I did not feel emotionally close to them. I had no interest in what they told me or asked me. I had become a very strange and weird thing. I didn't want to go back to my cell, but I felt lost, as if I were in a bizarre and alien world.

I was lucky to have my sons with me during these difficult times. Even though I was distant and often uninterested and unable to relate to them, they took me for walks, talked to me constantly, and tried to engage me in conversation. In the beginning, most of the time I just listened when they told me about things that had happened in Beijing while I was in prison. They explained that the Cultural Revolution had begun in 1966 and that Chairman Liu Shaoqi and Generals Peng Dehuai and He Long had been put in prison, where they had died. When my brother Chöm-pel visited me, he told me how our father had suffered and died in Batang. He also told me how our close comrade Topden had been hounded until he committed suicide during the Cultural Revolution. I was shocked to hear stories like these, yet oddly, I was also comforted. While I was in prison and cut off from any news of the world, I thought that my case was unique. Hearing about the fates of Liu Shaoqi, the generals, and my comrades made me realize that I was only one of many good cadres who had been wrongly persecuted and harmed.

Talking was hard for me for a long time. I could speak only a few words, and those with difficulty, and I could seldom describe my feelings accurately. (I learned later that one of the problems was that my vocal cords had been damaged by my years of silence in prison.) After a while, however, as I made progress, I began to ask my sons where their mother was. Whenever I did, they always changed the subject and became uneasy. Even in my dazed condition, I could see that they were hiding something from me, so I kept asking them. Finally Pengang told me that she had died during the Cultural Revolution, and it suddenly struck me that all the people who had been closest to me—my father, my mother, and my wife—were now gone. I felt a sense of despair that was almost suffocating.

Looking back at this difficult time, I think there were two things in particular, besides the constant attention of my sons, that helped me regain my balance and my interest in life. The first was being able to write. The dialectical theories I had formed so carefully in prison had literally preserved my sanity. I used to console myself with the thought that someday I could present my work as a gift to my father and my relatives. I even fantasized about being released and immediately sending a telegram to my father. In it I imagined saying proudly, "Father, though I have spent many years in prison, I have brought a gift for you, which will bring honor to Tibetans." Because I had not been allowed to preserve my theories and the written record of my reasoning processes, one of my greatest fears had been that I would forget the key ideas. Therefore, I tried to memorize the most important of them, and each day in my cell

I recited my findings, as if I were chanting the words of a Buddhist prayer. When I arrived in Zigong County, I immediately asked my sons to get me some paper, and I started to write down the main ideas. When I completed this task, I felt enormous relief, because I knew then that I could not lose or forget the results.

The other thing that helped me focus and regain my strength was my deep sense of the injustice I had suffered, and my commitment to redress the wrongs that had been done to me. I wanted the government and the party to admit their mistake and restore my previous status. My sons had told me of a few cases in which previously purged leaders had appealed to the central government for redress and been cleared of unjust accusations. When my other children came to visit me from Beijing, we also discussed the changes that were going on there and the many new examples of people who had suffered unjustly during the Cultural Revolution and had successfully petitioned for redress. Their visit fired my desire to make an appeal myself.

The question then became what to do next. It was obvious that I couldn't do much from a remote area like Zigong and that my best chance would be to try to get to Chengdu and launch my appeal from there. How to get there was the problem. I knew I could never get the officials overseeing me to let me simply relocate. Fortunately, however, after spending several months in Zigong, my relationship with them was good. They knew I was not crazy, and they had even intimated to my son that they thought I might really be innocent. At that time, stories of many innocent people who had been treated like me had come to the public's attention. I hoped, therefore, that because they liked and trusted me, the local authorities might be willing to look the other way.

My plan to get to Chengdu was simple enough. I had frequent problems with my feet swelling, and the next time a flare-up occurred, I went to the local hospital several times, and then told the local officials I would like to go to Chengdu to check with doctors there. I said I would take one son with me (leaving the other son there, as I feared that if I said I was taking both, they might suspect me of planning to run away). Typically, they made no response, but one day they sent a car for me and we went to Chengdu to see a doctor. I made several follow-up visits, and each time I was careful to return promptly. Then on one trip, my son and I decided to stay for a month. When the Zigong authorities said nothing, I decided I could be even bolder and make my appeal in Beijing itself. I quietly summoned my other son, and together we got on a train to Beijing. That was in February 1979.

The visit to Beijing rehabilitated me in many ways. I stayed at my children's apartment and almost immediately began to have visitors and meet old friends. I met Ngawang Kesang, who had been kept in my prison for two and a half years and then sent to a prisoners' road construction site in Sichuan for sixteen years. It was wonderful to see him and others again but sad to hear of their experiences in prison. Everyone in our party had suffered so much, so needlessly, but we had many experiences in common, which was a great help. We discussed my case, and encouraged by my good luck so far, I composed an appeal and sent my petition to the new top leaders, like Deng Xiaoping, Hu Yaobang, and Chen Yi.

Weeks went by with no response, and during that time I continued to talk with and meet more people than I had seen in decades, sharing experiences and catching up on the past twenty years. Then, one day in late March 1979, Xue Jianhua, the director of the Nationalities Bureau of the United Front Work Department, came to see me and told me that the Dalai Lama's older brother, Gyalo Thondup, had just arrived in Beijing as a guest of the central government. "He says that he must see you, and I think you should meet with him," Xue said. "Since you are staying with your children and have no apartment of your own, we suggest that you meet him at the Nationalities Palace Hotel, where we will get a room for you." I told him that whatever he wanted was fine with me. Actually, I thought it would be wonderful to meet somebody important from exile like him and learn what had happened to them all. The next day, Xue came to tell me that Gyalo Thondup insisted on meeting me at my residence (not in the Nationalities Palace), so I should prepare for the visit there.

This visit was one of the results of Deng Xiaoping's assumption of power in 1978. He changed the course of Chinese history, ushering in a new era in politics, society, and the economy. The kind of ultraleftist thinking that had produced the Antirightist campaign and the disastrous Cultural Revolution was now suppressed, and those who had previously been imprisoned were being released—if, like me, they were still alive. One dimension of Deng's new policy was the attempt to resolve outstanding "international issues," such as Taiwan, Hong Kong, and the Dalai Lama and the exiled Tibetans. Inviting Gyalo to visit Beijing was part of this shift.

When Gyalo Thondup arrived at our apartment, he explained the background of his visit. Some officials from the Xinhua News Agency in Hong Kong (who were representing the PRC in Hong Kong) had invited him to visit China. This seemed an overture with political implications, so he went to India to discuss the trip with the Dalai Lama and ask his

Figure 23. Phünwang, Gyalo Thondup, and Tseden Yangdrön (Phünwang's second wife), Beijing, 1999.

permission to accept. The Dalai Lama told him he should go, but that he had to make sure he did two things. One was that he could listen to anything, but not talk politics himself or negotiate. The other was that he was to try to find out where I was and what I was doing. He said the Dalai Lama had worried about what had become of me.

I was deeply moved by the Dalai Lama's concern and briefly filled Gyalo in on my story from 1958 to the present, including the fact that I was in the process of appealing my case to the central government. In return, he gave me a brief overview of what had happened to the Tibetans in exile, emphasizing that attitudes had changed from the old society. (For example, he said that many Tibetan children were now going to school.) He also said that he had met with many top officials, including Deng Xiaoping, who said that the party had made serious mistakes in Tibet (and China), but now things were different. Deng himself, he said, told him that except for independence, anything was open for discussion. It was heartening to hear this and exciting to be a part of his perhaps historic visit. Everything was changing so quickly.

Before he left, Gyalo said he wanted to meet my children, so I called them from their room. They discussed their experiences, and when my daughter began to cry, I could see tears well up in Gyalo's eyes. At that time, all but one of my children had active cases of tuberculosis, and he said that he would ask the government to let them go abroad to get medical treatment. If they did not agree to this, he said, he would buy medicines in Hong Kong and send them to us.

I later learned that Gyalo Thondup's visit was very beneficial to me. After he left, the top government leaders who dealt with nationality issues, like Ulanhu (director of the United Front Work Department) and Yang Jingren (the head of the State Nationalities Affairs Commission), started to pay serious attention to my appeal. At that time, Deng Xiaoping wanted to develop closer relations with the Dalai Lama and was even hoping it might be possible to settle the Tibet Question and have him return to China. They believed, I learned, that if the Dalai Lama was interested in my whereabouts and welfare, the government should also pay attention to my situation. The visit was also very helpful to my children. Although the authorities did not respond to the request to let them go abroad, about ten days after Gyalo Thondup left, we received a shipment of medicines from him that were not available in China.

Not long after Gyalo Thondup's visit, the Panchen Lama visited me as well, and we had a long conversation. "My friend," he said when he saw my situation—the poor conditions I was living in—"the two of us have spent many years in prison because of our interest in helping our nationality. You spent about eighteen years in prison, and I was kept over ten years in detention. We did not do anything illegal; we merely worked for the interests of our nationality. I have just been released and I have no power, so it is hard for me to help you politically. However, in terms of livelihood, I can help you with whatever you need. Eventually, when things get better, I will help you more."

The fact that the Panchen Lama had come to visit me in person and offered to help meant a lot to my family and me, and was another sign that coming to Beijing had been the right strategy. But it also reminded me that my immediate need was to secure full restitution from the party and the government. I began to worry about whether my petition had reached the top leadership, and decided to visit Ngabö and ask him to help, as he knew my situation well. (He had been fortunate and had not suffered during the intervening years.) I gave him a copy of my petition and asked him to pass it up the line. He said he would.

I also went to see Feng Weibing, the secretary of the general office of the Central Committee of the CCP, for the same reason. Though I did not know him personally, I was persistent in asking for a brief meeting. When he finally agreed, I told him that I had sent letters to Deng Xiaoping, Chen Yi, and Hu Yaobang, but that I was not sure whether they had received them. I asked him to speak with his superiors and requested that I be allowed to meet with Deng Xiaoping. "Deng knows me," I said. "If you mention my name to him, that will be good enough."

I brought a picture of me with Deng to prove that I knew him personally. That impressed Feng, and he seemed to pay more attention to me afterward. I also presented him with a copy of my petition. He told me that it was hard to predict whether Deng would be able to talk with me. He had great responsibilities now and was always extremely busy. But he did guarantee that he would give him my petition. Sometime later, Feng told me that he had done this, so I did not need to worry about its being seen. He also hinted that there would soon be a day when my status would be rehabilitated. That was the best news I had had in years. For the first time, I believed that my situation would finally be resolved.

In the fall of 1979, while my petition was still going forward, Deng Xiaoping invited the Dalai Lama to send a delegation to China to visit Tibetan areas. I became involved when Yang Jingren invited me to attend a banquet he was hosting for them. It was the first public event I had attended since my release, and I was encouraged by what the invitation seemed to imply about the government's attitude toward me. Although I was not actually rehabilitated, they arranged for me to sit at the second table, where most of the people from the United Front Work Department were seated. Yang Jingren and the members of the exile delegation were at the first table, but the Tibetan exile delegation frequently came to my table to offer toasts with me, and the exile delegates later told me in private that they had especially praised me in their talks with Yang and other officials. I enjoyed meeting with the exile delegates, whose subsequent trip to Tibet was a real eye-opener.

This was the first Tibetan exile delegation to visit Tibetan areas, and the government wanted to ensure they had a positive experience. It sent instructions to the areas they would visit, instructing the leadership to carefully inform the local people and cadres to give the delegates a warm welcome. (The United Front Work Department believed that the Tibetan masses were still very bitter about the old society, and feared they might treat the exile delegates rudely as class enemies and separatists.) In Lhasa, the local officials went so far as to hold neighborhood meetings warning the people not to throw stones or spit at the delegates.

As it turned out, they could not have been more wrong about what Tibetans thought and felt. When the delegation arrived in Tibet, the local people greeted them with a remarkable display of enthusiasm and support. The same Tibetan masses who had seemed adamant in their condemnation and hatred of the "exploiting classes" after the 1959 uprising and during the Cultural Revolution now welcomed them as returning heroes. Several thousand people in Lhasa presented ceremonial scarves to the delegates, and many people embraced them and shed tears of joy. People tore pieces from the belt of Lobsang Samden, the Dalai Lama's brother, to use as protective amulets, and some ordinary Tibetans shouted, "Free Tibet!" and "Long live the Dalai Lama!"

When they returned to Beijing, the delegation members told me that many cadres and local Tibetans had presented them with religious statues and religious scroll paintings they had saved from destruction during the Cultural Revolution, asking that they be given to the Dalai Lama. Everything that happened made it painfully obvious how little the government was in touch with Tibetans' real feelings. The delegation's experience showed vividly that the government had in a sense been fooled by its own propaganda. It was now clear that ethnicity, not class, was the dominant factor in Tibet. This was totally unexpected and sent shock waves through the leadership in Beijing.

It surprised me, too. From what I had read in newspapers while in prison, it seemed that Tibetans welcomed the policy of class struggle. Sitting alone in Qingchen Prison, out of contact with friends and the world, I had believed what I read. I never actually thought that the Tibetan masses would throw stones or spit on members of the exile delegation, but the degree of spontaneous welcome and support they exhibited went far beyond anything I would have imagined. And it made me feel proud. I thought that there was still hope for our nationality. All those years had not extinguished Tibetans' love of their culture and identity.

All of this got me thinking about political and nationality issues once again. I had always thought that a fundamental issue was developing a proper relationship between *two nationalities and two cultures*—Chinese and Tibetan. The central government had misunderstood this when they allowed the reforms to go forward in Kham in 1956, and now it was obvious that they had also erred when they suppressed traditional culture during the Cultural Revolution. They would have to reexamine what had transpired in Tibet since 1959 and decide what kind of nationalities policy they should employ in the new China. I thought I understood the problem and could play a role in this process.

For me, the response of common Tibetans to the Dalai Lama's representatives revealed the extent to which China's nationalities policy had been hijacked by ultraleftists. It was bad Marxism, and it had produced a bad result. Since the late 1950s, the original policy of equality of nationalities had been suppressed in favor of what we in the party used to call Great Han Chauvinism, that is to say, the ethnic Chinese (Han) controlling and dominating the minority nationalities, which in turn undermined the local minorities' autonomy and culture. Notwithstanding much rhetoric about equality, the fact was that over the past twenty years, the relationship between Chinese and Tibetans had devolved into a master/servant relationship.

In Marxist ideology, all minority nationalities should have true equality with the majority nationality in all spheres. This is a defining difference between capitalist and socialist states. And when a society or state reaches the final level of true communism, there should be no difference between nationalities in that nation, since nationalities A, B, and C will mesh to become a new, socialist nationality, D. However, that is not what had been happening in China. Instead, under the pressure of Han Chauvinist policies, nationalities B and C were being forced to become nationality A, that is, to become like Han Chinese. This was bad for the country and bad for the minority nationalities, and it was the reason, I thought, for the anger of Tibetans despite their dislike and rejection of the oppressive traditional feudal system.

When the exile delegation returned to Beijing, they visited me. After telling me in detail about their experiences, they mentioned that the Dalai Lama trusted me, so if I had anything to tell him, I should prepare it and they would pass it on to him. This was potentially important but also tricky. I thought carefully about what I should say, and after securing permission from the government, on December 5, 1979, I conveyed my thoughts to the delegates at my home. They made a written record of my ideas. (I later submitted a report to the party on what I told them, which was published the following year [September 20, 1980] as a supplement to the Central Party School's periodical *Materials for the Study of Theory* [see appendix B].)

Of course, I was careful about what I said, but I was also frank. The Tibetans' warm reception of the delegates and the thinking it had made me do were both much on my mind. I thought it would be important to try to ground my opinions in broader historical and theoretical contexts, and so began by telling the delegation that Marxism-Leninism is totally opposed to one nationality oppressing others and believes there should be real equality between the nationalities. In fact, I said, when such equality is absent, Marxism considers that the minority nationalities are justified in seeking separation.

Since the founding of the new China, I said, although there had been many improvements regarding the equality and unity of nationalities,

Figure 24. Tibetan exile delegation, Beijing, 1979. *From left:* Lobsang Targye, Phüntso Tashi, the Panchen Lama, Thubden Namgye, and Phünwang. *Kneeling:* Lobsang Samden.

there had also been many serious mistakes and much suffering. And, of course, there were still many problems. However, the top leaders of China recognized these mistakes and were attempting to correct them. Therefore, I said, I was convinced that the many new reform policies being instituted had made it feasible now for Tibetans to obtain real equality. Consequently, I believed that at this juncture the best path for Tibetans was to unite and cooperate with the Han (and other minority nationalities) under the leadership of the Communist Party. I asked them to report to the Dalai Lama and other friends overseas that if they really cared about the interests of today's Tibetans, they should study the current situation and examine carefully the essential question—was seeking alliance or division (separatism/independence) more beneficial for Tibetans as a nationality? I said I firmly believed that the correct answer was alliance. It felt good to engage my mind with ideas like these and to feel I was again playing a role in nationalities issues at a critical time in Tibet's history.

Four months later, in April 1980, Yang Jingren informed me that I was officially rehabilitated. All the false accusations against me were rescinded, and my membership in the Communist Party, as well as my official rank, was restored to the same level as before I was arrested. Yang told me to read the party's documents to catch up with what had been going on, and not long afterward I was selected as a deputy to the Fifth National People's Congress and a member of the Standing Committee of that body. At the same time, I was appointed deputy director of the Nationalities Committee of the National People's Congress.

Yang Jingren himself hosted the banquet at which my official rehabilitation was announced. At the start of the evening, he stood up and toasted me. "First," he said, "I would like to congratulate you, Phünwang, because from today on you are completely rehabilitated politically." Then he invited me to comment on my conversations with the Tibetan exile delegates. "When Gyalo Thondup and the subsequent exile delegation came to Beijing," he said, "they visited the Panchen Lama, Ngabö, and you. You had conversations and exchanged ideas with them, and though at present you have no special responsibility concerning Tibet affairs, in the past you were the senior Tibetan official and know the situation well. Moreover, even though the exiles visited the Panchen Lama and Ngabö, their attitude toward you was much more positive than it was toward the others, so you therefore probably know better than anyone else what they really think. Tell us, then, what you think is most important to them and how they see the future."

I felt many conflicting emotions as I rose to speak. It was hard to believe that after eighteen years of prison, I was actually being toasted and asked to speak at a meeting like this. I was grateful to have my life back and honored to have my opinions sought again, but I was also still dissatisfied because Yang Jingren had made no public apology for the government's misconduct toward me or for my eighteen years in solitary confinement. Consequently, I was careful *not* to thank them for my rehabilitation and said only, "Today Yang Jingren formally declared that I am politically rehabilitated. I am very happy about this."

I paused.

"Regarding his second point," I said, "when Gyalo Thondup and the others came to Beijing to visit me, these were not political visits. However, we did have some conversations in which they talked and I listened, and I will be happy to tell you my perceptions. I think their main aim is to have a united autonomous region that would comprise *all* Tibetans in the Tibet Autonomous Region as well as those in the provinces of Sichuan, Qinghai, Gansu, and Yunnan. They do not seem intent only on independence. They did not explicitly tell me this, but from their conversation, I think a united region with real autonomy is their main hope for the future."

"If that is want they want," said Yang Jingren, "then this is a matter that can be dealt with within our country."

Xue Jianhua immediately disagreed. "A united autonomous region of all Tibetans is the exiles' first step toward independence," he said sternly. "Their real purpose is independence."

Yang Jingren did not respond, so I replied, "I do not agree. I believe that what they really wish is to have all Tibetan areas united. If they achieve this, then I think they will give up their goal of independence. On the other hand, if they cannot achieve a united autonomous region, then I fear that they will continue to work hard for Tibetan independence for as long as it takes. There are two paths open to them, a fact that we should keep in mind as we formulate policy."

As I thought the next day about the banquet, I found my situation astonishing. Less than two years before, in a dazed and disoriented state, I was released from prison after eighteen years and exiled to a remote part of Sichuan Province. Now I was living in Beijing. I had been visited by the Dalai Lama's older brother, the Panchen Lama, and the first official delegation sent by the Dalai Lama to China. I had been officially declared rehabilitated, reinstated to my old rank and status in the party, and yesterday I had been toasted and my opinions sought by party officials at a banquet in my honor. It was wonderful but hard to digest how fast everything was changing. These were exciting times.

A few months after this, the general secretary of the party, Hu Yaobang, made an unprecedented inspection trip to Lhasa, during which he criticized earlier policies there and called for a new approach that would give Tibetans authority and power, as well as allow them to preserve their culture and practice their religion. I knew I had an obligation as a Tibetan intellectual to be a strong voice that would convey the perspective of Tibetans. But while I also knew there were many officials both in Beijing and in Tibet who were opposed to Hu Yaobang's ideas, I did not realize how quickly I would be caught up in this struggle.

CHAPTER 24

A New Struggle

Deng Xiaoping broke radically with the past by acknowledging that Mao was human and that some of his policies and decisions had been mistakes. However, the changes and new perspectives that Deng was implementing in the rest of China were slow to reach Tibet. No meetings were convened to state publicly that the Cultural Revolution in Tibet had been a mistake, and Ren Rong, the first party secretary, stubbornly followed the old policy commonly know as the "Two Whatevers." (After Mao's death, the new chairman of the CCP, Hua Guofeng, had stated, "We will uphold firmly *whatever* policies Chairman Mao made and follow forever *whatever* instructions Chairman Mao gave.") By the end of 1979, the Central Committee had recognized the problem, and in late May 1980, Deng sent Hu Yaobang to Tibet to end the "Two Whatevers" approach and begin a new, more culturally sensitive policy.

Hu's visit was historic. In a major speech delivered soon after he arrived, he severely criticized the policies of the past twenty years and promised that the government would make a major effort to improve economic development and create a Tibet that was more Tibetan in character. The speech contained a powerful vision of a strongly ethnic Tibet Autonomous Region. Tibetans, he said, should be able to exercise more autonomy, and there should be more cultural, linguistic, and religious freedom. Chinese cadres working in Tibet should learn the Tibetan language. A change of focus from class struggle to issues of ethnicity seemed genuinely to be occurring. (To show that he meant business, Hu not only replaced Ren Rong but also insisted that Ren physically leave the country with him. The symbolism was powerful.)

Hu publicly announced a liberal six-point reform program on Tibet, which included among its salient points:

(1). Full play must be given to the right of regional autonomy of minority nationalities under the unified leadership of the party Central Committee. . . . The right to decide for oneself under unified leadership should not be abolished. It is necessary to exercise this right fully and independently. Anything that is not suited to Tibet's conditions should be rejected or modified, along with anything that is not beneficial to national unity or the development of production. The autonomous region should fully exercise its right to decide for itself under the unified leadership of the party Central Committee, and it should lay down laws, rules and regulations according to its special characteristics to protect the right of national autonomy and its special national interests.

(2). . . . Compared with other provinces and autonomous regions of the country, it is conspicuous that in Tibet the people's living standards lag far behind. This situation means that the burden of the masses must be considerably lightened. The people in Tibet should be exempt from paying taxes and meeting purchase quotas for the next few years. . . . All kinds of exactions must be abolished. The people should not be assigned any additional work without pay. Peasants' and herdsmen's produce may be purchased at negotiated prices or bartered to supply mutual needs, and they should be exempt from meeting state purchase quotas. . . .

(3). Specific and flexible policies suited to conditions in Tibet must be carried out on the whole economic front of the region, including the agricultural, animal husbandry, financial and trade, commercial, handicraft and communication fronts, with a view of promoting Tibet's economic development more rapidly. . . .

(5). So long as the socialist orientation is upheld, vigorous efforts must be made to revive and develop Tibetan culture, education and science. The Tibetan people have a long history and a rich culture. The world renowned ancient Tibetan culture included fine Buddhism, graceful music and dance as well as medicine and opera, all of which are worthy of serious study and development. All ideas that ignore and weaken Tibetan culture are wrong. It is necessary to do a good job in inheriting and developing Tibetan culture.

Education has not progressed well in Tibet. Taking Tibet's special characteristics into consideration, efforts should be made to set up universities and middle and primary schools in the region. Some cultural relics and Buddhist scriptures in temples have been damaged, and conscientious effort should be made to protect, sort and study them. Cadres of Han nationality working in Tibet should learn the spoken and written Tibetan language. It should be a required subject; otherwise they will be divorced from the masses. Cherishing the people of minority nationalities is not empty talk. The Tibetan people's habits, customs, history and culture must be respected.

(6).   The party's policy on minority cadres must be correctly implemented and the unity between Han and Tibetan cadres must be even more closely enhanced. . . .

Full time cadres of Tibetan nationality should account for more than 2/3rds of all government functionaries in Xizang, within the next 2–3 years.[1]

Not long after Hu's return to Beijing, the Central Committee continued its new policy for Tibet when it approved a new directive, known as "Document Number 31." It stated that under the unified leadership of the central government, Tibet could exercise true autonomy, including the right to make its own decisions. For example, all central government guidelines, policies, instructions, and regulations could be refused or adapted if they did not conform with the practical conditions in Tibet, although for important cases, Tibet would have to ask permission from the central government. The new document also stated that when Han officials were transferred to Tibet, the principle of "few and outstanding" must be adhered to; that is to say, their numbers should be limited and those sent must be talented individuals with special knowledge and

---

1. Quoted in Melvyn Goldstein, *The Snow Lion and the Dragon* (Berkeley: University of California Press, 1997), pp. 64–65.

ability. Later, the Central Committee formulated "Document Number 46," concerning Xinjiang, which went further. It said that in the future, in special nationality areas like Xinjiang and Tibet, the central government would retain authority over only three areas: foreign relations, national defense, and veto power. All other rights belonged to the minority areas.— Goldstein, Sherap, and Siebenschuh

In June 1980, about ten days after Hu Yaobang returned from Tibet, I received a message from the State Nationalities Affairs Commission saying that Hu wanted to meet with me. I knew Hu personally. We had been members of the Southwest Bureau in the 1950s, and we both had been associated with the Communist Youth League. When we met, he smiled warmly and said, "To find you still alive is a great victory."

Hu quickly explained that the main reason he wanted to talk with me was his concern about some Tibetan officials. "Many of them simply do what the Chinese cadres tell them," he said. "They don't speak up on behalf of their nationality, and so they can't really be called *Tibetan* cadres, since they don't express or advocate the thoughts and concerns of Tibetans." I agreed that this situation had to be remedied if Tibet was to move forward. That was when the surprise came.

"We are bringing Tian Bao back from Tibet to work here in Beijing," he said, "and we would like you to go to Tibet in his place as governor. After a couple of years," he added, "the secretary position will be filled by a Tibetan." In context, I understood him to be suggesting that after two years I could be appointed the first party secretary of the TAR. I was stunned. I had never anticipated anything like this, and at first I had no idea what to say.

My strongest instincts told me to decline, and I did so, telling Hu that at this time I thought it would be better for me to stay in Beijing. During the eighteen years I was in prison, I explained, I had read widely and developed a theory about dialectical materialism that I wanted to spend the next year or so turning into a book. I said I thought my work on the book would be more beneficial for both the party and the country than anything I might be able to do in Tibet. We talked a bit more, and as I was leaving, I told him that I had thought a great deal about Tibetan affairs while I was in prison and would like to meet with him again some time and report on these issues. He said he would be happy to talk with me.

I left with a dozen ideas swirling in my head, but after I had some time to think about it, I decided I had made a good decision. I chose not to take a job in Tibet in part because I really did want time to refine and write up my thoughts on dialectics and continue my work. I believed that not to do so would mean that my eighteen years in prison had simply been wasted time, whereas to complete the study would mean that I had transformed something negative into something positive. But there were other issues.

I did not think I was the right person to go to Tibet just then. I had only recently been released from prison and didn't know the Chinese working in Lhasa or what had been going on since I had last been there, in 1958. If I tried to implement major changes, I would certainly encounter opposition and conflict from the Chinese cadres who supported Ren Rong. And if I went with a big title and did nothing new, I would anger the Tibetans, who would be looking for changes. The time was simply not right, and I thought it was best for me to take things slowly and wait until I knew more about the situation in both Tibet and Beijing. But that did not mean I intended to keep quiet about nationalities policy. I was very encouraged by the bold direction of Hu's proposed reforms and decided I should speak out and try to influence policy.

By 1981, my views had become well known among the elite. Some of my ideas on nationality equality and the place of nationality minorities in China had appeared in September 1980, when the comments I had made to the Tibetan exile delegation in 1979 were published [see appendix B]. A few months later, Hu invited me to dinner, along with a number of prominent Tibetan and Chinese officials from Tibet. (Other guests included Ngabö; Pasang, then secretary of the TAR Party Committee; and Yin Fatang, then the current Han first party secretary.) It was primarily a social event, but I took the opportunity to say some things I thought Hu and the others needed to hear.

First, I commented on the need to reopen the assessment of the 1959 revolt. I argued that there were significant discrepancies between what I had heard happened in 1959 and what had been officially written about the uprising, and I suggested that the Central Committee should form a small committee to take another look. Many people, I said, had erroneously been given negative political labels, and their histories needed to be reviewed and rectified. For example, some Tibetans had gone to Norbulingka in 1959 not to join the rebels but simply for a religious visit. I pointed out that we should not have labeled them as being "involved in the rebellion" simply because they happened to be there at the wrong time. "Consider," I said, "that Ngabö was preparing to go to Norbulingka for a Council of Ministers meeting when word came that demonstrators had killed a Tibetan official. Had that message not come and had he gone to the meeting, he might have been labeled a counterrevolutionary too."

I also pointed out that some officials in Tibet were still saying that we should not totally deny the Cultural Revolution. They were arguing that while some of its activities were wrong, some were correct, and we should give credit to the correct ones. I thought this attitude was wrong. Since the Central Committee had totally denied the Cultural Revolution, none of the major leaders of the Tibet Autonomous Region should be saying that some parts were good. This was extremely important, I said, because if the TAR's leaders were not in agreement on this, how could they carry out the government's new policy?

Finally, I said I thought it was a serious mistake to use the army to put down rebellions and do police work in minority areas. We may have felt that what we were sending was a "people's army," but because the soldiers were virtually all Han Chinese, when they arrived in the minority areas the ethnic population considered them a Han Chinese army. The situation then quickly became one in which Han Chinese with guns were viewed as suppressing the ethnic minority. This in turn only increased the opposition between the Han Chinese and the minority nationalities. "Rebellions and disturbances," I said, "should be put down peacefully and politically, through both sides discussing and coordinating. There should also be a local police staffed with ethnic citizens for such work."

When I had finished speaking, Hu nodded. The others said nothing, and their silence was an accurate prediction of events to come.

Reaction came quickly. Rumors spread in Tibet that I had sent a report to the Central Committee attacking the activities involved in putting down the 1959 rebellion and was instigating Tibetans to seek a "Greater Tibet." The latter accusation originated in the United Front Work Department. It had received a petition from six Tibetan cadres in Gansu asking for the creation of a single unified Tibet Autonomous Region, or if not that, then at least a unified Eastern Tibet Autonomous Region that would include all the Tibetan areas in Qinghai, Gansu, Yunnan, and Sichuan. These Tibetans had given me a copy of their petition on a visit I had made to Qinghai and Gansu at the end of 1980, but by that time it had already been submitted to the United Front Work Department in Beijing, so I really had nothing to do with its creation. Nevertheless, the United Front sent a team to Gansu to try to get people to say that I had been encouraging the six cadres to make this request. They did not succeed. The former charge was a total distortion of my comments, and the latter was simply untrue. But vague accusations like this prompted some reactionary leaders in Tibet who did not want to reform policy to think of me once again as a dangerous nationalist.

I learned that this was going on in the summer of 1981, when I went to Lhasa for the first time since my imprisonment. On the surface, all went nicely and the party and government in Tibet held elaborate receptions for me. But beneath the surface, I was under serious attack by the leadership of the TAR. I discovered this indirectly when a Tibetan named Ngawang Tenzin (the vice director of the Xinhua News Agency in Tibet) came to talk with me. I knew immediately that he wasn't there on an ordinary courtesy call, because he was extremely nervous and kept looking around to make sure no one was watching or listening.

I took him to the back of my house, where he handed me a document that had been written at the end of 1980 by Sheng Wuangqi, his boss. It was labeled in Chinese as a *dong tai qing yang* document, which meant it was circulated only among a very restricted level of top party members. Ngawang Tenzin said he had noticed it some months earlier when he went to get something out of the safe in his office. He said that when he read the letter, the contents shocked him, and at considerable personal risk, he copied it because he thought I needed to see it. He had held on to it until now, he said, since he didn't know anyone going to Beijing whom he trusted to bring it to me.

The letter shocked me as well, bringing back terrible memories. It said that there were three Tibetans who were harming the party's work in Tibet—the Dalai Lama, the Panchen Lama, and me. Outside of the country, it said, the Dalai Lama was traveling all over the world working for Tibet's independence. Inside the country (but outside the party), the new reforms had allowed the Panchen Lama to become arrogant. And within the party, it said,

> Phünwang has been rehabilitated, but he is still talking about Tibetan independence and does not acknowledge that the disturbance of 1959 was a true rebellion. He is "wagging his tail" [arrogantly criticizing and talking back]. There is talk that he will become the Governor of Tibet. Many of the Tibetans who were with him when he first came to Tibet now occupy critical posts in the government and party—many are at the level of directors of offices—and since they all have frequent contact with him and are his people, unless we are careful about this there is a danger for the party.

This was strong language and very serious, since it was not casual gossip. Although the letter was signed by Sheng Wuangqi, it certainly had been approved by Yin Fatang, the first party secretary. Was the past about to repeat itself? I could not help wondering whether this was the beginning of the same kind of process that had previously led to my arrest. But I was not as young or naïve as I had been then, and I decided I must take immediate steps to counter the rumors/accusations (which had never been made publicly to me).

I thought carefully how this could have come about. There was no history of bad relations between Yin Fatang and me, so he couldn't be attacking me because of a personal insult or grievance. I decided, therefore, that he must have approved this letter based on my comments at Hu Yaobang's dinner and other rumors he had heard about what I was thinking and advocating. Consequently, what I needed to do was convince him that my views were not a threat to the party's work in Tibet. The trick was going to be to do so *without* revealing that I had seen the report. Fortunately, I was scheduled to leave Lhasa on a tour of other parts of Tibet, so I had time to think about how best to respond.

When I returned, I asked Yin to convene a meeting so I could speak to the party leaders about the things that I had seen in my travels. My plan was to use the opportunity to address the charges in the secret document. I had given careful thought to what I needed to say, and told the meeting first that I had not come to Tibet with the idea of joining the government here. I said frankly that Hu Yaobang had asked me to become the governor in Tibet, but I declined and explained the reasons I had given to Hu—in essence, that I had been out of circulation for too long and the efficiency of the administration would surely suffer.

"Second," I said, "there are many rumors floating around Lhasa that concern Tibetan independence, and I would like to comment on that important issue. In 1949, we were reborn as a nation under the Communist Party. Under the old system, during the reign of the Guomindang, the leaders considered Han Chinese superior and oppressed and exploited the other nationalities. However, under the new, communist system, oppression and exploitation of the nationalities has become constitutionally illegal. In the new China, the relationship between the nationalities is diametrically opposite to what it was under the Guomindang.

"From the inception of the People's Republic of China," I said, as categorically as I could, "I have rejected the idea of independence for individual nationalities. I have always advocated the idea that all nationalities must strive together in harmony and equality." I spoke for about two hours, elaborating on my thinking. At the conclusion of my talk, no one made any comment. "That was a good meeting, and now it's time to eat" was Yin Fatang's only response.

On the way to dinner, I went to the restroom, where Yangling Dorje, a Bapa friend who was a deputy secretary in the Tibetan government, joined me. Speaking in the Batang dialect so no one else could understand, he told me my talk had been excellent but that Yin had not said anything about it after the meeting. Yin, he said, had given no inkling of what he thought. Then, at dinner, Yin made a toast. "Today our comrade Phünwang gave a very important speech," he said. "We have all learned a great deal. On behalf of everyone here, thank you. I hope you will come to Tibet again every year."

I had not expected Yin to say anything explicitly about the accusations in public. My hope was that he would say something indirectly, and then come to see me later in the evening to talk about them. Nothing happened, however. Although by now he should have realized that the accusations in the document were groundless, nothing I said in my speech seemed to have made any impression.

I was discouraged. After discussing the problem again with Yangling Dorje, I decided I had no choice but to raise the issue directly with the central government, which I did as soon as I was back in Beijing. Because the initial report had been sent from the Xinhua News Agency office in Lhasa, I went to see Zheng Tao, who was the director of the entire Xinhua News Agency, and asked him to pass on my complaint to Ulanhu, the director of the powerful United Front Work Department.

Consequently, as fall 1981 arrived, notwithstanding all of Deng Xiaoping's and Hu Yaobang's reforms, I was again in the middle of a potentially serious struggle about my views on Tibet and nationalities policy in China. I suppose if I had been determined to be careful, I would have tried to lie low and do nothing further to draw attention to myself. But I had spent too many years in prison thinking things through; too much had gone wrong with the party's nationalities policy, and I thought the party's top officials needed to hear my Tibetan Marxist perspective. And so, whatever the cost might be, I decided to continue to play an active role.

CHAPTER 25

Nationalities Policy

In late 1980, I decided to participate actively in the major discussions that were in progress regarding revising the national constitution. I had experienced firsthand how individual leaders could ignore or reverse policies with relative ease, so I wanted the government to add clauses to the constitution that clearly spelled out the rights of nationalities. If this was done properly, these rights would not just be policies, they would be the *law*, and they would stand regardless of subsequent changes in leadership or future political campaigns.

This debate over the constitution was a natural venue for me because I was a vice director of the Nationalities Commission of the National People's Congress, and so was directly involved in discussions of legislation relating to minorities. I thought a great deal about the new constitution, and then decided to present my thoughts verbally at a meeting of cadres in my work unit.

I decided that rather than just listing proposed clauses, I would start by discussing more broadly how Marxism deals with the issue of nationalities, and particularly the relationship between majority and minority nationalities. Many Chinese leaders criticized minority nationalities like Tibetans for pursuing separatist ideas. (That is what was bothering the officials in Lhasa who were attacking me.) However, I believed that they did not understand Marxist theory on this issue.

In Marxism, the relationship between nationalities in multiethnic states should be one of complete equality. However, Marxism draws a basic distinction between nationalities embedded in class-based societies and those in communist societies. In class-based societies, separatist activities by minority nationalities are not considered negatively because they are caused by the oppressive policies of the majority nationality and the government it monopolizes.

In such societies, the ruling (i.e., oppressing) nationality typically emphasizes in its rhetoric the unity of all nationalities [ch. *minzu tuanjie*], and it vigorously opposes the struggles of minority nationalities against the state, labeling these pejoratively as "splittist" activities that seek to destroy the nation. However, from the Marxist standpoint, the struggle of minority nationalities against oppression by the majority nationality is correct and justified because there is no equality. In the absence of true equality, splittism is a valid response for minority nationalities in class-based societies. It is, in fact, characteristic of class-based multiethnic nations. By contrast, in socialist states, the majority nationality does not (or should not) oppress the minority nationalities. All should be equal, and there should be complete unity and cooperation among nationalities. Nationality unity, therefore, requires not suppression but new policies that provide real equality.

But what does equality of nationalities mean? Lenin, I said, wrote, "We require that there be *sovereign* [ch. *zhuquan*] equality between nationalities in a country" (*The Collected Works of Lenin,* vol. 19). True national equality, therefore, means that the party/state should admit and respect the rights of the minorities to *make decisions* in the fields of politics, economy, culture, and so on. "Only this," he wrote, "will solve the issue of separatist feelings and activities" (ibid.). This being the case, I suggested that a number of specific items be added to the nation's constitution. [Phünwang's entire essay is found in appendix C.]

First, I suggested that the new constitution include a phrase stating that *"the self-governing nationality is the major power body and should shoulder the responsibility of managing local affairs."* If such were the case, each nationality would have the right to be involved in the management of its area and the development of its own politics, economy, and culture.

Second, I suggested that nationality populations should be combined into larger political units wherever possible. I pointed out that the current system of dividing nationalities between different regions interfered with the party policy of protecting the equality and unity of nationalities and would harm the interests of minority nationalities in the long run. I did not specifically mention a "Greater Tibet" because I thought it would anger or threaten people. But I crafted this point so that if it were accepted, it would include all Tibetans.

Third, as I had mentioned to Hu Yaobang, I thought the constitution should stipulate that the army should not be used as a police force in minority areas. While it is the nation's right to direct the military and foreign affairs of the whole country, in minority autonomous regions, there were problems that needed to be addressed regarding relations among the army, the local government, and the local people. Because the majority of soldiers were Han Chinese, the relationship between the army and the local people was often considered synonymous with the relationship between the Han Chinese and the minority. Therefore, I suggested the following article be added to the constitution:

> The national defense of our country should be controlled by the highest national authority (the National People's Congress) and the highest national administrative organization (the State Council). The army defending our country is responsible for fighting invading forces but is not responsible for maintaining public order in autonomous regions. In autonomous regions, public order should be maintained by the local minority forces. The national defense army stationed in autonomous regions should respect the right of the local autonomous government organizations and obey their orders concerning nationality autonomy.

Finally, I emphasized the essential need for a statement about the rights of minorities to use their own languages. Lenin, I pointed out, said, "Those who do not agree with and support the equality of nationalities and languages and those who do not fight against nationality oppression and inequality are not Marxists or even socialists" (*The Collected Works of Lenin,* vol. 20). And Stalin asked, "Why should people of a certain nationality use their own language? It is because using their own language is the only way for them to develop their culture, politics, and economy" (*The Collected Works of Stalin,* vol. 11).

In our country, I said, we have had a succession of different policies regarding the languages of minority nationalities. Before liberation, the Guomindang practiced Han Chauvinism and nationality assimilation. They attempted gradually to replace minority languages with the Chinese language, and sought eventually to wipe out minority languages. By contrast, immediately after liberation, the Chinese Communist party adhered to the principle of nationality equality and unity, and respected the right of minorities to use and develop their own languages. However, under the influence of the extreme left, the CCP went back to the old approach. "During the ten-year calamity" of the Cultural Revolution, I wrote, "minority languages were 'sentenced to death.'"

After the overthrow of the Gang of Four, however, the CCP began to rehabilitate the language rights of minorities, although in some areas officials still dreamed of eventually replacing minority languages with the Han language. The fact that this kind of Han Chauvinism exists in some places is one of the most serious hindrances to our nation's current work on nationality relations. Therefore, I suggested that the following article be added to the constitution:

> The nation protects the right of minorities to use their own language as the major language in their autonomous region, and the Han language should also be taught. It is prohibited to replace minority languages with the Han language. National laws, policies, regulations, and orders should be translated into minority languages. Detailed policies should be formulated to make sure that minority languages are used for minority students in the entrance examinations to secondary schools and colleges, and not replaced by the Han language.

After I finished speaking, Li Gui, the head of my office, praised my views and asked me to write them down. He then distributed them to a number of important officials, including Ulanhu, who also liked my essay and distributed it further to other offices and officials. In general, however, the essay raised a storm of controversy and led to a major debate within the party, because until then, no one had ever seriously criticized the party's policy on nationalities affairs. Ulanhu had raised some issues while he was working in Inner Mongolia, and Liu Geping had also made some criticisms when he worked in the Ningxia Hui Autonomous Region. But none of these critiques had gone to the core of the party's ideology on minority nationalities, as mine did.

Within the party, I was attacked by important officials like Yang Jingren, Jiang Peng, Xue Jianhua, and Huang Chou. I learned later that a group of about thirteen cadres got together and worked for five months to rebut this essay and my other discourses, such as the conversation I had had with the exile delegation. They produced a ten-thousand-character attack on my thinking, which they presented under the name of Li Weihan, the aging Marxist theoretician who, among other positions, had headed the Seventeen-Point Agreement negotiations in 1951 and the United Front Work Department.

It was infuriating. The attack had ten points in all, most of them forced and misleading. For example, one point said that I hadn't specifically mentioned that the imperialists had invaded and suppressed the nationalities of China, including the Tibetans. And because I had said that nationalities had initially had their freedom and then were forcefully put under one nationality's control, they accused me of denying that Tibet was historically part of China. Another point attacked what they called my reservations about the quelling of the 1959 uprising. Still another said that I had taken the side of the Dalai Lama's brother, who criticized Tibetan officials for just doing what they were told rather than representing the interests of Tibetans; and still another said that I had been inciting Tibetans to seek a Greater Tibet. There were even completely ridiculous suggestions that I was in league with the Tibetan exiles. But the main thrust of their attack concerned my argument about the need for what Lenin had called "sovereign equality between nationalities" in a country.

They totally rejected my case for the sovereignty of nationalities. Their essay said that there was a fundamental difference between national sovereignty [ch. *guojia zhuquan*] and nationality sovereignty [ch. *minzu zhuquan*]. The concept of "sovereignty" is relevant only between nations. They said there was no such thing as sovereignty among the different nationalities that comprised a nation, so they rejected the model represented by the Soviet system of "republics" and, by extension, tried to attack the theoretical legitimacy of the case I had laid out for the full autonomy of minority areas like Tibet.

I learned of this report only when a copy was delivered to me with a summons to appear at a meeting the next day (June 18, 1982) to answer questions about it. On such short notice, I decided not to try to respond in detail, but I also thought I should have something to give them, so I quickly wrote a one-page statement. In it, I tactfully said that while I hadn't had time to study and digest Li Weihan's comments, Li had been my senior leader in the past, so they could be sure I would consider his arguments carefully. I also said, however, that my cursory reading of the report revealed many points that were factually incorrect, and I promised to examine everything thoroughly and make a detailed written report. I put this brief statement in my pocket and went to the meeting.

From the moment I entered the room and saw a tape recorder and several microphones in the center of the table, I knew it was not going to be an ordinary meeting. Seven or eight people were already there, including Yang Jingren, but nobody came to meet me or shake my hand. They looked up when I entered but said nothing. I sat down quickly, and for a few minutes nobody spoke. We just sat silently, looking at one another. They weren't openly hostile, but they definitely were not friendly.

Before long, Li Weihan came in, helped by two people. He was eighty-six and not in good health (he was living in a hospital and would die two years later, in August 1984). He had been attacked and demoted during the Cultural Revolution, and this was the first time he had been at the United Front Work Department since his rehabilitation. I was moved when I saw him and immediately rose, shook his hand, and told him how sorry I was to have been the cause of his having to come today. Then we all sat down, and the meeting started.

"Phünwang," Li Weihan began, "thirty-one years ago you made a great contribution by helping to bring about the Seventeen-Point Agreement and the return of Tibet to the great motherland. But recently, people are saying that your understanding of Marxist theory is seriously flawed. I have examined what you said and have written a report about it. Have you seen that report?"

"Yes," I said, "I received the document and I have looked at it." Then I took out the statement I had prepared and read it.

I could tell from their expressions that Yang Jingren and the others were displeased when I said that I would not respond to Li's criticisms at this time. I directed my next remarks to Li.

"Director Li," I said, "you have just said that thirty-one years ago I made a great contribution. Do you know what happened to me after that?"

"No. Please tell me."

"Not long after my great contribution," I said, "I was accused of being a 'local nationalist' and imprisoned for eighteen years."

"Were you really imprisoned for eighteen years?" he asked. "You must have suffered terribly." He seemed stunned and said he hadn't known. At that time, he himself had been under attack, so probably he hadn't heard about any of it.

Yang Jingren and the others didn't like this turn of events at all, and Yang interrupted.

"Phünwang," he said sharply, "you promised to prepare a detailed written response. When, may we ask, will that be?"

"You have written a ten-thousand-character document," I said coolly. "It will take me some time to study it and respond."

"It will take some time, will it?" Yang hissed angrily. "You don't seem to realize that you have not been accused of minor mistakes. Li Weihan is a famous Marxist theoretician. He is the one who has criticized your ideas, and so your mistakes are extremely serious. Moreover, it is Deng Xiaoping who is really confronting you today. He was too busy to come himself, so he asked Xi Zhongxun [vice chairman of the National People's Congress] to handle the matter for him, and Xi is the one who chose Li Weihan to examine your writings."

I did not lose my composure. I simply said, as if it were the most obvious thing in the world, that it would be difficult to specify a time when I would be finished with my detailed response. "Director Li has thought carefully about his criticisms, and his points deserve equally careful examination."

At that, they all spoke at once, all trying to criticize and attack me, until finally Li intervened.

"Listen, everyone, please!" he said with some emotion. "I believe Phünwang should be given time to write his opinions in full. He may criticize my report or even rebut it, and he should be given all the time he needs to do it."

He paused and then smiled, saying, "I am pleased today. When I came, I thought I would have to argue with Phünwang, but we got along very well. Now let's all go to eat."

He took my hand as we left the room, and I sat beside him at the meal.

My strategy had worked. They had wanted to attack me at the meeting and afterward report either that I accepted my mistakes or that I tried to argue back. I would have lost either way. If I had accepted my errors, they would have said that I was persuaded of my mistakes by Li Weihan. If I hadn't, they would have said that Li Weihan advised me kindly and tried his best to educate me, but I stubbornly refused to listen. However, because Li himself made the suggestion that I be given more time and clearly seemed to have affection for me, there was nothing they could do, and so the meeting was concluded.

A week after the meeting, I sent a letter to Hu Yaobang. By then, I had begun my detailed response, and I estimated now that it would take some weeks to finish. So I sent Hu something brief to explain that Li's report had many points that were not factually accurate, and to request that the Central Committee investigate it carefully. I wanted to buy myself some more time, and I didn't want the only voices he heard to be those of my enemies.

It took several more weeks to finish my response, which ended up containing twenty-five thousand characters. I sent it to Li Weihan and also to Deng Xiaoping, Hu Yaobang, Zhao Ziyang, Xi Zhongxun, and others because I was afraid that Yang Jingren wouldn't allow my comments to be passed along. I therefore thought that I had assured myself a fair hearing at the highest levels. I soon found out differently.

On July 27, 1982, Li Weihan sent a letter to Deng Xiaoping, along with a brief summary of our meeting, his ten-thousand-character document, and my one-page response—but not my full-length rebuttal. I learned that Deng Xiaoping himself saw all these documents and sent them to Hu Yaobang with a note saying, "Comrade Li Weihan has made a good presentation. Please distribute these documents to each member of the Central Committee and to the officials of the Secretariat of the Central Committee." Hu did so, in accordance with Comrade Deng's order.

I was, of course, upset because the documents now being distributed at the highest levels did not contain my full-length response to Li's criticisms. I subsequently wrote letters requesting that my complete response be read together with Li's comments, and I went to visit Li in the hospital, because I had suspicions I hoped to confirm.

I found him sitting on a sofa. I shook his hand, sat down next to him, and said, "Director Li, you knew me well. I served under you in 1951 and in 1953. I have the greatest respect for you. If I had made mistakes in my thoughts and you had critiqued me honestly, I would have listened to you. I believe, however, that the ten-thousand-character critique was made by the people who put me in prison in the past. Now they want to attack me again. They are using your name to attack me, and I believe that you never saw all of the things I wrote. Therefore, I felt I had no choice but to respond strongly to your critique. But I want you to know that my comments are not aimed at you but at them." He didn't say yes or no, he just nodded his head.

Then things got worse. The packet of materials—again without my response—was sent to Yin Fatang, the head of the party in Tibet. Yin immediately distributed it to the members of the TAR Party Leaders Committee and called a big meeting to discuss it. Many Tibetan and Han officials criticized me strongly at this meeting. Only Yangling Dorje did not follow the party line. I was told later that he stood up and said, "If Director Li is correct, then Phünwang has made a serious mistake. However, in the one-page letter Phünwang submitted, he said that many things in Li's essay are not factually correct and that he will submit a detailed written argument that responds to these inaccuracies. I think we need to read Phünwang's response to know the whole story."

Yin Fatang did not appreciate Yangling Dorje's interference, calling his attitude ambiguous and later accusing him of being my "representative" in Tibet. Yin went on to distribute the materials to officials at the county level, where more meetings were held to attack me. It was a smear campaign, and it was extremely troubling.

In Beijing, I wrote several letters to the Central Committee telling them that I had written a twenty-five-thousand-character response to Li Weihan's ten-thousand-character essay and suggested that they ought to be evaluating the two arguments because this was not a trivial debate. Until now, I said bluntly, there had been no comparable debate in the party on nationality affairs. I stressed that the outcome was likely to have a huge impact on future work in minority nationality areas, and I therefore requested that the Central Committee set up a small investigation group to evaluate both Li's and my arguments. I sent letters making the same request to Deng Xiaoping and Hu Yaobang.

While waiting for an answer and preparing to attend the Sixth National People's Congress (which was to start in mid-1983), I got another shock. One day, quite by accident, I met Wang Guangmei, the widow of Liu Shaoqi. She told me that my name was not on the list of Sichuan delegates. I didn't pay this much attention, since what she said seemed impossible, but the following week, I met her again and she reiterated that she had checked and my name was not on the list. "You should pay attention to this," she said. This time I did.

Since I was a deputy party secretary of the Nationalities Committee of the National People's Congress, I had access to the list of representatives. As she had warned, I found that my name was missing and realized that this was another attempt to push me aside. Angry and frustrated, I immediately called Xi Zhongxun and asked for a meeting.

Xi, who was one of the top leaders in the party and a member of the Politburo, didn't know what I was talking about.

"No changes have been planned," he said. "You are still a member of the Standing Committee of the National People's Congress and a deputy party secretary of the Nationalities Committee."

"Then why has my name been dropped from the list of Sichuan representatives?" I asked.

Instead of responding, he turned to the lists, I think to show me that my fears were groundless. But the lists were so long—filling between ten and fifteen volumes—that while I sat sipping a glass of tea, he stopped searching through them and called Yang Jingren directly.

"What happened to Phünwang's status as a delegate to the National

People's Congress from Sichuan?" he asked bluntly. "Did you forget to put his name on the list?"

"I reported this to you some time ago," Yang said smoothly.

"That report was so long I didn't read it all. Can you tell me what happened?"

"As you know," said Yang, "Phünwang has been accused of being one of three people harming the party's work in Tibet. Then there were his comments about adding nationality clauses to the constitution, and finally there was the debate with Li Weihan. For these reasons, I have withdrawn him from the coming National People's Congress and instead have placed him as a candidate for membership on the Standing Committee of the Chinese People's Political Consultative Conference."

"Why didn't you discuss such an important thing with me first?" Xi said angrily. "And why did you bury an important decision like this under thousands of names on your endless list?" He paused, and continued, "You made a big mistake. Phünwang's position should not be changed. I am going to report this to Hu Yaobang! You must reinstate Phünwang immediately. Do you understand?"

After the phone call, I had a serious talk with Xi.

"Till now," I said, "I have never asked for a personal favor. However, as you can plainly see, the people who attacked me before are attacking me again. I have a right to be a delegate for the Tibetan people to the National People's Congress. You said just now that you will report this matter to Hu Yaobang. I will also report this to Hu—and to Deng Xiaoping himself if necessary—and I will fight to represent the Tibetan people."

After I left Xi, I did write letters, and so, I believe, did Xi. And before long, Hu Yaobang and Deng Xiaoping sent a message informing me that they had instructed Yang Jingren not to change my position as a member of the Standing Committee of the National People's Congress. The decision meant a great deal to me, and soon my fortunes began to improve on another front.

My detailed criticisms of Li Weihan's report posed a difficult problem for the party. Li had made his judgments on behalf of the Central Committee, which in a sense meant that he represented Deng Xiaoping. Thus, if the Central Committee said I was right, it meant Li—and by extension Deng—was wrong. They came up with an interesting solution.

At the National People's Congress, Xi Zhongxun, representing the Central Committee, made a speech introducing the members of the Standing Committee. When he introduced me, he praised me as a party member who had done good revolutionary work for many years. "He has made a great contribution," he said, and then he added, "In our party, there are different thoughts on ideology, and according to the party's constitution, one has the right to hold different views." He didn't mention my name, but what he was talking about was clear to those who knew of the dispute. And it was now clear to me what the Central Committee had done. Indirectly and cleverly they had declared that Li Weihan and I had the right to hold our different views. It was not necessary to decide whether one was right and one wrong. I wasn't declared right, but in this battle of criticism and debate, I felt I had won a victory against enormous odds. Not only had the party leadership declined to support the attack on my views, but they also sent a message that people in the party like me were free to speak their minds.

I also had an impact on the constitutional front. I didn't get the specific clauses I had suggested accepted, but I was able to persuade Peng Zhen, Politburo member and chairman of the National People's Congress (and de facto head of the Constitution Revisions Committee), to phrase a section of the preamble so that the word "equality" preceded the words "unity" and "cooperation." I thought this made a big difference in orientation because without equality first there cannot be unity. The final version, approved on December 4, 1982, said, "The People's Republic of China is a unitary multinational state created jointly by the people of all its nationalities. Socialist relations of equality, unity, and mutual assistance have been established among the nationalities and will continue to be strengthened." [The previous 1978 constitution had said only, "The unity between all nationalities of the country should be strengthened."]

On the other main front—the "three enemies of the party" campaign against me—I also eventually was vindicated.

In spring 1984, a number of TAR officials (including Yin Fatang, Ragdi, and Yangling Dorje) came to Beijing. During this visit, Yangling Dorje met with Premier Zhao Ziyang, whom he knew well from their days together in Sichuan. At their meeting, Zhao asked him about Tibet, and Yangling Dorje told him frankly, "After the Third Plenary Session of the Eleventh Central Committee of the Party in 1978, the whole nation shifted its priority away from political struggle to issues concerning economic development. However, Yin Fatang and others in Lhasa continued to proceed on the assumption that in Tibet the priority was political struggle. They have said that the primary targets of this political struggle are the Dalai Lama, the Panchen Lama, and Phünwang. They also criticized Phünwang's views on nationality theory without even reading his response to Li Weihan."

"What is going on in Tibet is wrong," Zhao said. "Economic development is the work priority for the nation—including Tibet. Phünwang and the Panchen Lama are both our people, and we are trying to win over the Dalai Lama. Therefore, it is wrong to make them objects of political attack."

The next day, Yangling Dorje went to see Hu Yaobang, and when Hu heard what he had to say, he became angry. "Economic development is the priority of the whole nation," he said. "Because of class struggle, our country has had very hard times. If we do not pay attention to economic development in Tibet and improve the people's living conditions there, we will never achieve the kinds of political results we want." He also said that it was wrong to single out three people and make them targets of political struggle.

I didn't know about any of this until one afternoon when there was a knock on my door. It was Yangling Dorje, and he was smiling broadly.

"*A rog,*" he said [*a rog* is a term of greeting that means roughly "my friend" in Khampa dialects], "I no longer need to be afraid to visit." (He meant, of course, that while I was under political attack, it was a risk for anyone to seem too close to me.)

"Today," he continued, "I bring two swords in my hands. One is from Hu Yaobang, and the other is from Zhao Ziyang. They are the ones who have asked me to visit you." He then proceeded to tell me about Hu's and Zhao's responses.

Not long after these events, the Central Committee actually criticized Yin Fatang publicly for his attack on the "three enemies," and then one day in early April 1984, Yin Fatang, Ragdi, Yangling Dorje, and Dorje Tseden (a top Tibetan cadre in the TAR government) unexpectedly came to see me. They came to tell me that the Central Committee had told them their campaign against me was wrong. They had visited the Panchen Lama yesterday, and today they had come to apologize to me. They admitted they had made a mistake!

It was more than I ever dreamed would happen.

Finally, in the fall of 1985, I also got closure on the status of our Tibetan Communist Party. When I had contacted the Chinese Communist Party in Yunnan in 1949, the local party leader agreed to accept me and the others in my party as members of the CCP but said that the date when our party membership should start would have to be decided later by the Central Committee. It was the mid-1980s now. Many of our members were close to retirement, and there was still confusion about the date at which their party membership had begun. Therefore, the United Front Work Department and the State Nationalities Affairs Commission conducted an investigation and reported their results to the Central Committee.

In a document that was signed by Xi Zhongxun, Hu Qili, and others, the Central Committee determined that after I met with Ye Jianying in Chongqing in 1940, I established a Communist Party in Tartsedo and Lhasa and enrolled many members. My revolutionary work therefore officially began in 1940. I thought that they should consider my relationship with the Chinese Communist Party to have started when I met with Ye Jianying in 1940, but they said that because Ye Jianying, who was then in his nineties, could not remember our meetings, they did not accept us as part of the CCP until 1949, when I arrived in Yunnan. I decided not to contest this. I was satisfied that they had officially recognized our Tibetan party as a Communist Party, and it did not matter to me whether it belonged to the Soviet Communist Party or the Chinese Communist Party or was its own Tibetan party.

And so events had finally come full circle. I had not only been rehabilitated, but now my revolutionary work since 1940 had been accepted. The terrible years in prison could not be wiped away, but the historical record was now clean.

AFTERWORD

Melvyn C. Goldstein, Dawei Sherap, and
William R. Siebenschuh

From 1985 until 1993, Phünwang continued to serve as a deputy director of the Nationalities Committee of the National People's Congress. He was also a close advisor to the late Panchen Lama, working with him in a number of ways on behalf of Tibetans. The latter's untimely death in 1989, coupled with the death of Hu Yaobang, the demotion of Zhao Ziyang after Tiananmen, and the imposition of martial law in Tibet in 1989, led Phünwang to concentrate on bringing to a conclusion the work on dialectics that he had begun in prison. In 1990, his major (eight-hundred-thousand-character) study *New Exploration of Dialectics* was published by the Tibetan People's Publishing House. This work was widely acclaimed in China and led to a conference on the book and the publication of the proceedings.

In 1994, his second book, *Water Exists in Liquid Form on the Moon,* was published by the Sichuan Science and Technology Publishing House. Using a dialectical perspective to study astronomical problems, it argued correctly for the presence of water on the moon. Two years later, in 1996, his third book, *Further Exploration of Natural Dialectics,* was published by the Chinese Social Science Publishing House.

While all this was happening, Phünwang met and married Tseden Yangdrön, a Tibetan born in Lhasa. They live in Beijing, where she assists Phünwang in his research and writing. Without her tireless support and assistance, he would not have been able to complete all of these studies.

Although Phünwang, at this writing, is now eighty-four years old, his deep feelings about Marxism and the Tibetan nationality continue to keep him active in current Tibet policies. He remains a critical Tibetan voice advocating a new policy in which Tibet will be granted greater autonomy. His opinions on Tibet are often solicited, as was the case in 1998, when he met with President Jiang Zemin and discussed nationality issues with him for two hours.

Phünwang is currently engaged in a variety of research efforts, including comparative research on the famous Chinese classic *The Book of Changes* and his own *The New Investigations into Dialectics.* At the same time, he is working on a history of revolutionary activities in the Tibetan region.

At present, Phünwang is a professor and tutor to doctoral students in the Chinese Academy of Social Sciences graduate school and is the first Tibetan doctoral tutor of philosophy.

It seems fitting to close this story of the life of Phünwang with his account of an important conversation he had with Hu Yaobang in late 1983, in which he laid out many of his ideas on the place of Tibetans within the People's Republic of China:

> Hu Yaobang asked me about Tibet, and I laid out my views on what needed to be done. Before I started, though, I told him that if he had a little time, I would present my thoughts in some detail, but if he was very busy, I would tell them briefly. Without hesitation Hu said, "No problem, take your time. My feet hurt a bit, but if I keep them up on a chair, I will be fine." So he put up his feet, lit a cigarette, and then listened to me. I spoke frankly, laying out a number of issues I felt were critical for creating and maintaining good relations with minority nationalities, especially Tibetans. During the conversation, time and again he would nod his head in agreement. He did not once say "no" or indicate disagreement.

Figure 25. Phünwang *(left)* discussing Tibet with Jiang Zemin, Beijing, 1998.

In general, I said we must work hard to treat minorities like Tibetans as genuine equals to Han Chinese in all ways. We must give them the power and authority to develop themselves as socialist parts of China, but with an ethnic flavor, as Tibetans.

Specifically, I said that it is critical that we do not criticize or stigmatize nationality officials for making comments or suggestions that further the interests of their nationality. It was wrong in 1958 to victimize thousands of local minority cadres by applying the label "local nationalism" to them. They were just raising real problems the minorities were experiencing. By contrast, there was not a single Chinese who received the negative label of "Great Han Chauvinism." We cannot have close unity among the nationalities in China, I said, if there is no equality and if Tibetans and other minorities have to subordinate their views and identity to those of the Han Chinese.

Second, I said, it is not enough just to appoint officials from the minority ethnic group. These officials have to have real power and authority, not just fancy titles. Everywhere there are complaints that minority officials were and are under the thumbs of their Han colleagues, who do not pay much attention to their viewpoints. This situation reached its peak during the Cultural Revolution and has remained largely unchanged since then. It cannot continue like this. Minority officials must have dominant power and decision-making authority in their regions. Equality means that minorities have the basic power to control their areas and their lives.

Third, I conveyed my views on the importance of not using the army to put down rebellions and do police work in minority areas . . . [presented in chapter 24, page 290, and earlier in this chapter].

Fourth, there is a problem with Chinese migrant laborers. They are spreading helter skelter into minority areas, and this is not good. In the Inner Mongolia Autonomous Region, for example, the Chinese population is now 87 percent of the total population, while the ethnic Mongolian population is only 13 percent. Not surprisingly, there have been many student demonstrations there. Xinjiang experienced a similar situation, and most of the best land in Xinjiang has been converted into farms for the PLA. I told him that I understand that China has a big population with a small territory, while the minority nationalities have a small population in a big territory. Thus it may be necessary to transfer some Han Chinese to minority areas, but it is not good to just let Han Chinese go wherever they want. The transferring of Han Chinese to Tibet must be incorporated into a national plan and should be conducted in a supervised and step-by-step fashion. The most important thing to keep in mind is that the Chinese population must not harm the local minority nationality's survival and interests, either economically or culturally.

Then I used Tibet as an example of problems with current policy. Before Tibet was liberated, I said, I could count the total number of Chinese in Lhasa on my hands. And when I first went to Shigatse in 1943, there was only one Chinese shop, with one Chinese shopkeeper. Now there are huge numbers of Chinese workers and cadres, as well as their families, not to mention the Chinese army.

This influx of Han Chinese has meant that many local occupations are being swallowed up by people from outside Tibet. This has not only been an economic hardship, but has also created many social problems, since it has attracted riff-raff who break laws and harm local security and ethnic relationships. If the central government does not pay immediate attention to this, there is a danger that in twenty or thirty years, only the Potala Palace will be left in Lhasa as "Tibetan." The rest of Lhasa will be filled with Chinese-speaking people. If this comes to pass, Lhasa, an object of worship and veneration by all Tibetans for thousands of years, will become extinct. And the term "the new democratic and socialist modern Tibet" will become an empty slogan. We will be fooling ourselves and others with such terms. This would become the Chinese Communist Party's biggest mistake in the international Communist Party movement.

There is a danger of this. Right now, the minority nationalities are being assimilated into Han Chinese society one by one. Some minorities in China have only their names left, but no cultural identities. If things continue like that, the Chinese Communist Party will go down in history as having made an unforgivable mistake. The basic characteristic of socialism is that all ethnic groups in socialist states prosper and have happiness. The central government should strictly control the influx of population to ensure that the majority of the residents in cities like Lhasa are Tibetan.

Fifth, the economic construction of the country is dependent upon the rich resources found in the areas inhabited by ethnic groups. They will need to be exploited. However, when these resources are utilized, the interests of local ethnic groups must be respected, in accordance with the constitution and the laws regarding ethnic autonomy. The impact of resource exploitation on the minorities' production and life must be taken into full consideration, and the income derived from any use of resources must be allocated proportionally in a reasonable manner. It cannot simply be taken away in the name of the "nation" or the central government. National interests and public ownership cannot be overemphasized without giving adequate regard to the interests of the local ethnic groups.

Ultimately, the issue of assimilation and loss of ethnic identity is at stake. If policies are not altered, I said, there is a danger that larger nationalities, like Tibetans, will end up like some of the smaller ones in having a nationality name but no language or distinctive culture. If the minority nationalities in our country are assimilated into the Han nationality one by one, then how can we say that there was and is equality among the nationalities under socialism and the Chinese Communist Party?

A Comment by Phünwang

In 2002, Melvyn Goldstein asked Phünwang if he would be willing to write an epilogue for this book. Two days later, Phünwang gave him the following statement.

You asked many questions about my life, and I have tried to answer them. Now, at your request, I will make a few points to sum up.

First, in the decade between 1939 and 1949, we struggled to achieve progress and development for the Tibetan nationality, social reforms in Tibet, the happiness of the Tibetan people, and the reunification and liberation of the entire Tibetan nationality. Although we did our best, under the prevailing historical conditions, we failed to make much progress.

After the new China was founded in 1949, I continued to work unwaveringly for the progress and development of the Tibetan nationality through new channels, in new ways, and with new methods under the new historical conditions.

As is known to all, the constitution of the new China and the fundamental policies of the Communist Party of China clearly stipulate that all those systems in the old China that were designed to oppress minority nationalities must be abolished and that all nationalities, big or small, are equal and should cooperate with one another so they can prosper together. Therefore, I believe that under today's historical conditions, Tibetans and other minority nationalities should unite with (not separate from) the powerful Han nationality for their mutual benefit. This has been my basic point of view since the founding of the new China.

After the Third Plenary Session repudiated the Cultural Revolution in the early 1980s, the party stipulated new guidelines and policies for working with nationalities. Based on this, I repeatedly emphasized that our Han brothers should treat their brother nationalities with sincerity and allow each of the fifty-five minority nationalities to have a relatively compact homeland in which they can truly be their own masters and carry out their own reforms and development. Only in this way will the interests of the nationalities and the country be united, and only in this way will the thoughts of dissension and discord be eliminated and true national unity and stability be realized. However, many obstacles and difficulties have been encountered due to the influence of traditional Han Chauvinist thoughts, feudalism, and hegemonism. The new guidelines and policies stipulated by the Central Committee have not been thoroughly carried out. Continuous effort is still needed to realize them.

Second, during my life I was in charge of launching the Tibetan communist movement and establishing relationships with the Chinese Communist Party, the Soviet Communist Party, and the Indian Communist Party. Because of this, I was expelled from the Guomoindang's school by Chiang Kaishek and pursued by the Guomindang police. Then I was deported from Tibet by the Tibetan government.

After this, I was a participant and witness to the Seventeen-Point Agreement, which brought Tibet back to the big family of new China. I worked hard for the liberation of the Tibetan nationality and for national unity in the new China. I was the interpreter when the Dalai Lama and the Panchen Lama, the traditional spiritual leaders of the Land of Snow, talked with Mao Zedong, Zhou Enlai, and other leaders of the central government. But I was later held in solitary confinement and cruelly tortured for eighteen years in the Communist Party's Qingchen Prison.

Nevertheless, as Liu Zongyuan of the Tang dynasty once said, "Everyone knows the harm enemies can do, but not how much benefit they can bring." I have a profound understanding of those words. After I was released from prison, Deng Xiaoping told me, "You have suffered a lot!" Indeed, the hardship of solitary imprisonment is beyond description. But, on the other hand, if I had not been sent into Qingchen by those leaders, I might have taken my last breath long ago during the chaotic Cultural Revolution. Fortunately, I am a Khampa who grew up on barley, beef, and mutton, and I managed to overcome unendurable difficulties though my extremely strong will. I survived Qingchen. Beethoven said, "I will seize fate by the throat. It won't lay me low." That is what I believe I did. I did not let my suffering lay me low. I did not disgrace my dear parents, countrymen, and the Tibetans of the Land of Snow.

I read widely when I was in prison. Einstein said, "Philosophy is the source of all scientific research." I believe that dialectics, the highest form of thinking in philosophy, is the crystallization of human wisdom and the science of sciences. For centuries, philosophers have thought that everything is changing according to different rules. Proceeding on such an assumption, I developed a new theoretical system of dialectic reasoning that incorporates the logical formulas of the structures of everything in terms of their spatial extensionality, the cyclical law of their movements in terms of temporal continuity, and the law of dialectically stratified differentiation. I carefully recorded my thoughts about these matters in what might be said to be my dissertation—completed after eighteen years at the "Qingchen Party School."

After I was released from prison, I wrote *New Exploration of Dialectics,* which deals mainly with social structures and is about eight hundred thousand characters long; *Water Exists in Liquid Form on the Moon,* which is about two hundred thousand characters long; and *Further Exploration of Natural Dialectics,* which is about six hundred thousand characters long. The scientific conclusion that I came up with for the first time—that liquid water exists on all the planets, including the moon—was verified several times by NASA in the United States. Overall, Qingchen Prison did me more good than harm.

Third, in 1980, I was invited to a meeting convened by the Society for the History of Marxist Philosophy in Luoyang at which, at their request, I made some comments. I said, "When I was in prison, I had time to read several times through all the classic works of Marxism, as well as other works on modern science and technology. Other people might not have had this opportunity. I am not saying that I am erudite because of that. On the contrary, I feel ignorant. However, I feel I have the right to make two comments. First, if they were alive today, Marx and Engels would negate some of their past viewpoints and proclaim that they had shortcomings and were imperfect. And second, they would amend and perfect some others, although the fundamental philosophical dialectical and economic viewpoints would be upheld. All theories are generalizations and summaries of social practices, and thus are subject to the constraints of the times. If Marx and Engels were still alive, they would proclaim that the policies and actions of communists all over the world today, including the Chinese communists, are not always in accordance with their thoughts and principles. When Marx was alive, he announced more than once to those who claimed to be Marxist organizations and parties that they were not what he would call Marxists."

When I said this, hundreds of Chinese experts and scholars—who had just gone through the hardships of the catastrophic ten-year Cultural Revolution, during which they had proclaimed that Marxism and Mao Zedong's thought had reached its "acme"—applauded warmly.

Marxism is meant to emancipate the human race, lead to universal harmony in the world, and establish a just, reasonable, and healthy social system in which there is no exploitation of man by man or oppression of weak nations by powerful ones. It has progressive thoughts that support the lofty cause of human beings.

However, as Deng Xiaoping emphasized, practice is the sole yardstick of truth. Under the guidance of this thought and under the third generation of leadership, with Jiang Zemin at the head, China has experienced new changes daily and has attracted the admiration of the world. But the relationship between Han and Tibetans, as well as that with other minority nationalities within the borders of China, needs to be improved.

A few years ago, General Secretary Jiang Zemin talked to me for about two hours [on Tibet]. During this time, I handed him a letter I had once written to the Central Committee about the importance of nationalities work in light of the collapse of the Soviet Union. Many people who have been involved in nationalities work for a long time and have a broad vision are concerned by the fact that while things superficially look harmonious in China, there are actually numerous points of conflict between the Han and Tibetans (as well as other minority nationalities). They are dissatisfied with various actions that are irresponsible, such as focusing on short-term rather than long-term goals, treating symptoms but not real causes, reporting good news but not bad, and even fabricating facts, telling lies, and achieving personal gain at the cost of the public interest.

There is hope that the Central Committee, after twenty years of reforms and the opening up of China to the world's economic structure, including joining the World Trade Organization, will [now] carefully analyze the relationships among the various nationalities, learn from the disintegration of the Soviet Union, and develop new policies and guidelines with regard to the work on nationalities, as it did in the early 1980s. As a result, it is to be hoped that the areas inhabited by minority nationalities will be granted rights to political, economic, and cultural autonomy, so that relationships between the Han and other nationalities will be fundamentally improved and genuine national unity, as well as true social peace and stability, will be achieved.

I often worry about the future and fate of the Tibetan nationality (as well as other sibling nationalities). When General Secretary Hu Yaobang met with me twenty years ago, I made many suggestions, one of which was that Lhasa should never change. It has been the sacred city of the Tibetans of the Land of Snow for hundreds of years, playing a role for Tibetans like the one Mecca plays for Muslims. If the Potala Palace were ever to be shouldered aside by new high-rise apartments and large numbers of Chinese-speaking residents, the Chinese government would have made a historic mistake with serious consequences. Since the Central Committee is now responsible for the Tibetan people and their history, I hope it will think carefully about its responsibility and reverse any policy with such [negative] consequences. However, I am disturbed that after twenty years, the situation is not improving. I founded the Tibetan Communist Party in the early 1940s and feel I have a historical responsibility to pay attention to this issue. Engels once said, "History will eventually put all the incorrect and abnormal phenomena back on the right track." I believe his words apply to national and ethnic relationships.

Finally, Mr. Wang Lixiong, a well-known Han author who has been to Tibet seventeen times and has traveled to every corner of the region, wrote a book entitled *Sky Burial—The Fate of Tibet*. He knows the truth of Tibet and the feelings and thoughts of the Tibetan people, and his book has attracted intense attention both at home and abroad. Recently, he also wrote an article for the benefit of both Tibetans and Han people, particularly the Han, which was entitled "The Dalai Lama Is the Key to the Issue of Tibet." This article has been translated into English and Tibetan and has been widely acclaimed.

A famous foreign writer said to me that Wang's work was very well written, but if a Tibetan had written what Wang did, the Han Chinese would certainly have said many things in disapproval and, at the minimum, would have thought it was biased. Similarly, if a foreigner had written it, the Han Chinese would have disapproved of it and, at the least, would have claimed that he failed to grasp the situation in Tibet correctly. However, since it was written by a well-known and knowledgeable Han writer, what can they say?

The Tibetan people living on the roof of the world have for many years combined their own culture with the Tibetan tradition of Buddhism that flourished in India, merging them like water seamlessly mixing with milk. The ensuing unique culture of Tibet greatly influenced the Tibetan people, so they strongly opposed the harm and destruction caused by the wrongful line of "Leftism" in the late 1950s (after the PRC was founded). Furthermore, they also strongly opposed the wounds caused by the disasters of the Cultural Revolution (1966–1976) and the remnants of the Cultural Revolution still existing in Tibet.

Therefore, most people in Kham, in [Central] Tibet, and in Amdo miss their spiritual leader, the Dalai Lama, from the bottom of their hearts. They trust and rely on him and ask him to grant favor to them and pray for them.

As all of you know, from ancient to modern times, the historical record inside the country and abroad has proven that the victory or loss of political power depends on the way people think. Therefore, Wang Lixiong's article has great significance for how to think about settling the issue that concerns all Tibetans.

In the past, Comrade Deng Xiaoping put forward a correct principle regarding Tibet when he said, "Outside of independence, we can talk about all the other matters." Similarly, the Dalai Lama has also declared repeatedly, "We don't want independence; we want genuine autonomy." One side wants the unification of the nation, and the other side wants autonomy. These two positions do not contradict each other and therefore are absolutely compatible. This basic viewpoint is very clear.

Mr. Wang Lixiong wrote a new book in 2002 entitled *A Conversation with the Dalai Lama*. In this book, he summed up his four visits with the Dalai Lama:

> I have three points to tell the political power holders:
> First, after visiting the Dalai Lama and investigating the issue, I can declare that he sincerely wants to take the middle path [autonomy], and I can repudiate the viewpoint that his talking about "the middle path" is merely an evil trick.
> Second, the Dalai Lama is very healthy. Consequently, those people who are thinking that the physical and mental condition of the Dalai Lama is declining day by day and are trying their best to delay the settlement of the Tibetan issue until his death should reconsider.
> Third, in Western society, the Dalai Lama is regarded as a great and famous person. Therefore, whoever puts the Dalai Lama into the position of his enemy [let alone becoming the opponents of the Tibetan people inside the country], they become the opponents of the Western world.

Based on these three points, Wang said that the Dalai Lama is the key to the issue of Tibet. If China would talk with the Dalai Lama and they were able to settle the issues that concern all Tibetans, then the central government would at last be able, with a single stroke, to achieve a tremendous success [regarding this issue].

In the past, an intellectual said, "A viewpoint based on bias and prejudice is further from the truth than one that is simply factually mistaken." Thus, there is a big difference in the impact of speech and ideas, depending on whether the person is prejudiced or just mistaken. On the issue of Tibet, the prejudiced view consistently held by the relevant parties must be considered in this light.

Here I have to clarify one thing. Today, we should recognize that the Dalai Lama is the key to the issue of Tibet; he is the main effective factor upon which [the Tibetan issue] depends. Therefore, it is extremely important to investigate the trends regarding the Dalai Lama and his position.

History has proven that the separation of religion and politics was an inevitable trend of society. Likewise, it has shown that there is an inevitable trend for political feudal autocratic systems lasting more than three hundred years to develop into democratic modern societies. Similarly, the system of having reincarnations like the Dalai Lamas is also like that.

Regarding this, the Dalai Lama himself has repeatedly spoken out. He has said that if the middle path [not wanting independence, but only genuine autonomy] that he adheres to was realized, and if there was a genuine democratic autonomous government of a united Tibetan nationality within the big family of the PRC, then he would leave political life and become a simple monk concentrating on his religious activities.

Consequently, there is no reason to have suspicions regarding the intentions of the Dalai Lama, and no reason to distort his sincere, selfless thought and attack his incomparable character. To the contrary, as Mr. Wang Lixiong has said, he is the key to settling the Tibet issue.

Original Charter of the Eastern Tibet People's Autonomous Alliance

The original copy of the charter of the Eastern Tibet People's Autonomous Alliance was found among GMD documents after the establishment of the PRC. It reads as follows.

POLITICAL PROGRAM OF THE EASTERN TIBET PEOPLE'S AUTONOMOUS ALLIANCE (OCTOBER 1946, DEQEN)

Chapter One

The alliance is temporarily named the Eastern Tibet People's Autonomous Alliance and will be formally announced after being discussed at the First Representative Meeting of the Alliance.

Chapter Two

The highest principle of the Eastern Tibet People's Autonomous Alliance is to set up a new government of the Eastern Tibet People's Autonomous Region under the Three Principles of the People put forward by Dr. Sun Yatsen. According to the Three Principles of the People, the decisions on nationalism mentioned in the announcement of the First National Representative Meeting of the Guomindang, and the promise of realizing nationalism and protecting world peace made by Chairman Chiang Kaishek at the Central Executive Committee Meeting in Chongqing on August 24, 1945, we should try our best to do the following:

1. All the people in Eastern Tibet should be united and fight together for freedom. The forces of the feudalistic warlord Liu Wenhui must withdraw and stay out of Eastern Tibet.

2. An Autonomous Region government must be set up. The government should be politically controlled by all the people in Eastern Tibet. All its government officials should be elected by the people in Eastern Tibet, and the government will oppose any invading power that does not follow the Three Principles of the People or attempts to control the region.

3. Abolish the corvée labor system and cancel all exorbitant taxes and levies. Exploit resources, construct roads, and develop farming and herding in order to rapidly improve people's lives.

We will fight through to the end to realize the above promises and improve the political, economic, military, and cultural life of the people in Eastern Tibet.

Chapter Three

Members' regulations:

1. Sincerely follow all rules mentioned in this program
2. Absolutely obey the orders of the Central Committee of the Alliance
3. Never go against the interests of the homeland
4. Never go against the interests of the people of Eastern Tibet
5. Never betray the interests of the Alliance
6. Care about the interests of the local people
7. Respect other people's religious beliefs
8. Love and help comrades like brothers
9. Accept well-meaning criticism
10. Correct mistakes bravely
11. Work hard to acquire new knowledge
12. One's own interests are secondary to the interests of the whole
13. The minority should submit to the majority
14. Try to get rid of unhealthy habits
15. Attend meetings of different levels

Chapter Four: The Oath

I am one of the people of Eastern Tibet. I am determined to love my compatriots and join the glorious revolutionary army to complete the historical commission. I will obey orders from the Central Committee of the

Alliance and will fight bravely for it till the last day of my life. If I fail to follow this oath, I will deserve the most severe punishment.

Name: _____.

Chapter Five

1. The highest authority of the Eastern Tibet People's Autonomous Alliance is the Representative Assembly of all the members.

2. Ten to twelve members will be elected from the Representative Assembly to form the Central Committee, which will be the highest authority between sessions of the Representative Assembly.

3. The Central Committee will appoint five to eight members to form a Standing Committee, and one member will be appointed as the chair of the Standing Committee.

4. Eastern Tibet will be divided into three bureaus [ch. *ju*]: Jiangdong (east of the river [the Drichu]), Jiangxi (west of the river), and Xiajiang (the lower reaches of the river). Each bureau will have a local government organization consisting of five to seven officials, one chief secretary [ch. *shuji zhang*], one general secretary [ch. *zong ganshi*], and several secretaries.

5. Each area will have a county branch consisting of three to five officials, one chief secretary, and several secretaries. The county branch will be under the guidance of the area government and be responsible for following the orders of the higher authorities.

6. There will be a district branch under the county branch, a township branch under the district branch, and several groups under the township branch.

7. The General Assembly Meeting of the Alliance will decide on the strategies and political lines of the Alliance and will be held at irregular intervals, depending on the situation. Each bureau will have a representative meeting once a year, each county will have a representative meeting every six months, each district will have a representative meeting every three months, each township will have a representative meeting every month, and each group will have three meetings every month. At the representative meetings, working experience will be exchanged and orders from the higher authorities will be passed on.

8. The basic unit of the Alliance is the group. For each township [ch. *xiang*], there will be one elected representative; for the representative meeting of a bureau [ch. *ju*], each township will elect two representatives; for the representative meeting of a district [ch. *qu*], each township will elect two representatives. Members of a group must attend the group meeting. Each group will have five or fewer people.

9. Members of the Central Committee, the Standing Committee, and the chairman will be elected once a year at the Representative Assembly of the Alliance. They can renew their term of office if reelected.

10. The person responsible for the area will be appointed by the Central Committee.

11. The head of each county branch will be recommended by the government organization of the area and announced with the approval of the Central Committee.

12. The head of each group will be elected by the group meeting and will be reported to the branches at township and county levels. Group leaders are subject to recall by the higher authorities.

Chapter Six

In order to accomplish assignments rapidly, a military general head-quarters will be set up under the Central Committee of the Alliance. The organization and management of the military general headquarters will be discussed in a separate document.

Chapter Seven

If necessary, other items will be added to this program at any time.

The above chapters will become effective immediately upon approval at the First Representative Assembly of the Eastern Tibet People's Autonomous Alliance.

Appendix to Chapter Seven: Military Affairs Program

Concerning military affairs [tib. *dmag don*] of the Eastern Tibet People's Autonomous Alliance:

In accordance with the situation inside and outside China and the situation in Eastern Tibet, organizing our military power is an absolutely necessary and urgent responsibility. Therefore, based on the political environment, the economic conditions, and the present real power in the early stages of development of our General Command, it is necessary to make Deqen the main base.

At present, given the work that has been started, the current geographic situation, and many special conditions, three subcommands should be established under the general command: the lower reaches of the Drichu, the west side of the Drichu, and the east side of the Drichu.

All subcommands should efficiently start work according to the present situation. The three subcommands' duties in the early stages of activity are given below.

> Lower reaches of the Drichu (including Deqen, Gyeltang, Weishi, Gyungdrang, Yongding, etc., of the Khampa ethnic areas in Yunnan).
>
> East side of the Drichu. This subcommand's activity is in the area under the 24th Route Army [of Liu Wenhui]. We will decide on the work based on the situation of the GMD.
>
> West side of the Drichu [the Chamdo area]. In order to achieve our final central task and to expand our work in Tibet, at present the most meaningful and urgent work is to build up a military force on the west side of the Drichu.

In accordance with the above, we should develop relations with young people, women, monasteries, schools, people from the upper classes [tib. *mtho rim mi sna*], and local military organizations, and propagandize them. We should also investigate the enemy's power.

Regarding organizing guerrilla power: We have made a detailed plan for military power. The main strategy comes from the writings of Mao Zedong, Zhu De, and Peng Dehui. For example,

1. If one doesn't have much military power, one should pretend to have it. And we should not focus on only one area, but should go all over.
2. If the enemy enters, we should retreat. If the enemy retreats, we should enter. If the enemy stays in an area, we should harass them. If the enemy gets weak and tired, we should attack.
3. We should destroy their transportation and steal their supplies, and we should make it so that there is no place for the enemy to stay.
4. We should spread out our many military units. And our forces who are scattered, we should collect them into units. And when we fight, we should fight swiftly and in a manner that is beyond the imagination of the enemy.
5. We should not be involved in very tough battles, and we should not have the idea of destroying a large number of troops at one

time. We should fight quickly. We should keep our locations secret from the enemy.

6. We should investigate the enemy's situation, conquer less with
   more, use ambushes to destroy the enemy, and surround and
   annihilate the enemy.

7. We should treat prisoners well. We should pursue the enemy to
   win them over. We should give gifts to enemies who defect.

Summary of Talks with Tibetan Exile Delegations

The complete title of this document is "Summary of Talks Between Phüntso Wangye [Phünwang] (Chinese Communist Party Member) and the Delegation of Returning Tibetans and Personages" from a supplementary issue of Materials for the Study of Theory (published by the Theory Study Office of the Central Party School), September 20, 1980.

[Journal editor's note:] Comrade Phüntso Wangye sent us a summary of several talks between him and the delegation of returning Tibetans and other personnel. We believe that this summary will help us understand current issues concerning Tibet and other nationalities. Thus it is published for reference.

SUMMARY OF TALKS WITH DELEGATION SENT BY DALAI LAMA AT THEIR REQUEST (DECEMBER 25, 1979)

The Delegation of Upper-Level Tibetans Returning from India visited me again on December 3 and told me in detail about the warm welcome they had received during their visit to the Tibetan areas. They hoped that I could commit some time to talking about my past and present in more detail and say something to overseas Tibetans headed by the Dalai Lama. They said that they would take notes on the main points and report to the Dalai Lama in detail when they went back to India. I asked the United Front Work Department of the CCP Central Committee what I should talk about and was told that I could decide on the contents. Because the time to leave Beijing was pressing, the delegation chose the Dalai Lama's brother-in-law, Phüntso Tashi, the security minister of the government-in-exile, and Lobsang Targye, the vice chairman of the People's Parliament, to talk with me at my residence on the afternoon of December 5. They treated me to dinner that night at the Friendship Restaurant in the name of the delegation.

First of all, they repeatedly asked me to talk about my personal experiences, in particular about my "vanishing" from the political scene for the past twenty years or so. I briefly recounted my experiences of going to school in the inland area and, from the time I was eighteen years old, pursuing the revolutionary truth of Marxism and Leninism and exploring the path of national liberation. In order to fight against the nationality oppression policy of the Guomindang, I established the Tibetan Communist Revolutionary Group in the Mongolian and Tibetan Affairs Commission school, and its peripheral organization, the Student Association of Tibetan Youth in Chongqing. After I was expelled from the school, I joined the revolutionary movement led by the Communist Party of China and was engaged in national and democratic revolutionary activities in Tibetan areas until 1949, when the new China was born. During that period, I organized such revolutionary organizations as the Spark Society, the Plateau Communist Youth Alliance (a.k.a. the Plateau Communist Movement Group), the Tibetan National Unification and Liberation Alliance, the Eastern Tibet People's Autonomous Alliance, the Batang Underground Party or Kang-Tibet Working Committee of the Communist Party of China, and its peripheral organization, the East Tibetan Democratic Youth League. During the same period, I also requested the Tibetan Kashag government, through Governor-General Dorje Yuthok and Council Minister Surkhang, to exercise democratic reform, alleviate the people's burden in Tibet, and fight against imperialism and the Guomindang government outside Tibet. Because of my national and democratic revolutionary activities, I was placed on the wanted list of "communist bandits" by the central government in old China and was expelled by the Tibetan Kashag government as a communist.

Starting in 1950, all the nationalities should have united in accordance with the party's policy of national equity, and endeavored to build a prosperous and strong socialist family together. In order to realize this lofty revolutionary goal, I participated in the peaceful liberation of Tibet and did other work for the development of Tibet, and made my best effort. But, unfortunately, I was framed by certain leaders in 1958 who deceived their superiors and the people. I was transferred out of Tibet under the pretext of a fabricated accusation called "local nationalism thinking." In 1960, I was put into the Qingchen Prison under the pretext of "examination in isolation," which lasted for eighteen years.

At present, thanks to the concern of the Central Committee of the Communist Party of China, headed by Chairman Hu, a new team has been formed to reexamine the issue. As my issue involves several hundred Tibetan Communist Party members recruited by me, it [the resolution of the issue] might take some time. According to the responses I have received from concerned departments, it is progressing in a timely manner. I believe that it will be resolved soon in the spirit of the Third Plenary Meeting of the party [the Eleventh CCP Central Committee]. The truth of my issue was explained to the central government, relevant leaders, and relatives and friends after I was released from the prison. The public has its own opinion of what is right and what is wrong; people know in their hearts what is crooked and what is straight. I express my cordial gratitude to the Dalai Lama and all of you for your concern.

The following are answers to their questions and some of my personal views or opinions for reference or correction:

I

I was and am still a communist who believes in Marxism. Although I suffered from eighteen years of extreme hardship, I also enjoyed the greatest pleasure at the same time. The second part of the sentence refers to the fact that I had a chance to study, which people normally could not have, and to read through more than once all the works of Marx and many other classic works of philosophy. I benefited tremendously. I hope to have time to put in order the results of my research. It is not an exaggeration to say that until now I did not have a firm understanding of how to be a strong Marxist with the right attitude toward Marxism, of how to be a communist who can use the fundamental theorem of the foundation of Marxism, which is materialist dialectics, as a guide to correctly understand various Marxist viewpoints. Nor did I understand how to adhere to the principle of seeking truth from facts, to be good at thinking on one's feet, to correctly deal with Marxism, non-Marxism, and anti-Marxism, and to be a communist soldier who pursues more advanced and more reasonable objective laws that are in conformity with historical development and the struggle for them.

Interestingly, I learned from foreign reports that the Dalai Lama said that he is now "a loyal follower of communism." I hope to have an opportunity to exchange ideas with him with respect to this.

2

Allow me to answer a thorny question that many of my relatives and friends are discussing. I am a communist, true, but I was also in solitary confinement in a communist prison for as long as eighteen years and suffered from both mental and physical torture. But I was definitely not put in jail for violation of party discipline or the laws of the country; instead, I was put into prison by people who executed the laws, broke the laws, and violated party discipline and the laws of the country. Therefore, it is not the responsibility or the fault of the party; it is not my fault, but it is my misfortune. The unusual, astonishingly protracted solitary imprisonment itself says enough about the problem. Such aberrant historical tragedies, in violation of the socialist political system, became routine during the chaotic Cultural Revolution. You may have read in the newspapers the fate of many people who were known both at home and abroad to have made lasting contributions to the party and the people. Yes, not only was I imprisoned, but many were also implicated for my sake. Among them was my younger brother, Thubden Wangchuk, who was imprisoned for fourteen years. My wife, Tsilila, died from persecution. My children were also imprisoned and went through forced labor for many years (my eldest son, Phüngang, was jailed for six years). My father, Gora Ashi, died from anxiety. A few dozen relatives were imprisoned. Topden, my comrade-in-arms, and some other comrades died from persecution. Comrade Ngawang Kesang was imprisoned and forced to labor for sixteen years. Indeed, our experience stands out among Tibetans. Therefore, after I was released from prison, many veteran comrades told me, "Survival is the greatest triumph." I agree with the party's call to take into consideration the entire situation and look forward.

3

I mentioned that I came to understand the Dalai Lama over many years of acquaintance, and he also understands me. Although we have different world views, we both eagerly hope that our backward Tibetan nation will prosper and the people will be happy along with other nationalities. Although we have lived apart for more than twenty years, I am convinced that his wish has grown stronger and more determined. He not only enjoys traditional prestige and has the most devout belief in the eyes and hearts of the Tibetans. . . . (Mr. Phüntso Tashi interrupted: The fact that we were warmly welcomed by the people and that the Dalai Lama was warmly received by Mongolians in Outer Mongolia is evidence of this.) Personally, I respect the Dalai Lama, as mentioned above, because he can elevate himself above extremely high secular prestige and has lofty beliefs. For these reasons, when his second-eldest brother, Mr. Gyalo Thondup, visited Beijing the last time and solicited my advice on his behalf, I analyzed the situation both at home and abroad and frankly suggested, "You should put an end to the isolation from the government of the PRC, initiate dialogues, and send some people back to look around and listen. It wouldn't hurt even if the Dalai Lama himself comes back to look around and listen sometimes." Any choice should be based on an understanding of the basic conditions and entire situation. I heard that the Dalai Lama's third-eldest brother, Lobsang Samden, had visited Hong Kong and explained to the central government about the Dalai Lama's attending the Peace Conference in Mongolia via the Soviet Union. I am very happy that you are here and that you all are major leaders. I have heard about your trip to the Tibetan areas. The enthusiasm of the masses provides answers to many questions that deserve to be pondered. I heard that when they met with you again yesterday, Vice President Li Xiannian and Vice Chairman Ulanhu said, "There are flaws and mistakes in our work in Tibet, and we will correct them." I personally think that the remarks are sincere and responsible to the interests of the people, including our Tibetan people, as well as you. I believe that you can correctly understand the meaning and spirit of the talks of central government leaders.

4

I've read the two Tibetan pamphlets you gave me, which were written by the Dalai Lama. There is a paragraph talking about me. (Phüntso Tashi and Lobsang Targye said, "Right, it's about you.") Yes, I agree that I was the "red Tibetan" who led the "red Han" into Tibet. To be accurate, I led the People's Liberation Army. (Mr. Phüntso Tashi recalled, "The vanguard of the Liberation Army was carrying big portraits of Chairman Mao and Commander in Chief Zhu when they entered downtown Lhasa in 1951. Wang Qimei and you were walking at the very front, right after the band.") I was the Tibetan who guided the people who, in the words of Chairman Mao, were there to help the Tibetans—the brotherly Tibetans—to stand up, be the masters of their own homes, reform themselves, and be engaged in construction to improve the living standard of the people and build a happy new society. But I was never meant to lead the Han people into Tibet to establish rule over the Tibetans by the Han people. If so, the "red Han," the Liberation Army, and the "red Tibetans" who were their guides are all phony communists.

As we all know, of all the truths that the communists believe in and would sacrifice their lives to fight for, the primary and fundamental one is opposing the domination and oppression of one nationality by another nationality in any form. For this reason, any thoughts, remarks, or actions that support the control or ownership of one nationality by another nationality are as incompatible with true Marxism—the principles followed by true communists and the lofty beliefs and goals aimed at realizing the principles—as fire and water. Therefore, if the essence and goal of our guiding the Han into Tibet was for the Han people to rule the Tibetans or that the Han themselves wanted to rule the Tibetans, we would have been traitors to Marxism and traitors to the Tibetan nationality and people. In order to be responsible to the party, the people, and history, I must clarify our goal.

By the same token, it was also to achieve this goal that Han people entered into other regions inhabited by brotherly minority nationalities. Minority nationalities, including us Tibetans, were in great need of the help of our Han brothers in terms of both human and material resources. It is not enough to depend solely upon ourselves. (I gave the example of constructing the highway between Lhasa and Kongpo, which cost more than eight million yuan.) However, the essence is help and assistance, and their status is as advisors and consultants, and the goal is that we stand on our own, "walk on our own legs" (Stalin), be the master of our own homes, and build a better life. It is not the contrary. The clarification of this point is not only of theoretical significance, but also of realistic significance. Practically, it will impact the distant future and decide the quality and success of our revolutionary cause. It has very great strategic significance.

5

I talked about the Dalai Lama's remarks regarding the "red Han" and the "red Tibetans" just now. Of course, what one says about one's goal is one thing; what actually happens in reality is another. Subjective wishes are important, but objective results determine everything in the end. Therefore, when Tibetans, like other brotherly nationalities, are today united in the big socialist family under the leadership of the Communist Party, prospering as a nation and the masters of our own homes, when the society is progressing, the living standard of the people is improving and people are happy, we the Tibetans who guided "Han people into Tibet" or cooperated with Han people have made more or less historical contributions to the cause and interests of our nationality and people. Simply put, we are good guys. On the contrary, if things turned out to be the opposite, we the Tibetans who guided Han people into Tibet or cooperated with Han people would have sinned against our nation and our people, and would be bad guys. I believe that all the red Han, the red Tibetans, and the Tibetans cooperating with them should and will surely endeavor to become the former and not the latter. As for myself, I've always been the former (including eighteen years of unwavering struggle in prison), and will spare no effort to work and struggle for it in the rest of my life.

Engels said, "History will eventually put everything on the right track." This is also true with the issue of nationalities. Therefore, under the leadership of the Communist Party, the Tibetan people and other brotherly nationalities will overcome all difficulties in the course of progress, and march toward a bright future of national prosperity and happiness.

6

Because of the fundamental conditions of social progress, which are economic activities (production and exchange), the gradual unification of the nations and countries from both inside and outside is historically inevitable. For example, even in the capitalist world, the European Common Market and other economic communities are all working toward alliance and unification, not to mention the various nationalities in socialist China. Of course, the alliance and unification should be based on absolute equality, mutual help, and mutual interest, and only in this way can they be strong, long-lasting, dynamic, and in conformity with objective rules. On the contrary, anything forced upon others, whether it is economical, political, cultural, or ideological, can only last a very short period of time, with the cost oftentimes outweighing the gains, and it will end up in disagreement and separation, causing certain abnormal historical phenomena. Therefore, the principle of equality of nationalities, which is "the basic principle of socialists" (Lenin), should be adhered to not only nationally but also internationally. Today, in the long-term and fundamental interests of ourselves and on the basis of national equality, we Tibetans should not only unite closely with our big brother Han and other brotherly nationalities with whom we have had close economic, political, and cultural ties in the course of our historical development to build a prosperous socialist big family, but also establish friendly relationships with neighboring nations, such as India, Pakistan, Nepal, and Burma.

Each nationality, in the course of its development, was originally free and independent. However, the strong prey on the weak and the fit survive. Various eras of history have witnessed domination by the strong, which has resulted in abnormal and inappropriate historical relationships of conquering and being conquered between the nationalities. The adversarial relationships, which are not the mainstream form of relationships between nationalities in the development of human society, should not become the foundation on which people justify and rationalize their historical and realistic behaviors. These are the product of hegemony. It is the fallacy of the ruling class within those ruling nationalities that conquer other nationalities, and it is historical prejudice. These traditional perspectives and the historical prejudice in favor of one nationality's domination or ownership of another nationality, which are embellished by all kinds of sacred language, are not conducive to the establishment of normal and reasonable relationships in practice, which should be based on the principle of equality of nationalities, but rather will lead to and deepen the separation between nationalities. Therefore, when it comes to historical relationships between nationalities, neither side should base their arguments on the abnormal rule-and-ruled relationship, which is not the basic form of relationships between nationalities. Instead, they should base their arguments on the normal and reasonable economic, political, and cultural relationships between nationalities that have gradually formed in the course of protracted mutual exchanges. They should focus on the basic trend of relationships between nationalities and historical motion. Also, the guiding principle of the arguments should not rely on things that have already passed away, but rather on the analysis of the strict following of the principle of equality of nationalities in the fields of economy, politics, and culture in the common interest of all nationalities.

The revolutionary (Engels) denied the old system qualitatively, and the communists (Marx, Engels) "broke absolutely with the old system of ownership." If one needs to quote documents that the ruling class of the ruling nationality, such as kings, emperors, ministers, and generals, used the power of "virtue" or "awe" to conquer and rule other nationalities, it can only use them to an extremely limited extent; it should use them as negative teaching materials but not positive evidence. Otherwise, one will not only run counter to his own revolutionary principles and historical facts, but will also fall into logical contradictions and confusion arising from the loss of a Marxist stand regarding nationalities and classes. (According to the fundamentals of Marxist theory, oppressing nationalities are distinguished from the oppressed nationalities, exploiting classes from exploited classes, and one should observe and deal with the issues regarding nationalities and classes from the standpoint of the oppressed nationalities and exploited classes.) The purpose of examining nationality relations in the past is to effectively form a reasonable relationship today and a more reasonable relationship in the future.

I once read about the Dalai Lama's talks saying that Tibet has been a sovereign country since ancient times, and his recent article published in the *Wall Street Journal*. (I also read works written by Shakabpa and other people.) I completely understand the point regarding nationality and class on which he based his arguments. I've already talked about my viewpoints regarding the treatment of historical relationships between nationalities. In my opinion, neither side should base its arguments on the old relationships, especially abnormal and inappropriate relationships, but rather should base its arguments on today's new, normal and appropriate relationships. Even when one looks back, the purpose is to look forward, and reasonably and appropriately adjust existing relationships. In my humble personal opinion, one should focus on today's realistic situation; one should not be obsessed with wishful thinking and subjective imagination, but should analyze the balance of objective and subjective forces; one should not be biased or blindfolded, and overestimate his abilities; one should know oneself as well as other people, have visions, have insight into the current situation and future trends, and balance benefits with cost. In sum, one must not separate subjective wishes from reality or split ideals from reality.

Based on the above analysis, I believe that the most realistic, beneficial, and optimal solution is that Han, Tibetans, and the over fifty other brotherly nationalities exercise the right to alliance and, under the leadership of the Communist Party and on the basis of the equality of nationalities, help and cooperate with one another and work together in the big socialist family of the People's Republic of China. This is in the common interests of people of all nationalities in our country, including Tibetans. Indisputably, every nationality has, in theory, the right to determine its own fate. This is a principle that even a democrat acknowledges, not to mention socialists. However, to be responsible for the fate of one's own nationality, the right of national self-determination cannot be abused, and the rights cannot be taken advantage of by a handful of people for the selfish interests of their group.

To be responsible for the fundamental interests of the nationalities and as long as we conduct an objective, thorough, and truthful analysis, we can draw a correct and feasible conclusion: under the historical conditions of today's China, it is better for all nationalities to be united than to be separated. Unity is beneficial, and separation damages. Today, the CCP, which represents the interests of the people, does not advocate separation, for separation will not benefit the people of all nationalities. And the broad masses of people, who are the majority of every nationality and have the most right to voice their opinions and make decisions, will not agree with separation either, because of their own fundamental interests. Taking one step back, if we think twice, it is impossible to separate today. Comrade Ulanhu once said, "Outer Mongolia, which was separated from the mainland, exists only in name today under the control of Soviet imperialists." In sum, we should proceed from reality and not imagination, and understand that alliance is the trend of historical development. Of course, I have clarified the prerequisites for unity: it should be genuine, not fake, and sincere, not superficial. The primary condition is the genuine and earnest equality of nationalities, that is, recognition of the sovereign equality of nationalities. Any theory or action that goes against the equality of nationalities is actually the cause of national division. It is the subjective idealism of the nationalists in the ruling nationality to blame the results while being oblivious to or ignorant of or disregarding the causes of division. It is the prejudice of the ruling class. Only fools do not understand this and go against it.

I would like you to think about my opinions above and tell them to the Dalai Lama and other friends overseas. If we really care about the interests of Tibetans, we should carefully study the current situation and give a correct answer to the essential question—which is more beneficial, alliance or division?

7

Since the founding of the new China, great achievements have been made regarding the implementation of the policies of equality and unity of nationalities made by the Central Committee of the Party and Chairman Mao. However, there are still many problems, both in theory and practice. During the Cultural Revolution, these shortcomings, due to the disturbance and destruction of Lin Biao and the Gang of Four, caused a catastrophe, and the loss is unfathomable. You must have seen this in the Tibetan areas. Comrades Ulanhu and Yang Jingren pointed out the causes of the problems at the meeting on the Work of the Minorities this summer. On the other hand, great achievements have been made in every field since the founding of the new China. When he visited the interior areas, the Dalai Lama saw the achievements and spoke highly of them. However, things began to go awry after the Antirightist movement in 1957, and the situation was extremely severe during the Cultural Revolution. Comrade Ye Jianying made a very important summary of this in a speech in celebration of the thirtieth anniversary of the country. From our talks, I learned that you paid close attention to the current situation in various Tibetan areas, which is surely the right thing to do. However, Tibet is just one of the minority nationalities of our country, and you have to learn more about the general situation of minority nationalities in order to have a clear vision of the issue of Tibet. Therefore, you should study the above-mentioned speeches of Comrades Ulanhu and Yang Jingren. Meanwhile, the issue of nationalities is an issue for the entire nation. I suggest that in order to have a clear picture of the current situation of the whole issue of nationalities, you study the important speech by Comrade Ye Jianying. The two important reports regarding the issues of nationalities and country are of great necessity and importance for you to truly understand and thoroughly analyze the situation in the country today and yesterday and to correctly decide your future actions.

Our nation has made some detours, made some mistakes, and suffered from losses in the past. However, mistakes usually come before correctness, and failure is the mother of success. Today, the Central Committee of the Party, led by Chairman Hua, is rectifying the mistakes, and everything is progressing on the right track. Although there remain obstacles and difficulties on our way ahead, the prospect for the realization of the Four Modernizations [the modernization of industry, agriculture, national defense, and science and technology] is bright and assured. In one word, practice tests all theories. The faith and strength of the people will continuously change everything. Although the road is crooked, the future will be bright and beautiful.

8

Finally, I'd like to answer your question about my responsibilities when I was working in Tibet. Of course, what I will tell you is only my personal viewpoint. In addition to working on the Tibet Work Committee of the CCP (I was the only Tibetan member), I participated in the meetings between central government leaders and such upper-level Tibetan personnel as the Dalai Lama (I was the interpreter when Chairman Mao, Premier Zhou, Vice Premier Deng Xiaoping, and Vice Premier Chen Yi talked with the Dalai Lama and other upper-level personnel). Overall, the spirit and policy of the Central Committee of the Party headed by Chairman Mao with regard to Tibet are correct (instructions concerning concrete work should be analyzed on an individual basis). That is to say, Han and Tibet are equals and not subordinate or one the ancillary of the other. The purpose of Han people entering Tibet, which I discussed above, was also clarified several times by Chairman Mao and Premier Zhou to both religious and secular officials and other representatives in Tibet. National equality or national subordination? Helper, advisor, consultant, or the opposite? These questions are key to the relationships between Han and Tibet, and thus to the entire issue of nationality relationships in our country; they are the dividing line between two absolutely different stands, viewpoints, and methods regarding the issue of nationalities; they are the touchstone of true Marxism and the Communist Party; they are two guidelines regarding the issue of nationalities, and therefore the roots of the success or failure of the work on nationalities. Therefore, if there has been this or that deviation or mistake in Tibet in the past (reasons and explanations can be found in Ye and Ulanhu's reports), as far as I know, it was to a great extent the fault of local leaders (Han cadres). Those leaders either did not report the truth about the local situation to the higher authorities, or purposefully or inadvertently deviated from and even disobeyed the guidelines and policies of the Central Committee of the Party and Chairman Mao, or gave forceful orders without regard to practical conditions in Tibet. I am one of the people in the know. I would like to explain this situation to the Dalai Lama in person when there is a chance. In this way, it would be clear that the problems regarding the work in Tibet cannot be attributed to the

Central Committee of the Party and Chairman Mao, let alone to the principles of Marxism and the policies that should have been carried out.

At the end of the meeting, they asked me again to go to India to meet with the Dalai Lama. I said, "I will listen to the opinion of leaders of the Central Committee about this." Meanwhile, I said that my greatest personal wish was to meet with the Dalai Lama in Beijing and accompany him to visit Tibetan areas as well as provinces and cities in the interior areas again, as I had accompanied him to visit provinces and cities in the interior areas before. I am looking forward to such an opportunity.

Some Opinions on Amending the Constitution with Regard to Nationalities

In late 1980, Phünwang gave a powerful lecture to the Nationalities Commission of the National People's Congress, laying out many of his ideas on minority nationalities in China.

I

As we all know, in a class society, the relationship between nationalities is that of ruling and ruled, and the relationship between classes is that of exploiting and exploited. The Marxist ideology of nationality struggle and class struggle is based on the standpoint of the oppressed nationalities and the exploited classes.

Generally, the ruling (oppressing) nationality emphasizes unity and alliance ("the unity of nationalities" [ch. *minzu tuanjie*]) and opposes struggle and antagonism ("nationality separation and independence"). On the other hand, the oppressed nationality emphasizes struggle and antagonism and opposes unity and alliance. This difference is based on the interests of the different nationalities. It is the same when it comes to class relations. Therefore, when there is oppression between nationalities, the theory of "unity of nationalities" is the argument of those who oppose nationality struggles, and the theory of "nationality separation and independence" is the argument of those who support nationality struggles.

Under the historical condition of nationality equality, the theory of unity and cooperation between nationalities is progressive and revolutionary, whereas the theory of nationality separation and independence is retrogressive and reactionary. However, when there is more serious nationality oppression from outside, struggles between nationalities within a country will decrease, and all the nationalities may unite to fight the invading nationality oppression. This is the positive significance of unity between oppressed nationalities under particular historical conditions. These are the principles of Marxism concerning nationality struggles and nationality equality, which should be used differently under different historical conditions.

It is obvious that unity and equality between the oppressing and oppressed nationalities would be absurd under the historical condition of nationality oppression. However, it is also absurd that under the historical condition of nationality equality (e.g., a socialist country led by the Communist Party) one would oppose the unity and cooperation of nationalities and support nationality separation and independence. It is absurd in theory and harmful in practice to support "nationality unity" or "nationality separation" without discriminating between oppressing and oppressed, or recognizing the historical conditions. Lenin said that if one is not able to theoretically analyze nationalities and classes, that person will be fooled by himself or by others.

The unity of nationalities is the fruit of nationality equality and is predicated on nationality equality. Nationality unity cannot exist without nationality equality. If there is no unity of nationalities, nationalities can hardly be equal, and there will be nationality oppression and discrimination. (Some people who use the name of nationalism to call for "nationality independence" and harm the interests of the nationalities are excluded.) Therefore, nationality equality is the cause of nationality unity, and nationality separation is the result of nationality oppression. The causal relationship between the two could be reversed under certain circumstances. Failing to recognize the causal relationship, considering the effect as the cause, and/or deliberately causing harmful results are cognitive mistakes and sources of all the abnormal phenomena in nationality relationships. In history, they were usually the bias of the upper levels of the controlling or big nationality. Without nationality equality, the unity of nationalities can only cause nationality disagreements, or be used by national capitulators to betray their own nationality.

The bottom line of real unity and cooperation of nationalities is absolutely true national equality. This is the most basic principle for socialists (Lenin). Real unity of nationalities is based on true national equality and is actually the product of the willing and self-motivated alliance between nationalities. Such an alliance is not aimed at hurting, enslaving, or even killing each other, but rather at friendly cooperation and mutual benefit. It is a solid and long-lasting relationship. Unfortunately, many people of the larger nationality do not understand such an easy theory.

What are the characteristics and principles of nationality equality? Lenin said, "We require sovereign equality of nationalities in a country and the protection of the interests of the minorities" (*The Collected Works of Lenin*, vol. 19, p. 100). This means that we should admit and respect the rights of the minorities to make decisions in the fields of politics, economy, and culture, and so on (*The Collected Works of Lenin*, vol. 19, p. 238). In a socialist country led by the Communist Party, people of all nationalities share common interests and should be united to fight against nationality separation and independence in order to construct a new socialistic society. This is our historical responsibility and glorious career. This is also an authentic characteristic of the Communist Party and socialism. Nationality oppression, exploitation, discrimination, domination, and especially nationality assimilation are as absolutely incompatible with this as fire with water. In a true socialist and democratic country, this is exactly the reason and basis for the willing unity and alliance of all nationalities.

As mentioned above, when it comes to relationships and problems between nationalities, the dividing line between genuine and fake Marxism, communism, and socialism is whether it is admitted and respected that each nationality has the right to make decisions on its own. Alliance and cooperation should be based on such an acknowledgment. Recognizing this principle is particularly important when dealing with problems of nationalities.

To some degree, a nation's foreign policies reflect its state policies. Admitting and respecting the rights of other nations and countries are the results of admitting and respecting the rights of all the nationalities within a nation. (The Soviet Union's revisionism toward other countries results from Russian chauvinism within the country.) Therefore, admitting that all nationalities within a country are equal and constructing a cooperative relationship between nationalities are the bases of respecting the rights of other countries. It is, therefore, internationally significant that our nation should respect the rights of every nationality, and it is necessary to guarantee that our nation will never seek revisionism and domination.

This year, two important documents were issued by the Central Committee. They are the "Notice of Forwarding the 'Summary of the Meeting on the Work in Tibet' " (the important talks given by Comrade Hu Yaobang and Comrade Wang Li in Tibet) and the "Summary of the Discussion of Work in Tibet at the Meeting of the Central Committee Secretariat." There are also the talks given by Zhao Ziyang and Ulanhu at this year's meeting of the Nationalities Committee of the National People's Congress. All these talks and documents are guiding principles in dealing with problems of autonomy and the independent management of nationalities in our country thirty years after it was founded. They are also a scientific summary of history and the present. They are in line with Marxism's principles of nationality, as well as the current situation of our country's nationality relationships. Therefore, they are the guiding principles of our work on nationalities under the new historical conditions. However, all the principles protecting the right of minorities should be included in national laws and regulations. "The right of minorities can only be protected in a democratic country where all the nationalities are equal and the rights of minorities are demonstrated in national laws." "The rights of the minorities should be included in the laws at regional, city, or even village levels" (*The Collected Works of Lenin*, vol. 20, p. 28).

Therefore, the following item should be added to the General Principles of the Constitution:

- The People's Republic of China is a multinational country. Each nationality should strictly adhere to the principle of nationality autonomy, oppose nationality oppression and discrimination, and support nationality equality. All nationalities should work together to protect the unity of the country and the unity of nationalities in order to construct a modern socialist country.

2

At present, autonomous regions in China fall into the following two categories:

1. The minority nationality that is self-governing in an autonomous region comprises the majority of the population, while the Han nationality is demographically a minority. As the characteristics of any issue are decided by the majority (the biggest portion), this type of autonomy is theoretically a genuine

autonomy, and the controlling system employed in that region is in line with its name.

2. The minority nationality in an autonomous region has less population than the Han nationality living in that region. This type of autonomy is theoretically not a genuine autonomy and does not deserve the name "autonomous region." As the majority of the population in such a region is not the controlling minority, there must be abnormal measures taken to make the region appear to be a qualified autonomous region. For example, the minority population may be exaggerated to meet the standards of an autonomous region.

Therefore, the first type of nationality autonomy is theoretically correct because its characteristic is decided by the majority of its population. The second type is theoretically incorrect because its characteristic is usually decided by fake population numbers. As it is theoretically incorrect, the second type of nationality autonomy will lead to mistakes and chaos in practice. What we should do is to change the situation of the second type to fit the first type.

Based on the above reasons, the following items should be added to the revised Constitution:

- As a way to carry out nationality autonomy, each region where minority nationalities reside should have an autonomous organization. In such a region, the self-governing nationality is the major power body and should shoulder the responsibility of managing local affairs.
- In a region where the major nationality does not comprise the majority of the population, the system of dividing up regions should be adjusted and other reasonable measures taken to help the population of the major nationality become the largest in that region.
- In adjacent areas where minority nationalities and the Han nationality cohabit, coautonomous government organizations, which are an alliance of all nationalities, should be set up.
- In a region where various minority nationalities and the Han nationality cohabit, autonomous government organizations, which consist of representatives of each nationality, should be set up.
- Local governments of provinces, autonomous regions, cities, and villages should be responsible for protecting the rights of minority and Han citizens scattered in their regions. Those citi-

zens should be encouraged to get involved in managing local affairs. Nationality discrimination, humiliation, and oppression are not allowed.

3

The socialist period is a time of development, prosperity, and advancement for all nationalities. In order to achieve this goal, especially to help the minority nationalities to develop and set up centers of their own politics, economy, and culture, and to diminish nationality oppression, discrimination, and assimilation left by the old society, adjustments should be made to the current system of dividing minority nationalities into regions. The current region-dividing system was set up on the basis of the old, unreasonable system and was the fruit of the Han Chauvinism employed by the reactionary Guomindang. The system is contrary to the characteristics of the new China that is led by the Communist Party and is always trying to provide all the nationalities with equal rights. Neither is the system in line with nationality relationships in our socialist country, which is a coexisting, codeveloping relationship based on public ownership of property. The nationality relationships in our socialist country are more reasonable and more advanced than the ones based on private ownership. However, the current region-dividing system plays a negative role when implementing party policies like "protecting the equality and unity of nationalities" and will do harm to the interest of minority nationalities in the long run. Lenin said, "There is no doubt that it has significant meaning to set up an autonomous region that is ruled by the minority nationality living in that region. Such a region, even though it may be very small in size, plays an important role in diminishing nationality oppression" (*The Collected Works of Lenin*, vol. 20, p. 33). Therefore, the following item should be added to the Constitution:

- Various minority nationalities cohabiting in geographically adjacent regions should gradually set up individual autonomous government organizations ruled by each minority nationality.

4

As explained above, summarizing the problems in the work of nationalities during the thirty years since the founding of the nation, we can see clearly that it is absolutely right for the nation to have central control over the military and foreign affairs of our country. However, in autonomous regions, there are problems that need to be solved, for example, the problems between the army and the local government and the problems between the army and the local people (e.g., the army takes the power from the minority forces to maintain public order in a minority region; problems concerning land and pasture for horses owned by the army but located in minority regions, etc.). As the majority of the soldiers are of Han nationality, the relationship between the army and the local people is often considered as a relationship between the Han nationality and the minorities. Regarding such problems, it is necessary to clearly define the responsibilities and the limitations on the responsibilities of both parties.

Similarly, the foreign affairs of the country, which concern the minorities on the borders, should not be decided by the highest national authority until they have been discussed and approved by the relevant minority people and their autonomous government organizations. The interests of the nation should be combined with the interests of the related minorities when handling foreign affairs. Therefore, the following items should be added to the Constitution:

- The national defense of our country should be controlled by the highest national authority (the National People's Congress) and the highest national administrative organization (the State Council). The army defending our country is responsible for fighting invading forces but is not responsible for maintaining public order in autonomous regions. In autonomous regions, public order should be maintained by the local minority forces. The national defense army stationed in autonomous regions should respect the right of the local autonomous government organizations and obey their orders concerning nationality autonomy.
- The highest national authority (the National People's Congress) and the highest national administrative organization (the State Council) have central control of the nation's foreign affairs. All foreign affairs concerning the interests of minority nationalities living near the borders should be discussed by the relevant minority people and their autonomous government before being raised with the National People's Congress.

5

The Guomindang practiced Han Chauvinism and nationality assimilation before liberation. They attempted to gradually replace minority languages with the Han language and eventually wipe out minority languages. After liberation, our party has adhered to the principle of nationality equality and unity, and has respected the right of minorities to use and develop their own languages. However, influenced by the extreme left, we did once go back to the old Guomindang system and emphasized "revolution" and "socialism" instead of respecting the language rights of the minorities. During the ten-year calamity, minority languages were "sentenced to death." After overthrowing the Gang of Four, and especially after the Third Meeting of the Central Committee, the party started to work on rehabilitation, and the language rights of minorities received more attention. However, some people still dream of eventually eliminating minority languages, and they are still working on it in many minority regions. Minority languages have not been completely liberated yet, and the tendency to replace them with the Han language still exists. This is one of the most serious problems of our current work on nationality relations.

"Those who do not agree with and support the equality of nationalities and languages and those who do not fight against nationality oppression and inequality are not Marxists or even socialists" (*The Collected Works of Lenin,* vol. 20, p. 11). "Why should people of a certain nationality use their own language? It is because using their own language is the only way for them to develop their culture, politics, and economy" (*The Collected Works of Stalin,* vol. 11, p. 30). For each and every nationality, using and developing its own language is the fundamental issue concerning the fate of the nationality and also a question of principle concerning its dignity and interests. In our country, it is necessary for minorities to learn the Han language, but the Han language should not replace the languages of the minorities. Therefore, the following item should be added to the Constitution:

- The nation protects the right of minorities to use their own languages as the major language in their autonomous regions, and the Han language should also be taught. It is prohibited to replace minority languages with the Han language. National laws, policies, regulations, and orders should be translated into minority languages. Detailed policies should be formulated to make sure that minority languages are used for minority students in the entrance examinations to secondary schools and colleges, and not replaced by the Han language.

6

Summarizing the above items, the following items should be added to the General Principles of the Constitution:

- The People's Republic of China is a multinational country. Each nationality should strictly adhere to the principle of nationality autonomy, oppose nationality oppression and discrimination, and support nationality equality. All nationalities should work together to protect the unity of the country and the unity of nationalities in order to construct a modern socialist country.
- As a way to carry out nationality autonomy, each region where minority nationalities reside should have an autonomous organization. In such a region, the self-governing nationality is the major power body and should shoulder the responsibility of managing local affairs.
- In a region where the major nationality does not comprise the majority of the population, the system of dividing up regions should be adjusted and other reasonable measures taken to help the population of the major nationality become the largest in that region.
- In adjacent areas where minority nationalities and the Han nationality cohabit, coautonomous government organizations, which are an alliance of all nationalities, should be set up.
- In a region where various minority nationalities and the Han nationality cohabit, autonomous government organizations, which consist of representatives of each nationality, should be set up.
- Local governments of provinces, autonomous regions, cities, and villages should be responsible for protecting the rights of minority and Han citizens scattered in their regions. Those citizens should be encouraged to get involved in managing local affairs. Nationality discrimination, humiliation, and oppression are not allowed.
- Various minority nationalities cohabiting in geographically adjacent regions should gradually set up individual autonomous government organizations ruled by each minority nationality.

- The national defense of our country should be controlled by the highest national authority (the National People's Congress) and the highest national administrative organization (the State Council). The army defending our country is responsible for fighting invading forces but is not responsible for maintaining public order in autonomous regions. In autonomous regions, public order should be maintained by the local minority forces. The national defense army stationed in autonomous regions should respect the right of the local autonomous government organizations and obey their orders concerning nationality autonomy.
- The highest national authority (the National People's Congress) and the highest national administrative organization (the State Council) have central control of the nation's foreign affairs. All foreign affairs concerning the interests of minority nationalities living near the borders should be discussed by the relevant minority people and their autonomous government before being raised with the National People's Congress.
- The nation protects the right of minorities to use their own languages as the major language in their autonomous regions, and the Han language should also be taught. It is prohibited to replace minority languages with the Han language. National laws, policies, regulations, and orders should be translated into minority languages. Detailed policies should be formulated to make sure that minority languages are used for minority students in the entrance examinations to secondary schools and colleges, and not replaced by the Han language.
- The nation should set up special grants or adopt other measures to help minorities to develop their politics, economy, culture, science, education, and health, in order to eliminate the existing inequality between the various nationalities.
- With the help of the nation, each minority nationality should set up its own center of politics, economy, and culture in order to achieve prosperity and development.

7

In our country, the minority nationalities occupy a vast territory (70 percent of the entire nation) that has abundant resources. However, the more than fifty minorities have only small populations (50 million altogether, about 6 percent of the entire population of the nation). In order to protect the interests of the nation, as well as those of the minorities, the nation's highest authority, the National People's Congress, should have the right to reject motions not in line with the interests of the nation. Similarly, minority representatives in the government should have the right to reject motions that do not protect the interests of the minorities. Minority representatives can exercise the veto by holding "small meetings" of minority representatives only and voting down motions at those meetings. According to Marx's theory, we cannot consider truth in terms of absolutes because there are always exceptions. Under most conditions, the minority should submit to the majority. However, under special circumstances, the minority may not need to submit to the majority. When it comes to equality of nationalities, small size should not mean less power. Members of every nationality in the country should have equal rights. The following items concerning the nation's power organizations should be added to the Constitution:

1. The quota for minority representatives in the National People's Congress:

(1) In principle, each minority nationality should have a certain number of representatives in the National People's Congress.

(2) In a local People's Congress of a minority autonomous region, besides representatives of the ruling minority, there should be representatives of other minorities living in the region.

(3) In the local People's Congress of a province containing minority autonomous regions, each minority in the province should have a certain number of representatives.

2. The functions and powers of the People's Congress at various levels:

(1) The National People's Congress has the right to vote down motions raised by the local People's Congress of a minority autonomous region if the motions go against the interests of the nation. Representatives of minority nationalities have the right to vote down policies formulated by the National People's Congress at their "small meetings" if the policies contradict with the interests of the minorities.

(2) The People's Congress of a minority autonomous region has the right to vote down motions raised by the People's Congress at the lower level if they go against the collective interests of people in the whole region. Policies formulated by the People's Congress of a minority autonomous region concerning the interests of minorities other than the

ruling one in that region could be voted down by representatives of the related minorities at their own "small meetings."

(3) The People's Congress of a province containing minority autonomous regions has the right to vote down motions raised by the People's Congress of a minority autonomous region in the province if the motions go against the interests of all the people in that province. Policies formulated by the People's Congress of a province containing minority autonomous regions could be voted down by representatives of the minority autonomous regions in that province at their "small meetings" if the policies go against the interests of the minorities.

In a region where various nationalities cohabit, policies formulated by the local People's Congress concerning the interests of any of the nationalities or relations between the nationalities have to be discussed and approved by the representatives of all nationalities.

Local governments should be responsible for protecting the rights and interests of the minority and Han citizens scattered in their regions (e.g., helping them find jobs and respecting their customs, religious beliefs, and political rights).

The above suggestions are for reference only.

Glossary of Correct Tibetan Spellings

Amdo	a mdo
Apo Raga	a po rab dga'
Baiyü	dpal yul
bajo	spa lcog
Bami Tseden	'ba' smad tshe brtan
Bapa	'ba' pa
Barkor	bar skor
Batang	'ba' thang
Chagö Tomden	bya rgod stobs ldan
Chamdo	chab mdo
Changöpa	byang ngos pa
Chanju-la	byang chub lags
Chapa Kesang Wangdü	cha pa skal bzang dbang 'dus
chemar	phye mar
Chöde	chos sde
Chödrak	chos grags
Cholo	chos blo
Chömpel	chos 'phel
cho rombo	jo bo rin po che

Chumik Khangsar	chu mig khang gsar
chupa	phyu pa
Chushigandrug	chu bzhi sgang drug
Chushul	chu shur
Damshung	'dam gzhung
Dargye	dar rgyas
Darjeeling	rdo rje gling
Dawa	zla ba
Dawei Senge	zla ba'i seng ge
Demo Rimpoche	bde mo rin po che
Dengko	'dan khog
depa	sde pa
depön	mda' dpon
Deqen	bde chen
Derge	sde dge
Derge Sey	sge dge sras
Dorje Tseden	rdo rje tshe brtan
dotse	rdo tshad
Dramdul	dgra 'dul
Drepung	'bras spungs
Drichu	'bri chu
Drug Chompel	'brug chos 'phel
Drung Ashi	drung a shi
Dunglung	mdung lung
Dünjom Rimpoche	bdud 'joms rin po che
Dzachu	rdza chu
dzasa	rdza sag
Dzayü	rdza yul
Gamtok	skam thog
Ganden	dga' ldan
Gangtok	sgang thog
Ganze	dkar mdzes

Gara Lama	mgar ba bla ma
geshe	dge bshes
Geshe Chödrag	dge bshes chos grags
Giamda	rgya mda'
Gombo Tsering	mgon po tshe ring
Gönchen	dgon chen
Gonggar Lama	gong dkar bla ma
Gongjo	go 'jo
Gora Ashi	sgo ra a shes
Gyalo Thondup	rgya lo don grub
Gyantse	rgyal rtse
Gyeltang	rgyal thang
Jagpori	lcags po ri
jamchung	ljam chung
Janglojen (Kung)	lcang lo can (gung)
jigyab khembo	spyi khyab mkhan po
Jisungang	spyi srung sgang
Jo	jo bo
Jomda	'jo mda'
Kalimpong	ka lon sbug
kalön	bka' blon
Kapshöpa Sey	ka shod po sras
Kashag	bka' shag
Kesang Namgye	skal bzang rnam rgyal
Kesang Tsering	skal bzang tshe ring
Kesang Wangdü	skal bzang dbang 'dus
Kesang Yeshe	skal bzang ye shes
Kham	khams
Khampa	khams pa
Kheme (Sonam Wangdü)	khe smad (bsod nams dbang 'dus)
khenjung	mkhan chung
Kongpo	kong po

Kumbela	kun 'phel lags
Kuncho Tashi	kun mchog bkra shis
Kundeling Dzasa	kun bde gling rdza sag
Kyidöpa	skyid stod pa
Labrang	bla brang
Laga Lama	la kha bla ma
Langdün	glang mdun
Lhalu	lha klu
Lhamön	lha smon
Lhasa	lha sa
Lhautara	lha'u rta ra
Litang	li thang
Liushar (Thubden Tharpa)	sne'u shar (thub bstan mthar pa)
Lobsang Gyaltsen	blo bzang rgyal mtshan
Lobsang Namgye	blo bzang rnam rgyal
Lobsang Samden	blo bzang bsam gtan
Lobsang Targye	blo bzang thar rgyas
Lobsang Tashi	blo bzang bkra shis
Lobsang Thundrup	blo bzang don grub
Lowang	blo dbang
Lukangwa	klu khang ba
Maja Thundrup	rma bya don grub
Markam	smar khams
mendre densum	mandal rten gsum
Milarepa	mi la ras pa
momo	mog mog
Mucha	mu bya
Nagchuka	nag chu kha
Namgye Dorje	rnam rgyal rdo rje
nangmagang	nang ma sgang
Natöla (pass)	rna thos la
Ngabö	nga phod

Ngawang Kesang	ngag dbang skal bzang
Ngawang Namgye	ngag dbang rnam rgyal
Ngawang Norbu	ngag dbang nor bu
Ngawang Tenzin	ngag dbang bstan 'dzin
Norbulingka	nor bu gling kha
Norgye Lobsang	nor rgyas blo bzang
Nyarong	nyag rong
Nyingmapa	rnying ma pa
Panda Raga	spom mda' rab dga'
Panda Tobgye	spom mda' stobs rgyas
Pangtsiwaka	spang rtsi wa kha
Pasang	pa sangs
Pema	pad ma
Phagpala	'phags pa lha
Phala	pha lha
Phari	phag ri
Phembo	'phan po
Phula	bu lags
Phuntob	phun stobs
Phüntso Tashi	phun tshogs bkra shis
Phüntso Wangye	phun tshogs dbang rgyal
Pöba	bod pa
Potala	po ta la
Ragashar	ra ga shag
Ragdi	rag ti
Reting	rwa sgreng
rimshi	rim bzhi
Riwoche	ri bo che
Sadam	sa tham
Sampo Sey	bsam pho sras
Sandutsang	sa 'dul tshang
Sera	ser ra

Seshin	zas zhim
Seshü	se shul
Shakabpa	zhwa sgab pa
Shasur	bshad zur
Sherap	shes rab
Sherap Gyatso	shes rab rgya mtsho
Shigatse	gzhis ka rtse
Shökhang	zhol khang
Sonam Lobsang	bsod nams blo bzang
Sonam Tomjor	bsod nams stobs 'byor
Songtsen Gampo	srong btsan sgam po
Surkhang	zur khang
Takla	stag lha
Taktse Rimpoche	stag rtse rin po che
talama	ta la ma
Tartsedo	dar rtse mdo
Tashilhunpo	bkra shis lhun po
Tashi Tsering	bkra shis tshe ring
Tashi Wangchuk	bkra shis dbang phyug
Tharchen	mthar phyin
Tharchin	mthar phyin
Thöndrupling (pass)	don grub gling
Thubden Lengmön	thub bstan legs smon
Thubden Namgye	thub bstan rnam rgyal
Thubden Wangchuk	thub bstan dbang phyug
Thuwang	thub dbang
Tomjor	stobs 'byor
Tomjor Wangchuk	stobs 'byor dbang phyug
Topden	stobs ldan
Topgye	stobs rgyas
Trayab	brag g.yab
Trendong Sey	mkras mthong sras

Trijang Rimpoche	khri byang rin po che
Trimön	khri smon
Trinley Nyima	'phrin las nyi ma
Tsachuka	tshwa chu kha
Tsadrü Rimpoche	tsha sprul rim po che
Tsakalo	tshwa kha lho
tsampa	rtsam pa
Tsang	gtsang
Tsarong Dzasa	tsha rong rdza sa
Tseden Yangdrön	tshe brtan dbyangs sgron
Tsering Tshomo	tshe ring mtsho mo
Tsilila	mdzes legs lags
Tsögo	mtsho sgo
Tsuglagang	gtsug lag khang
Ü	dbus
ula	'u lag
Wangye	dbang rgyal
Wangye Phüntso	dbang rgyal phun tshogs
Yadong (Tromo)	gro mo
Yangling Dorje	yang ling rdo rje
Yapshi Depön	yab gzhis mda' dpon
Yurubön	g.yu ru dpon
Yuthok, Tashi Thondrup	g.yu thog bkra shis don grub

Index

Page numbers in italics indicate illustrations and maps.

Text: 10/13 Sabon
Display: Sabon
Cartographer: Bill Nelson
Compositor: Binghamton Valley Composition
Printer and Binder: Thomson-Shore, Inc.